Robert Arold Walters
2005

ALESSANDRO MANZONI'S

The Count of Carmagnola and *Adelchis*

ALESSANDRO MANZONI'S

The Count of Carmagnola and *Adelchis*

Introduced & Translated by

Federica Brunori Deigan

THE JOHNS HOPKINS UNIVERSITY PRESS
Baltimore & London

© 2004 The Johns Hopkins University Press
All rights reserved. Published 2004
Printed in the United States of America on acid-free paper
2 4 6 8 9 7 5 3 1

The Johns Hopkins University Press
2715 North Charles Street
Baltimore, Maryland 21218-4363
www.press.jhu.edu

Library of Congress Cataloging-in-Publication Data

Manzoni, Alessandro, 1785–1873.
[Conte di Carmagnola. English]
Alessandro Manzoni's The Count of Carmagnola ; and Adelchis / introduced
and translated by Federica Brunori Deigan.
p. cm.
ISBN 0-8018-7881-0 (alk. paper)
1. Manzoni, Alessandro, 1785–1873—Translations into English.
I. Title: Count of Carmagnola. II. Deigan, Federica Brunori. III. Manzoni, Alessandro,
1785–1873. Adelchi. English. IV. Title: Adelchis. V. Title.
PQ4714.A24 2004
853'.7—dc22
2003018059

A catalog record for this book is available from the British Library.

The frontispieces to the plays are from Opere Varie di Alessandro Manzoni, *Milan, 1845.*
Courtesy of University of Chicago Library.

Contents

Translator's Note

My guiding principle throughout these translations has been to remain as close as possible to the figures of speech present in the original. Furthermore, I have aimed at a stylistic compromise similar to the original. Manzoni intended to innovate from within the tradition of the tragic genre. Accordingly, when composing the tragedies' dialogues, he could not but opt for the *endecasillabo sciolto*, the meter traditionally employed in tragedy. However, he avoided the artificiality in which Italian poetry had fallen over the previous few centuries by eliminating Latinisms in both lexicon and syntax and by using words and constructs that his contemporary readers could understand. In my translation, therefore, I employed the blank verse for the dialogues, which oftentimes entailed resorting to the emphatic form for the possessive ("own") or to the emphatic use of "do" in order to meet the demands of the meter. However, I avoided archaic forms such as the use of "thou" or the ending "-th" in verbs for the third person singular. I restricted the use of learned words and inverted syntax to a few cases of brief replies in the dialogue, where it was necessary to heighten the stylistic level from an excessively prosaic tone. Also, for the future tense, I used the auxiliary "will" when volition was intended, "shall" in the other cases.

Whereas the blank verse was the obvious choice to render the Italian endecasillabo sciolto of the dialogues, the three choruses (one in *Carmagnola* and two in *Adelchis*) posed a serious challenge. In all three cases, Manzoni resorted to rhythms and rhyming patterns of Latin hymns and melic poetry to forcefully convey his own message to the reader. While the tragedies' characters speak in the solemn meter traditional of this genre—a flow of unrhymed lines, often run-on lines, akin in stress to natural speech—the corner reserved for the author's view (Manzoni's definition of the chorus) resonates with more musical, repetitive accents. In the tragedies' choruses Manzoni continued the poetic experiment that he had begun with the *Inni sacri*. As Andrea Ciccarelli has remarked in his analysis of Manzoni's poetic style, the author's religious hymns marked an important point of departure from the classicist tradition in Italian poetry. Not only the material's disposition but also the lexicon and, above all, the meter of the *Inni sacri* were innovative attempts at recuperating the poetic forms of popular tradition, with a view to creating a modern poetic medium, both poignant and pensive. The poet's voice was to be not only understandable but also morally meaningful to the average person. Thus in the tragedies, diverse metrical choices set the choruses apart from the dialogue.

After a few attempts at reproducing the complex rhyming patterns in the translated choruses, I decided, for the sake of readability, to sacrifice the rhymes in *Carmagnola*'s chorus and in the first chorus of *Adelchis*, opting for lines reproducing the rhythm of the original.

In the case of *Carmagnola*'s chorus, I rendered the Italian anapestic decasyllable lines (the same meter used in "La passione," one of the *Inni sacri*) with their English equivalent. A comparison with Milman's translation of the same chorus, which appeared in his 1820 article for the *Quarterly Review* (see introduction) and attempted to reproduce the rhyming pattern of the original, confirms in my mind that rhyming has negative impact on readability and rhythm.

Similarly, in the case of *Adelchis*'s first chorus, I reproduced the meter of the original, dodecasyllable or alexandrine (iambic hexameters), focusing on keeping the rhythm unbreached, maintaining caesuras, and rendering closely the highly visual lines of the original.

In the case of *Adelchis*'s second chorus, known as Ermengarde's chorus, I attempted to preserve the rhyming pattern, opting for a variant of the English ballad meter, an alternation of octosyllabic and mostly hexasyllabic lines. Sometimes, in my translation, the shorter lines (the even ones) are four, five, or seven syllables long. In the tradeoff that rhyming entails, the foot is not regular. A trochee, however, often starts the line, which is mostly dominated by an iambic rhythm, thus making the translation a little bit closer to the original in rhythm. Although the original meter is very regularly iambic, there is a trochaic substitution at the beginning of each line. The rhyming pattern of the four-line stanza of a ballad (*abcb*) is close to the original (*abcbde*), which in fact dictated, together with other considerations, the choice of the ballad meter in my translation. This meter presents even lines always rhyming, the odd ones usually but not always in rhyme. Coleridge's *Rime of the Ancient Mariner* is generally deemed the most perfect example of ballad with such a pattern, mostly *abcb*, with variation in some

longer stanzas. In disregard of the ballad meter and in observance of the original, the last line of each stanza rhymes with the last one of the next stanza, so
as to form twin stanzas (*strofe geminate*, also used in "Il natale," "La risurrezione,"
and "La Pentecoste") throughout. This coupling pattern is important, as the
stanzas do proceed in pairs as far as content is concerned, with the extreme cases
of the period running over from one to the next, in the concluding part of the
chorus. The last two stanzas are matched by a word rhyme ("serene"), in order
to highlight the symmetrically opposed lots of Ermengarde and the "pious peasant." There are cases of assonance or consonance instead of rhymes that could
not be eliminated. And I am aware that sometimes rhyming is obtained by
stretching the orthodox use of the language.

As far as the characters' names are concerned, I anglicized them, with some
exceptions. In *Carmagnola*, I left "Doge" unchanged to distinguish clearly between
the Venetian supreme authority and the Duke of Milan. I decided to leave
unchanged all the last names, including Visconti, since most of the last names
identify the military officers in the two camps. In *Adelchis* instead of "Albinus"
I used "Alcuin," more recognizable, to readers of English, as the name of Charles's
personal advisor.

In *Carmagnola*, I have translated *condottiere* with "military chief" or "captain,"
as I find in the *Oxford English Dictionary* that this word indicated "a military leader,
commander of a body of troops" from c.1370 to c.1850 and "a military leader of
skill and experience" from c.1590 to c.1860.

In *Adelchis*, I left unchanged the few feminine proper nouns, except for the
heroine's name. The English equivalent was readily found in Shakespeare, *Henry
V* (I.i.83) where a homonym of the Lombard princess appears in the same list of
names with Charlemagne. The spelling in Shakespeare is "Ermengare," in Shakespeare's source, Holinshed, "Ermengard." I opted for "Ermengarde," consistent
with the spelling of her rival's name, "Hildegarde," as it appears in English history texts.

The present translations were copyrighted in 1999, after I defended my doc-
toral dissertation, which consisted of the first-ever unabridged English translation of Manzoni's tragedies and their critical assessment. In 2002 another English translation was provided by Michael J. Curley in *Alessandro Manzoni, Two
Plays* (New York: Peter Lang).

I wish to thank my mentor and friend Pier Massimo Forni for reviving my interest in Manzoni during my graduate years at the Johns Hopkins University, and
for all his invaluable advice.

I also wish to thank the following persons for their generous help at various stages of the book: Andrew Bradley, Mauro Colombo, Stuart Curran, Alice Deigan, Gianmarco Gaspari, and Walter Stephens.

Finally, I wish to thank my husband, Richard, and my family for their patience and constant support throughout the writing of this book.

Alessandro Manzoni's

The Count of Carmagnola and *Adelchis*

Introduction

MANZONI'S LIFE AND WORKS

Alessandro Manzoni was born in Milan, on the 7 March 1785, the only child of Pietro Manzoni and Giulia Beccaria.

The Manzonis' noble titles dated as far back as the seventeenth century. When his father died in 1807, Alessandro was left sole heir to the family assets. He lived as a man of independent means, in the lifestyle typical of the aristocratic class in which he had been raised. However, whereas Manzoni's father and uncles had tried to keep the tradition of nobility alive, Alessandro did nothing to claim his feudal rights and always rejected the title of "Count" with which some admirers would address him.

His mother, Giulia, was the daughter of possibly the most famous representative of the Italian Enlightenment, Cesare Beccaria, author of the pamphlet *Dei delitti e delle pene* (On crimes and punishments, 1764), which advocated the abolition of torture and the death penalty. In his youth Alessandro was known to proudly associate his maternal grandfather's last name with his own; in his letters he consistently added "Beccaria" to his signature until mid-1809.

The marriage of Alessandro's parents was arranged by Count Pietro Verri, who, together with his brothers, belonged to the Milanese Enlightenment circles Giulia attended. Whereas she enjoyed an intense social life, her husband, twenty-six years her elder, was taciturn and solitary. Their union proved unhappy and they separated in 1792. Alessandro was born three years into their marriage. He was baptized Catholic and sent to a wet nurse in the countryside. He then attended religious boarding schools from age six to eighteen. At fifteen, he composed a long poem in terza rima, *Il trionfo della libertà* (Liberty triumphant), in which historical figures, appearing in a vision to the young poet, celebrated the liberty brought about by the French Revolution and decried tyrannical regimes, as well as the repressive influence of the Church. In the following years Alessandro devoted his poetic creativity to the idyllic genre and to satire, adopting the neoclassical style of his maestro, Vincenzo Monti (1754–1828).

After a sojourn in Venice (1803–4), in 1805 Manzoni joined his mother (whom he had not seen since his childhood) in Paris, where she had moved after her divorce. Giulia lived *more uxorio* with a wealthy Milanese intellectual, Carlo Imbonati, who invited Manzoni to join him and his mother but died before Alessandro could arrange the travel. So when twenty-year-old Manzoni went to Paris for the first time, he went to accompany his recently bereft mother and to offer her solace after the loss of her beloved companion, for whom Alessandro composed a poem, the first of his work to be published. The *carme* (a solemn lyrical poem), *In Memory of Carlo Imbonati*, was published in Paris in 1806, in four different editions. In it the poet engaged in a visionary dialogue with the spirit of the deceased, who bequeathed him maxims on which to model his life in a world devoid of morality. Some of these maxims extolled Truth and Virtue as supreme values, while others exhorted him to care for earthly things as little as possible. While some maxims bordered on moral neutrality and indifference and would be abandoned in time, the recommendation "feel and meditate" was to remain at the core of Manzoni's poetics. This carme has been seen as a mirror of a moral evolution, anticipating Manzoni's religious conversion. Ugo Foscolo (1778–1827), a famous poet of the time, considered the lines of this carme worthy of quotation, accompanied by a commendatory mention in a footnote, in his poem *I sepolcri* (The sepulchers, 1807). The relationship between these two poets soon cooled, though, because Foscolo felt that Manzoni, while seeking the appreciation of others, was unwilling to reciprocate. A lasting friendship began instead between Manzoni and historian and philologist Claude Fauriel (1772–1844). Manzoni's mother was welcomed in the house of Sophie de Condorcet (widow of Marquis de Condorcet, the philosopher and mathematician who died during the Terror) where republican intellectuals would gather for their discussions. It was there that Manzoni met and made friends with Fauriel, who was then Madame de Condorcet's lover.

Traveling across the border between France and Italy was easy during the height of the Napoleonic empire, and Alessandro and his mother went repeatedly back and forth between Paris and Milan in those years. In 1807, when Pietro Manzoni died, they went to Milan to settle the estate. Other travels were for the purpose of finding a suitable wife for Alessandro. In 1808, in Milan, he married

Enrichetta Blondel, the daughter of a weaver of Swiss origin who was acquainted with Imbonati. Manzoni agreed to a Protestant wedding at her family's request. Soon after their wedding, Alessandro and Enrichetta, accompanied by Giulia, moved back to Paris. Their first daughter was born in December 1808. Through the years, Enrichetta gave Alessandro numerous children, nine of whom survived past childhood. Giulietta, the first child, was baptized with Catholic rite. The Manzonis then applied with the Holy See for the permission to celebrate their wedding in the Catholic Church as well. The permission was granted in 1809, and the rite was celebrated in Paris the following year. Enrichetta wished to be instructed in the new religion, and she finally converted in a solemn church ceremony in May 1810. During this period Manzoni and his mother also returned to practicing Catholicism. Obeying their deep-felt need for a quiet retreat, the Manzonis moved from Paris to the Brusuglio villa (Imbonati's legacy to Giulia) near Milan and sought the spiritual guidance of the abbé Luigi Tosi. In 1813, Manzoni bought a house in downtown Milan, in Via Morone (today a national monument, library, archive, and center of Manzonian studies known as Casa del Manzoni), where he resided the rest of his life, with the exception of a second sojourn in Paris in 1819–20. Today the daily train connecting Milan to Paris bears the name "Alessandro Manzoni," in memory of the Milanese author's love for the French capital.

Early in 1812, Manzoni began composing religious poetry, the *Jnni sacri* (Sacred hymns). In 1815 he published the first four hymns: "La risurrezione" (The resurrection), "Il nome di Maria" (The name of Mary), "Il natale" (The Nativity), and "La passione" (The Passion). In these poems, Manzoni developed an entirely new poetic style, shunning mythological ornaments and aiming at linguistic incisiveness and clarity. In the hymns, the poet illustrates the main tenets of the Christian belief through a celebration of the main liturgical solemnities of the Catholic holy days. A fifth hymn, "La Pentecoste" (The Pentecost), begun in these same years, was completed in 1822.

Over the years during which the *Jnni sacri* were composed (1812–22), Manzoni experienced a unique period of creative fervor. In that decade, besides the five hymns, he wrote two tragedies, *Jl Conte di Carmagnola* (The Count of Carmagnola, 1820) and *Adelchi* (Adelchis, 1822), a philosophical tract on the Catholic morals, *Osservazioni sulla morale cattolica* (Remarks on Catholic morals, 1819), and a historical tract on the Lombard domination in Italy, *Discorso sopra alcuni punti della dominazione longobardica in Jtalia* (Discourse on some aspects of the Lombard rule in Italy), which accompanied *Adelchis* upon publication. He also wrote two essays on drama, the preface to *Carmagnola*, published with the tragedy in 1820, and the

"Lettre à Monsiuer Chauvet sur l'unité de temps et de lieu dans la tragédie" (Letter to Monsieur Chauvet on the unity of time and place in tragedy), which appeared in Paris in 1823; the famous ode to commemorate Napoleon's death, "Il cinque maggio" ("The Fifth of May," 1821), and a political poem on the patriots' attempt to deliver Italy from foreign domination, "Marzo 1821" ("March 1821," 1848). As he was completing *Adelchis,* he conceived a third tragedy, on the rebellion of the Roman gladiator Spartacus (some sketchy notes for this drama exist), but he decided instead to focus on a historical novel, which he had also begun before the completion of his second tragedy (the manuscript is dated 24 April 1821). In 1823, Manzoni finished a first draft of the novel, (bearing the tentative titles *Fermo e Lucia* or *Sposi promessi*), and, after major revisions, submitted to the printer a copy entitled *I promessi sposi* (The betrothed) in 1824. The novel was finally published in 1827.

With the completion of the novel, Manzoni's creative whirlwind abated. In 1827 he made the first of his three trips to Florence, by which he intended to acquire the linguistic expertise for revising the novel's language after the Tuscan idiom. In 1840, he began publishing in installments the linguistically revised version of the novel, enriched with vignettes illustrated by Francesco Gonin, with substantial input by the author. In an appendix to the 1840 version of the novel, Manzoni published *Storia della colonna infame* (The column of infamy, 1842), a historical tract on the seventeenth-century trial of the anointers, the men whom the populace believed involved in a conspiracy to poison Milan with the plague.

In order to preempt unlicensed or pirated printing, Manzoni attended to the publication of his complete works with the Milanese publisher Redaelli. The *Opere varie,* published in installments over ten years (1845–55), contained everything Manzoni had written, except for *The Betrothed* and *The Column of Infamy.* It also contained an essay entitled *Del romanzo storico* (On the historical novel, 1845), centered on the ethical values of historical fiction, and a philosophical dialogue on art and morals, *Dell'invenzione* (On invention, 1850). This dialogue shows the influence of philosopher Antonio Rosmini, one of Manzoni's closest friends during this period. The tragedies were linguistically revised for the 1845 edition and illustrated by the artist Roberto Focosi.

In 1830, Manzoni began a book on the Italian language, and, as years went by, this topic increasingly captured his interest. In parallel with his linguistic concerns, Manzoni's devotion to historical issues is further documented by a comparative historical study, *La rivoluzione francese del 1789 e la rivoluzione italiana del 1859* (The French Revolution of 1789 and the Italian Revolution of 1859), which he left unfinished; it was posthumously published in 1889. In 1868, the minister for education appointed Manzoni chair of a committee whose task was to report on the unification of the national language. The report, eventually published also in book form, was entitled *Dell'unità della lingua e dei mezzi di diffonderla* (On the unity of the language—and on the best means to divulge it).

Manzoni died on 22 May 1873, at the age of eighty-eight, having mourned the loss of his two wives (Blondel died in 1833; his second wife, Teresa Borri, died in 1861) and seven of his nine children. Milan's municipal council sponsored an elaborate funeral, decreed to name a central street after the author, and allotted a sum for a commemorative statue, which was unveiled ten years later and is situated to this day in Piazza di San Fedele. In paying solemn homage to its beloved citizen, the city of Milan was recognizing the wide renown Manzoni had earned, not only in Italy, but in Europe and beyond.

MANZONI AND THE MAKING OF ITALY
1800–1815: Early Civic Poetry

In his youth, Manzoni witnessed the clash between the Austrians and the French over the rule of his native region, Lombardy. Throughout the centuries history had shown that control of this prosperous northern Italian land afforded a great staging ground to those who wished to dominate the Italian peninsula. After ruling Milan for almost a century, the Hapsburgs were ousted from the city and its surrounding region by Napoleon and his army in 1796. The following year the French set up the Cisalpine republic, with which poets of Manzoni's older generation, such as Foscolo and Monti, eagerly collaborated. The Austrian emperor Francis II formally recognized the Cisalpine republic and pledged to maintain peace with it, but instead he occupied it militarily, with the help of the Russians, in 1799. Napoleon vanquished the Austrians and Russians at the battle of Marengo in 1800, thus securing French domination over Lombardy (Luneville treaty, 1801). In these same years, Manzoni wrote the terza rima long poem *Il trionfo della libertà*. In it, the French Revolution (which Manzoni will later unfavorably compare to the Italian national revolution) serves as a model that Italians should follow to liberate themselves from tyrants, and Marengo is synonym with "liberation" from the "German greedy beasts" (the Austrians). However, young Manzoni does not fail to denounce the glaringly contradictory behavior of the French rulers in Lombardy: they are gentler than the Austrians, yet still greedy and still strangers, and terribly hypocritical to boot. The spirit of Insubria (Lombardy's ancient name) speaks in the following lines, addressing the oppressed land:

Kind bandits in your villas now reside
Where wild ones used to live; and yet your will,
Even your strength, remain the slaves of strangers.
The populace is hungry, cries for bread,
While in revels and banquets spend their time.
The chiefs and their lost women, a vain crowd,
feeding on empty luxury and pride,
who scorn the lower classes whence they came,
to whom they still proclaim "Equality!"[1]

In a similar tone, thirteen years later, Manzoni denounced the injustice and the hypocrisy of the French regime in his first civic ode, "April 1814," celebrating the fall of the Napoleonic rule in Milan after Emperor Napoleon (king of Italy since 1805) abdicated in Paris on 7 April, 1814. Manzoni painted a dark picture of the "Liberator's" government in the Lombard city: an atmosphere of suspicion and fear; spying; arbitrary abolition of, or disrespect for, existing laws; and rhetoric of freedom masking a reality of exploitation. French propaganda claimed Napoleon had given the Italians their political independence when he created the Italian republics and their legions (bearing the three-colored flag that was in fact to become Italy's flag), but in reality the price tagged to this budding independence was high. The French levied heavy taxes on the Italians and drafted them for their wars of conquest. This state of affairs, denounced in Manzoni's ode, was unmistakably revealed when the French minister of finance was lynched in a popular riot in downtown Milan on 20 April 1814, within earshot of the horrified Manzoni family, who lived nearby. In "April 1814," Manzoni, eager to celebrate the end of such a rapacious and hypocritical regime, went so far as to call the Austrians and Russians who had defeated the Napoleonic army "handsome fighters" and "God-assisted."

That poetic compliment could hardly mean that Manzoni welcomed the return of the Austrians as rulers of Lombardy, however, as his maestro and fellow poet Monti would soon do. After Napoleon's abdication, Manzoni actively engaged in trying to earn international acknowledgement of Italy's right to national unity and independence. An acceptable solution for the group of patriots who called themselves the Italici was to have Napoleon's viceroy for the Italian kingdom, Eugene Beauharnais, as king of a national and constitutional monarchy, despite the unpleasant legacy this monarch would bring with him from his Napoleonic past. The municipality of Milan organized an interim government in the vacuum of power that followed the popular riot, as the French were rapidly dismantling their administration in Milan. When the Lombard Senate (an ancient body that had recently been filled with pro-Napoleonic senators) decided to avoid asking the anti-Napoleonic powers for Beauharnais to become king of Italy, the Italici challenged the validity of the senate's decision and initiated a petition with the interim city government for the convocation of the electoral bodies that would put a new senate in place. Manzoni's signature is on this petition. The interim government, in the meantime, sent a delegation of patriots to Paris to plea with the European powers in favor of Italian independence under a constitutional monarchy, relying on the personal sympathy that the viceroy enjoyed among the royalty and nobility of Europe. Count Federico Confalonieri, a friend of Manzoni's, and Manzoni's cousin, Giacomo Beccaria, were two of the seven members of the delegation. The final two stanzas of Manzoni's ode "April 1814" express the joyful hope that this delegation may obtain what it is seeking, the fulfillment of "the ancient Italian desire" for national unification and independence.

The delegation's requests were denied, as the European powers favored instead the Austrians' return in northern Italy. The viceroy renounced his royal aspirations and signed off the territory of the former Italian kingdom to the Austrian army, which entered Milan early that May. At the end of the month, all the bodies of local government were dissolved. In June the Austrians posted leaflets announcing to the Lombard population "their happy lot" for having been given the Austrian emperor as their ruler. But the Lombards were far from being happy with the return of the Austrians. "On 14 June, at the theater 'alla Cannobiana,' an improviser was given as a theme *The Battle at Leipzig*. While the improviser praised, as he was expected to do, the anti-Napoleonic allies, the audience started to whisper and then to boo, so loudly that the actor could not go on. The theater was evacuated by the authorities. One should not mistake this popular protest for a reborn love toward the one who had been vanquished at Leipzig, Napoleon. But the Austrians interpreted it that way and circulated vulgar caricatures of the general reduced in exile on the tiny island of Elba. In the city of Milan all toponyms recalling the Napoleonic past were rapidly erased."[2]

The following April the national hopes of the Italians were indeed pinned again, although briefly and indirectly, onto Napoleon. Gioacchino Murat, Napoleon's brother-in-law and king of Naples since 1808 (the French-supported Partenopean republic had ousted the local dynasty of the Bourbons in 1799), had always harbored the dream of becoming king of Italy, rival in this to Viceroy Eugene. After the fall of the Napoleonic empire, the great powers had left him on his throne in Naples. When Napoleon returned to power in Paris from Elba (the so-called One Hundred Days, March–June 1815), Murat joined forces with him against the anti-Napoleonic alliance, declaring war against the Austrians. He invaded the region of Marche in central Italy and on 30 March issued a call to action circulating a passionate speech from Rimini, in which he exhorted all the Italians to join him in the fight for Italy's independence: "From the Alps to the Sicilian strait, may one cry only be heard: 'Independence for Italy!'" Manzoni responded with enthusiasm. His second civic ode, "April 1815," or "Il proclama di Rimini" (The speech of Rimini), celebrates Murat as a second Moses, entrusted with the God-ordained mission to lead Italy's fight for unification. The poem features a famous line, a motto of the Risorgimento: "*Liberi non sarem se non siam uni*" (We can no freedom have until we are one).

But Murat was defeated by the Austrians in May and had to renounce the crown. He was later deceitfully enticed to land in Calabria, captured, and summarily sentenced to death in October 1815.[3] When the news of Napoleon's defeat at Waterloo in June 1815 reached him, Manzoni, who was at a bookseller's, fainted from emotional distress. Sitting as winners at the negotiating table of the Congress of Vienna, the Austrians were able to incorporate Lombardy and the Veneto region as lands of the empire and to gain near total control of the Italian peninsula through dynastic and defensive alliances.

1816–1818: The Romantic Debate and *Il Conciliatore*

In its first years, the newly reestablished Austrian rulers in Milan tried earnestly to enlist the support of the local intellectuals. The government asked even Foscolo, a fiery defender of liberty and a well-known republican sympathizer with a Jacobin past, to head the *Biblioteca italiana,* a journal that the Austrians sponsored in the hope (at first secret, later more and more patent) of winning the consensus of the young men of letters in Milan. Foscolo did not refuse at once, but on the eve of being sworn in the ranks of the Austrian administration, he fled from Milan. The Austrian police persecuted him in Switzerland and only London proved a secure haven for him. Monti, on the other hand, celebrated the return of the Austrians through poetry and theatre pieces and became one of the editors of *Biblioteca italiana.*

A celebrity of European literature, Madame Germaine de Staël (1766–1817) was invited to write for the opening issue of the journal, and she sent an article entitled "On the Usefulness of Translations," which was published in January 1816. In this article she advocated the opening of stale, rule-ridden, and provincial Italian literature to the German and English influences by means of translations. This line of thought was initially more or less encouraged by some officials of the Austrian government; the opening to the "Teutonic" culture advocated by Madame de Staël could foster an admiration for the German culture and diminish the patriotic feeling in the Italians, thus favoring the maintenance of the Hapsburgs' multiethnic empire. Ironically, however, things went in the opposite direction. Madame de Staël's article was at first harshly criticized by the supporters of the classical culture and style, according to whom the desirable renewal of Italian literature could and had to take place exclusively through deeper study of the Greek and Latin traditions, as well as of the greatest Italian classics. These traditionalist, "classicist" articles attacking Madame de Staël sparked in turn the production of the so-called manifestos of Italian romanticism by Ludovico di Breme, Pietro Borsieri, and Giovanni Berchet, who was a personal friend of Manzoni's. Berchet, in his "Lettera semiseria di Grisostomo al suo figliolo" (Semi-serious letter of Chrysostom to his son) staunchly defended Madame de Staël's ideas. Berchet defined "classicist poetry as 'the poetry of the dead' and, conversely, romantic poetry 'the poetry of the living,'" that is, the poetry expressing "the civilization of the living century." He advocated immediate action in creating "a common literary fatherland to comfort us in our wretchedness," implying that modern literary creations by talented and open-minded Italians would pave the way to patriotic political action, liberating Italy from the present "wretchedness" of division and consequent subjugation to the foreigners.[4]

Manzoni did not publicly enter this controversy between romanticism and neoclassicism. In the year of the romantic manifestos, 1816, he circulated among his friends a poem, "L'ira di Apollo—Per la lettera semiseria di Grisostomo" (The wrath of Apollo—over the semi-serious letter of Chrysostom), in which he parodied the use of mythology in poetry.[5] But most importantly, in these same months of 1816, Manzoni conceived his first tragedy, *The Count of Carmagnola*, as we know from a letter to Fauriel, to whom the tragedy is dedicated.[6] That letter reveals how Manzoni planned to defy the rules of the neoclassical tradition at the time of the tragedy's conception. Four years later he would write his preface to *Carmagnola*, a philosophical refutation of the neoclassical dramatic rules, which was to be one of the author's most important public contributions to the debate over romanticism versus neoclassicism.

In 1817, the society of the *Biblioteca italiana* was dissolved, and although the journal continued to be published by a few pro-Austrian editors, it lost its spotlight in the Milanese literary life. The debate initiated by that journal—in which the discussion of literature hinted at the debate on Italy's national destiny—continued into a new publication, *Il Conciliatore*, first published on 3 September 1818. Silvio Pellico (1789–1854) was the founder and editor in chief of this biweekly *foglio* (sheet) printed on azure paper. He had moved to Milan from his native Piedmont in order to follow his literary and patriotic aspirations, instead of the career in commerce his family had wanted for him. Pellico's collaborators included Ermes Visconti, a friend of Manzoni's from boarding school days, the three authors of the romantic manifestos (Berchet, Borsieri, and di Breme), Federico Confalonieri, and others.[7] These young men, well-versed in the humanities and the sciences, advocated new cultural ideas that indirectly promoted the cause of liberty and independence for Italy. They needed to muster all their resolve for this enterprise because they faced the Austrian police that made use of both smearing propaganda, like a paper parodically called *L'Attaccabrighe* (The "quarreler," to mock the romantic appellative of *Reconciler*), and routine censorship.

Mainly through reviews of books on commerce, agriculture, history, education, literature, and drama, and sometimes through essays, the *conciliatoristi* would harp on the same basic principles: first and foremost, the ideal of liberty in every aspect of civic life; then, the idea that literature, as part of the dissemination of culture, had a civic role no different from school education, effecting an amelioration of people's moral, and therefore, social behavior. These Enlightenment ideals cohabited with patriotism and national aspirations in their writings. Love for one's *patria* ("fatherland," but feminine in Latin and Italian, being the adjective in agreement with the word *terra*, "land," and often metaphorically referred to as "mother"; see, for example, Marino's speech in act IV, scene iii of *Carmagnola*) meant neither isolation nor will of encroachment on other nations but rather a necessary step in a civilized progress that would make Italy an equal with the other nations in Europe.[8]

In the chorus of his first tragedy, *The Count of Carmagnola*, Manzoni clearly mirrored this ideal inspiring the circle of *Il Conciliatore*, by which it was altogether possible to harmonize the love for one's nation with universal love and love for other nations. Firmly convinced that Italy could be free only if it could be politically unified from north to south, Manzoni throughout the whole chorus reflects on the ruinous division of Italy into many warring city-states in the fifteenth century. At the end of that same century, because of those inner wars, Italy became an easy prey for foreigners bent on military conquest. The allusion to the present state of Italy—still subjugated to strangers as a result of those fratricidal wars of four centuries before—would not be missed by the sympathetic eye of patriotic contemporary readers:

All these fighters belong to one land,
They all speak the same language, and "brothers"
Is the name that the foreigner gives them;
The same traits appear on all faces,
The same land has nurtured them all,
This land that their blood now submerges,
And that nature from others divided
By the girth of the seas and the Alps.

Then, in the last stanza, Manzoni puts his desire for the independence and unification of Italy into a universal, ethical, and religious perspective:

We are all made in the image of One,
We are all children of a sole Redemption,
And no matter in what epoch, in what region,
We all pass through this ether of life,
We are brothers, we are tied by one pact.
Cursed be those who infringe such a pact,
Those who rise by trampling the weak,
Those who sadden an immortal spirit.

The Gospels taught Manzoni the democratic principle of equal dignity, not only for all individuals, but also for all nations: "The [Christian] Religion has equal consideration for all nations, it does not aim at the power or splendor of any one of them."[9] In the first of the two stanzas of *Carmagnola*'s chorus quoted above, the word "brothers" means people belonging to one nation, one by language and natural borders. In the second stanza, the same word means all human beings recognizing their brotherhood with Christ.

Il Conciliatore reviewed Manzoni's *Inni sacri*, although they had been published four years earlier. Manzoni's poetry was praised precisely because, with an admirable simplicity of style, the national language had been employed for a subject that could morally elevate the reader, making him into a better citizen. The conclusion of Giovan Battista de Cristoforis's review is exemplary of the democratic principles *Il Conciliatore* shared with Manzoni, as well as of its position on literature as a means to improve the moral composition of its readers: "Thus [Manzoni's] religious poetry, deeply felt and understood by all, has raised the highest interest in worship. The prayer, no longer mechanically mumbled by people who do not know what they are saying, has risen most warmly from adoring hearts; and the ensuing respect of religious and political laws has in turn reinforced the universal exercise of social virtues."[10]

The *Inni sacri* marked the beginning of Manzoni's quest for a popular literary language. Over the last two centuries Italian literature had grown to be an elitist enterprise, an exercise in a language so archaic and bookish that it was incomprehensible to most readers. In the years that led to the composition of *Carmagnola*, Manzoni and Fauriel frequently discussed the status of their respective national languages, as Charles de Sainte-Beuve summarizes:

> [Manzoni] saw clearly how in Italy, for several reasons, poetry could not accomplish its most natural task, that is to be the mirror of the national and social life. Italy's fragmentation in many states, the lack of a national center, together with laziness, cowardice, ignorance, or the self-aggrandizing of provincial people— all these things had caused the written language to become very different from the language as it was spoken in the diverse parts of the peninsula. The written language had been over time so intentionally transformed into a dead language that it now failed to affect the people in a direct, immediate, and universal way . . . [Manzoni] could not help experiencing a certain pleasure mixed with envy every time he saw the Parisian audience react uniformly to the performance of Molière's comedies. Such an immediate and intelligent communion of a whole people with the production of a genius—which is the ultimate proof of existence of the genius to himself—seemed to him precluded to his nation, divided and almost segregated into many parts owing to the dialects. This man, who was eventually to unite all the intelligent minds of his nation into a unanimous sentiment of admiration, could not then himself believe that such a unanimity would ever be achieved.[11]

Manzoni eventually formed a very simple view on the century-old "question of the language": the Tuscan idiom, in the form in which it was spoken by educated people in Florence's everyday life, was a viable standard to which all other variants of Italian could and should adapt. Manzoni himself, who could speak and write French as a native, was more versed in Milanese dialect than in Tuscan and constantly applied himself to mastering the Tuscan idiom. Throughout the years of Italy's political making, Manzoni became increasingly aware of his own personal mission: his contribution to the national unification could be in renewing the Dantean effort to give Italians a national, popular literary language.[12]

1819–1821: Attempted Expatriation, *Carmagnola*, and "March 1821"

The Austrian authorities exerted increasingly heavy censorship on the pages of *Il Conciliatore*, which would often go to press with several blotted-out paragraphs. On 18 October 1819, after the censor had heavily rebuked the editors' political effrontery, the publication was altogether suspended.

Manzoni was a personal friend of some of the conciliatoristi—Visconti, Berchet, Luigi Porro, Confalonieri—but did not participate in the publication of the paper. His friends were frequent visitors to his house in the city and in the countryside villa, and he would circulate the drafts of his writings among them. However, Manzoni, not unlike exiled Dante, "made himself a party of his own." He would not partake in the social evenings at La Scala and in 1817 initiated a petition for a passport to travel to Paris.[13]

Carlo Dionisotti argues that Manzoni kept his distance from the conciliatoristi for a precise reason, although the exchange of ideas with them was otherwise vital to his literary production. The conciliatoristi invited the Swiss historian Sismonde de Sismondi (1773–1842) to submit an article for the opening issue of *Il Conciliatore*, also asking him to be a regular foreign contributor. For that first issue Sismondi wrote a review of an 1817 edition of the Portuguese epic poem *Os Lusiadas* (1572) by Luis de Camoens. The historian elaborated on the history of Portugal, pointing to the stark contrast between the past glorious achievements of that nation and its present decadence. The allusion to Italy's similar lot was clear. Sismondi's ideas, however, did not sit well with Manzoni. In a chapter of his popular *History of the Italian Republics in the Middle Ages* (1809–18), the Swiss historian blamed the Catholic Church for the moral corruption of the Italians. Sismondi's statements occasioned Manzoni's rebuttal in an apologetic writing that went to form his *Osservazioni sulla morale cattolica*, composed between 1818 and 1819, just at the time when his friends were engaged in the publication of *Il Conciliatore*. Unlike his friends, Manzoni was not ready to renounce his southern European and Catholic roots by blindly espousing the ideas of Sismondi, who, like Madame de Staël, ultimately advocated the superiority of the freer Protestant cultures of northern Europe.

So, Dionisotti argues, Manzoni eagerly took the road to Paris in 1819 (when the Austrian authorities finally granted him and his family a passport), most probably for the need of distancing himself from Milan and its circles, whose public debates were not attuned with his more heartfelt questions and spiritual visions. In the beginning of his Parisian sojourn, Manzoni entertained the idea of moving to the French capital permanently, probably thinking he could find there an intellectual atmosphere more suited to his own literary and spiritual quests. The publication of his apology for Catholicism could not have met the approbation of the conciliatoristi. At the same time, the impending publication of *Carmagnola* would greatly please them, as it conveyed a patriotic message and was the first serious challenge by an Italian author to neoclassical theatre. But Manzoni did not want to earn a public recognition as the master or leader of the group from which he rather wanted to keep his independence.[14]

Paradoxically, this second—and last—Parisian sojourn brought Manzoni much closer to northern European literature, since it is there and then that he was introduced to the historical novels of Walter Scott (1771–1832). As a catalyst for Manzoni's ideas on historical fiction, Scott's works had almost as profound an influence as Shakespeare's histories and tragedies. Moreover, in Paris, Manzoni got acquainted with historian Augustin Thierry (1795–1856)—a friend of Fauriel's and the one who recommended Scott's novels. Thierry, whose ideas and historiographic method, very different from Sismondi's, inspired Manzoni for his second historical tragedy, *Adelchis*, as well as for *The Betrothed*.[15]

Apart from these fortunate personal and literary encounters, Manzoni's second stay in Paris turned out to be a disappointment from both an intellectual and spiritual point of view:

> During his last stay in Paris, Manzoni realized how things had deeply changed in France, like in Italy, after the fall of the Napoleonic empire, in both the doctrine and practice of religion and literary culture. He felt, in other words, that his duties as a Christian and as a writer were calling him back to Milan. The Christian came back disappointed, as we gather from this letter to Tosi [his spiritual adviser] dated 7 April 1820: 'Who could have told me that the situation in France would make me appreciate with joy the predicament of the Religion in Italy?' The writer went back to Milan with a rested and enriched soul. He could not know it, but it was as if he were sensing that his temporary, freely chosen and leisurely expatriation would soon be a term of historical comparison, first with Foscolo's definitive and sad self-exile and then with the inevitable, harsh, and long exile of the people convicted for the attempted patriotic riots of the years 1820–21.[16]

Manzoni went back to Milan in the summer of 1820 to engage in new literary enterprises and become one of the most beloved writers of the Italian people. And Milan in 1820 was not an easy place to go back to for a person who was on friendly terms with the conciliatoristi. By publishing, at the beginning of that year, *The Count of Carmagnola*—an "irregular," "romantic" tragedy—with the same printer, Vincenzo Ferrario, who had produced *Il Conciliatore* during its brief existence, Manzoni implicitly acknowledged his kinship with the romantic and patriotic group. The Austrian authorities were conducting inquiries and judicial procedures against the Carboneria, the secret sect that tried to organize a national unification movement among the noble and professional classes. In August 1820, the Austrian government instituted capital punishment for membership in any secret sect, equating such membership to an act of high treason.

In October 1820, Pellico was arrested for conspiring with the *carbonari*. He was condemned to death, but his sentence was commuted to life in prison. After nine years in the Spielberg jail in Moravia, he suddenly received an imperial pardon. He retired to Turin, abstaining from politics but not from literature. He published his memoirs, *My Prisons*, in 1832. Although the book narrates the spiritual evolution of a soul who finds comfort in God, the resigned, tranquil tone with which the hardships of imprisonment are recounted paradoxically made the book a vehement public indictment of Austrian tyranny. Pellico's sufferings touched his fellow patriots deeply, not only in Italy and Hungary, which were part of the Hapsburg empire, but also in Greece, until recently ruled by the Turkish empire, and Poland, under the Russian empire.

Manzoni's many-layered first tragedy, published a few months prior to the arrest of Pellico, profoundly resonated with the contemporary scene. The Republic of Venice in the drama represented in certain respects the Austrians, with their pompous ceremonies advertising to the world their Catholic orthodoxy, which was actually used as a convenient screen for hiding injustice. The Count of Carmagnola, summarily sentenced to death by the Venetians, foreshadowed many generous but reckless patriots who made themselves vulnerable to the repressive machine of the Hapsburgs. In Mark, the count's friend, Manzoni strikingly anticipated the sad character of those who recanted and betrayed, as they were unable to be loyal to their fellow patriots when caught by the Austrian police. Pietro Maroncelli, the carbonaro who first enmeshed Pellico into the activities of the sect, cowardly denounced his friends to the authorities when apprehended, whereas Pellico firmly maintained his silence.[17]

While the Austrians reinforced the coercive measures in the Lombardy-Venetia, in July 1820 Neapolitan army officers and judges affiliated with the Carboneria organized a successful rebellion in the Southern Kingdom (then called "of the two Sicilies," as it included the lands on both sides of the Messina Straits), which had been restored, after Murat's definitive demise, to the Bourbons' absolutist rule. The patriots' political agenda, modeled on the Spanish rebellion of 1812, was the creation of a constitutional monarchy, with a statute allowing the formation of elective legislative bodies. As the rebels had the upper hand militarily and enjoyed a wide popular consensus, King Ferdinand of Bourbon granted a constitution, solemnly swearing to uphold it. But the Austrians convened a meeting among the European powers, to which Ferdinand fled (leaving his son Francesco as a "vicar" on the throne) to condemn and undo a constitutional regime that represented a dangerous precedent and a threat to all the other absolutist monarchs, in Italy and throughout Europe. In March 1821 the Austrian army, after defeating the Neapolitan patriots, put an end to the regime of constitutional monarchy. Ferdinand resumed his place on the throne and ordered executions of the patriots who had not managed to flee.

A similar pattern, also in March 1821, followed the patriotic rebellion in the kingdom of Piedmont and Sardinia, where students and military officers rioted and requested that a constitution be granted. The patriots' insurrection prompted the king, Vittorio Emanuele I, to abdicate. Since his brother Carlo Felice—next in line of succession to the throne in the House of Savoy—was absent, the Prince of Carignano, Carlo Alberto, a known liberal sympathizer, took the regency at the king's command and granted a constitution on 14 March 1821. In the meantime, the Piedmontese rebels concerted with the Lombard patriots (carbonari and *federati*), led by Confalonieri, a joint armed effort to liberate Lombardy and Venetia from the Austrians. But this attempt failed as, upon his return to Piedmont, Carlo Felice repealed the constitution, Carlo Alberto left the kingdom, and the Austrians aided the Piedmontese king in orchestrating the repression of the patriotic insurrection.

Manzoni celebrated the attempted liberation of Lombardy in a poem, "March 1821," which he did not publish but circulated privately. The poem's dedication reads: "To the illustrious memory of Theodore Koerner, poet and soldier of the German independence, who died on the battlefield at Leipzig on 18 October 1813, a name dear to all nations who are fighting to defend or reconquer a fatherland."[18] In the last stanza, Manzoni seems to hint at the goodness of his recent personal decision to come back to Italy from Paris and be part of the momentous fight for national independence:

> *O the days of our redemption!*
> *O forever regretful those who*
> *From afar, from the lips of another*
> *Today gather this tale, just like strangers;*
> *who, when telling their children one day*

will confess with a sigh: 'I was elsewhere';
who will not have saluted that day
our blessed and victorious flag.

Soon after its composition, Manzoni burnt the manuscript of the poem, preferring to commit it to memory rather than risking imprisonment because of it, at a time when the Austrians never ceased looking at him with suspicion. On the occasion of the extensive rebellion of Lombardy-Venetia in 1848–49, which was again aided by the Piedmontese troops (with a more decisive intervention by Carlo Alberto, this time), Manzoni published his patriotic ode, devolving the sale profits to the refugees of the Veneto.

Harsh repression followed the attempted rebellion of 1821. Two other conciliatoristi, Confalonieri and Borsieri, were arrested at the end of that year. Manzoni helped Confalonieri's wife to write petitions for pardon to the emperor. Like Pellico's, Confalonieri's death sentence was commuted to life in prison; however, he was detained for a longer period in the Spielberg jail. In 1830 Teresa Confalonieri died of heartbreak for her worries over her husband's well-being. A handwritten inscription, dated 1836, that Manzoni sent inside a book to Confalonieri, testifies to our author's care for his friend during the long, terrible imprisonment. Confalonieri was finally released later in 1836, on condition that he leave Europe. He was readmitted to Italy in 1840 and died in 1846.

1822–1860: *Adelchis, The Betrothed,* and the Italian Unification

During 1821 Manzoni was tending intermittently to the composition of his second tragedy, *Adelchis.* In April he began working on the historical novel, *The Betrothed,* and in July he wrote the ode commemorating Napoleon's death, "The Fifth of May."

As *Carmagnola's* historical background clearly conjured up, in more than one way, reflections on Italy's current predicament (its inner division as cause of foreign subjugation, the count and the Republic of Venice hinting at the patriots and the Hapsburgs, respectively), so the topical allusions in *Adelchis* were fairly easy to detect for Manzoni's contemporaries.

After ruling out the subject that Fauriel proposed to him—the thirteenth-century anti-Hapsburg candidate to the imperial crown, Adolph of Nassau—Manzoni found what he claimed would be a much more popular subject: the end of the bicentenary Lombard rule over Italy (568–774).[19] The tragedy in its final form focused on the events of the last two years of the Lombard domination, directly leading to its fall during the joint reign of Desiderius and his son Adelchis,[20] at the hands of the king of the Franks, who came later to be known as Charlemagne. The war between the Franks and the Lombards in the tragedy naturally called to mind the recent clash between the French and the Austrians over the possession of Lombardy—the name of the region, deriving from that of the German population, provided in itself an immediate connection with the present—and control of the whole Italian peninsula. But this was only one way of interpreting the tragedy as a political allegory. Manzoni composed this work while the Neapolitan and Piedmontese constitutional rebellions were under way. In the first draft (which is extant), Adelchis is featured as a ruler who, although of German stock and therefore a stranger to the subjected Romans or Latins (the forefathers of the Italians), takes it upon himself to act as king of both the conquering Lombards and the native, vanquished people. Manzoni's own historical research showed how the Italians were utterly deprived of any rights under the Lombards, and, on revising the first draft, the author felt that the decrees and actions of the two last Lombard kings (Desiderius and Adelchis), who perpetuated that state of affairs, could not historically warrant an idealization of Adelchis.

At the end of 1821 Manzoni redrafted the tragedy, substantially changing the role of the tragic hero. He reduced the young king's dream of becoming the just ruler of a cohesive kingdom to a concise plan for a change in the dynastic strategy: "Let us return / the lands to the Romans, let us be friends / with Hadrian: he too so wishes" (I.ii). When Desiderius obstinately insists on his reckless course of land conquest, which he sees as the only means of keeping the kingdom together, Adelchis capitulates in the name of filial respect, and his capitulation is the beginning of the end for the Lombard domination over Italy. Gian Piero Bognetti convincingly maintains that contemporary history, rather than the author's historical research, must have catalyzed Manzoni's final portrayal of Adelchis.[21] Bognetti feels that Manzoni obviously chose this subject from national history with a view to addressing his fellow patriots. Both in Naples and in Piedmont, the patriots had relied on the favor of the younger member of the royal families to achieve their goal of setting up a constitutional monarchy. Francesco in the Southern Kingdom and Carlo Alberto in the kingdom of Piedmont and Sardinia, both played an ambiguous role in helping the patriots, ultimately failing to maintain the constitutions that the rebels had obtained from the elders of their royal houses. Adelchis, as he appears in Manzoni's first draft, might have reflected the initially promising patriotic role that these princes seemed to be willing to play in their openings to the patriots in the initial phases of the 1821 rebellions, while the Adelchis of the definitive version appears to mirror those princes' historical failures.

Bognetti also suggests another connection with contemporary events, that *Adelchis* was written to reconcile the patriots with the Church, at a time when many of them shared the opinion that the popes were chiefly to blame for Italy's political fragmentation. Manzoni's artistic treatment of the Church, however, developed beyond the possible oratorical concerns of *Adelchis*. The theme of the Church's role in Italian history, as well as in history *tout court*, forms a central concern in *The Betrothed*.[22] It is also not by chance that Manzoni's fifth of the *Inni sacri*, "La Pentecoste"—celebrating the foundation of the Church fifty days after Christ's passion and resurrection—appeared the same year *Adelchis* was published.

Manzoni wrote the first chorus of *Adelchis*, which praises the Franks' vigor and reviles the Italians' haplessness, after having completed the whole tragedy, in the dark months of winter 1822. *Adelchis* was finally published, again with the printer Vincenzo Ferrario, in October 1822. Manzoni then decided to abandon the genre of historical tragedy (sparse notes over historical sources and an outline for a third drama, *Spartacus*, are extant), with its oratorical references to contemporary events, and to devote himself to the composition of a novel.[23] However, he kept his subject strictly historical and national, as it had been for the tragedies. *The Betrothed* is set in the seventeenth century, during the Spanish domination over the dukedom of Milan and southern Italy. Taken with the two tragedies, the novel completes a trilogy that depicts the salient epochs in Italian history prior to the unification.[24]

When in 1827 Manzoni's *The Betrothed* was finally published, it became immediately popular: even the poorest scrambled for money to buy the three volumes, and the first two thousand copies were sold out in two months. In subsequent years the novel was illustrated, put in music, performed in marionette theatres, used to advertise consumer items such as matches, and adopted for reading in schools. As if in fulfillment of Berchet's 1816 appeal to create a literary patria in the absence of political unity, Manzoni made it possible for Italians to experience a sort of spiritual unification. Before becoming citizens of the same nation, many Italians, from north to south, were able to enjoy a book whose subject—drawn from national history—and lexicon—echoing the spoken language—they could understand and appreciate. The political meaning of Manzoni's novel was recognized (and prudently stated, for fear of the censor) by Pellico, who was in prison when he first read *The Betrothed* and wrote to Confalonieri, also languishing in the same jail: "In his two tragedies Manzoni was much greater than our petty critics would concede back then, but even if those works failed for some reason to be recognized for what they were—the highest expression of romantic theatre—this novel, I believe, will not fail. In this work he has achieved his goal fully; [in the tragedies] he was a man of remarkable stature, in the novel he is a giant. O dear, dear Manzoni! . . . Works like this deserve the greatest success, as they educate the mind and refine the mores; works like these can be rightly called 'beautiful deeds.'"[25]

While Italy was finally being unified politically, Manzoni was indeed given the respect due to a spiritual forerunner of the Risorgimento. In the year of the national revolution, 1859, a delegation of statesmen went to Manzoni's house to bestow on him an honorary title that came with a yearly state pension. In 1860, Savoy's prime minister and Italian minister of interiors Cavour accompanied with a warm personal letter the notification of the royal decree by which the author was appointed senator for life of the newly formed Italian Senate. In 1862 Giuseppe Garibaldi paid a visit to Manzoni at his house in Milan, and in 1868 Giuseppe Verdi tributed his personal homage to the author whom he had deeply admired since his youth (he read *The Betrothed* when he was sixteen). In the same year, Manzoni accepted to chair a parliamentary committee on the unification of the language and the means to divulge it. Giancarlo Vigorelli comments on Manzoni's ever-increasing interest for linguistic issues following the publication of his novel:

> Nobody can deny the almost obsessive nature of Manzoni's works on the language. But his was not a crisis, which can be altogether normal and legitimate for some writers, as was the case, for example, with Joyce, and, in Italy, with Gadda. Manzoni's correction of his *Betrothed* after the Tuscan idiom and all his painstaking work on the language were not dictated by a drought of his expressive power, but were rather an effort to contribute to the Risorgimento, to give linguistic unity to a nation laboriously endeavoring to achieve political unity. Manzoni's linguistic work ultimately contributed to our democracy, by greatly helping to forge a language for "the people with no name."[26]

RECEPTION OF MANZONI'S TRAGEDIES

The Count of Carmagnola—A Tragedy was released in Milan in the first days of January 1820, while its author still lingered in Paris. The Milanese readers were astir with the novelty produced by this work. In fact, they had been expecting this tragedy, as we know from a letter of Stendhal, who was living in Milan at that time, to his friend Baron de Mareste, dated 2 November 1819:

You have had there in Paris for two months, now, Monsieur Manzoni, a deeply devout young man who last spring composed two very long acts on the death of General Carmagnola, grandfather of the "Carmagnola" [a song of the French Revolution named after the village where the general was born], born at Carmagnola, in Piedmont, and *fatto morire* [sent to his death] in Venice by the Council of the Ten. These two acts were written for the closet only. He interrupted this work to translate Lamennais' book *On Indifference in Religious Matters* and to refute the impious statements by Sismondi. Ermes Visconti has then exhorted [Manzoni] to write a tragedy for the stage, so he has redone the two acts, and written the last three, in just three months. This "Death of Carmagnola" is in print now *e desta la più alta aspettazione* [and is raising the highest expectations]. All I fear is that it will displease ... because it is Romantic. At a certain point, soldiers are fighting, and a solitary man stops them: "Aren't you all Italians, all children of the same fatherland?" They say this passage is sublime.[27]

Other than mistakenly believing that Manzoni was translating Félicité de Lamennais' (1782–1854) book (which he never produced and most likely never undertook),[28] Stendhal was otherwise well informed. He even knew ahead of time the content of the tragedy's patriotic chorus, in which the wars among the fifteenth-century Italian city-states—which served as a backdrop for the tragedy of the mercenary captain Carmagnola—occasioned the author's allusive lament over contemporary Italy, still as divided as it had been four centuries before, and, accordingly, still easy prey to foreign domination. As we know from a letter to Fauriel, Manzoni did interrupt the tragedy's composition to write the *Osservazioni sulla morale cattolica*, which was finished in July 1819.[29] Having resumed and rapidly brought *Carmagnola* to conclusion, Manzoni left for Paris in September 1819, entrusting the manuscript of *Carmagnola* to Visconti, who helped with clearing it through the office of the Austrian censor and with printing.

Visconti must have felt proud of the mission entrusted to him by his friend. Manzoni had indeed produced in *Carmagnola*, as Stendhal hinted in the letter quoted above, a "romantic" drama, meaning, among other things, that Manzoni had written a tragedy without submitting to the rules of the unities of time and place. This was a stunning innovation, considering that in Italy, like in France, major dramatists had not produced anything else but "regular" tragedies for more than the last two centuries.[30] One year to the month before the publication of *Carmagnola* Visconti had published in *Il Conciliatore* two articles in form of dialogue on the unities of time and place in drama, demonstrating their irrationality, arbitrariness, and therefore their uselessness.[31] The unities of time and place had been made into a tenet of European drama since the rediscovery of Aristotle's *Poetics* during the Renaissance.

In 1823, in the first of three articles hailed as "the first major statement of the new Romantic school in France"[32] (later published in book form with the title *Racine et Shakespeare*) Stendhal modeled the dialogue about the dramatic unities between "the romantic" and "the Academic" on Visconti's 1819 dialogue.[33] Stendhal's article (occasioned by the necessity of defending the right to perform Shakespearean works on the Parisian stage) appeared in the *Paris Monthly Review of British and Continental Literature* just one week before the publication of Fauriel's French translations of Manzoni's two tragedies.[34] Fauriel's translations were accompanied by Manzoni's essay on the dramatic unities, which the author wrote in French while still in Paris, in 1820, to respond to a negative review of *Carmagnola* published by Victor Chauvet on the influential *lycée français*. The French critic found the tragedy's subject interesting but ruined by the disregard of the unity of time and place. He went so far as to indicate to Manzoni how he could and should have reduced the seven-year-long chain of events leading to the demise of the tragic hero to the traditional twenty-four-hour time-span, through a compact, more narrative organization of his material. Manzoni's reply was entitled "Lettre à Monsieur Chauvet sur l'unité de temps et de lieu dans la tragédie" (Letter to Monsieur Chauvet on the unities of time and place in tragedy). In it, his analysis of Shakespearean plays (*Othello* and *Richard II*) illustrates the "historical system" that contemporary dramatists should follow, while Voltaire's and Jean Racine's neoclassical tragedies exemplify the moral weakness of a theater based on the unities, which was to be abandoned. The juxtaposition of Racine and Shakespeare as models for the neoclassical and romantic dramatic schools respectively emerged as an evident common theme in major pieces of romantic dramatic theory in both France and Italy.

In Milan, a few days after the publication of *Carmagnola*, Pellico thus wrote to his brother:

8 January 1820

I am sending you Manzoni's wonderful tragedy *Carmagnola*, by the Monday coach. It seems to me a thing divine. Here it has been generally praised, and Monti himself has no other criticism but for its prosaic style; but Manzoni did not adopt that style unwittingly. He chose it as the most suited to a non-ancient subject, in which the characters' speech should not differ much from today's ordinary way of speaking. The advantage of such a style, which refrains from constructs and words too far from prose, is to endear the work also to those who are not conversant in the poetic language. Most Italian women, for example, have a hard time reading Italian poetry (except for Metastasio): Why? Because Italian poetry is couched in a language unknown to them. Give the poetry a known language and it shall acquire many readers of both sexes.[35]

Pellico and Manzoni were certainly of one mind and felt strongly about the mission of communicating their ideas to the largest number of readers, to reach out to mainstream Italians, the multitudes who remained outside the parlors of the learned elite.

Most local reviews of Manzoni's tragic art, however, did not have the appreciative tone of Pellico's letter and harped on the same point raised by Monsieur Chauvet in France: Manzoni's failure to comply with the dramatic unities. In the *Gazzetta di Milano* of January 1820, Francesco Pezzi "defended classicist ideas and tried to refute Manzoni's arguments against the unities. He then harshly criticized the tragedy for its boringly long dialogues, lack of tragic spirit, incoherence of plot, weakness of the hero, low moral stature of Mark [the count's friend]." In its February 1820 issue, the journal *Biblioteca italiana* criticized the language of the tragedy, defining it as *triviale* (coarse, vulgar), as well as the tragedy's structure and the supposedly wrong choice of illustrative episodes from the life of the general.[36] Other important, and also negative, contemporary reviews of *Carmagnola* and *Adelchis* are found in the *Commentari dell'Ateneo di Brescia* for the years 1821 and 1823.[37] In these *Commentari*—scripts of yearly speeches by the chair of the *Ateneo* (university) of Brescia—the chair criticized a too appreciative judgment of Manzoni's tragedies by one of the Ateneo di Brescia's members, Giambattista Pagani, who had been a personal friend of Manzoni's since their school years. The chair praised Pagani for having defended Manzoni against the disgraceful mockery contained in some of the attacks on his tragedies, but he substantially objected to Pagani's approval of his friend's elimination of the dramatic unities. The chair thought that this elimination was tantamount to going backward on the path of literary progress.

Soon after his return to Milan from Paris, Manzoni received the greatest reward he could want for his first endeavor in dramatic literature: Wolfgang von Goethe (1749–1832) published highly appreciative reviews of *Carmagnola* in *Ueber Kunst und Alterthum*.[38] The old poet—the Nestor of European literature, as he was called, after the elderly sage and warrior of the Homeric epics—using all his great literary and spiritual authority, praised Manzoni's tragic art. The Italian poet and dramatist was, in Goethe's view, the true heir of the historical drama that he and Schiller had initiated in Germany. Goethe had words of admiration

for all aspects of Manzoni's tragedy: its structure was devoid of the useless unities; the characters were nuanced, even the secondary parts; the wording was so
concise it was impossible "to detect either a redundant or a missing word"; the
meter, "whose alternating caesuras and numerous enjambments make it sound
like a freely versified recitativo, suitable to be passionately declaimed by the intelligent actor and accompanied by music."[39]

Although *The Count of Carmagnola* had bad fortune on the stage in its century
(see below), Manzoni's first tragedy was highly appreciated in artistic and patriotic circles. In the pages of his memoirs dated "Milan, June 1820," Venetian
painter Francesco Hayez (1791–1882) wrote: "Colonel Arese gave me the com-
mission for the painting of a scene from *The Count of Carmagnola*, the famous
tragedy of Alessandro Manzoni that had been recently published and had produced much sensation."[40] Hayez's painting *The Last Day of Count Carmagnola* was
exhibited at the Brera Gallery in July 1821 to great public acclaim.[41] At the end
of that same year, Francesco Arese, the colonel who had commissioned Hayez's
painting, was among those arrested by the Austrian authorities in connection
with the patriots' attempted rebellion in March. His arrest occurred in the same
wave of repressive measures that led to the arrest of Confalonieri and Borsieri,
among others. Hayez's painting and the arrest of its illustrious commissioner
"certainly amplified the allusions to the thorny questions of contemporary history contained in Manzoni's historical drama."[42]

A very close friend of Manzoni's, novelist Tommaso Grossi (who authored
in 1820 a historical novella in verse, *Ildegonda*, and some cantos of the epics *The
Lombards at the First Crusade*, later made popular by Verdi's opera) consented to
pose as Gonzaga in the painting. This practice, which derived from the Renaissance tradition, favored the involvement of the contemporaries in the portrayed
historical scene and was therefore perfectly in line with the spirit of civic engage-
ment present in Manzoni's historical drama.[43]

Manzoni later thanked Hayez with some lines of poetry, which he sent along
with a copy of his second tragedy:

> So vividly you painted for the eye
> What confusedly had dawned within my mind!
> Another formless, fleeting idea now
> Timidly I send to your imagination:
> Welcome it gladly, and out of it create
> Immortal figures of wonder and pity,

While I could only give it with my verse
A few despised days, and then oblivion.

But Hayez was not to immortalize *Adelchis* on canvas. Instead, he made another painting from *Carmagnola* for the 1824 exhibit at Brera. The painting depicted the count being led to his execution. The work was commissioned by Marquis Maurice Bethmann of Frankfurt, which suggests that Manzoni's tragedy was known in other parts of Europe. Even Stendhal, in his *Salon de 1824*, wrote that "all Italy speaks of this young Venetian painter's [Hayez's] work, exhibited in Milan, entitled *The Count of Carmagnola as He Goes to His Death, Receiving the Last Salutations of His Wife and Daughters*."[44]

Adelchis, unlike *Carmagnola*, did not cause much sensation, either on its publication, in 1822 or in the following years.[45] "Historical painting, which was by then bound to stay in the circuit of public exhibits, strictly obeyed market rules: no painter would have staked his reputation on such an unpopular, irksome, and unpleasant protagonist as Adelchis. This aspect of the tragedy, combined with its lack of clearly indicated solutions to the contemporary historico-political questions, caused Hayez and other painters of the historical school to steer clear of Lombard themes more or less directly inspired by Manzoni's second tragedy."[46]

In early 1824 *Biblioteca italiana* published a late and very unfavorable opinion on Manzoni's second tragedy along antiromantic, pro-neoclassicist lines. Again Manzoni was criticized for his lack of respect of the unities of time and place. A strong refutation of the *Biblioteca italiana* criticisms and a defense of Manzoni's second tragedy came one year later in the *Nuovo Ricoglitore*, from the pen of Niccolò Tommaseo, a linguist, novelist, and patriot, who was a friend of Manzoni's and an early admirer of his art.[47]

In France, Fauriel published his translations of Manzoni's tragedies, with a laudatory preface, as early as 1823, and Goethe saw to it that Manzoni's collected works, including *Adelchis*, were made available to the German public, although not in translation (except for some excerpts) in 1827. In the foreword to Manzoni's second tragedy, published in the 1827 volume of collected works, Goethe again bestowed his highest praises on the Italian author, particularly commending the rare and perfect fusion of poetry and history in *Adelchis*.[48] In England, while *Carmagnola* was timely reviewed (in September and November of the publication year by the *London Magazine*, and in October by the *Quarterly Review*, about which see below), no article on *Adelchis* appeared in literary periodicals before 1826–27. As Dionisotti has argued, in those years, "The Fifth of May" was published in English translation, spurring a renewed interest in Manzoni's literary enterprises, including *Adelchis*. Those late reviews, however, were substantially negative. Dionisotti argues that while *Carmagnola* fully responded to the English taste and expectations about Italy, the nation appeared in too problematic a light in *Adelchis*. Moreover, "The Fifth of May" reinforced Manzoni's image, in the English mind, as a great lyric poet, not as a dramatist.[49]

As for the reception of Manzoni's tragedies in the United States, Murray R. Low could not find any articles on Manzoni in major literary periodicals prior to 1833: "No mention was found of his tragedies and poems before the American translations of *I promessi sposi* [two in 1834] ... The two translations of the novel seem to have actually caused an interest in Manzoni rather than being occasioned by an existing interest."[50] The year 1834 was Manzoni's annus mirabilis in American criticism: three reviewers in particular praised Manzoni the tragedian as an innovator, indeed the creator of Italian romantic drama. One of them, Elizabeth Ellet, in her article in *American Monthly Magazine*, explained the plot in detail and translated passages from both tragedies in blank verse. In the following year, Edgar Allan Poe published a very positive evaluation of Manzoni's novel.

Stage Performances of the Two Tragedies

In 1828 the censor of the Grand Dukedom of Tuscany, Attilio Zuccagni Orlandini, asked Manzoni for permission to stage his dramas. In his reply, Manzoni kindly but firmly refused, reiterating what he had already stated elsewhere, that his two tragedies were not suitable for the stage. Through a keen stylistic analysis of all the passages where Manzoni refers to his tragedies as closet drama (see one of these in the preface to *Carmagnola*), Paolo Bosisio remarks how the author, in each case, is being either modest about his own work or polemical with the existing constraints of the literary and theatrical conventions of the time.[51] Based on his technical analysis of Manzoni's successive drafts of the two dramas, Bosisio concludes that one should not take at face value Manzoni's declarations about his tragedies' lack of stage qualities because they were indeed composed with a view to their theater performance. Several stage productions have indeed been attempted:[52]

1828. Luigi Vestri, an accomplished and famous actor, staged *Carmagnola* at the Teatro Goldoni in Firenze. It was a flop, with the audience mocking the actors on stage. The majority of the actors, except Vestri and Carolina Internari, who took the leading roles, were inexperienced amateurs. Only the last act and the chorus were appreciated.

1834. Gustavo Modena, one of the most famous actors of his times, recited the
. speech of Deacon Martinus in *Adelchis,* act II, at the Teatro Re, in Milan. An unverifiable source records that Manzoni was among the audience and embraced the actor on stage at the end of the recital. The tale of Martinus became, after that night, part of Modena's repertoire.

1839. A mixed company of professionals and amateurs gave a performance of *Carmagnola* at the Teatro Ducale in Parma, for which no reviews or testimonies are extant, only the poster announcing the show. In the same year, Gustavo Modena staged the last scenes of *Carmagnola* at the Teatro S. Benedetto in Venice; the day-after review described Manzoni's tragedy as "sublime."

1843. The Compagnia Reale Sarda (Royal Company of the Kingdom of Sardinia and Piedmont) staged *Adelchis* at Teatro Carignano in Turin. It was the first attempt at staging Manzoni's second tragedy, and it was very badly received. Pellico, who went to see the performance, was saddened by the disrespectful behavior of the audience, but he expressed doubts about the intrinsic stage qualities of *Adelchis.*

1873. A few months after Manzoni's death, the famous actor Ernesto Rossi appeared in *Carmagnola* staged in Naples at the Teatro dei Fiorentini (Compagnia Alberti-Majeroni). The reviewer for the daily city paper described the staging as excellent but the actors' performance as poor.

1874. At the Teatro alla Cannobiana in Milan, *Adelchis* was unsuccessfully staged by an actor who botched the text.

1875. In Milan, at the Teatro Fossati, *Adelchis* was performed amid the respectful attention of the audience, notwithstanding the bad delivery of the text by the actors.

1938. Director Gualtiero Tumiati successfully staged *Adelchis* in Milan, at the Teatro Lirico, with Filippo Scelzo in the leading role.

1940. *Adelchis* was performed with great success in the outdoor scenery of the Giardino dei Boboli in Florence. The director was Renato Simoni, and Salvo Randone was cast as King Charles.

1960. *Adelchis* was brought to stage by Vittorio Gassman (who starred in the leading role) with the company Teatro Popolare Italiano. The cross was the central symbol of Gassman's stage production, employed to connote "the heroes' death" as well as "the [spiritual] death from which the Italian people seem unable to wake up." Adelchis was given speeches from the first draft of the tragedy in which he is depicted as a king with a mission to unify Lombards and Romans; both choruses were recited by Gassman as Adelchis.

1973. To commemorate the centennial of Manzoni's death, director Ruggero Rimini presented a performance freely drawn from *Adelchis* at the Teatro Uno in Florence. It was successful and toured some Italian cities in that year.

1984–85. In the occasion of the bicentenary of Manzoni's birth, Carmelo Bene (who vied with Gassman for the recognition as the best actor of the Italian stage during the twentieth century) created a recital from *Adelchis* for two voices (Bene as Adelchis, and Anna Perino as Ermengarde), accompanied by much music and drums. Bene—who collaborated with Giuseppe Di Leva in the creation of the recital's script—was convinced that there was no other way to stage such a tragedy. The actor reprised this recital several times, with variants (and with Elizabetta Pozzi as feminine voice), during the 1980s and 1990s. *Carmagnola* was staged twice in 1985: in Busto Arsizio (Varese) at the Teatro Sociale, by director Delia Cajelli, and in Milan, in the inner yard of the Senatorial Palace, by director Giuseppina Carutti.

1989. Director Lamberto Puggelli produced *Carmagnola* with the Teatro Piccolo company in Milan, obtaining mostly very favorable reviews. The tragic hero was portrayed with a mixture of violent passions, love for glory and hate for his former master. The members of the audience in the first row were invited to wear the red robes of the Venetian senators, to create a bridge between the two sides of the curtain. The scenery (Venice and the boggy battlefield at Maclodio) included much water. The chorus, which the director deemed to be the climax of the performance, was recited twice: at the end of the first part of the performance (after the first two acts) by the whole company, literally in a chorus, and at the beginning of the second part by an actor (Tino Carraro) in bourgeois attire. Puggelli's *Carmagnola* toured Italy. In the same year, famous actor and director Giorgio Strehler composed a recital from *Carmagnola* and *Adelchis* for his solo performance, at the Teatro Studio in Milan.

1992. Federico Tiezzi staged *Adelchis* with the Teatro Biondo di Palermo company featuring famous actors in the cast, such as Arnoldo Foà. In the production, Adelchis was conceived as a hero of modernity, with his dilemmatic, introspective personality and Anfrid, his squire, as his soul's mirror. Adelchis also fought for justice, as the patriots in Manzoni's times did. The scenes and costumes therefore were in the Risorgimento fashion, and the music was Verdian. But most reviewers (Tiezzi's *Adelchis* toured the main Italian cities) did

not appreciate the superimposition of nineteenth-century posturing and costumes (the uniforms of the Austrian and Piedmontese armies) over the war
between Lombards and Franks. Most, however, appreciated Ermengarde's
death scene, set in a war hospital, in line with the setting of the Risorgimento
wars.

1993–96. Renato Borsoni created a cycle of yearly performances drawn from
 Adelchis and set among the historical monuments of Brescia, the city where
 Ermengarde died. Originally planned to last until 2000 (the city administration cut funding in 1996), each year part of the cycle was performed with a
 different focus and a different director.

On balance, although the preference for selected recitals drawn from the
tragedies has continued from the nineteenth into the twentieth century, directors have begun to uncover the dramatic power of the unabridged works. This
seems especially true of Puggelli's *Carmagnola.* However, their dramatic power appears to be still largely untapped. A survey of the twentieth-century reviews of
performances (see bibliography) reveals the persistence, with very few exceptions, of a misguided interpretation, in directors and reviewers (journalists and
scholars) alike that Manzoni's tragic heroes are innocent victims, Christlike sacrificial figures. Tiezzi's *Adelchis* especially went a long way in trying to promote
admiration for the supposedly modern, dilemmatic nature of its title character.
It is my conviction—and Puggelli's *Carmagnola* confirms it—that an altogether
different interpretation of Manzoni's tragic heroes is needed to stage these historical tragedies successfully (see below).

Manzoni and Historical Drama
History on Stage: A "Revolution in Drama"

Manzoni's essay "On the Historical Novel—and, in General, on Literary Works
Resulting from the Mixture of History and Fiction," published in 1845, while
expressing deep reserve as to the ethical nature of the historical novel, cast historical drama in a more positive light.[53] Evaluating the impact of history on
drama that he himself both witnessed and fostered, Manzoni wrote words somewhat out of character with his usually prudent and measured style: "history had
not to wait long before initiating the revolution in drama that we now see triumphant."[54] He indicated, somewhat humorously, the fathers of historical
drama (those who were in fact his own models and masters) and the great resistance the genre had to confront at its inception:

In Germany . . . Goethe . . . , in taking the path of the historical drama marked out by the "savage genius" [Shakespeare], and in taking it—as happens with great talents—without intention or fear of imitating, from his first steps forward imposes the rationale of history on his nation at the expenses of the two unities. But in France, long proud of poets who had taken the other path, and in Italy, also proud of a recent poet [Alfieri], it was a different story. "What!" they said. "The rules to which a Corneille, a Racine, a Voltaire, an Alfieri submitted . . . now seem a burdensome constraint on genius, an obstacle to perfection! How the proving grounds must have narrowed!" I do not know whether proposing that those rules be abolished seemed more an intolerable temerity or a wretched folly. But for history to burst into tragedy as it intended, it actually had to knock down that bulwark [of the unities], and it did.[55]

And he concludes: "Now . . . poets . . . , when history books lack details, search them out in any available kind of document to amplify or even to locate their subject. They are very happy if they manage to produce a more complete idea of the historical fact they are depicting, and even happier if they come up with a new idea different from the one commonly held."[56]

Manzoni is here describing what he did when he composed *Carmagnola* and *Adelchis*. The historical dramatist, before penning his verse, dons the garb of the modern historian, who compares all extant evidence with a critical eye and then tries to reconstruct the historical truth, challenging, rather than adapting to, conventional interpretations.[57] This approach is more conspicuous for *Adelchis*, which was published together with a historical tract inspired by an original historiographic hypothesis. But even in *Carmagnola* the historical research was meant to produce not only a historical play but a new interpretation of a famous event in Italian history.

In its last sentence, the preface of *Carmagnola* introduces the historical notes and alludes to the author's preoccupation with mixing history in fiction, which would be developed in "On the Historical Novel": "The tragedy is preceded by some historical notes on the character and the events that form its subject. I conceived such a premise thinking that whoever resolves to read a work resulting from the mixture of historical truth and fiction, may like to be able, without lengthy inquiries, to discern what was preserved in it of the real facts." The historical notes Manzoni prepared for *Carmagnola* and *Adelchis* were an absolute novelty in Italian literature. The closest precedent was in Germany, where Friederich Schiller (1759–1805) had been, among other things, both a historian and a dramatist. He had written *The History of the Thirty Years' War* (1791–93) before com-

posing the theatrical trilogy *Wallenstein* (1796–99), centered on the imperial gen-
eralissimo in that war.

Manzoni's aesthetic results were also stunningly new: his historical tragic
heroes were highly individualized characters, whose actions and reactions the
reader comes to understand, not only from the facts and descriptions of the historical setting in the author's prefatory notes, but by an essential and cinematic
presentation of the most important scenes reconstructed from the last years of
the heroes' lives.

Georg Lukács devoted a chapter to historical drama in *The Historical Novel* (a
classic in the academic realm since the 1960s). In it, he recognizes Manzoni's
foremost importance in promoting historicism in literature, especially in drama,
where the masterpieces, in Lukács's view, have been much rarer than in the narrative genre: "Manzoni, the most important exponent of historical drama at the
time [romantic period] in Western Europe, very consistently sees its mainspring
in this [Goethe's, in *Goetz von Berlichingen*] individualization of characters and destinies; and this kind of historical drama he polemically opposes to the abstract-
ing method of classicism." Lukács mentions Manzoni's first tragic hero together
with Alexander Pushkin's and George Büchner's as successful embodiments of
romantic historical drama: "Dimitri, Boris Godunov, Carmagnola or Danton are
portrayed as historical heroes in whose personal lives just those features are un-
derlined and explained which have made them the concrete [Hegelian] 'world-
historical individuals' they are, and which cause their tragic rise and fall. . . . The
dramatic greatness of [historicism in drama] lies in its successful translation
of social-historical driving forces into the interplay of contending, concrete
individuals."[58]

This passage may well serve as an effective definition of historical drama.
Lukács devotes much attention to historical fiction because his thesis is that the
historicization of literature by romantic authors such as Scott, Pushkin, and
Manzoni, paved the way for social realism, the literary form Lukács most admires. Simply put, without a Walter Scott there would have never been a Honoré
de Balzac.

It is not surprising that a Marxist scholar like Lukács, provided he could
eschew Manzoni's theme of nationhood, as he did, could find himself in close
agreement with the Christian dramatist's view of history and literature. Both
Lukács and Manzoni conceive history teleologically, as the unfolding in time of
an impersonal shaping force. For the Marxist scholar that force is the dialectic,
or conflict of social classes that will ultimately bring about the classless society
of communism; for Manzoni that force is Divine Providence, which has a plan

for the world as a whole and for every individual in it. Both the Marxist and the Christian are keenly interested in the interaction between the universal plan and the individual's existence—as seen through personal decisions and actions— what Lukács calls the Hegelian world-historical individual and Manzoni, the human being endowed with free will and the knowledge of moral precepts. It is precisely this interaction that proves to be the center of artistic and ethical interest in historical fiction for both Lukács and Manzoni.[59]

Romantic historical drama has been more recently defined from the standpoint of the theme that Lukács deliberately avoids, the theme of nationhood. European theater scholar Marvin Carlson has rightly pointed out the link between nationalism and romantic drama: "The roots of modern nationalism and romanticism are closely intertwined. The romantic dramatist found in national history, legend, and myth a fertile source of subject matter, and in the struggles for national freedom and identification [the dramatist found] important sources of dramatic power. The emerging nationalist consciousness found in the romantic drama a highly useful means for encouraging national enthusiasm, pride and solidarity."[60] To illustrate the Italian romantic stage in its connection with the national theme, Carlson mentions Pellico, Manzoni, and Gian Battista Niccolini (1782–1861).[61] He also reviews examples from the German, Spanish, Russian and other European national theaters. Notwithstanding the great variety of the examples encountered in his survey, he concludes: "The historical drama with a specific nationalist focus was, however, a particular concern of the romantic period when the modern concept of nation-state was developing."[62]

A third way of defining romantic historical drama—besides indicating in Goethe its father and in Shakespeare its archetype (as both Manzoni and Lukács do) or pointing to the common subject of a theme of nationhood (as Carlson does)—is to pit it against the neoclassical dramatic tradition of Racine, Voltaire, and their followers, as the romantics did. Although not all the romantic authors of historical dramas were of one mind on the question of the unities of time and place and might advocate, one way or another, a continuity with the tragic genre of Aristotelian descent, this negative definition—romantic historical drama as a reaction to the high-flown style, ancient setting, and abstract method of neoclassicism—holds true for all the most renowned historical dramas composed by authors as diverse as Goethe, Schiller, Manzoni, Victor Hugo, Alfred de Musset, Byron, Pushkin, and Büchner, from the end of the eighteenth century to the first decades of the nineteenth.[63]

Reforming Neoclassical Drama:
Pellico, Foscolo, and the Alfierian Legacy

In Italy, the neoclassical tradition was indeed hard to die, as the cold reception of *Carmagnola* and *Adelchis* demonstrated and as Manzoni remarked many years later in his essay on historical fiction. When *Carmagnola* was first published, even a fellow romantic like Pellico, admirer of Shakespeare and Schiller, failed to see, at first, the depth of Manzoni's revolutionary use of history in drama. Pellico addressed the question of history in a letter to his brother (dated 20 February 1820) in which he somewhat revised his initial positive judgment of Manzoni's *Carmagnola.* This tragedy failed to create a passionate response in the reader, he wrote, because "heroes are left too similar to their historical selves. Poetry is a more beautiful world than the real one, and the inhabitants of that world should have a higher stature than ours, in either love, or wrath, or political virtues, and so on. But please do keep this opinion of mine to yourself because nothing would sadden me more than earning the fame of being envious of Manzoni's merit. This is the reason why I do not dare to criticize his tragedy."[64]

Pellico had been the regular reviewer of dramatic works for *Il Conciliatore* in the previous year and was a tragedian himself, whose fame had been secured by his *Francesca da Rimini* (1815 on stage, 1818 in print). The novelty of Pellico's tragedy consisted in its setting, the Italian Middle Ages, instead of ancient Greece or Rome. The author, however, had not defied the respect of the classical unities, nor did he consult chronicles and documents of Italian history. The plot borders therefore on national legend, rather than national history, since it was drawn from Dante's famous episode of Paolo and Francesca in the *Inferno,* a story whose historical authenticity cannot be corroborated by any document other than Dante's literary creation. In writing his tragedy, Pellico, unlike Manzoni, did not seek historical plausibility, let alone accuracy; rather, he aimed at exciting strong passions in the audience. In the unhappy story he chose there was much love, to which Pellico added wrath, melancholic despair, and paternal sorrow. In order to excite these stormy passions, without forgetting to insert "political virtues," Pellico invented anachronistic and implausible aspects for his historical characters: Paolo was not only the unfortunate lover and brother-in-law of Francesca but also a mercenary captain who regrets having to fight for nations other than his own fatherland. At the end of the tragedy's twenty-four hours Lanciotto, lord of Rimini, kills his brother Paolo and his wife Francesca, mistakenly thinking they are lovers (a major change from the *Inferno,* in which the adultery is real). But early that same day the brothers are warmly affectionate with each other, as they are joyously reunited after Paolo comes back to Rimini from vaguely indicated "wars" fought for "Byzanthium," (although a previous version reads "Germany"). Paolo tells Lanciotto:

> *From now onward we'll never part again.*
> *I am tired of the vain visions of glory.*
> *I shed my blood for the throne of Byzanthium,*
> *Defeating cities that I did not hate.*
> *I earned renown, the emperor bestowed*
> *On me plentiful honors. Yet all these*
> *Universal praises made me uneasy:*
> *For whom was my sword stained with slaughters' blood?*
> *For the foreigner. As if I did not*
> *Have my fatherland, who holds most sacred*
> *The blood of all her citizens! For you,*
> *My Italy, with your courageous sons,*
> *I will fight, if offense moves your will at last.*
> *Aren't you indeed the gentlest land among*
> *All those the sun illumines every day?*
> *Aren't you mother of all the arts, o Italy?*
> *Is not your dust the dust of noble heroes?*
> *My fathers had from you wisdom and power;*
> *Your bosom hosts all that I have most dear. (I.v)*[65]

As Pellico's tragedy premiered on 18 August 1815, a little over a year after the Austrians had regained possession of northern Italy, we can imagine how the Milanese audience sitting that night at the Teatro Re, could have easily read between the lines of Paolo's patriotic tirade, which was not connected in any way to the central plot, not even to the contiguous dialogue with Lanciotto. Paolo's speech was rather the dramatist's own disguised speech aiming at keeping alive in the Italians their patriotic hopes, even in the face of the restored Hapsburg domination. With its mixture of unhappy love and patriotic messages, the popularity of this tragedy was vast and lasting, beyond the enthusiastic acclaim at the premiere (which Pellico relates in a letter to his brother), for decades to come.

In October 1820, the authoritative English journal *Quarterly Review* decreed Pellico's *Francesca* the best of three recent attempts at reviving Italian tragedy, the other two being Manzoni's *Carmagnola* and Ugo Foscolo's *Ricciarda*. The reviewer,

Rev. H. H. Milman, Oxford professor of poetry, summarily wrote that "*Carmagnola* wants poetry," labeled the work "feeble," and judged that much more originality was needed for an Italian author to be able to abandon the dramatic unities with good results. The reviewer extolled Manzoni's chorus and translated it entirely. He advised Manzoni to forsake drama and go back to the composition of odes in which he could truly excel. Foscolo and Pellico, on the other hand, had done exactly what he, the reviewer, would expect Italian tragedians to do: keep the unities—which are somewhat necessary for the untidy Italian spirit—and draw the subjects from some of those novellas that had made the fortune of many an English dramatic work.

According to Milman, Foscolo with his *Ricciarda* (1813) had produced a "regular" good tragedy about a Romeo-and-Juliet type of story set in southern Italy. But "Signor Foscolo" did not get the palm of victory among the three tragedians considered in Milman's article, although that Italian poet was at the time living "among us," that is, in London, where he expatriated in 1816 (crossing paths with Byron, by the way, who moved to Italy the same year). Pellico had done even better than drawing his subject from novellas or history (Milman is not sure if Foscolo's characters are also historical). By resorting to Dante, Pellico had set the best example yet for young Italian tragedians to follow: "Why should not Dante be to them what Homer was to the Greek tragedians?"[66] In this review (which occasioned Goethe's second article on *Carmagnola*, on which see above) Manzoni's fundamental innovations—eliminating the unities and allowing history to be center stage—were overshadowed by Foscolo's and Pellico's moderate attempts at reforming the tragic tradition.

With *Ricciarda*, Foscolo tried his hand at a national setting drawn from a vaguely defined Middle Age. His previous two tragedies had an ancient subject in rigorously neoclassical style: *Thyestes* (1796), which followed Seneca's tragedy of the same name, and *Ajax* (1811), recreated from Homer's epic. Foscolo dedicated his first dramatic work to the master of Italian neoclassical tragedy, Vittorio Alfieri (1749–1803), who read it and found it promising. Alfieri's twenty-one tragedies, all composed in the 1770s and 1780s, formed an inescapable paradigm for anyone attempting to write in the tragic style in Italy at the turn of the century. Alfierian emulators included not only Foscolo, but also his friends, the Pindemonte brothers, Giovanni and Ippolito, Monti, and a host of minor poets.

Aesthetically, Alfieri aimed at bringing Racine's neoclassical tragedy to a higher level of discipline and restraint, not only by a strict observance of the unities of place and time but also by reducing the number of secondary characters. As for subject matter, Alfieri's tragedies, mostly drawn from the Greek tragic cycles and Roman history, focused invariably on the conflict between the individual and the political power that curbs freedom by its laws. Similar to Alfieri's treatise on tyranny (1778), in which the characteristics of the tyrannical regime are infrequently illustrated by historical episodes (and the few that are are taken from ancient history), historical events and circumstances in his tragedies serve only as a pretext for a display of stoicism or strength of will in the tragic hero; they never become part and parcel of the character's motivations. German scholar August von Schlegel (1767–1845), in his influential *Course of Lectures on Dramatic Art and Literature* (lectures held in Vienna in 1808–9, published in Heidelberg in 1809–11, translated into French in 1814), harshly criticized this latest production of Italian tragedy when he came to review Alfieri, precisely because of Alfieri's utter disregard for historical sources. It was this disregard that produced rigid, black-and-white characters who merely illustrated abstract principles. Schlegel compared Alfieri's *Octavia*, allegedly based on Tacitus, with Racine's *Britannicus:*

> Racine appears here before us as a man who was thoroughly acquainted with all the corruption of a court, and had beheld ancient Rome under the Emperors reflected in [Tacitus'] mirror of observation. On the other hand, if Alfieri did not expressly assure us that his *Octavia* was a daughter of Tacitus, we should be inclined to believe that it was modeled on that of the pretended Seneca [*Octavia*, sole extant classical tragedy of contemporary Roman history, attributed to Seneca]. The colors with which he paints his tyrants are borrowed from the rhetorical exercises of the school. Who can recognize in his blustering and raging Nero the man who, as Tacitus says, seemed formed by nature "to veil hatred with caresses?"[67]

Schlegel found that Alfieri had "succeeded best in painting the public life of the Roman Republic" in *Virginia.* Conversely, the scholar was unimpressed with Alfieri's depiction of Imperial Rome in *Octavia*, of the Jewish people at the time of their first king in *Saul*, and of the Greeks and their "heroic magnificence" in *Agamemnon* and *Orestes.* Schlegel also disapproved of Alfieri's few tragedies with a "non-ancient subject":

> If Alfieri has in [*Octavia's*] case been untrue to Tacitus, in *The Conspiracy of the Pazzi* he has equally failed in his attempt to translate Macchiavel [*sic*] into the language of poetry. In this and other pieces from modern history, the *Filippo* for instance, and the *Don Garcia*, he has by no means hit the spirit and tone of modern times,

nor even of his own nation: his ideas of the tragic style were opposed to the observance of everything like *a local* and *determinate costume.* . . . While the Unity of Place is strictly observed, the scene chosen is for the most part so invisible and *indeterminate*, that one would fain imagine it is some out-of-the way corner, where nobody comes but persons involved in painful and disagreeable transactions. Again, this stripping his kings and heroes, for the sake of simplicity, of their external retinue, produces the impression that the world is actually depopulated around them.[68]

In his book, a cornerstone of European romanticism, Schlegel makes it clear that the recent attempts by Racine and Alfieri "to restore the ancient stage"[69]— which had been, at best, a mirror to the Greek civilization, forever lost since the advent of Christianity—were dead ends in literary history. The dramatic art of the present age needed rather, in Schlegel's view, a rediscovery of the essence of "the romantic." He cautions, however, that this essence is not in the beautiful folklore being rediscovered by poets, such as ballads, narratives of the Middle Ages, and the like, but rather in national history:

We have lately endeavored in many ways to revive the remains of our old national poetry. These may afford the poet a foundation for the wonderful festival-play; but *the most dignified species of the romantic is the historical.* In this field, the most glorious laurels may yet be reaped by dramatic poets who are willing to emulate Goethe and Schiller. Only *let our historical drama be in reality and thoroughly national; let it not attach itself to the life and adventures of single knights and petty princes, who exercised no influence on the fortunes of the whole nation. Let it, at the same time, be truly historical, drawn from a profound knowledge, and transporting us back to the great olden time.* In this mirror let the poet enable us to see, while we take deep shame to ourselves for what we are, what the Germans were in former times, and what they must again be.[70]

When the *Course on Dramatic Art* started to circulate in Italy, Schlegel's negative judgment on Alfieri came to many, even in romantic circles, as an unpleasant surprise. Alfieri was a national glory. His *Myrrha* and *Saul* remained popular stage productions throughout the nineteenth century. His other ancient heroes, endowed with stern and firm purposes in the face of tyrannical rulers had enjoyed great popularity in the years following the French Revolution, as they embodied the budding, still confused aspirations to freedom and independence harbored by Foscolo's generation.[71]

Il Conciliatore, true to its name announcing a conciliatory line, paid to Alfieri the homage due to a great Italian author, interpreter of national aspirations and one who, in many respects, was impossible to equal. Pellico defended Alfieri in these terms in the first issues of the foglio, in which he sided with the refutation of a critic who had accused the poet of being just a minor imitator of French neoclassical tragedians.[72] At the same time, Il Conciliatore was receptive of Schlegel's criticism of the major Italian tragedian. In his essay entitled "On Tragic Poetry, as Well as on Romanticism," Giuseppe Nicolini saw a great future for the tragic genre freed from the neoclassical yoke: "The independence from the unities of time and place resulting from the current literary debate, mostly revolving around drama, opens up a new road to follow for the young writers of genius. This road is free from those hurdles that had been created by a school to which Alfieri wanted to enslave his creative genius, and can lead to a sort of artistic beauties to which he could not necessarily aspire."[73]

Conversely, Foscolo remained the staunch defender of the Alfierian legacy. In 1827, in a lengthy essay, On the New Italian Dramatic School (published as an article in London and posthumously in book form), he maintained that Alfieri was the sole touchstone in the tragic genre, praising and justifying his choice of ancient Greek and Roman subjects. Foscolo was horrified that Manzoni, leader of the "new dramatic school," only mentioned Alfieri disparagingly as the author of the Misogallo (The hater of the French) in his lengthy essay on drama. This was, Foscolo thought, because Alfieri was identified as the master of the "old school," that is, the neoclassical.[74] Foscolo's article was mostly a dismissive reading of Carmagnola. As a Venetian, Foscolo thought he knew more than Manzoni about that city-state and its ways and history, and he devoted himself to a fastidious, and inessential, analysis of the play. Foscolo also took issue with Manzoni's enterprise to bring history onto the stage. Foscolo thought that as a genre historical tragedy "does not benefit history and harms poetry alike": "The historian guides us by presenting events and by reasoning over them; the poet guides us instead by means of the imagination and of the very strong feelings that this faculty, almost almighty in man, can at all times excite, provided it is handled with mastery. Poetry aims at making us feel intensely our existence and lifting it up from its annoying problems; history intends instead to direct our lives so that we can avail ourselves of its vision of the world as it is."[75]

Both Foscolo's and Pellico's criticism of Manzoni's drama posit the shallow conflict of reason versus passion (or reason / reality versus passion / feelings / ideal) that is stereotypically "romantic." They both put historical accuracy on the side of the mortifying elements (reason, facts) set against the more vital parts of man (passions, feelings). One of Manzoni's many aims in his tragedies was to debunk these simplistic dualisms of the romantic stereotype. But most importantly, in refusing to employ the unities Foscolo and Pellico kept using, Manzoni was targeting exactly what those two dramatists, like most dramatists at that time, held most dear: the centrality of passions in drama. Manzoni's reason for eliminating the unities was strictly connected with shifting the focus of tragedy away from an abstract and absolute treatment of human passions and toward historical truth. In *Carmagnola*'s preface and historical notes, Manzoni implicitly connects the refutation and elimination of the unities in the form of the tragedy with the necessity of historical accuracy in its content. Manzoni refused to cater to the facile enjoyment of love stories. National history, political justice, history as God's plan, free will—these are some of the themes that Manzoni submits to his audience for reflection and judgment.

Manzoni's "Schlegelian" Dramas

Manzoni had carefully read and profoundly admired Schlegel's *Course on Dramatic Art* in its 1814 French version. He proclaimed "excellent" the lesson in which the German author discusses the use of the unities in drama.[76] In fact, in his preface to *Carmagnola*, Manzoni declares that his discourse on the refutation of the unities is just "a little appendix" to what has been so amply and well discussed by recent writings on this topic. Schlegel is the only modern author quoted in Manzoni's preface to *Carmagnola*, once in connection with the refutation of the Aristotelian origin of the two unities and once for his ideas on the chorus in tragedy.

If we consider the emphasized sentences in Schlegel's quotes above, we will realize how Manzoni's tragedies perfectly corresponded to the kind of drama the German author envisioned for their present age. The stories of Carmagnola and Adelchis were drawn from national history, and they were not "the life and adventures of single knights and petty princes, who exercised no influence on the fortunes of the whole nation," as, for example, was Foscolo's "prince of Salerno" in *Ricciarda*. Manzoni's tragedies deal with momentous events in Italian history and their tragic heroes play important roles in them.

In the first tragedy, Carmagnola could have become ruler of Milan, as another captain, Francesco Sforza (featured in act II), did a few years after Carmagnola's death. Having married into the Visconti family (as Carmagnola had also done) and having earned the merits of defending the city against the Venetians, Sforza ousted the consolidated Viscontean rule in 1450. Moreover, Manzoni's Carmagnola hints at Italy as a divided nation (act I, scene 4), and this hint makes us perceive that this is an unnatural division that only benefits mercenary captains like himself who try to sell themselves to one of Italian rulers, either princes or republics. The tragic hero's lucid view of Italy occasions reflections on the ever-present idea of Italy as a nation throughout the centuries, as well as on the power of armies and their generals in the life of nations. Could the audience miss the allusion to the recent vicissitudes of Napoleon? Could they ignore the importance of military force if Italy had to be politically unified?

Even if Carmagnola did not become a ruler like Sforza, he did exercise "influence on the fortune of the whole nation" because he was the general for the Republic of Venice at the crucial battle of Maclodio (see act II). By winning this battle, thanks to the new military techniques invented by their general, the Venetians started steadily to gain power on the mainland at the expense of the Dukedom of Milan. Therefore Carmagnola reinforced the Venetians' power and strengthened their foothold in northern Italy for many centuries to come. These territorial changes among the Italian city-states set the stage for the chaotic situation that would develop after 1498, when the French started their "Italian wars" and the peninsula fell prey to foreign domination. The Republic of Venice was then fully equipped to participate, with all the other major Italian city-states and dukedoms—the Republic of Florence, the Dukedom of Milan, the Papal States, the Southern Kingdom, and Carmagnola's native Piedmont under the Duke of Savoy—in the reckless game of shifting alliances with the French or with the Hapsburg emperor, whichever would suit them better. Every hope of unification and freedom from foreign rule the Italians might have had was buried by the fratricidal wars that started in 1400s. These wars formed the background of *Carmagnola*. That hope had to wait for centuries, and was in fact still waiting at the time when Manzoni's tragedy was written, when the geopolitical map of Italy closely resembled what it had been four centuries before.

Adelchis had even a greater influence on the "fortunes of the whole nation." The last king of a people, the Lombards, who ruled over northern and central Italy for two centuries could have created a peaceful and prosperous Italian kingdom if he had firmly opposed the customary barbarian policy pursued by his father. When Charles, king of the Franks, intervened to defend the Pope from the Lombards, renewing Pepin's glory in his descent into Italy, he inaugurated a tradition, lasting into Manzoni's days, by which the French could intervene in the affairs of the Italian peninsula in order to defend the Papal States.

Manzoni conducted extensive historical research for both tragedies, so that they might be "truly historical, drawn from a profound knowledge, and transporting us back to the great olden time." The tragedies' scenes were no longer fixed, but rather precisely "determined," and they would change depending on what the action required: the Senate hall in Venice, the battlefield at Maclodio, the count's house in Venice; the Lombard court in Pavia, the Frankish military camp, the abbey of San Salvatore in Brescia. Manzoni reconstructed "the local customs" (those that Schlegel found deplorably lacking in Alfieri's tragedies) by means of historical research and explained them to the reader in the historical notes, details on the life of the mercenary soldiers in *Carmagnola*, for example, or on the customs of the Lombards in *Adelchis*. Finally, in both tragedies the choruses voice the concern, common to the author and his fellow patriots in the audience, over the nation's destiny.

History in Manzoni's Dramatic Theory

Historical Subjects and the Classical Unities

Manzoni implicitly addressed the pivotal point of his poetics—the unities of time and place are incompatible with history in drama—in his preface to *Carmagnola* and amply clarified it in his "Lettre," his most important writing on dramatic theory.

By attacking the unities in his preface, Manzoni intended to tackle a much bigger question than the incidental and academic issue of theater aesthetics. Opposition to the unities was not an absolute novelty by 1820, as we have seen. Indeed, many an essay had already dealt with the subject, which had thus lost its flavor of rebellion to tradition in dramatic theory.[77] If Manzoni wanted to renew the attack on the unities in his preface to *Carmagnola*, it was in order to add a new dimension to the debate, namely the elaboration of a moral role for the dramatic art through the historical genre.

"Historical truth is a type of verisimilitude," we read in a note for an essay Manzoni never published, which was to be entitled "On the Moral Aim and Aesthetic Perfection of Tragedy."[78] In the preface to *Carmagnola*, Manzoni questions the notion that the unities are an effective means to create this central necessity of any work of art, verisimilitude. He hints at a better alternative to create verisimilitude in drama, based on human rationality rather than on human passions and sensations.

The intention of the unities is to enhance the verisimilitude of dramatic works by making the time the spectator is watching the performance coincide with the time in which the *entire* action takes place (unity of time); likewise for place: the *whole* action happens on the same scene, the material space within the sight of the spectator. Thus the spectator can supposedly "enter" the performance and totally identify with those on stage, if the illusion of reality is maintained.

But, Manzoni objects, if the aim is to preserve an illusion of reality in the spectator, this is breached in many other instances besides the unities of time and place, for instance, when the actors on stage pretend that the spectator is not there while confiding a secret to each other. The use of the unities can also backfire, making the whole action appear absurd because of its artificial constraints of time and space. Therefore, the unities represent an attempt to create verisimilitude with the wrong means, that is, by trying to make the spectator "feel" that he is a material eyewitness to the story he sees enacted on stage. If we posit instead that the spectator knows at all times that he is watching a performance and is therefore outside, not inside, the performance, we have to look for other means to create verisimilitude. This must rest, Manzoni argues, on the shared rationality of spectator and author, their "mind contemplating from outside," which conceives human behavior in the terms of cause and effect and provides the true unity of action. The "contemplating mind" can provide the unity of action in detecting the causal connections between the events and the reaction of the hero to them, over time and wherever the hero will happen to be during that time.

The conclusion of the "Lettre" spells out these ideas, summarized above, already present in the preface of *Carmagnola*. It elaborates on the notion of historical truth as a type of verisimilitude and as a warranty for the unity of action:

Any poet who has a good grasp of the unity of action will see the right measure of time and place appropriate to the chosen subject, and after receiving from history the idea for the drama, he will endeavor to render it with faithfulness, so as to make the moral effect ensue. The real part played by passions in the development of facts will emerge clearly once the poet is no longer obliged to make facts take place in a sudden and abrupt fashion. Once he is sure he can win the spectator's interest with the help of historical truth, he will not feel the need to inspire passions in the spectator in order to seduce him and he will not have much to do but to preserve history's more serious and poetic trait, impartiality. It is not by sharing the anguish, the desire, and pride of the characters on stage that one experiences the highest degree of emotion; it is rather above this narrow and agitated sphere, in the pure regions of disinterested contemplation that the vision of useless suffering and vain joys of fellow human beings causes us to be most forcefully seized by pity and terror for ourselves.... It is from history that the tragedian can make human sentiments come forth, without artificiality.[79]

Vice versa, if tragedians keep the unities of time and place, they will inevitably end up resorting to a monotonous depiction of love. Tragedy purports to portray a reversal from a happy state of things to suffering and unhappiness. The passion of love, with its vicissitudes characterized by swift changes, is best suited to form the main subject of "regular" tragedies and dramas because it is adaptable to the narrow space allowed by the classical rules. Conversely, "The great historical actions have an origin, motivations, aims, and hurdles very different and far more complex [than those dictated by love]; they do not let themselves be easily reduced, in art, to conditions that they did not have in reality."[80]

Once the focus of a tragedy is no longer on surprise, on the suspense created by a petty fight between protagonist and antagonist, once the spectator is no longer steeped in the small and meaningless oscillations of a single passion (be it love, wrath, jealousy, envy, and so forth) observed under the forced vacuum created by the unities, the spectator can follow the reactions of the tragic hero to historical events, his moral development prompted by the historical circumstances, and his choices in response to them. For Manzoni, the primary example of this kind of tragedy is Shakespeare's *Richard II*, discussed at great length in the "Lettre" (see below for the influence of this drama on *Adelchis*). Subjects drawn from history allow the poet to find unity of action just by following and highlighting the causal sequence of events reconstructed through historical sources. The gradual fall of the hero, explored in his psychological-moral motivations as they develop in time (and not in twenty-four hours) will produce a much deeper reaction of Aristotelian "pity and terror" in the spectator.

Some sentences from the outline of Manzoni's unpublished essay on morality and tragedy, have, in recent years, become very popular: "[The French dramas] make the spectator sympathize with the passions of the characters, thus making him into an accomplice. One can make the spectator experience separate feelings with respect to the characters on stage, so that he might rather become their judge. Paramount example: Shakespeare."[81] Gilberto Lonardi has compared these sentences, reiterating with conciseness Manzoni's rationale for eliminating the unities, with Bertold Brecht's conception of the epic theater. The difference between the two authors, however, is that Manzoni wants to make the spectator aware not only of a political truth, as Brecht intended, but also of a moral and metaphysical one.[82]

The Tragic and Comic

Another important point that Manzoni touches in the "Lettre" is his refusal to mix comic and tragic elements in his historical dramas, after the fashion of Shakespeare. Schlegel recommended such a mixture in his *Course on Dramatic Art,* as it was a trait of the indigenous romantic drama of the English and Spanish theaters. Victor Hugo did the same in his preface to *Cromwell* (1827), and he practiced it in his historical dramas. Although he felt he could not advocate this as a generally valid precept, Manzoni found that the mixture of comic and tragic, or burlesque and grave, was detrimental to the "unity of impression, necessary to produce the emotional and sympathetic effect."[83]

Consistent with this theoretical assumption, Manzoni termed his two dramatic works "Tragedy."[84] His choice of that ancient word, without even the qualification of "historical" (which Byron chose to label his Venetian tragedies), and his numerous explicit references to Aristotle's definitions of tragedy in chapter 13 of *Poetics* clearly indicate that Manzoni wanted to keep the traditional traits of the genre. Tragedy deals with suffering, a reversal from happiness to unhappiness. The tragic hero is a great, illustrious person, not inherently evil; he commits a fatal error, which brings about his demise, evoking terror and pity in the audience left to contemplate the tragic ending. For Manzoni, reader of the seventeenth-century French moralists and Christian apologists such as Blaise Pascal and Pierre Nicole, the traditional fatal flaw is the direst of the seven deadly sins, pride, which in turn generates what Aristotle calls *hamartia,* an error of knowledge, a wrong evaluation of the circumstances on the part of the hero. When the spectator has a full grasp of the moral development of a character and listens, in the last act, to the hero's late lament upon realizing how much good life has been wasted, the moral effect is assured. Sin is somber; the effect of tragedy should be as somber, and hence there is no place for comic relief in Manzonian tragedy.

HISTORY AND TRAGEDY IN *Carmagnola* AND *Adelchis*

Carmagnola

Historical Tragedy as an Appeal Trial

Manzoni's historical notes for *The Count of Carmagnola* resemble a skilled plea by the defense attorney in a judicial procedure. The author musters all the evidence he can to show the opposite of the commonly held opinion, that his tragic hero, the Count of Carmagnola, was guilty of high treason against the Republic of

Venice. After examining a variety of primary historical sources, Manzoni shows how Carmagnola's guilt is far from proven, unlike what many historians, were ready to admit.[85]

As the author reports the various historical sources that helped form his opinion on the case, the historical notes serve the purpose of making plausible the motives that the tragedian attributes to his characters. The paranoid fear (the obverse of the omnipotence delirium) of the Venetian state and the towering pride and haughty ways of the military chief Carmagnola, as we learn from these sources, jointly bring about the tragedy of the count's unjust condemnation. Moreover, in presenting one of the sources, Manzoni hints at the justification for the overall strategy of his historical drama: the end of the Republic of Venice, which occurred in Manzoni's lifetime (1797), may appear a retribution for its unjust judicial practices in the past. Although Manzoni warns that he is not moved by a feeling of "vengeance" in recounting the death of Carmagnola, he makes a point of reminding us, in the last paragraphs of the historical notes, of the first great defeat suffered by the Venetians in their attempt to expand their inland territorial conquests, when the other Italian states joined with France and the Hapsburg Emperor in the League of Cambrai against the Serenissima.

The debate over historical sources leading to opposite opinions in the historical notes prepares us for the trial scene in the final act of the tragedy. In reality, the count was never allowed a public trial but was rather put in the hands of the Secret Council, which sentenced him to death in closed-door hearings. This lack of public procedures is one of the institutional sins of the republic. Manzoni gives Carmagnola a second chance to be heard and this trial scene literalizes Manzoni's metaphor of dramatic theory in which the spectator should be a "judge," rather than "an accomplice," of the tragic action. In act V, scene i, the count appears in front of the Senate, thinking he has been recalled there from the battlefield in order to consult on the possibility of a peace in the ongoing war with Milan; instead, the doge informs him that he has been accused of high treason. It is in this scene that the audience is transformed into a jury, the stage being the second chance for a public acquittal of the count. The hero metatheatrically addresses the audience, mentioning history and the writing of history, "the annals." Thus Carmagnola speaks to the doge, who has ordered the soldiers to deliver the count to the Secret Council:

> *Listen first, a brief word: you have decreed,*
> *I can see it, my death sentence. Thus you*
> *At once condemned yourselves to eternal shame.*

The ensigns bearing the Lion now do fly
Upon towers beyond the ancient border,
And Europe knows 'twas I who infixed them there.
No one will say this here, yet all around you,
Beyond the silence of your reign of terror,
Someone will ponder this and chronicle
The deed and its reward in lasting words.
Think of the annals, think of the future.
You shall presently need another warrior,
But who will be yours? You alarm the men of arms.
I am now at your mercy, it is true,
And yet from where I come you should remember.

The doge is not impressed by Carmagnola's admonishments. However, the most warlike region in Italy, the count's native Piedmont, will indeed seek vengeance against Venice for the killing of their fellow countryman (see historical notes). The doge then accuses the count of trying to delay, with his speech, his impending death out of fear. Here, again, Manzoni's Carmagnola metatheatrically breaches, briefly and indirectly, verisimilitude to make the spectator reflect on the grand scheme of history and on his own contemporary scene. Carmagnola tells the doge, upon being escorted out:

O unworthy man, you have restored me now
To my true self. You thought that I was begging
For your mercy. Indeed you dared to think
That a brave man was trembling for his life!
O, you shall see how nobly one can die.
When in your coward bed death finds you at last,
You will not meet it bearing such a brow
As I bear now in facing this base death
To which you are dragging me.

The mention of the bed in connection with the Doge's death is important in these lines. In the last days of the Serenissima, in 1797, as the Venetian government dealt with the approaching French troops and bargained with Napoleon:

The desire not to lose the possessions on the mainland played a part in the decision not to put up any resistance, as the nobles feared their confiscation. But it was in any case a forced choice. All the final acts of the drama are marked by the fear and physical terror of a ruling class that was by now irremediably outmoded. *Thus the Doge*, on learning on the 30th of April of billeting of enemy troops at Marghera, *declared that one could not feel safe even in one's own bed that night*. When General Junot entered the hall of the Great Council [on 12 May] he found it hard, as he himself relates, to suppress his laughter when he, the son of a revolution that had changed the history of the world, saw the Doge and the Signoria dressed in the costume of another age and clearly showing their anxiety and fear.[86]

The last doge of Venice feared indeed to be surprised by death in his "coward bed." By a subtle and "estranging" allusion to an anecdote of contemporary history, one that his contemporaries would not miss, Manzoni's text makes the spectator perceive the reversal of roles of accuser and accused between the count and the republic that will occur over the centuries. Seen from this epochal perspective, the tragedy appears to feature two tragic heroes, an individual, General Carmagnola, and an institution, the Republic of Venice.

Byron's, Shakespeare's, and Manzoni's Venice

Manzoni's Carmagnola is closely echoed by another character condemned for high treason by the Republic of Venice, although his guilt, unlike Carmagnola's, was proven: Marino Faliero in Byron's homonymous historical tragedy, composed just six months after *The Count of Carmagnola*, in June 1820, while the English poet was living in Ravenna.[87] Like Manzoni's Carmagnola, Byron's Faliero is a valiant soldier and military chief. Once he becomes doge, he discovers that this is more of a figurehead role than one with decision-making power. Faliero is tormented by the dream of becoming king, although he has sworn allegiance to the republic. He becomes involved in political conspiracy with the populace, and he is discovered, condemned, and beheaded, like Carmagnola. Byron, like Manzoni, resorts to the post-factum prophecy of Venice's inglorious end for Faliero's last speech in the Senate, in more explicit, blunter terms:

> I am not innocent, but are these [the Senators] guiltless?
> I perish but not unavenged; far ages
> Float up from the abyss of time to be
> And show these eyes, before they close, the doom
> Of this proud city. And I leave my curse

On her and hers for ever! Yes, the hours
Are silently engendering of the day
When she, who built against Attila a bulwark,
Shall yield, and bloodlessly and basely yield,
Unto a bastard Attila, without
Shedding so much blood in her last self-defense
As in these old veins, oft drained in shielding her,
Shall pour in sacrifice.—She shall be bought
and sold and be an appanage to those
Who shall despise her!—She shall stoop to be
A province for an Empire, petty town
In lieu of capital, with slaves for senates,
Beggars for nobles, panders for a people! (V.iii)[88]

In reviewing Pierre Daru's *History of the Republic of Venice* (Paris, 1819) for *Il Conciliatore*, Pellico, in his opening sentence, remarked: "Of all the empires that time and violence have undone, no other fell with less noise than the Republic of Venice, surrounded with less regret, with less attention, and more devoid of any hopes of being one day restored."[89] Pellico explains the reasons why his contemporaries have shown such a lack of sympathy for the fall of Venice. That state had never allowed its institutions to be renewed over the centuries. Venice was unable to change until it became an anachronism in a world where nations were politically organized in either monarchies or democracies. Both of these modern political systems, explains Pellico, abhor the oligarchy, the republic of aristocrats that Venice was. Hence, "the peoples who saw Venice assaulted in her old age could not feel any pity for her," but now that the "great building" has been demolished, Pellico continues, it is more than ever an object of study and meditation for historians.[90] A few months after this review appeared in *Il Conciliatore*, Manzoni and Byron composed their Venetian historical tragedies, confirming the reviewer's impression of a great revival of historical interest in the Serenissima, as well as the lack of sympathy for its liquidation.

Daru's *History* is one of the sources that Byron quotes in his preface to *Marino Faliero*, and most likely the French historian influenced the English poet's vision of the doge as victim of the aristocrats. Although Byron never mentions Manzoni, a comparative analysis of the prefatory texts and of the trial scenes in *Carmagnola* and in *Faliero* shows that Manzoni's work must have had at least a catalyzing effect on Byron's conception of his first Venetian historical tragedy.[91] In *The Two Foscaris* (1821), his second, very different Venetian historical tragedy, Byron inserts Carmagnola's story into a dialogue between two noblemen, the naïve Barbarigo and the cynical Loredano:

> BAR: *And yet he [Doge Foscari] seems*
>   *All openness.*
> LOR: *And so he seemed not long*
>   *Ago to Carmagnuola.*
> BAR: *The attainted*
>   *And foreign traitor?*
> LOR: *Even so: When he*
>   *After the very night in which "the Ten"*
>   *(Join'd with the Doge) decided his destruction,*
>   *Met the great Duke [sic] at daybreak with a jest,*
>   *Demanding whether he should augur him*
>   *"The good day or good night?" his Doge-ship answered,*
>   *"That he in truth had passed a night of vigil,*
>   *In which (he added with a gracious smile)*
>   *There often has been question about you."*
>   *'Twas true: the question was the death resolved*
>   *Of Carmagnuola, eight months ere he died;*
>   *And the old Doge who knew him doomed smiled on him*
>   *With deadly cozenage, eight long months beforehand,*
>   *Eight months of such hypocrisy as is*
>   *Learnt but in eighty years. Brave Carmagnuola*
>   *Is dead. So is young Foscari and his brethren—*
>   *I never smiled on them.*
> BARB: *Was Carmagnuola*
>   *your friend?*
> LOR: *He was the safeguard of the city.*
>   *In early life its foe, but in his manhood,*
>   *Its savior first, then victim.*
> BAR: *Ah! That seems*
>   *The penalty for saving cities! (IV.i)*[92]

Byron's compacted narration of Carmagnola's story within the text of *The Two Foscaris* testifies, as do the paintings by Hayez at Brera, to the popularity enjoyed by the subject in the months and years following the publication of Manzoni's Venetian tragedy.

Byron presents Venice as a city of amazing contrasts and contradictions in the famous opening lines of *Childe Harold* canto IV (1815–18): "I stood in Venice on the Bridge of Sighs; / A palace and a prison on each hand." The beauty and majesty of the Ducal Palace is offset by the horror and cruelty of the dungeons called Piombi. The people who were indicted within the palace, in those terrible secret hearings in which torture was used, would go to the prison through the covered bridge designed to conceal them from the eyes and ears of the populace. In *The Two Foscaris* we find the contrast of Venetian beauty and horror within the young tragic hero, Jacopo, who is homesick for his fair native city even though its authorities (including his father, who is the doge) are torturing him and keeping him in the dungeon. Byron's depiction of Venice and its contrasts responded to a popular taste for the sensational and was very lasting.[93]

Manzoni was fascinated by Venice in a different way. In 1809 he intended to write a poem on the founding of Venice, as the subject appeared to him to be central in the national history of Italy.[94] The French version of Shakespeare's works by Pierre Le Tourneur, which he was reading at the time he conceived his first tragedy, in 1816, opened with *Othello, the Moor of Venice*, in the first of the twenty volumes, right after the biography of the Bard.[95] In the first act of that tragedy, Manzoni could find an insightful depiction of the Venetian "State." This single capitalized word, by which all the characters in both the French version of Shakespeare's *Othello* and Manzoni's *Carmagnola* refer to the Serenissima, best illustrates Manzoni's vision of Venice: the republic was the only Italian political entity in which one could see all the traits of the modern impersonal state, endowed with an apparatus of institutions methodically geared to its self-preservation.

Beyond the popular legend of Venice filled with romantic and decadent contrasts—queen of the sea and commerce, city of sensuous beauty but also of horror, vice, and cruelty—Venice represented for Manzoni a specimen of the modern impersonal state, and as such it afforded material for political reflections not only on the contemporary scene but on political justice. Just as he was conceiving *Carmagnola*, he could find in Shakespeare the dramatic juxtaposition of an impersonal state, Venice, and a military chief whose mentality was centered on the notion of personal honor and glory achieved through war. Othello, the valiant general, defines himself in the end "an honorable murderer:" "for naught I did in hate, but all in honor" (V.ii.295–96). The Venetian State, on the other hand, does everything in pursuit of power and self-preservation. This is well known to the Shakespearean spectator, who remembers the ways of the Venetian senators in act I, with their lack of loyalty to Brabantio, their peer, and their time-serving pardon of Othello, which is granted just for the sake of exploiting his military expertise in the impending attack by the Turks against Cyprus.

In *Carmagnola* Manzoni depicts the essential duplicity of Venice—on the one hand, a reality of mighty power, economical and political, and on the other, an empty rhetoric of pious intentions—by inserting two ideal characters in the midst of the historical ones.[96] These ideal characters are two senators of the republic, Mark and Marino, whose opinions and behaviors are diametrically opposed but who are equally instrumental in bringing about the demise of the tragic hero. The names of the two senators hint at an allegory on Venice: Mark—the naïve senator who thinks he can reconcile his friendship with the count and his loyalty to the Venetian state—is ironically named after the patron saint of the city; Marino, the staunchest and coherent supporter of the Venetian state in all its practices and institutions, is named after the very source of Venice's power throughout the centuries, *mare* (sea).

In *Othello*, the scheming Iago acts on the Moor's deep-seated insecurity, resulting from his being an outsider in the Venetian republic of the nobles. It is important to notice that the end of the tragedy emphasizes the inequality in the match between the general and the republic. The doge's messenger in Cyprus, Lodovico, stops paying any respect to the Moor: "You shall close prisoner rest / Till that nature of your fault be known / to the Venetian state. Come, bring away" (V.ii.335–37). Othello avoids the Venetian prison by killing himself, not without first reiterating his loyalty to the State. As it is customary in the genre of tragedy, in which the fall of the tragic hero is juxtaposed against the continuity of political power, while the Moor self-destructs, the statuesque "State" features, unchanged and unperturbed, in the final rhymed couplet of *Othello*, uttered by Lodovico: "Myself will straight aboard, and to the state / this heavy act with heavy heart relate."

The General and the State

In the Napoleonic era the eyes of the world were pointed toward the generals and admirals, authors of renowned exploits, not only Bonaparte but also Wellington, Nelson, Kutuzov, not unlike the World War II era, when everybody was familiar with the names and faces of Montgomery, Patton, Eisenhower, Rommel, and MacArthur. Manzoni gives in *Carmagnola*, among other things, a study of the military mentality that recent history had made vividly present in his contemporaries' minds. A hint at Napoleon's fulgurating military career (including its final disappointments) can be perceived in these lines uttered by the count:

When I was but a simple soldier, hidden
And lost among the thousands, when I sensed
That a low rank was not the place God meant
For me, when I breathed the heavy air
Of obscurity, when I strongly yearned
For the supreme command which seemed to me
So full of beauty, who would have told me
That I would one day achieve it, that I
Would be the chief of glorious officers,
Of so many trusted and brave soldiers,
And yet I would not be the happier for it. (IV.iii)

Against General Carmagnola, Manzoni juxtaposes the Venetian republic for its characteristics of the modern impersonal state, a similar contrast to that seen in *Othello.* The historical, moral, and political interest of the tragedy was to reside in the clash of the opposite sets of values held by the general and by the state. The conflict between the military mentality and political power was also at the heart of the German historical dramas by Goethe and Schiller, as Benjamin Constant indicated in a book that was published at the end of Manzoni's first stay in Paris. "Quelques réflexions sur le théâtre allemand" (Some reflections on the German theater, 1809) was a prefatory essay Constant wrote to introduce the French readership to his abridgement and translation of Schiller's *Wallenstein.*[97]

> The lifestyle of the sixteenth-century Generals gave their character a certain originality that we are unable to fully understand today. Originality always results from independence. As authority becomes more and more concentrated and centralized, the individuality gets lost. All the stones cut for the construction of a pyramid and modeled on the place that they have to fill acquire uniformity in their aspect. Individuality disappears within man as he becomes a means, no longer an end. However, individuality alone can raise interest. . . . This is why Goethe has depicted, in his *Goetz von Berlichingen*, the fight of the declining knighthood against the authority of the Empire; and Schiller has wanted, in a similar way, in his *Wallenstein*, to retrace the last efforts of the military to preserve the independent, almost savage life of their camps that the progress of civilization has forever substituted with uniformity, obedience, discipline.[98]

In this passage, Constant's reflections interconnect three realms: history (Germany in the first half of the seventeenth century), politics (the individual versus the centralized state), and art (what constitutes an interesting subject for a tragedy). In Manzoni's *Carmagnola*, we can see the artistic embodiment of Constant's reflections transposed into Italian history.[99] In fifteenth-century Italy, society was in the kind of political turmoil and fragmentation (similar to Germany prior to and during the Thirty Years' War) when there lived that type of men who "love war for war's sake and they look for it in a place when they cannot find it in another . . . men with no other mission than the sentiment of their talent and their courage [who rule over their soldiers] merely through their personal charisma."[100]

These synthetic remarks by Constant mirror closely Manzoni's broad conception of his first tragedy. The historical conflict features, on one side, a general, proud of the freedom of the military camps with their unwritten, customary rules—such as the release of war prisoners after victory—and on the other side, a highly centralized state such as the Republic of Venice, already a model of the modern, impersonal state, which regards the individuals as "stones cut for the pyramid." Carmagnola's fatal error of judgment is in ignoring this dimension of the Venetian republic. He is used to the ways of his old lord, Philip Visconti, a whimsical prince who governed his state without method. Feelings and impulses, not rational Machiavellian principles, rule Milan. In Carmagnola's eyes, the Republic of Venice is simply Philip's enemy, and his naïve zeal to serve the new master will prove fatal. Constant's considerations on the individual versus the state are relevant in weighing Carmagnola's pledge of loyalty to the Venetian state: "And my arm, my mind, and all I am / Are a *thing* in your possession" (I.ii).

Thus Carmagnola impulsively forgoes his human rights by demeaning himself to a "thing." He is the first to be blamed for lack of respect for his own individuality because his pent-up desire for individual freedom and independence will unavoidably reemerge, most forcefully in the question of the treatment of the war prisoners, but also in the overall conduct of the war against Milan. The disagreements with the Venetian commissioners (see act III) will be the beginning of his end.

Beyond the legal question of whether the count was innocent—Manzoni the historian thinks he was—the tragedy intends to raise interest in the deep-seated motivations of the characters. The count did not want to become "a stone in the pyramid," and this prevented him from granting the unconditional loyalty to the republic that he himself gave only impulsively in his initial pledge. As Roberto Alonge has remarked in his notes for Puggelli's 1989 stage production of *Carmagnola*, the hero was unconsciously entertaining a love-hate relationship with the prince, his former master Visconti. At the same time, even if the count never committed treason, the republic was right in perceiving faults in his "unlimited devotion" (Manzoni's words) to the business at hand—the conquest of the largest extent of territory beyond the Milan-Venice boundary. Moreover, the count's unconscious attachment to the old situation, evident in his pursuit of personal vengeance (II.v), prevents him from coldly evaluating the nature of the new masters. He confines himself to judging them noble because he is immensely flattered for having been welcomed into Venice's aristocratic senate and for having attained the personal friendship of one of the senators, Mark. The warnings of his faithful officer, Gonzaga, go miserably unheeded (IV.iii).

Not because Manzoni considers Carmagnola "a great man" does the playwright hesitate to show the unpleasant traits of his personality.[101] Carmagnola is a self-serving man, and although his courage and military valor are admirable, his dreams of glory are morally and physically pernicious. He cannot be seriously interested in heading a national unification (he hints at "this divided Italy" in act I, scene iv), just as Goethe's Egmont, in the homonymous tragedy, cannot with his flawed character be the liberator of the Dutch, whereas William of Orange will succeed as such.[102] The broader resemblance between Egmont and Carmagnola seems to be exactly their vanity and unwitting demagogy. They desire to be universally loved, Egmont by the people, Carmagnola by his troops; they also want to be loved by their superiors, the princes, because they unconsciously wish not only to preserve but also to increase their personal power. Caught between these opposite demands in their egos—to obtain the love of the people and the love of the powerful whom they have to obey—they will end up crushed by the powerful, duplicitous politicians, whom they naïvely trusted because they wanted to be their peers in greatness.

In his 1895 essay on Manzoni's first tragedy, Michele Scherillo, having verified the similarities between Carmagnola's and Egmont's farewells to arms at the end of their respective tragedies, suggested that both Manzoni and Goethe had in mind Othello's farewell to arms:[103]

> *O now forever*
> *Farewell the tranquil mind, farewell content!*
> *Farewell the plumed troop, and the big wars*
> *That make ambition virtue! O farewell!*
> *Farewell the neighing steed, and the shrill trump,*
> *The spirit-stirring drum, the ear-piercing fife,*
> *The royal banner, and all quality,*

Pride,'Pomp, and circumstance of glorious war!
(III.iii.347–54)

Scherillo's philological discovery illuminates the very core of Manzoni's tragedy. Manzoni could find in Othello's farewell to arms the clearest exposition of the soldierly mentality. Othello and Carmagnola alike "love war for war's sake" (as Constant observed about the tragic heroes of the German theater) in the belief that military deeds can raise ambition to the heights of virtue. Manzoni reproduces this love of war for war's sake in Carmagnola with many touches demonstrating the general's highest appreciation for his occupation, above all with the recurrent use of the adjective "beautiful" for the hero's reflections on war, on the battlefield, on his command. But this aesthetics of war is nothing else but the peculiar embodiment of the men-at-arms' pride. It is a blinding passion that prevents the tragic hero from reasonably calculating his odds of survival, or of unabated favor, in facing his powerful counterpart, the state of Venice. Carmagnola neglects his moral duty toward his wife and daughter, who depend on him for their well-being as he is undividedly involved in his quest of glory through war.[104] However, the spouses of Othello and Carmagnola, Desdemona and Antoinette, are fascinated by their husbands' aesthetics of war, and this causes their own final death or downfall to appear, from a moral perspective, justly deserved. They were proud to belong to these beloved, popular warriors, and they cannot but share in their demise as well.[105]

Manzoni's focus in the tragedy, therefore, is not on Venice as symbol of "unjust rule," or on the Count as a Christlike victim.[106] Rather, this seems Byron's approach in his Venetian tragedies. The English poet engages in a criticism of the Venetian institutions (chiefly through Faliero, Loredano, and Marina) and is at times very preachy in scolding the Venetians (and, allegorically, the British) for the shortcomings of their institutions and behavior. Although Faliero is guilty of high treason, he is depicted as a sacrificial victim of the noble class; the nobleman Leoni is only likable because he is aware of his city's decadent mores; and young Jacopo Foscari, appears, throughout his ordeals, very much like a Christ figure.

Even if he is convinced of the count's innocence, Manzoni shuns the aggrandizing of the victim's status and puts in place a very refined psychological characterization that permeates every word of the tragedy's poetry. The final suffering and death, traditional to the tragic genre, must be brought about by the reactions of the tragic hero to the events, and the tragic hero must have a fatal flaw that leads to his own downfall.[107] In a letter, Manzoni defined the republic's ways in dealing with the count as "malicious," and this has led many critics to conclude that Venice's Machiavellian ways were a target of reproach on Manzoni's part.[108] But although *Carmagnola* is certainly an anti-Venetian work, one should not assume that Manzoni would take it on himself to write such a tragedy to demonstrate the commonplace that Machiavellism is immoral.[109] The republic is what it is because institutions are given, not readily modifiable by the good will of one single individual. The republic will pay over a longer time than the individual tragic hero for its institutional sins. Rather, the focus of the tragedy for Manzoni is the confused behavior of the tragic hero—a self-absorbed soldier with a high self-esteem and the highest consideration for his trade—vis-à-vis the institution—a specimen of the impersonal state positing its own self-preservation as its highest priority—as Constant indicated in the German authors that Manzoni himself admired.

While the general's moral fallacies are his consuming desire for glory and his neglect of his familial duties, the state's sin is that of believing itself to be like God. The frequent occurrences of the dismembered eye associated with the state must be considered together with two other images connoting the Venetian institutions.[110] While reasserting that the state knows Mark's conduct better than Mark himself, Marino mentions the state's "book" where everything is unfailingly recorded: "Time has perchance erased much / From your memory, but *our book* leaves / *Nothing* to oblivion" (IV.i).[111] Here is an echo of the Book of Life of Revelations (20:12), mediated by Dante's lines in *Paradiso* XIX: the unjust rulers of the Christian world will be liable of reproach by the heathen ones when these, on Doomsday, "*vedranno quel* volume *aperto / nel qual si scrivon* tutti *i suoi dispregi*" ("shall see the open book / in which *all* misdeeds are recorded," 113–14). In *Carmagnola*, the context is ironically reversed: the unjust Christian ruler, the Republic of Venice, claims to be the holder of the Book of Life, the all-inclusive record of human deeds, thus revealing its presumption to be like God.

Another, clearly recognizable, iconographic trait of God is conjured up when Gonzaga compares the judicial procedure of Venice's Secret Council to the lightning bolt launched from an invisible hand behind the clouds: "Down strikes the lightning bolt, hidden remains / Among the clouds the hand which sent it forth" (V.iii). By characterizing the Venetian republic with Godlike attributes—the Book of Life, the hand among the clouds, and the recurrent watching, dismembered eye—Manzoni is undoubtedly pointing to the sin of the state of Venice in Pascalian terms: suppressing human feelings and presuming to have become like God.[112]

The Fine Line of Justice

The central question of how to treat the war prisoners, in act III, illustrates the tragedy's theme of justice as a fine line, as it touches the quick of the conflict hero versus the state, while revealing the hero's blindness to the conflict itself. The republic paid for the wars, therefore it had a right to decide about the lot of the war prisoners; the Venetian commissioners who demand that the prisoners not be set free are "good men, perfectly worthy of their mission," as Goethe observed in his review; in other words, they are doing their job. The count cannot see their point of view because he conforms to the unwritten rules of his trade. Customarily, prisoners of war were released after the battle. As Manzoni remarks in his historical notes, this custom originated in the mercenary soldiers' fear that all wars, the source of their earnings, would end if all the combatants were retained as prisoners by opposing parties, and that the populace would then order the soldiers back to tilling the land, with the motto, recorded in history, "Back to the hoe, soldiers!" Manzoni provides this explanation in the historical notes because he wants to indicate the individuals' contribution to the sad state of inner warfare in Italy. The Italian peasants seemed to be attracted more to the trade of mercenary soldier than to that of farmer. This point is subtly illustrated in the tragedy's chorus by the juxtaposition between the images of land cultivation and agriculture and the physical and spiritual ravages caused by war.

Once we see the mercenary wars in the light of Manzoni's historical explanation, as well as through the author's poetical commentary provided in the chorus, we understand better the rationale of the count's attachment to his trade. We can then comprehend why one of the Venetian commissioners, whose priority is to protect the interests of the state, admonishes the count that the present war is not a joust for his private pleasure. The admonishment falls on deaf ears. The count imposes his own policies dictated by the old custom of mercenary war, by which war prisoners are released after the battle. The count does not bother to seek a compromise. The commissioners then pretend to go along with the count's decision, but they secretly plan to study his moves and report his suspicious conduct to the Venetian senate (III.iv). The immorality in their conduct is not their pursuit of their contractual rights, but rather their resolution to put on a false façade of gladness, which will lead the count to believe that his decisions sit well with the Venetians after all.

As this case demonstrates, the characters in *Carmagnola* are divided into two groups, but not on the basis of goodness and villainy. Rather, they are divided relative to their practice of either concealing or disclosing their intentions. Manzoni methodically uses the metaphor of the "heart" for the characters' inner-most feelings and intentions.[113] The doge, the senators, and the commissioners are able to conceal their "hearts" and are, in different measures, proud of their ability to do so. Secrecy and concealment are repeatedly indicated as the most important values demanded by the republic of its loyal members, the dominant traits of the Venetian life. On the other hand, the count, Antoinette, and Mark champion the opening of the heart to the world.

The character of Mark also illustrates very well how Manzoni conceives of justice as a fine line. He functions in the tragedy as the deadly *trait d'union* between the general and the state, mirroring and amplifying the moral confusion of the tragic hero. Swaying the count's mind toward blind optimism, Mark's lofty words act as a poison on the count's soul from the moment of their first utterance in act I, scene iv, until the count's decision to return to Venice in act IV, scene iii. The count will not hesitate to return to Venice, in the end because a friend—he remembers Mark's lofty words at his house—sits in the senate and would surely warn him if a plot were ordained against him. Mark's ambiguity is imme-diately manifest in his first words uttered in the text. The doge expresses con-fidence in Venice's ability to discover a possible treason by the count: " . . . do we lack / *An eye* that might soon alert us to his ways, / And *an arm* that might invis-ibly reach him?" (I.iii). Mark concedes that Venice can spy on the count, as the doge has suggested, but also exhorts the State to be trustful: "And now, for pru-dence's sake, let *the eye* watch / But may *the heart* repose in utter trust" (I.iii; empha-sis added).

By recommending the doge to have a trustful heart, Mark annuls the con-cession to typically Venetian prudence (the watching eye). His rhetoric, making contrary opinions coexist in a single sentence, denounces his inconclusive stance, his only partial adherence to Venice's Machiavellian principles, and the velleity of his optimism. In the end, the state will force Mark to choose a terrible act of concealment: he is informed in advance of the Council of Ten's indictment of the count with high treason, but if he warns his friend he will be killed. When confronted by such a tough choice, he becomes a coward, preferring to save his life rather than tell his friend about the impending danger. Mark's problem is that he does not see his tragically conflicting desires of wanting to be a friend to the count and remaining a loyal senator of the Venetian republic. He does not see the tragic conflict because he is proud of his liberal heart, of his own good-ness; he wants to do good at all costs and conversely ends up contributing to the hero's fall. Manzoni is indicating through this character the damage that moral confusion and the consequent bending of rules can cause to the good life.[114]

Moral ambiguity is worse than the clear-headed cynicism of Marino. When, in act I, scene ii, the count opens his heart to the Venetian senators, Marino takes advantage of Carmagnola's readiness to disclose his most intimate thoughts and feelings. After analyzing the count's words, Marino detects in him pride and a touchy nature, and he would like therefore to eliminate the count's candidacy to be Venice's general in the present war. Reading the heart that Carmagnola had voluntarily opened (not an immoral act, therefore), Marino puts his psychological insight at the service of the State, concluding that it would be better to choose another general. If Marino had won the senate's consent on this issue, there would have been no tragedy.

The demise of the tragic hero and his friend, champions of open hearts and transparent minds, ultimately shows that anti-Machiavellism does not lead necessarily to just and good results, if by these we mean, for example, individual self-preservation, which is a duty for each person. Nor is anti-Machiavellism, intended as transparent intentions, conducive in any way to an amelioration of the unjust institution. Unrestrained and advertised feelings can be as deadly as murderous intentions concealed in the heart.[115] At the same time, the practice of hiding affections and intentions in one's heart is not as great an object of Manzoni's moral judgment as the judicial procedures adopted in the Venetian state. The republic is guilty of the practice of spying—prying into the individuals' hearts with its terrifying eye—usurping, in so doing, a role that belongs only to God. The State deliberates in secret over the life or death of people—another prerogative of God. In *The Count of Carmagnola*, the political entity that traditionally survives the tragic hero is tainted with horrible moral faults. No wonder that the epilogue provokes the most somber horror. The audience, however, knows that Venice is doomed in turn to fall tragically for its own fatal flaws.

The entire picture is dark in the tragedy's ending. Yet God is still a hope for the count, and Manzoni imagines that he repents before dying, thus restoring the individual wholeness and dignity on which he had let his masters trample. This is one fundamental symmetry between the tragedy and its chorus, whose final stanza recommends the Christian ethics as the only viable solution to mediate the historical conflicts between nations and individuals alike.

Napoleon's Shadow

The tragedy's ending makes reference to contemporary history, by which we see once again Napoleon's shadow behind Carmagnola. This time the count in the Venetian prison mirrors Napoleon in perpetual exile on St. Helen's island.

In his first Venetian tragedy, Byron wants us to see Napoleon's figure behind the tragic hero, Faliero, with his glorious military past in defense of the republic, his personal aspirations, indeed his ambition, and his desire for the crown, although he had sworn allegiance to republican institutions. Another important author of historical drama in this period, Victor Hugo, follows Byron in the way he projects Napoleon onto his Cromwell.[116] Manzoni, however, has an altogether different focus in hinting at the Napoleonic epic in the life of his Carmagnola. Whereas Byron and Hugo are interested in Napoleon's ambition and greed for personal power, and we are therefore supposed to see Bonaparte in Faliero's and Cromwell's dilemmatic consideration of republic versus monarchy, Manzoni is instead interested in the soldier's courage and love of war that made the man "great" and, at the same time, in his dramatic fall from power, the tragic reversal in the exceptional man's lot from the highest summits of human glory to humiliating defeat. These are the themes of the ode commemorating the death of the general-emperor, "The Fifth of May," published in 1822.[117]

In the ode, Manzoni refrains from any past polemics or political criticism. His interpretation of the Napoleonic epic is rather a Christian one: God put on the stage of history a man bearing in himself "a stronger mark of the creating spirit," able, with his exploits, to hold the gaze of sympathizers and opponents alike, in order to teach through him a lesson on the human predicament and the power of grace:

> Was it real glory?
> Posterity will say.
> We bow our forehead
> To the Highest Maker,
> Who willed to leave on him
> A greater mark
> Of the creating spirit.

Manzoni imagines Napoleon in remote Saint Helen's island trying to write his memoirs. But this last enterprise turns out to be almost impossible for the general-emperor. He is often paralyzed by despair when he measures his past power and glory on the battlefields and the present misery in solitude and inactivity. His mind is assaulted by

> The memories of camps,
> and trenches conquered,

the glittering squadrons,
The onrushing tide of horses,
And agitated orders,
Swift words of compliance.

In his last hour in prison, and with words that, as we have seen, were modeled on Othello's farewell to arms, an anguished Carmagnola remembers his military past:

Alas
The open fields, the shining sun, the clangor
Of weapons, the thrill of perils, the trumpets,
The warriors' cries, my steed . . . To die amidst
All this would have indeed be beautiful. (V.iv)

Abandoned by men, Napoleon finally finds faith in God. The world learned about Napoleon's Christian devotion in his last days and stood to ponder "that superb human highness" bowing to "the scandal of the Golgotha," as Manzoni puts it in the last stanzas of his ode. Under the adverse circumstances of his end, the count too finds at last in God the strength to be a moral support not only for himself but for his wife and daughter when they come to see him for the last time in prison:

Nay, men did not invent death; it would be
Full of rage, unbearable. From Heaven
Death comes to us, and Heaven sends with it
Such solace that men cannot give nor take. (V.v)

Appropriately, in Hayez's painting, which is a commentary to this very scene, the general's eyes are not on his wife and daughters (Hayez added a daughter for compositional reasons) but rather look upward. In both Manzoni's reconstruction of Carmagnola and interpretation of Napoleon's epic, the greatness of the man of arms has turned at last into the greatness of a Christian soul that believes in its final celestial abode, as their warlike courage becomes the theological virtues of hope and faith in facing death.

Adelchis

Political Justice and Historiography

In *Adelchis* the problem of political justice acquires even more centrality than in *Carmagnola*, as the tragic hero is a king who loses his kingdom. The author's historical notes contain the timeline of facts and the description of customs, the data strictly necessary to evaluate the mixture of history and fiction in the tragedy, according to the formula already tested in *Carmagnola*. In addition to the historical notes, however, Manzoni felt the need to devote a separate essay to a discussion of what other historians had written on the Lombards. This essay, published with *Adelchis*, was entitled *Discorso sopra alcuni punti della dominazione longobardica in Italia* (Discourse on some aspects of the Lombard rule in Italy).

In his critical examination of historical sources, Manzoni discovered that many celebrated historians of the eighteenth century advocated the optimistic thesis that the Lombards had harmoniously blended with the Italians (also referred to as Latins or Romans) to form one people on one land. Manzoni objected that nothing in the careful interpretation of both the extant documents and the early historians could indicate such a happy state of things. On the contrary, from many clues Manzoni inferred that the Lombards kept the indigenous population, the Italians, in a state of slavish subjection, not only during the regime of the dukes (the first part of the Lombard domination), but also after the establishment of kingship. For instance, the judges in each city were exclusively Lombards, and the laws issued by the Lombard kings explicitly stated that they concerned only the Lombard nation, not the Italian one. Augustin Thierry's theory concerning the separation of the races of the conquerors (the Germanic Franks) from the conquered (the Gallo-Romans) in Medieval France served probably as an inspiration for Manzoni's lengthy refutation, in the first part of the *Discorso*, of the thesis that envisioned a Lombard-Latin fusion.[118] Accordingly, as the tragedy's chorus is reserved for the personal voice of the dramatist (see the preface to *Carmagnola*), Thierry's influence can be easily detected in the two choruses of *Adelchis*.[119]

Because of inaccurate interpretations of the documents' language, or perhaps simply because of their optimistic bias as to the Lombards' goodness, the eighteenth-century historians wrote "not only apologies, but veritable panegyrics on the Lombards."[120] These historians discarded the popes' declarations of the Lombards' cruelty because they thought that the popes did not speak in good faith, but rather were trying to mar the reputation of their rivals in a bid for territorial supremacy over the Italian peninsula. Thus, in the *Discorso*, while refuting the generally accepted thesis on the Lombard domination over Italy, Manzoni comes to tackle other related questions. One was the role of the popes in the history of the nation, a thorny problem at the time when the Papal States were an objective hindrance to national unification and many for this reason were unleashing sweeping attacks on the popes' role in Italian history.[121] Apart from any political bias and generalization dictated by contemporary politics, Manzoni the historian concludes that Pope Hadrian benefited the Italians when Charles (later Charlemagne), the Frankish king, responding to the pope's call for help, put an end to the Lombard domination over Italy. The contemporary political debate was so heated that Manzoni had to issue a formal disclaimer, in the quick of the tract, concerning the aims of his historiographic discussion:

> This author declares therefore that his judgment over the disputes between the Lombards and the popes, deriving from the careful consideration of the facts at hand, is decisively in favor of the latter. The author declares that it is his intention to prove that justice (not absolute justice, which cannot be found in human affairs) was on [Pope] Hadrian's side, while Desiderius was wrong, nothing more. The author furthermore declares that it is not his fault if those who defend one pope are regarded as the apologists for all the popes have done, or was done in their name; and it is not his fault either if many cannot conceive that one might want to prove that one man, one institution, was right in one case without necessarily deeming that institution and its cause righteous at all times, as one monolithic block. The author's aim is to tell what he deems to be the truth and to proclaim it all the more forcefully because it has been suppressed.[122]

Another question Manzoni tackled indirectly was what constitutes a just government, not in abstract terms but under specific historical circumstances. Alien to any utopian formulation, Manzoni had always nonetheless been very interested, as his actions and civic poetry show, in dealing with the question of political justice. As we can see from the above quote, he did not believe that absolute justice was of this world, but he was far from being apolitical, or "quietist," as many have accused him of being. On the contrary, Manzoni thought it was good—in fact necessary—to seek relative political justice by choosing among the available alternatives at any given moment in history. What was the best rule, or the least damaging, for the well-being of the Italians under the historical circumstances in A.D. 774? Manzoni answers after taking a close look at the facts and the men involved: Desiderius and Adelchis on one side, Charles and Pope Hadrian on the other. These were the leaders from whom the silent mass of the

Romans might expect a just government. Thus, beyond the Thierrian question of the racial separation between Lombards and Latins, the focus of *Adelchis*, as well as the focus of the last chapters of its accompanying historical tract, is on kingship, on what makes a desirable ruler, the one who will ensure the politically just solution at a given moment in history.

The Inept King and the Christian King: Shakespeare's Richard II and Henry V

The end of the Lombard domination in Italy somewhat ameliorated the plight of the Italians who could look at the pope and Charles as benevolent rulers, at least able and willing to protect them from the fierce Lombards.[123] This Manzoni writes in so many words in the last chapters of his *Discorso*. It seems hard to imagine that Manzoni did not intend to incorporate the conclusions of his historical research into the tragedy, but some scholars did imagine this, as they were led astray by what they saw as a positive portrait of Adelchis.[124] The tragic hero is a Lombard, endowed with a noble, Christian soul and seemingly a victim of historical circumstances. In fact, the last king of the Lombards, the hero of the tragedy, has a fatal flaw that is even morally graver than General Carmagnola's pride and ambition: Adelchis is a king and as such he is responsible for unleashing war or constructing peace for a multitude of people. Therefore, more so than in *Carmagnola*, Manzoni in *Adelchis* is far from aggrandizing the status of victim for the tragic hero. Instead, he makes sure that we condemn the hero's victimism by showing how this attitude can serve as a cover for failure to fulfill one's moral duty. As he does in *Carmagnola*, Manzoni portrays the tragic hero with that mixture of defects and gifts that every human being has. As he commonsensically remarked to his stepson inquiring on the ultimate meaning of *Adelchis*, "righteousness is never all on one side in human affairs."[125]

Several commentators have referred to Adelchis as "the Lombard Prince," thus falling into the author's trap. In his sheepish compliance with his father's will, Adelchis behaves like a prince in line for succession on the throne at his father's death, but he is in fact a ruling king. The play's first two lines make it clear that there are two kings reigning jointly over Italy, something that Manzoni had verified in a first-hand examination of historical documents, namely royal decrees that Adelchis would sign in discharging his royal functions (see the historical notes). Further on in the first scene of act I, we hear how Desiderius made Adelchis king because of his military valor, and again in act III, scene ii, Desiderius reminds us that Adelchis is his "peer in kingship." The weakness with which Adelchis defends his alternative plan—to surrender the territory over which disputes arose and start a diplomatic policy of friendship with the Pope, avoiding war with the Franks—to his father's reckless policy is a veritable regression to the position of prince, and is indeed his guilt. His moral duty as a king demands that he tend to the preservation of his kingdom, to the well-being of his subjects, Latins and Lombards alike. If he really wants to have a beneficial effect on the land that Heaven, in his own words, entrusted to his rule, then he should begin at once, not await better times as Anfrid flatteringly advises him to do in act III, scene i. If we see Adelchis from this perspective—as a neglectful, inept king—we will begin to pass upon him, not on Charlemagne, a stern moral judgment.[126] Adelchis, for all his pure-hearted filial love, will appear guilty of grave moral omissions in his kingly duties.

Thus, in *Adelchis* the moral and the political levels of meaning dovetail in the figure of the king. In this respect, the Shakespearean kings were certainly a model. In *Richard II*, for example, on a literal, historical, and political level, the king's will was instrumental in determining the fate of a nation; on a metaphorical-moral level, the king stands for Everyman.

In chapter 6 of the *Discorso*, entitled "On the general reason for Charles's effortless conquest," Manzoni considers how, in the Middle Ages, what made a king was just the "moral superiority" of the man.[127] There were no constitutional charters to regulate the king's action and jurisdiction, but rather only customs; the true decisive force in resolving conflicts over political power resided in "the strongest will,"[128] such as Charles's: "Whoever wants to grasp the meaning of the word 'king' in the barbarian age should not look for it in institutions that either were not there or were still nascent and weak. One should rather inquire upon the character and actions of each of those kings, only to discover that this word had in each case a different meaning. *The crown was a metal circle, which was worth as much as the head girded by it.*"[129]

The image with which Manzoni concludes his argument on the king's will recalls the words of Shakespeare's Richard II (translated by Le Tourneur) when the king, having lost his power, considers the vanity of royal pomp and customs, nullified by incumbent death: "*La mort a etabli sa cour dans* le cercle de cette Couronne, qui ceint le front mortel d'un Roi . . . *Banissez le respect, les formalités, le cérémonies, tous ces vains égards transmis par la coutume*" [Death has established his court within the circle of this Crown, which girds the mortal head of a king. Banish reverence, formalities, and ceremonies, all these vain honors that customs prescribe].[130] At this point in the play, Richard has just received the news that his beloved courtiers, his mates of revels, have been killed. He can see that his deposal from the throne, as well as his own death, are now only a matter of time.

Richard II is replete with instances when kingship is a metaphor for the human predicament. Under the impression of his own fall, the inept king becomes an existentialist philosopher, with a meaningfully sudden transformation that Manzoni did not leave unnoticed in the "Lettre."[131] The attentive analysis that Manzoni devotes there to *Richard II* clearly indicates that he knew the play very well. Manzoni borrows for Adelchis the blasphemous self-identification of Richard with Christ.[132] This self-identification marks them out as inept kings to the attentive spectator who recognizes the irony of the biblical quotations.

However, the spectator's judgment on the moral shortcomings of the falling kings does not rule out a sense of pity for them as they die. Adelchis's final moments elicit the pity that everybody feels for a soul, full of dignity in its sorrow, departing from life, the same pity that Charles, in his magnanimity, is showing him once he has vanquished him as his enemy. Do we not feel pity for Richard when he is brought to the Tower of London, and when he is killed in prison? We certainly do. Bolingbroke-Henry could have probably reigned in peace without having Richard killed. But was Richard a good king? No; his deposal freed England from his squandering of public money, from his capricious favors to his flatterers and his likewise capricious, unjust treatment (including murder) of innocent noblemen, all causes of civil strife. Shakespeare's scriptural quotations, concerning the archetypal Judeo-Christian victims and their killers, are meant to make the audience ponder the problem of victim and villain in politics.[133] It will prove impossible to sort out neatly the bad from the good on the basis of those quotations; but they do show that acting is evil when perpetrated for unjust aims or at best as a neutrally judged practice, which comes with government, when carried out for just purposes. These same considerations apply to Manzoni's strategy of quotation from the Scriptures in his second tragedy.

The history of Richard II's successors to the English throne was the subject of Shakespeare's *Henry IV*, Parts I and II, and *Henry V*, forming a tetralogy of which *Richard II* was the first part. What Manzoni could find in this series is a complex analysis of the question of the ideal ruler. Shakespeare's sources for *Henry V* included both Machiavelli's advice of practical prudence to the princes and Erasmus's moral precepts to the princes. These opposite sets of instructions were embodied in the oxymoronic ideal of the "Christian king." How can a powerful king be Christian? If the chorus calls Henry V "the mirror of all Christian kings" (*Henry V*, act II, prologue, 6), then that king could be interesting for Manzoni in re-creating the antagonist of the inept king in his second historical tragedy.[134]

Adelchis has a *pars construens* as far as political justice is concerned because, as it ends, Charles, known to future ages as "the Great," replaces the inept Lombard king, Adelchis. This contrasts with *Carmagnola*, in which the political power antagonizing the tragic hero is tainted with irredeemable moral flaws. Here is the uniformly positive portrait of Charles, conqueror of Rome, that Manzoni opposes to the historians who maintain that the pope called the Franks to fight against his own Italian subjects:

> What would the Roman citizens have said on hearing such a reproach? They were used to trembling, to seeking refuge in churches, to screaming in fright at the news of the arrival of a Lombard king. How different a spectacle the Frankish king offered, the victorious Charles, whose name they had learned just recently, but that already had a historic ring to it! They saw him reach the gates of Rome, ask meekly for permission to enter the city, take the pope's hand with sincere affection and awe, and then walk in with him, accompanied by Roman and Frankish judges. With his gestures of friendship, with his confident mingling with them, Charles gave a pledge of future peace to those who could not hope to win it by themselves.[135]

Charles was a devout friend of the pope. Manzoni writes in the note to this passage that the Frankish king was seen in tears upon learning of Hadrian's death. He had "the strongest will," as the previous quotation from the *Discorso* told us, and a "moral superiority" by which he could command total obedience from his people. That is why he proved victorious against Desiderius and Adelchis in Italy. But while the *Discorso* recounts and reasons on the historical events, only the tragedy fills in the details of Charles's thoughts and doubts, of that strong will in action, as it were.[136] In the tragedy we see how, in his Italian enterprise, Charles had to face ethical dilemmas at each step. First, he had to decide whether to try to maintain his position in the Alps against the impenetrable Lombard defensive line, while Adelchis terrorized his soldiers, thinning out their ranks with his forays. He had to consider retreating and abandoning the pope to the Lombards in order to spare his own people, the Franks. Then, when the way to Italy was providentially opened, he had to face the remorse of conquering the land that was the birthplace of the woman he married but soon repudiated—Ermengarde, Adelchis's sister. Then, how to deal with the Lombards who betrayed their kings to serve him? With flattery? Rewards? Humiliations? Finally, could he afford to let Adelchis live, once he had conquered the kingdom? When portraying Charles in his ethical dilemmas, Manzoni seems to have had in mind the way Shakespeare's ideal king, Henry V, went about solving his own.[137]

Agricultural Metaphors

The agricultural imagery in *Adelchis* clearly indicates that Manzoni adopted Shakespeare's tetralogy as a model, in which the fall of the inept king is followed by the rise of the ideal king. Manzoni's vegetation and agricultural imagery (already meaningfully employed in *Carmagnola*'s chorus) illustrates the political-historical thesis of the tragedy: Charlemagne represents the just ruler under the circumstances, and is modeled on Henry V; Adelchis represents an inept and blasphemous king, like Richard II, who only in the very end understands his fault and repents.

A passage from Le Tourneur's version of Henry V's monologue at the eve of the battle of Agincourt contains several poetic seeds for the imagery in *Adelchis*'s choruses. Henry V laments the king's lot, since the royal pomp

> *ne les fait dormir d'un sommeil aussi profond que le dernier des* esclaves, qui, *l'esprit vide et le corps rempli d'un pain amer de l'indigence, va chercher le repos; jamais il ne s'éveille et ne voit l'horrible spectre de la nuit, fille des enfers: le jour, depuis son lever jusqu'à son coucher, il se couvre de* sueur sous l'oeil brûlant du soleil, *mais tout la nuit il dort en paix dans un tranquille Élysée; et le lendemain à la naissance du jour,* il se lève, il aide à Phoebus à atteler ses coursiers à son char, *et il suit la même carrière pendant le course éternel de l'année, dans la chaîne d'un travail utile, jusqu'à son tombeau.*

> does not let the king sleep with a sleep as profound as the last of slaves, who with an empty spirit and the body filled with the bitter bread of poverty, goes to seek his rest at night; he never wakes up and never sees the horrible ghost of the night, the child of hell; during the day, from when he gets up until bedtime, he works *sweating under the burning eye of the sun*, but then all night he sleeps in the peace of tranquil Elysian fields; and the day after he gets up, *helps Phoebus attach the horses to his carriage*, and follows that road all year long, enchained a useful job, until he dies.[138]

This passage is structured on the comparison between the king's lot and the peasant's lot and revolves around the metaphor of the sun. The mindless physical labor of the humble subjects is connoted by the sweat, caused by the sun's heat. These images must be compared with the Italian peasants in the first two stanzas of *Adelchis*'s first chorus. Devoid of any spiritual dimension, they sprinkle the field's furrows with *servo sudor* ("slavish sweat"), although the sun that warms them up is only metaphorical—the pale sun of the past Roman glory, a sun choked by the clouds of present enslavement to the barbarians. A setting sun disentangling itself from the clouds brings "a day more serene" to the "pious peasant" in the last two lines of *Adelchis*'s second chorus. This "pious peasant" has often been seen as a representative of the nameless people of the first chorus. This is the only way to make sense of his unexpected appearance at the end of the elegy of the princess's death (the second chorus of *Adelchis* is often called Ermengarde's chorus).

The sun is associated with the king figure throughout Shakespeare's tetral-ogy.[139] In one of the most famous references, Prince Hal, future king Henry V, describes himself as a sun obfuscated by clouds that will shine more brightly once the clouds—his companions of revel—are dispersed (*Henry IV, part I* I.ii.201–8). The last lines of the passage quoted above speak of a peasant wak-ing up with the sun each morning to start his work day in useful alliance with that star. The early hour, rendered with an image of the peasant helping Phoe-bus attach the horses to the sun chariot, underlines the appreciation for the hum-ble, yet "useful," work of the peasant. The image seems to bespeak the friendly collaboration of the king-sun and the peasant on which the good life of a king-dom must be based. Let us posit that Manzoni adopted, for his own aims, the Shakespearean sun imagery. Following the metaphors, the last stanza of the sec-ond chorus means that the king, freeing at once himself from the clouds of sin through remorse (for the repudiation of the Lombard princess, Ermengarde) and freeing the Italians from their clouds of enslavement to the Lombards, brings "more serenity" to the Italian peasant. Charles does not bring perfect serenity to the peasant, but he is a welcome improvement over the Lombards, described in *Adelchis*'s second chorus as "savage oppressors." The close of this chorus mirrors a famous passage in the *Discorso* in which Charles's conquest of Italy is evaluated according to a criterion of relative justice ("a little justice").[140]

Furthermore, the setting sun of the last stanza of the second chorus must be compared with the scorching sun of the central stanzas in the same chorus. That sun metaphorically causes the death of Ermengarde, who is compared to sun-parched grass leaves. This burning sun symbolizes her passionate love for King Charles, a love that she finally reveals in her delirium in act IV. Manzoni imag-ines that Ermengarde falls passionately in love with Charles once they are mar-ried. Their marriage was arranged for the purpose of bringing peace between Lombards and Franks. For Charles the diplomatic marriage to Ermengarde is not emotionally significant, and he breaks it when he falls in love with Hildegarde. But that same marriage kindles the flame of erotic passion in Ermengarde, a passion that ultimately consumes her very life when she represses it, after being repudiated by Charles.

So the sun-king of the last stanza brings "more serenity" to the peasant (an interpretation not acceptable to many because it does not fit the generally negative interpretation of Charlemagne in the tragedy), but at the same time the burning sun, appearing in the central stanzas and representing erotic passion provoked by Charles, makes a victim of the grass-blade Ermengarde. The sun images in the second chorus convey the mixture of good and bad present in the Christian king. Despite destroying Ermengarde—her virginal purity stained by the passion inspired in her by the king—the sun brings a better life to the Italian peasant.[141]

The realistic images of the peasant, both in *Adelchis* and in Shakespeare's tetralogy, acquire more poignancy if considered against the backdrop of the agricultural imagery as metaphors of political government. There are several notable examples in Shakespeare's tetralogy. The gardener reproaches Richard II, overheard by the Queen, for not having cultivated his kingdom as he himself has done with the garden entrusted to his care. In the same scene, the names of the king's favorites—Green, Bushy, and Wiltshire—generate the metaphor by which their death is described: they were weeds to uproot (III.iv.52–53). France in the grip of war is rhetorically described, in a pompous speech by a French nobleman pleading for peace, as an uncultivated, overgrown field, while it was the most beautiful garden of Europe before the war (*Henry V,* V.ii.35–67).[142]

In *Adelchis,* on the eve of the invasion of Italy, Charles describes to his soldiers the land they seek to conquer as a fruit-laden, exotic orchard (II.v). Subsequently, two agricultural images show Adelchis's moral development. In the first of these two images, Adelchis describes his own life, wasted in idle kingship: "And my heart becomes dry, like to a seed / cast onto a barren ground and blown away / by the wind" (III.i). What is remarkable in this metaphor—amply quoted as a sample of beautiful romantic lyric—is that Adelchis lays the blame for his sterility as a king onto the land Heaven has entrusted to his care.[143] Ironically, that land is the symbol of a person's nature in Christ's parable of the sower (Luke 8:4–8, 9–15; Matthew 13:3–9). Christ himself is the sower and "the seed is the Word of God" (Luke 8:11), while the various types of terrain are the various human types who will be more or less receptive of the Christian message. Adelchis's simile may sound beautiful but is, in its unwitting reference to the parable of the sower, blasphemous. His heart—his intentions, motives, preferences—is like the seed—that is, like the Word of Christ; the bad results of his kingship therefore are not in the seed but rather in the land and in the wind, the historical circumstances. Prior to his fall, although he sees clearly that he should counter his father's policy of continual warfare for territorial conquest, Adelchis hides to himself his own duties as king by commiserating on Anfrid's shoulder. By this easily recognizable scriptural quotation, Manzoni wants the reader or spectator to see how playing the victim in order to shun moral duties can bring a person to a stunning and blasphemous self-identification with Christ.[144]

Adelchis's rhetorical turn in act III recalls Richard II' s velleitarian, pathetic apostrophe to the land when he sees his own demise approaching. The king exhorts the land to become sterile: "*Terre, amie de Richard, ne nourris pas l'ennemi de ton Souverain! Ne produis pas pour ces rebelles que de poignantes épines. . . . Cette terre aura de sentiments et ses pierres se changeront en soldats armés*" [Land, friend of Richard, do not nourish the enemy of your King! Produce but pricking thorns for these rebels. . . . This land will have feelings and its rocks will become armed soldiers].[145]

The second important occurrence of an agricultural metaphor in Adelchis's words is in act V. By this time, dying Adelchis's agricultural metaphor serves to illustrate his clear-headed analysis of the historical circumstances that brought about the Lombard fall:

> With their blood-stained hands our
> forefathers cast the seed of injustice;
> Our fathers manured it with blood
> And the land does not yield other harvest.
> (V.vii)

These words can be compared with those of the Bishop of Carlisle in *Richard II*, when, in a last-ditch attempt to rescue Richard from being deposed, he prophesies the bloody War of the Roses:

> *je vous predis que* le sang *anglois* engraissera cette terre . . . *Je tumulte, le desordre, les horreurs, les alarmes et la revolte habiteront dans ce Royaume et cette terre, blanchie des ossemens entassés de ses habitans sera nommée* le champ du sang. . . . *Opposez-vous à cette injustice; que jamais elle ne s'accomplisse, si vous ne voulez pas que les enfants de vos enfants crient contre vous: malediction sur nos pères!*

> I foretell you that the English *blood will manure this land* . . . The tumult, the disorder, the horrors, the alarms and the revolt will inhabit in this Kingdom and the land, whitened by the heaps of bones of her dead inhabitants, will be called "*the*

field of blood" . . . Oppose the present *injustice:* that it may never take place, if you do not want your children's children to cry against you "Curse be our *fathers!"*[146]

Manzoni adapts the land cultivation metaphor from the *post eventum* prophecy of the Shakespearean text for Adelchis's final evaluation of the historical causes of the Lombard kingdom's fall. This fact is evident if we consider that Le Tourneur has rendered with *champ du sang* the original "the field of Golgotha and dead men's skulls."[147] Whereas in the metaphor of the original work, people cultivate the land with blood and harvest skulls, in the French version, people cultivate blood and reap blood, just as in Adelchis's metaphor.[148]

Adelchis, like Richard II, does not until the drama's end lose his ineptitude masked by grandiloquent philosophizing. However, Adelchis's clear-headed diagnosis of the Lombards' historical failure as rulers of Italy shows the moral development of his character. By the same token, the final invocation to Christ appears as a penitential response to his blasphemous self-identification with Christ in act III. With the apostrophe to Christ, "O King of kings," Adelchis is humbly recognizing that he is one of many kings, one of many men, distinct from the One, the veritable King.

In order to add meaning to Adelchis's final invocation to Christ as "King of kings," in the second edition of the tragedy Manzoni modified the wording of Charles's speech to his counts and bishops in the close of act II. This is one of the only five major changes in wording (four changes in *Adelchis* and one in *Carmagnola*) that Manzoni effected while adjusting punctuation and orthography in the tragedies for the 1845 edition of *Opere varie.* In the modified passage, Charles is ordering bishops and priests in his camp to arrange a prayer service in which all soldiers will soon participate: "Just as my Franks prostrating in the dust / will bow their head before the King of kings / so our foes will yield to us in battle." In the 1822 version, Christ was indicated by a capitalized "Him" and the phrase "prostrating in the dust" was lacking. It is evident that Manzoni modified the lines' wording in order to accommodate Christ's designation as "King of kings" in Charles's speech, thus creating a proleptic echo for Adelchis's final invocation.

The Queen and the Garland: Ermengarde and Katharine of Aragon

Manzoni once declared to his stepson that he was very much in debt to Shakespeare's Katharine of Aragon in the play *Henry VIII* for the portrayal of Ermengarde.[149] At of the end of the nineteenth century, two scholars, Paolo Bellezza and Vincenzo Reforgiato, identified some of the elements in Katharine's character and story that inspired Manzoni while he was reconstructing the character of Ermengarde.[150] There are two main points, however, that remain to be made about Manzoni's appropriation of certain aspects of Queen Katherine in recreating his own tragic heroine.

Reforgiato and Bellezza have already shown that Shakespeare and Manzoni employed similar vegetation imagery to describe the queens' lots.[151] However, there is one common vegetation image, largely overlooked, that yields significantly different symbolic meaning in the two respective contexts.

Both Ermengarde and Katharine have supernatural visions right before they die, although in Ermengarde's case it is a vision of hell, whereas Katharine has a peaceful vision of a celestial banquet of white-robed angels. Whereas Katharine sees garland-bearers in her vision that she recognizes as angels,[152] Ermengarde becomes delirious and mistakes the white-robed nuns that are trying to revive her for the people of the Frankish court. She sees herself in the midst of a leering Frankish crowd before whom the king allows Ermengarde's rival to smile flirtatiously at him, thus humiliating the queen publicly. Ermengarde's delirious words let out all her pent-up passion. From details of her vision—and from the chorus that follows—we learn that her love for Charles is deeply passionate, that for her the repudiation was not just the breaking of a concerted marriage. Manzoni imagines that the passion she conceived for Charles continues to torment her even after she retreats to the monastery founded by her mother, where her sister Ansberga is the abbess. On recovering from her spell, Ermengarde, finally delivered of her burden of repressed feelings and memories, is grateful to be back among the nuns and can, at the very last moment, prepare for a Christian death.

In Shakespeare, the garland, prominent in Katharine's vision, is a visible prop and a clear symbol: it signifies forthcoming beatitude for the forsaken queen, which she yearns for as her hands stretch to reach the garland suspended by the angels over her head. In Manzoni, by contrast, we find the garland in a simile with which Ermengarde describes her own forlorn lot to her father and to her brother, in act I, scene iii. This is the first of the sole two scenes where Ermengarde appears in the tragedy. She is asking her father to be allowed to live far from the Lombard court in Pavia and to retire into the monastery where her sister is a nun:

> This court, where I grew up to be adorned
> With hopes, protected in my mother's bosom,

Cannot be my abode. What would I do
here now? Garland briefly desired, worn
on the brow for sport one festive day,
and soon thrown at the feet of passers-by.

The mirth of bystanders surrounding the repudiated queen links this simile of the garland with the madness scene of act IV—the mocking crowd in the delirium. Ermengarde is a weak, passive object for others to watch and judge. In contrast to Katharine's garland, which points upward to the spiritual heights to which each soul can soar, Ermengarde's garland points to the ground, to the dirt and dust of a road, and, above all, is worn by someone other than herself. She is that garland, a beautiful but passive entity, shortly lived, whose life in fact lasts as long as the desire of others lasts. Katharine's garland is symbol of the real crown to which everybody can aspire. It is the arrival point of her itinerary of Christian resignation, an itinerary suited to her as a mature woman. Ermengarde, by contrast, is just a young bride when she is abandoned. Manzoni conceives her on the model of Katharine but also individualizes her character respecting the historical facts known about the Lombard princess. Ermengarde cannot soar to spiritual heights because she never allows herself even to measure sincerely her own hidden passion, as Shakespeare allows Katharine to do. Moreover, as a tragic heroine, she shares in the tragic hero's traditional status as a flawed character. In this respect, however, it is important to emphasize that Manzoni indicates her fatal flaw not in her passion, which was kindled by the king, but rather in the pride that prevented her from confessing and acknowledging that passion and suffering for it.[153] Ermengarde prefers to repress her passion in the silence of melancholic brooding in the monastery. The secluded life, the attempt to live like a nun, has only exacerbated her pent-up passion. That is the conclusion of her sister Ansberga ("O poor sister! / This somber quiet brought you torments rather / Than relief"), and Ermengarde promptly acknowledges it. Only after this acknowledgement is her soul cleansed and she ready to die a Christian death.

Despite the difference between Shakespeare's elegiac treatment of Katharine and Manzoni's tragic portrayal of the young queen burning with nonconfessed passion, the essential similarity between these two repudiated queens remains. Both Katharine and Ermengarde are repudiated in favor of a rival that is younger or more beautiful or allegedly healthier. In Shakespeare's play Henry falls in love with Anne Boleyn; in Manzoni's tragedy Charles falls in love with Hildegarde. Both Katharine and Ermengarde are formally and falsely accused of being unable to satisfy the king's need for an heir. Although the consequences of these repudiations—both clearly shown to be dictated by the kings' lust—are dire for the two women in their earthly life, a beneficial effect ensues for the nations governed by the two kings. Shakespeare's play ends on the day Elizabeth, daughter of Anne Boleyn, is baptized, and the archbishop Cranmer utters a post-factum prophecy of the ascent of Elizabeth to the throne of England. Elizabeth would have never been born if Henry VIII had not, however unjustly, repudiated his first wife and married Anne Boleyn. England might have never seen then the Golden Age brought about by the Virgin Queen, "a thousand thousand blessings, / which time will bring to ripeness," as Cranmer says (*Henry VIII*, V.iv.20–21).

Similarly, in *Adelchis* the appeasement of the Franks devised by Bertrada, Charles's mother, and Desiderius, when they concerted the marriage between Ermengarde and Charles, would have meant the perpetuation of the terrible domination of the Lombards over the Italians. For the sake of the latter, it was good that Charles was free from any dynastic constraint when he intervened in Italy to defeat the Lombards, as the pope summoned him to defend his territories and the Italians from the Lombard fury. Elizabeth was good for the national life of England, and so was the reign of Charles for Italy, an improvement after the ravaging centuries of the Lombard domination. Manzoni and Shakespeare leave us thus to ponder on Ermengarde and Katharine—individuals whose earthly happiness was unjustly sacrificed, while another outcome of the same unjust act of which they were victims proved beneficial for large masses of people.

NOTES

1. For all quotations from Manzoni's poetry and tragedies, I translate from the edition by Pietro Gibellini and Sergio Blazina, *Poesie e tragedie* (Milan: Garzanti, 1990), which follows the edition by Alberto Chiari and Fausto Ghisalberti in vol. 1 of *Tutte le opere* (Milan: Mondadori, 1957). The Chiari-Ghisalberti edition reproduces Manzoni's 1845 revised version of the tragedies. For the *editio princeps* I consulted Gilberto Lonardi's editions. All English translations, from either Italian or French, in both notes and text of this introduction, are mine, unless otherwise stated. All emphasis in quotations is mine, unless otherwise stated.

2. Scherillo, *Il decennio.* In this paragraph, I am translating and abridging from pp. 89–91 of this invaluable essay, which reconstructs in detail Milanese political history and literary life in the decade 1812–22.

3. Scherillo (and others after him) suggested that in the many-layered text of Manzoni's historical tragedy, one could detect the figure of Murat behind Carmagnola, when the generously impulsive soldier finally ignores the danger to his person and goes to put himself in the hands of his enemies. Both Carmagnola and Murat were of humble origins, son of a cowherd and of a peasant, respectively; both were valiant generals who had led their armies to historically important military victories. Rumor had it that the former king of Naples was deceived into believing that he could safely land in Calabria from the French Riviera, were he was living as an outcast after the military defeats of the previous spring. Having landed there with a few faithful companions,

he was ambushed, apprehended by the Bourbon police, and kept prisoner in the castle of Pizzo. After his capture and during a brief arraignment, he never showed any sign of fear. On going to his execution, he said "Let the will of God be done." Before dying, he sent a letter to his wife asking that it be remembered that his life was never stained by any unjust act and recommending his memory to her and to the children. Scherillo is convinced that Manzoni could glean information from oral sources in the absence of published documents, given the closeness in time of the Murattian epic (ibid., 145–48).

4. All the quotations in this paragraph are from Avitabile, *Controversy on Romanticism*, 61; chaps. 2 and 3 of this excellent study are a synthetic report of the beginning of the Milanese controversy over classicism vs. romanticism.

5. In 1823, in the *Letter on Romanticism* (which was written originally as a private piece of correspondence and published only to remedy a printing problem in 1870), Manzoni reiterated Berchet's notion of romanticism as the dignified and reasonable literary expression of people living in touch with their own times.

6. Manzoni to Fauriel, Milan, 25 Mar. 1816:

> I am almost ashamed of telling you about my literary projects, after having conceived so many of them and carried out but a few. But this time I hope to bring to conclusion a tragedy that I have begun with much enthusiasm, and hope to produce something truly new here among us. I have my plan, I have divided the action into scenes, I versified some of them, and I have even prepared in my head a dedication to my best friend: do you think he will accept it? The subject deals with the death of Francesco Carmagnola; if you want to be reminded of his story in detail, consult the end of the eighth volume of the *Italian Republics* by Sismondi. The action starts with the war declaration by the Venetians against Milan at page 378 and ends with the death of Carmagnola described at the end of that volume. The action lasts six years. This is a huge blow to the rule of unity of time, but I know you are not going to be among those who will be shocked by this. After having well read Shakespeare, as well as some of the latest writings on theater, and after much reflection, my ideas have changed deeply on some reputations, and I do not dare to say more on this because I want to write a tragedy myself, and there is nothing more ridiculous than to speak ill of those who have composed works in this same genre and who are now deemed great masters in it. (*Tutte le lettere*, vol. 1:155–56)

7. Stendhal has left us a snapshot of this group in his Italian travel journal from 12 Nov. 1816:

> I go every day to the balcony of Monsieur de Breme at La Scala. It is a very literary company. One never sees women there. Monsieur de Breme has much learning, wit, and grand manners. He is a passionate admirer of Madame de Staël, and very committed to the arts. He is less solicitous with me now because I have dared to say that Madame de Staël has written but one work, *The Spirit of Laws in Society*. For the rest, she has done nothing but putting together and editing in beautiful style the ideas that she has heard during the evenings in her parlor. . . . Since de Breme is very kind, I continue to go almost every night to his balcony. I bring to that company the news from France and anecdotes on the retreat from Moscow, on Napoleon, on the Bourbons, and they repay me with news from Italy. In this balcony I met Monti, the greatest living poet but one who lacks logic. When something incenses him, his eloquence becomes sublime. Monti is still a handsome fifty-five-year-old man. . . . Silvio Pel-

lico, full of reason and good manners, has not as much poetic force as Monti. And in literature force is a synonym for influence, effect on the readers, and merit. Certainly Pellico is very young, and he is in the unhappy situation of lacking independent means; a barbarous destiny has allotted to him, instead of a bronze face—cheeky and defiant—typical of the plotter, a tender and generous soul. . . . In de Breme's balcony I often find Monsieur Borsieri. He has a French spirit, full of vivacity and daring. Monsieur the Marquis Ermes Visconti has very clear ideas, despite the fact that he admires Kant. If one wanted to meet the first Italian philosopher I believe one should choose between Monsieur Visconti and Monsieur Gioia. . . . Monsieur Confalonieri, man of great courage and who loves his fatherland, comes often into de Breme's balcony. Monsieur "Crisostomo" Berchet has translated very well some of Bürger's poems. He is *impiegato* [he has a job], and the good sense he infuses into his Italian verse, surprisingly containing ideas, could cost him his position. (Stendhal, *Rome, Naples et Florence*, vol. 1:70–74)

8. Avitabile, in *Controversy on Romanticism*, underlines the reconcilement of national aspirations with the ideas and ideals of the eighteenth century in the writings of the Milanese romantics (see 42 and 95).

9. Manzoni, *Opere inedite o rare*, vol. 3:308. From an unpublished essay entitled "On some particular aspects of the Christian religion in relation to the main social institutions."

10. Giovan Battista De Cristoforis, "*Inni sacri* di Alessandro Manzoni. Milano, dalla stamperia di Pietro Agnelli, 1815," in Branca, *Il Conciliatore*, vol. 3:28–33 (4 Jul. 1819), 33.

11. Sainte-Beuve, *Fauriel e Manzoni*, 5.

12. Manzoni compares the status of the French and the Italian national languages in a letter to Fauriel dated 3 Nov. 1821:

The French person wishing to express novel ideas can tap the resources of a language that has been spoken for a long time and forged by daily use, in many books, many conversations, many debates of all kinds. Moreover, there is a rule for the choice of expressions, and this rule he finds it in his memories, in his habits, which reassure him about the conformity of his style to the general spirit of the language. . . . Imagine now an Italian who writes instead in a language that he has almost never spoken, unless he is a Tuscan. And even if he is born in that privileged region, he writes in a language that only a few inhabitants of Italy speak, a language that is seldom used in conversations over important topics, a language in which works on moral sciences are very rare, and a language that has been corrupted and disfigured just by those writers who have written about the most important topics in a recent epoch. . . . The Italian who writes asks himself if the sentence that he has just written is Italian. How on earth can he ever hope to answer with precision a question that is itself vague? What does Italian mean in such a context? According to some it means what is enshrined in the *Crusca* [the dictionary compiled by the homonymous Accademia starting in 1612], according to others, it means something found everywhere in Italy, among the learned classes; most people do not associate that word with any clear idea. . . . Behind the ferocious and pedantic rigor of our *puristi* [the party that advocated a strict adherence to the pure language of the literary classics, first of all Petrarch and Boccaccio] there is, in my view, a very reasonable sentiment: it is the need for a certain norm, for a convention between the writers and the readers. I think that their error is in believing that a whole language can be contained in the *Crusca* and in the classic authors; even if that were the case, it would be impossible, as they believe, to find it, learn it and apply it drawing from that classic reservoir. The reason being that a sure, vast, and applicable knowledge of linguistic material cannot possibly result just from what one remembers of readings. And now tell me what an Italian should do when that Italian, not knowing how to do anything else, wishes to be a writer. As far as I am concerned, in the despair of finding a constant and special rule to do well in this trade, I have come to believe that there is for us too an approximate perfection of style and that, in order to transpose it as much as possible in our writings, there is a number of things we must do. We must think well on what we intend to say; we must read the so-called Italian classics, as well as the writers of other languages, the French above all; and we must have spoken of important questions with our fellow citizens. By means of these practices one can acquire a certain quickness in finding what one needs to express our current needs in the so-called good language, as well as a certain capability to expand the language by analogy, and finally a certain tact allowing one to draw from the French all that can be mixed with our language without shocking or incomprehensible effects. Here is how we Italians can succeed, although with toil and much perseverance, in doing what you French can do with much ease. (*Tutte le lettere*, vol. 1:254–247)

Manzoni used to engage in conversations with friends and family on the forging of a national and popular language, as can be seen in memoirs such as those collected in Bonghi, Borri, and Tommaseo, *Colloqui col Manzoni*. In these conversations the question of the language is the most frequently recurring topic, together with that of Italian unity and independence.

13. In his Italian travel journal, Stendhal records a sighting of Manzoni that gives us a sense of the author's isolation from the city. Writing on 14 Dec. 1816, the French writer reports his impressions on leaving Milan for southern Italy: "I have seen from afar Monsieur Manzoni, a strongly devout young man, who contends to Byron the honor of being the greatest lyric poet among the living. He has composed two or three odes that move me deeply and never give me the impression of a Monsieur de Fontanes rubbing his temples in order to produce poetry that sounds sublime, and who goes to see the minister in order to gain the title of baron" (*Rome, Naples et Florence*, vol. 1:153).

14. In this paragraph I have summarized the hypothesis of Carlo Dionisotti, "Manzoni fra Italia," 502–3, which is part of a larger analysis of Manzoni's relationship with France and the French culture. It is important to remark that, notwithstanding the fact that he distanced himself from the publishing enterprise of his friends, Manzoni felt that *Il Conciliatore* had had a very important role in the national literary life as a spearhead of the romantic movement. Writing at the end of 1820 to Fauriel, who wanted to publish a scholarly article on the Italian literary debate over neoclassicism vs. romanticism, Manzoni recommended that his friend consult all the literary articles from *Il Conciliatore*, which are "indispensable in order to have a complete vision of the romantic question in Italy" (*Tutte le lettere*, vol. 1:214). In the same letter, Manzoni states what he will repeat in his 1823 *Letter on Romanticism:* the romantics have been forced to keep a defensive posture by the obtuse attacks of the antiromantic critics, so that the romantics have been able to show just the *pars destruens* of their system, much less of their constructive ideas. Manzoni ascribes the stagnation of the debate to the repetitive and simplistic objections of the romantics' adversaries, who have "kept [the romantics] within the realm of too elementary ideas, which have remained too undetermined" (ibid.). A propos of the influence of *Il Conciliatore* on Manzoni, Dionisotti writes:

"If Manzoni arrived at Shakespeare through the mediation of French and German authors, the passage from lyrical poetry to drama, the assumtpion of Shakespeare as a model, and the justification of historical tragedy devoid of the unities of time and place—these momentous choices cannot be explained as resulting from individual elaboration, not even from the collaboration via correspondence with Fauriel in Paris. Manzoni's choices were rather the fruit of a different collaboration, that with the Milanese group who were bracing themselves for the romantic battle and were open not only, like Manzoni, to the German influence, but also to the English one" ("Manzoni e la cultura inglese," 254). Dionisotti emphasizes the fruitfulness of the dialectic stance Manzoni took toward his friends and acquaintances engaged in the romantic controversy and later in *Il Conciliatore:* Manzoni aimed at defending the peculiarities of the Italian culture, including its Catholic component, rather than surrendering to an unconditional dependence on northern European, Protestant culture, whose superiority was ultimately advocated by intellectuals such as Staël and Sismondi, respected masters of the conciliatoristi.

15. Dionisotti, "Manzoni e la cultura inglese," 256.

16. Dionisotti, "Manzoni fra Italia," 505.

17. In this connection, as Eurialo de Michelis has suggested in "Le tragedie," 106, the first stanza of Manzoni's first political ode, "April 1814," can be seen as a general statement on the individual's political conduct to be kept during the rule of an unjustly coercive and repressive regime (in this poem, Napoleon's):

> *As long as Truth was crime and Falsehood reigned*
> *Proclaiming everywhere with frowning face:*
> *"I alone can speak out, I am the truth,"*
> *My verse was silent, and I felt no shame.*
> *It was not shame, rather a noble choice:*
> *'cause being sincere is not alone praiseworthy,*
> *Nor is risk handsome for no noble cause.*

Among the many emotions and thoughts that went into the conception and composition of Manzoni's first tragedy, one cannot rule out the poet's reflections on his own attitude toward the political struggle of his times (the patriots against the Austrians), with its dramatic demands on individuals.

18. Koerner was also a dramatist whose historical drama *Zriny* was very popular in Vienna in 1812, as I found in Carlson, "Nationalism and the Romantic Drama," 143. Further research should clarify whether Manzoni only knew Koerner's war poetry or was also aware of his historical drama.

19. In a letter to Fauriel dated 17 Oct. 1820, Manzoni writes: "I have to leave aside the subject of Adolph, which you have suggested me, because I could not deal with it but in a way to which the public is very little used, and against which there are too many prejudices to overcome. What I am going to undertake now is much more popular, the fall of the Lombard kingdom, or better, of the Lombard dynasty and its extinction in the person of Adelchis, who was the last king with Desiderius, his father" (*Tutte le lettere,* vol. 1:215).

20. I follow the English form of the Lombard king's name as I found it in Paul the Deacon, *History of the Langobards.* For his 1823 French translation, Fauriel adopted "Adelghis," which is more similar to the Italian variant of the name, "Adalgiso." Manzoni justified his choice of "Adelchi"

with the fact that this was the form in which the young king signed official documents and royal decrees (see historical notes to *Adelchis*).

21. Bognetti, "La genesi." The essay was originally published in *Archivio Storico Lombardo* 3 (1953): 45–153, but the version I am summarizing from is an abridged version reprinted in *Adelchi. Dai Longobardi ai Carolingi*. Bognetti warns that the political allusions contained in Adelchis's character seemed leveled more at the Neapolitan rather than the Piedmontese prince. Many decades later, in his unfinished essay "On the Italian Independence," Manzoni in fact expressed vivid appreciation for Charles Albert's role in the 1848–49 events, as he greatly helped to foster in the Italians the perception that the House of Savoy was the most viable agent of national unification.

22. The novel's title, *I promessi sposi*, contains a religious allegory. One of the names of the Church is "Sposa di Cristo," "Bride of Christ," with reference of St. Paul's letter to the Ephesians (5:21–32) where the wedding of Christ to the Church is defined as "a great mystery." Paul indicates here that Christ's earthly institution, the Church, points to the mysterious link between God and man, between the eternal and the temporal, the mystery of history and time. Therefore the wedding of Manzoni's comedic novel, foregrounded in its title, refers to that of the young couple, Renzo and Lucia, with which it ends, but it also alludes to the renewed union of the faithful in Christ within their Church, which is led, in the darkest of times, by the illuminated action of exceptional ecclesiastical men such as Federigo Borromeo.

23. In the already quoted letter to Fauriel, 3 Nov. 1821, Manzoni announces the numerous literary projects he then had under way: "I am correcting *Adelchis* and the historical tract for the printing press; then I will draft an essay, which I have had in mind for a long time, on the moral effect of tragedy; after this, I will tend to my novel, or to another tragedy, on Spartacus, depending on my disposition toward either one of these two works" (*Tutte le lettere*, vol. 1:249).

24. Manzoni placed *Adelchis* before *Carmagnola* in the 1845 edition of his complete works. Egidi, introduction, vii, surmised that the new order was motivated not so much by the need to create a chronological sequence in the tragedies' content (Middle Ages in *Adelchis*, Renaissance in *Carmagnola*) as by Manzoni's intention to let the name of his beloved first wife, Enrichetta—to whom *Adelchis* is dedicated—appear on the first page of the volume. However, in explaining Manzoni's choice to change the compositional order of his two tragedies, one cannot rule out either the chronological reordering with a view to the tragedies' historical content or an aesthetical evaluation by the author.

25. Pellico, *Opere scelte*, 178.

26. Vigorelli, "*I Promessi Sposi* da ieri a oggi," in *Manzoni*, 146.

27. Stendhal's letter is quoted by Trompeo, *Nell'Italia romantica*, 88.

28. Ibid.

29. Manzoni to Fauriel, Brusuglio, 26 Jul. 1819:

> As for my tragedy, I suspended its composition for one year because of another work that I undertook and completed, and that I hope to send you together with this letter. I really hope that the person entrusted with the letter will also accept the book because if I simply told you the title of it now, it would engender, I feel, nothing but sad prejudices. The book is a "refutation," that is to say a genre in which, I believe, nobody writes anything anymore. And it is a genre in which the lowest passions of literature (mark this, now!) are there unleashed. I would like you to see this one so that you can judge the spirit that has dictated

it. I have resumed my Tragedy at the beginning of this month in order to finish it before my departure [for Paris] and to leave it here ready for the press. I had previously versified only two acts. I wrote the third act in twelve days, God knows how, and I am now well into the fourth act. I would not leave without finishing this work, because it would be unbearable to have to go back to working on it once more, and also because it must be printed here, for excellent reasons that I will explain to you. (*Tutte le lettere*, vol. 1:184)

30. With the exception of Venetian Carlo Gozzi, author of celebrated dramatic fables, who also wrote tragedies (far less known than his fables) that breached the dramatic unities. Carlson, "Italian Romantic Drama," 235–36, summarizes the Venetian polemics between Pietro Chiari, Carlo Goldoni, and Gozzi as the first however confused signs of a crisis in the neoclassical dramatic tradition. He also mentions Giuseppe Baretti and Alessandro Pepoli as the forerunners of the Italian romanticism in defending Shakespeare and attacking the neoclassical traditions, although their writings (dating 1777 and 1796 respectively) went unheeded when they were published (ibid., 236–38).

31. Ermes Visconti, "Dialogo sulle unità drammatiche di luogo e di tempo," *Il Conciliatore* 2 (24 Jan. 1819): 90–111; 2 (28 Jan. 1819): 112–17.

32. Carlson, "Italian Romantic Drama," 246.

33. See a textual comparison in Scelfo, *Le teorie drammatiche*, 107–18. Scelfo reprises in more detail Trompeo's comparative studies between French and Italian romantic authors.

34. Carlson, "Italian Romantic Drama," 246.

35. Pellico, *Opere scelte*, 104–5.

36. These excerpts of early reviews are translated from Vigorelli, *Manzoni*, 116, where both transcriptions and photographs of the original articles are reproduced. See also the negative judgment on *Carmagnola* by Giovita Scalvini, "Dalla *Biblioteca italiana.*"

37. See *Commentari.*

38. The first of these reviews, the one that Manzoni found upon his return from Paris, was published in 1820, in volume 2, issue 3, of the German journal. The second one was a response to the October 1820 negative review in the English journal *Quarterly Review* (about which see below).

39. Goethe, "Gli scritti critici," 247–48.

40. Hayez, *Le mie memorie*, 120.

41. Ibid., 125. There Hayez continues: "Among all the works [I brought to Milan for the exhibit] 'Carmagnola' was the most admired; but, except for some good expressions of the heads and for the composition suggested by the famous tragedy, I believe that the painting in itself did not have great merit." See the illustration on the play's title page in this volume for a fairly close reproduction of Hayez's painting in a drawing by Roberto Focosi, the artist entrusted with the illustrations of the 1845 edition of Manzoni's *Opere varie*. In copying Hayez's painting for the frontispiece of act V of *Carmagnola*, Focosi drew only one daughter instead of the two featured in the original so as to mirror more closely the letter of Manzoni's tragedy. Hayez's painting was lost during the bombing of central Italy in World War II and only a photograph and an engraving by a contemporary artist, faithfully reproducing the painting, are extant today.

42. Fernando Mazzocca, commentary on the displayed painting, in Vigorelli, *Manzoni*, 113.

43. See Gozzoli and Mazzocca, *Hayez*, 94.

44. Ibid.

45. Manzoni's brother-in-law, Giuseppe Borri, reported having heard him say that the coldness with which *Adelchis* was received discouraged him from carrying out his plan for a third tragedy, on Spartacus (Bonghi, Borri, and Tommaseo, *Colloqui col Manzoni,* 216–17).

46. Mazzocca, "La sfortuna visiva," 49. Mazzocca also remarks how *The Death of Ermengarde,* by the Florentine painter Giuseppe Bezzuoli, contained anachronistic details in its reproduction of the monastery of Saint Salvatore in Brescia, where the Lombard princess dies of heartbreak. More interesting is an 1828 engraving by Massimo d'Azeglio, Manzoni's son-in-law, painter, novelist, and statesman, depicting "Charlemagne overcoming the Lombard defense at the Alps," in which Mazzocca finds evident iconic quotations from *Adelchis* (Vigorelli, *Manzoni,* 134).

47. Vigorelli, *Manzoni,* 128, reproduces the frontispiece to these articles and provides a commentary. The articles in *Biblioteca italiana* were originally published anonymously, but the reviewer was identified in Paride Zajotti. See Zajotti, "*Adelchi,* tragedia." Tommaseo's judgment on *Adelchis* is included in "Alessandro Manzoni."

48. Goethe, "Gli scritti critici," 264–72.

49. Dionisotti, "Manzoni e la cultura inglese," 261. Dionisotti further remarks how, since *The Betrothed* was published shortly after the English translation of his ode on Napoleon, the image of Manzoni as a lyric poet influenced the initial reception of his novel. This was unresponsive. But after Charles Swan's translation was published, in 1828, the novel earned Manzoni great renown in England, as attested, after many decades, by obituaries in *The Times* and the *London Quarterly Review,* in which he was extolled above Byron and Scott.

50. Low, "Manzoni in the American 1830s," 52. Rocco Montano had previously confined himself to researching the fortune of the novel in America.

51. Bosisio, "*Il conte di Carmagnola.*"

52. In staunchly advocating the suitability of Manzoni's tragedies to the stage, Bosisio can also rely on Goethe's appreciation of the tragedies, in which he often refers specifically to their theatrical qualities. Mangini, in "Manzoni e il teatro," has an opposite view about the stage values of Manzoni's tragedies. He shares in actor Gustavo Modena's judgment that the two tragedies lack dramatic strength and cannot be successfully put on stage in their entirety. My reconstruction of the chronology of stage performances is based on both Bosisio's and Mangini's writings, as well as Vigorelli, *Manzoni,* 143 (where one can find also references for the few attempts to turn the tragedies in opera or melodrama), and on a first-hand consultation of brochures and reviews for the twentieth-century performances (see bibliography). For the theatrical works based on Manzoni's novel, see also Faitrop-Porta, *I promessi sposi. Riduzioni teatrali.*

53. In this essay Manzoni expressed concern for the future of the historical novel because he could see more and more novelists claiming to be teaching history through their creations, and he thought that the genre would therefore bring great detriment to historical accuracy. In the way history mixes with fiction to create historical fiction, there is, in Manzoni's view, a fundamental, structural difference between the historical novel and historical drama. In the latter, history enters only indirectly, by providing the subject and the characters through the sources. Since there is no narration but only dialogues, one can draw a clear-cut line demarcating what is historical and what is fictional in the plot of a drama; it is evident that the the plot is historical but the dialogue invented by the playwrights on the basis of plausibility or verisimilitude. In the novel, as in the epic, one cannot separate invention and historical facts because the narrator has to wear at all times the double-faced mask of historian and novelist. Thus Manzoni found a fundamental ethical fault in

the historical novel because it could hurt historical accuracy, especially if practiced with levity. Manzoni did not write fiction of any sort after the two tragedies and *The Betrothed*, devoting himself instead to historical tracts and linguistic studies.

54. Manzoni, *On the Historical Novel*, 120. In the section of her introduction entitled "*On the Historical Novel* Today," Bermann, the translator, rightly compares Manzoni's essay with twentieth-century classics on the theory of the novel, such as Georg Lukács's books and R. Scholes' and R. Kellogg's *The Nature of Narrative*.

55. Manzoni, *On the Historical Novel*, 122–23.

56. Ibid., 123–24.

57. Manzoni thus writes in the "Lettre": "History seems to have become, at last, a science; it is being rewritten in all of its parts, as one realizes that what has been taken to be history so far is actually nothing but systematic abstraction, a series of attempts at demonstrating either false or true ideas by means of facts, which are always more or less distorted by the biased intentions to which they are made to serve. It is conventional ideas coupled with the vain aspiration to reduce everything to one exclusive and isolated aim that have dominated and led astray the human spirit in its judgment over the past, its evaluation of ancient customs and mores, of ancient laws and people, as well as in the appreciation of past aesthetic theories" (*Scritti letterari*, 158). Manzoni is here targeting the presumption of that enterprise of the spirit called "philosophy of history." For him, history deserved painstaking accuracy to show its "impartiality." In other words, Manzoni was awed by history, as he saw in it the mysterious ways in which human free will and God's providential plan interweave to form the thread of time. The relationship between time, history, and eternity was for Manzoni, as for Dante, a rich mystery to ponder in its meandering, microscopic level of individual choices. No wonder that he abhorred any conceited attempt to flatten this infinite variety into a rigid, all-secular grand scheme. In a note for the never-written essay on morality and tragedy, Manzoni is explicit in leveling this accusation against the intellectuals of the previous century who invented the philosophy of history: "The fad of treating history philosophically has begun in this past last century, and such a habit is patently noticeable in many works of the last century. All writers, in greater or lesser degrees, consider the diverse epochs of history from the point of view of the eighteenth century. They consider irregular all that was not noticeable back then" (ibid., 72).

58. Lukács, *The Historical Novel*, 159.

59. Lukács analyzes Alfieri's *Myrrha*, using Manzonian categories, as a tragedy that vivisects passion and lacks any real drama because there is no interaction with the world outside. Manzoni could have fully subscribed to Lukács's analysis on 113–14. From these pages one has a clear sense that Lukács had read Manzoni's essays on drama very attentively, so much so that he adopts the Manzonian categories in his own analysis of dramas. Lukács does not mention which edition of Manzoni's essays he consulted.

60. Carlson, "Nationalism and the Romantic Drama," 139.

61. Having begun his creative career as a classicist tragedian, he later became an emulator of Manzoni's in historical drama. The two met in Niccolini's native Florence, where Manzoni went repeatedly to perfect his knowledge of the Florentine idiom. Niccolini's most important and successful historical dramas, composed before midcentury, were *Antonio Foscarini*, a tragedy set in 1450 Venice; *Giovanni da Procida*, on the Sicilian Vespers; and *Arnaldo da Brescia*, on a twelfth-century cleric and philosopher who attacked certain aspects of the temporal power of the Church for the sake

of a spiritual renewal and a revival of the republican institutions in Italian municipalities. See Zardo, "Due tragedie veneziane," on the fundamental differences between Manzoni and Niccolini in practicing historical drama.

62. Carlson, "Nationalism and the Romantic Drama," 152.

63. Following is a list of the most renowned historical dramas composed by romantic authors. Serving as models for many attempts to write in this genre were the two dramas on the Thirty Years' War, Goethe's *Goetz Von Berlichingen* (1773), and Schiller's *Wallenstein* (1795–99). Samuel Taylor Coleridge translated *Wallenstein* in 1800 and Benjamin Constant in 1809. Two other influential historical dramas by the two German authors were Schiller's *William Tell* (1804) and Goethe's *Egmont* (1789), which focused on the making of two nations, Switzerland and the Netherlands, respectively. Heinrich von Kleist's *The Prince of Homburg* (1810) reflected on the role of Prussia in the German unification. The Republic of Venice at the apogee of its splendor occasions political reflections in Manzoni's *The Count of Carmagnola* (1820) and Byron's *Marin Faliero* (1820) and *The Two Foscaris* (1821). Manzoni's *Adelchis* (1822) and Alexander Pushkin's *Boris Godunov* (1825) were drawn from crucial junctures of their authors' respective national histories. Victor Hugo's *Cromwell* (1827), a historical reconstruction of the English Puritan Revolution, was also a dramatic rendition of the debate between republic and monarchy, relevant to contemporary France. Likewise, Hugo presented the history of the Royal House of Spain from Charles V to late 1600s in *Hernani* (1830) and *Ruy Blas* (1838) as a reflection on kingship. The Italian Renaissance city-states and their rulers provided the setting for three famous, very diverse, historical dramas: Rome and Papal rule for Percy Bysshe Shelley's *The Cenci* (1819), Medicean Florence for Alfred de Musset's *Lorenzaccio* (1834), Ferrara and the Borgias for Hugo's *Lucrece Borgia* (1833). The latter could be grouped also with the historical dramas featuring female protagonists, such as Schiller's *Mary Stuart* and *Joan of Arc* and Hugo's *Marion de Lorme* and *Mary Tudor*. On the momentous events of recent history, the French Revolution and the Napoleonic age, were George Büchner's *Danton's Death* (1835), Coleridge and Robert Southey's *The Fall of Robespierre* (1794), and Alexandre Dumas's *Napoleon Bonaparte* (1831). Manzoni's remark at midcentury that history had produced "a revolution in drama" was undoubtedly occasioned by the great favor that the European historical dramas (many among the ones listed above) enjoyed with Italian opera composers (Verdi, Donizetti, Bellini), as well as by the events of neighboring France, especially the 1830 "battle for *Hernani*," with which Hugo and other romantics won lasting influence over the citadel of classicist drama, the theater of the Comedie française.

64. Pellico, *Opere scelte*, 105.

65. Ibid., 353.

66. Milman, "Article III," 101. The article was published anonymously. Its authorship is identified in a note in Goethe, "Gli scritti critici," 256. In 1816 Pellico had proudly informed his brother that Lord Byron, then in Milan, had taken an interest in his tragedy and intended to translate it. Pellico even hoped that Byron would bring the *Francesca* to the stage of the Drury Lane theater: "I am so sorry that Ugo[Foscolo] does not like my tragedy. He who had advised me to burn it will never forgive Lord Byron's bad taste" (*Opere scelte*, 86–87).

67. Schlegel, *Course on Dramatic Art*, 222.

68. Ibid., 223.

69. Ibid., 28.

70. Ibid., 528–29.

71. Alfieri, with his nobility of blood coupled with disdain for those he considered the tyrants of his age (the absolutist monarchs Frederick of Prussia, Catherine of Russia, Maria Theresa of Austria), his aloofness, his passion for horses, and his irregular but passionate dedication to a married woman, was a forerunner in Italy of the stereotypical romantic or Byronic hero. Manzoni was aware of this stereotype of the romantic / rebellious / heroic artist and parodied it in his tragedies, probably having in mind Alfieri and Foscolo (see below and n. 144).

72. Silvio Pellico, "Vera idea della tragedia di Vittorio Alfieri, ossia la dissertazione critica dell'avvocato Giovanni Carmignani confutata dall'avvocato Gaetano Marrè. 2 vols. Genova, 1817," *Il Conciliatore* 1 (27 Sep. 1818): 127–35; the first part of the article appeared in the issue of September 6, 1818.

73. Giuseppe Nicolini, "Sulla Poesia tragica, e occasionalmente sul Romantismo," *Il Conciliatore* 2 (3 Jun. 1819): 669–79, 672.

74. Foscolo, "Della nuova scuola," 583–84. Foscolo had quoted a line of Manzoni's early poem "In Memory of Carlo Imbonati" in his famous long poem *The Sepulchres*. But Manzoni did not encourage a friendship between them, and Foscolo was incensed by Manzoni's coldness. See Parenti, *Immagini della vita*, 60. When in England, Foscolo was responsible for ruining the relationship between Byron and the Italian conciliatoristi with whom the English poet had mingled while in Milan. For a review of the Italian contemporary literary scene to be included in a new edition of *Childe Harold*, canto IV, Byron relied on J. C. Hobhouse, who in turn relied on Foscolo, at that time living in London. Byron's notes conveyed a very unflattering portrait of the Italian romantics. Lodovico di Breme wrote Byron an angry letter criticizing the bad figure that his group cut in *Childe Harold*. This famous squabble is summarized in Carlson, "Italian Romantic Drama," 243. Carlson rightly remarks how Foscolo negatively affected the English reception of the Italian romantic works and ideas.

75. Foscolo, "Della nuova scuola," 565–66. Poet Giosuè Carducci reprised these arguments to detract from the unconditional praises that Giuseppe Rovani tributed to Manzoni's dramatic art in 1873. Carducci argued that the absence of passions, as well as the poetics of historical truth and the poet's moralizing, prevented Manzoni's tragedies from achieving truly great dramatic effects. Despite this critique, Carducci thought that Manzoni's tragedies were still to be regarded as remarkable achievements of the Italian theater: "Manzoni confined himself to composing historical drama tinged with idealization. The genre constraints on one hand, and on the other the author's own propensity to avoid passions and to moralize, prevented him from producing great, authentic drama. Carmagnola, Adelchis, Ermengarde, Svartus are beautiful figures that yet resemble statues: we can admire them but we have to look elsewhere if we want to find lively contrasts, passions, psychologic tragedy, historical heroism. This having been said, some parts of Manzoni's works are indeed beautiful" (Carducci, *Opere scelte*, 425–26).

76. Manzoni, *Scritti letterari*, 41.

77. See note 30 on the beginning of the debate over neoclassical drama.

78. Manzoni, *Scritti letterari*, 61.

79. Ibid., 159–60.

80. Ibid., 139.

81. Ibid., 55–56.

82. Lonardi, *Ermengarda e il pirata*, 105–7.

83. Manzoni, *Scritti letterari*, 101.

84. In the "Lettre" and in the essay "On the Historical Novel," Manzoni does use the terms "historical tragedy" and "historical drama" to designate the type of dramatic works that he authored. It is therefore all the more remarkable that he refrained from using the adjective "historical" for the subtitle of his dramatic works, preferring simply "tragedy," with the aim to state forcefully that it was possible, as he was doing, to provide a modern example of an ancient genre, that is, to innovate within the tradition.

85. Sismonde de Sismondi narrated the story of Carmagnola in the context of the wars among the Italian city-states in early 1400s in his *History of the Italian Republics in the Middle Ages,* chaps. 64, 65. He came to the same conclusion as Manzoni as to the lack of evidence about the count's guilt. In Sismondi, however, the various sources are used exclusively to reconstruct the chronological thread. The Swiss historian's impression that Carmagnola might have been innocent is apodictical, as there is no historiographic discussion of the sources consulted. In the Italian edition I consulted, *Storia delle repubbliche,* Carmagnola's story is in vol. 3:521–46.

86. Crivellari, *Venice,* 50.

87. Byron's preface to *Marino Faliero* confines the discussion of the dramatic unities to its last paragraph, as this was a question that the English poet did not consider central to the new "system," as he, like Manzoni, calls it, by which history is made the base for drama. In the last paragraph of his preface, Byron also advises the reader that the "real facts," namely excerpts of the historical sources he consulted, were to be found in the appendix to the tragedy. However, "real facts," in the form of a discussion of historical sources, occupy Byron's entire preface. In general, for the tone, method of discussion, and aims, Byron's preface to *Faliero* strikingly resembles Manzoni's historical notes for *Carmagnola.* Byron presents his historical hero through historical facts that he has ascertained, he says, through his own research of Italian sources close in time to the facts narrated. Byron's main preoccupation in his preface is to illustrate his own fidelity, in his portrayal of the tragic hero and his motives, to the "national" (namely, Italian) sources that he consulted, in polemics with all foreign historians. The modern historians—Daru, Sismondi, and Laugier—attribute the conspiracy of Faliero entirely to "jealousy," since the nobleman Michel Steno, while drunk, jokingly accused the doge's young wife of being adulterous, and this offense was not adequately punished by the Venetian senate. But Byron remarks that he was able to find another motive in the Italian sources, and he quotes in Italian from historian Sandi: "[Faliero's] innate ambition, by which he wished to become an independent prince" (*Works of Lord Byron,* vol. 3:268). Byron harshly criticizes the only English version of Faliero's story, Dr. Moore's account in *View of Italy,* as "false and flippant, full of vain jests about old men and young wives, and wondering at so great an effect for so slight a cause" (ibid.). Moreover, Moore states without certain proof that Marino in the end begged for his life, and at this Byron rages: "I know no justification at any distance of time, for calumniating an historical character: surely truth belongs to the dead and to the unfortunate; and they who have died upon a scaffold have generally had faults enough of their own without attributing to them that which the very incurring of the perils which conducted them to their violent death renders, of all others, the most improbable" (ibid., 270).

In his intricate syntax Byron is saying more than that one needs not speak ill of the dead. He is saying that those who die a violent death, like Faliero, have generally an excess rather than a defect of courage. It is daring that made Faliero incur the deadly perils leading to his condemnation, and therefore it is highly improbable that he begged for his life when confronted with the Venetian institution, the senate, that he had conspired to overthrow. We remember, in this connection, Carmagnola's indignant words to the doge when he suggests that the general is begging for his life.

88. *Works of Lord Byron*, vol. 3:364. A footnote by the author explains, for those who have missed it, the veiled allegory of Faliero's "prophecy," about the Campoformio treaty by which Napoleon yielded the newly conquered Venice to the Austrians. Byron adds in the footnote that "the Empire" of the Hapsburg will plunge Venice into "infernal tyranny." The literal Attila against whom the first settlers of the Lagoon Islands, the founders of Venice, were defending themselves, marks the glorious origin of the Venetian state in the fifth century A.D., and a "bastard Attila," obviously Napoleon, who was a son of the Mediterranean Sea, marks its shameful end. This post-factum prophecy is also briefly hinted at in Faliero's words to his wife in the previous scene, where again Venice is defined as "this proud city" (ibid., 361).

89. Silvio Pellico, "*Histoire de la République de Venise*. Par Pierre Daru. 7 vols. Paris, 1819." *Il Conciliatore* 3 (22 Aug. 1819): 218–27, 218.

90. Ibid., 219.

91. There is not, to my knowledge, a single mention of Manzoni's name in Byron's writings. From Teresa Guiccioli's memoirs we gather that Byron knew Manzoni at least by fame (see Guiccioli, *My Recollections*, 274–75). Scholars generally take at face value Byron's profession of being Alfieri's pupil (e.g., Brand, *Italy and the English Romantics*, 120–23), but some have doubts about it when they consider the sharp change in Byron's dramatic mode after *Manfred*:

> After completing *Manfred*, Byron's thinking about history, politics, and society—and about the connections between these and literary production—matured remarkably. In his next three dramatic poems (*Marino Faliero, Sardanapalus* and *The Two Foscari*) he abandoned the mythic scope of *Manfred* in favor of specific, if remote, historical situations, attempting to imagine the operations of social life within those situations and the demands and challenges that society-in-crisis pose for personal life. While the dramas lack the strong personality of a hero such as Manfred, they make up for this lack with an intelligent portrayal of the networks of power, strikers of belief, and categories of social life that both enable and constrain individual need, desire, and action. (Watkins, "Dramas of Lord Byron," 59)

With respect to *Manfred*, the novelty of *Faliero* in dealing with history must have come to Byron through Manzoni's first tragedy, not from the Alfierian tragedies.

> The characters [in *The Two Foscari*] are clearly motivated and our attention is directed to an array of obsessive predilections: Loredano's debt, Jacopo's homeland, the Doge's punctilious observance of the law; or accessible emotions: Marina's doughty but futile rage, Barbarigo's compromised decency, Memmo's sycophantic ambition. . . . This, and the unflinching presentation of the horror of political power, makes *The Two Foscari* the most Alfierian of Byron's tragedies; though he had taken Alfieri as his model in the earlier Ravenna dramas, there is only a tangential resemblance between them and the tragedies of the Italian poet. *Marino Faliero* is far too rhetorically elaborated and *Sardanapalus* too subtly characterised for Alfieri. *The Two Foscari* manages to achieve something of the terse, tense utterance and spare form of Alfieri. (Corbett, *Byron and Tragedy*, 117)

I completely agree with Corbett, and I argue that *Marino Faliero* is not "Alfierian" because it was, in all likelihood, directly influenced, in its final form, by Manzoni's *Carmagnola*.

92. *Works of Lord Byron*, 525–26. Byron condemns through Loredano the hypocrisy that was often seen as a dominant trait in the Venetian character, in this case in Doge Foscari. Manzoni's Carmagnola defies this, which he considers a stereotype in his dialogue with Gonzaga in act IV, scene iii, only to verify how true it is in act V, scene i, the "trial scene."

93. I think of those pages by Charles Dickens, slightly humorous, where the description of the city's dreamlike beauty is interspersed with the nightmarish visions of the people condemned and beheaded, like Faliero, in his *Pictures from Italy* (1846).

94. In a letter to Fauriel dated 1 Mar. 1809, Manzoni mentions the epic poem that he intended to write (but would never write) about the foundation of Venice, a subject he defines of "national import" (*Tutte le lettere*, vol. 1:89). Manzoni came to regard the Republic of Venice as one of the Italian states that could have accomplished an early political unification of the peninsula (see Bonghi, Borri, and Tommaseo, *Colloqui col Manzoni*, 234).

95. "After having carefully read Shakespeare . . . ," Manzoni to Fauriel, 25 Mar. 1816 (see above, note 6) (*Tutte le lettere*, vol. 1:155–56). Giovanni Getto, in "Manzoni e Shakespeare," has initiated the practice of verifying Shakespeare's influence on Manzoni's novel on the French version that the Italian poet read, Pierre Le Tourneur's *Shakespeare traduit de l'anglois*. Italian translations of Shakespeare were made available between 1819 and 1821 by Michele Leoni, but the tragedies were abridged to fit the neoclassical format, as I find in Carlson, *Italian Shakespearians*, 17.

96. Despite the authoritative opinion of Goethe, who criticized the insertion of ideal characters in the tragedy—claiming that there should not be such a partition between ideal and historical characters, since they all belong to the same historically reconstructed background—Manzoni kept these characters in place, although divided from the rest in the list of characters, when he reprinted the two tragedies for the 1845 volume *Opere varie*.

97. Lavinia Mazzucchetti, in "Federico Schiller e Alessandro Manzoni," has convincingly shown the similarities between *Carmagnola* and Schiller's *Wallenstein*, especially when compared to Constant's adaptation *Wallstein*. This was published in Paris in 1809, just at the time of Manzoni's first sojourn there. Mazzucchetti argues, based on Manzoni's mention of it in a letter to Fauriel written at the time of *Carmagnola*'s composition, that the author had a long-standing acquaintance with Constant's book. The next few paragraphs in this introduction will not deal with the resemblance between the tragedies, already clearly indicated by Mazzucchetti, but rather with Manzoni's interest in the historicopolitical remarks in Constant's preface. Cordié, "Alessandro Manzoni," 200, reports that Constant's book has been found in Manzoni's library; however, it does not have annotations or marks. A more recent book, Kostka, *Schiller in Italy*, deals with the influence of Schiller on Manzoni the dramatist in chap. 2, pp. 13–26.

98. Constant, "Quelques réflections," ix–x. This work hereafter will be referred to as "Reflections."

99. For a clear echo in Manzoni of Constant's "Reflections," see also a passage in the "Lettre": "*Je vois* ce qu'il avait d'individuel dans le caractère de Carmagnola *éclater et se développer par des incidens nés de cette lutte . . . entre le pouvoir civil et la force militaire, le premier aspirant à être indépendant, et celle-ci à ne pas obéir* [I see individuality explode and develop in the character of Carmagnola through incidents caused by the struggle between the civil power and the military strength, the former eager to be independent, the latter, eager not to obey]" (*Scritti letterari*, 129). These remarks on the influence of Constant's "Reflections" on Manzoni's conception of *Carmagnola* appear in the introductory paragraphs of Deigan, "General's Heart."

100. "Reflections," vii–viii.

101. In a letter to Gaetano Giudici (a man of letters close to the circle of *Il Conciliatore*), Paris, 7 Feb. 1820, Manzoni defines Carmagnola as "a man endowed with a strong and elevated spirit, striving to do great deeds." The letter touches on many important points: it asserts that the tragedy's focus is in the clash of the great man with the Venetian institutions and questions whether this really suffices to create drama; it also illustrates how the tragedy is meant to arouse the spectator's interest in the wars in which Carmagnola is enmeshed, while the chorus reviles those same wars. Manzoni thinks it is possible for the two sentiments to cohabit in the tragedy; he defines two types of interest that can be excited in the spectator: the first is interest in an ideal reality, which excites admiration "for those images of, and desires for perfection that we all harbor in ourselves"; the other is interest "in the true status of human things, which is a mixture of grand and petty, reasonable and crazy, the mixture that we all can see in big and small events of this world. This interest belongs to an important, eternal component of the human mind, animated by a desire to know the things as they really are, and to discern as much as we can about ourselves and our destiny on earth" (*Tutte le lettere*, vol. 1:193–94).

102. The existing comparative studies of Goethe's and Manzoni's tragedies are far from exhaustive, given the ample resemblance between these two authors. In 1907 Bonaventura Zumbini, in "L'*Egmont*," proposed a sketchy comparative study, but, to my knowledge, this line of inquiry has not been thoroughly pursued.

103. Scherillo, "La prima tragedia," 42.

104. When Mark recommends prudence to Carmagnola, he invokes his duties as paterfamilias to convince him: " . . . think of your wife, / Your daughter, whose sole hope you are; Heaven / Gave them a soul to sense the joy, a soul / That freely breathes in serene days, but that / Cannot act to win them. That you can do, / And you will" (I.v). In the tragic epilogue Antoinette echoes these words by Mark: "Love of my happy days, / you who are their maker . . . " (V.v).

105. Interesting comparisons to Shakespeare's feminine figures, among other things, are in Cazzato, *Appunti*, 4–40, and Marrapodi, "Carmagnola e Coriolano." Both authors suggest Shakespeare's *Coriolanus* as a possible source for *Carmagnola*. But beyond the links to Shakespeare, it is above all an allusion to Dante that alerts the attentive reader to the negative moral example that Antoinette, as a tragic heroine, must highlight. In protesting to her husband her deep sorrow and her continuing desire to be his, she says to him: "*il core / vedimi*": "Gaze at *my* heart" (V.v). Antoinette's words echo those uttered by Amore holding in his arms "the woman who brings salvation," Beatrice, in Dante's first dream in *Vita nuova* (chap. 3). In that dream, the first manifestation of a selfless love that will eventually help save the poet's eternal soul by leading him away from a narcissistic absorption in his own feelings, Amore has Dante's heart in one hand and shows it to him while saying: "*vide cor tuum*": gaze at *your* heart. Conversely, Antoinette points to her own heart with a narcissistic gesture that attempts to perpetuate the discourse of aesthetic love with the count in the last instants of his earthly life. The altered reference to Dante subtly accuses Antoinette's love as being the opposite of Beatrice's: Antoinette's love cannot save the count in either this or the next life.

106. The title of Gilberto Lonardi's essay "Il *Carmagnola*, Venezia e il 'potere ingiusto,'" quotes Manzoni's own words, "unjust rule," in chap. 2 of *Osservazioni sulla morale cattolica*, vol. 2:468–69. But in that passage Manzoni is asserting that personal contributions to the "unjust rule," in the form of the individual will breaching religious morals, are a *conditio sine qua non* for injustice to take

place within an institution. When speaking of moral responsibility, his focus is always on individuals who act within the institutions.

107. The count, the republic, and Mark have been indicated as the three tragic heroes in the deep structure of this tragedy, being each in turn "object and subject of injustice." The author of this excellent formula, so apt to define the Manzonian tragic heroes, is Mario Martelli, who was the first scholar to indicate how these heroes had to be considered as negative examples in Christian terms, on the basis of the refined arguments produced by the seventeenth-century Christian moralists Manzoni admired, such as Blaise Pascal and Louis Bourdaloue (Martelli, introduction, xli–lxiii). We can add that the Republic of Venice, which meets its death in a future time made present in the tragedy by the count's metatheatrical allusion, is fully entitled to the status of tragic hero.

108. Manzoni thought of Carmagnola's times as "weak and malicious" and the Venetian institutions, "petty, devoid of foresight, unreasonable, but already shrewd and fortified by custom and popular respect, as well as by the interest of those who have the power" (Manzoni to Giudici, Paris, 7 Feb. 1820, *Tutte le lettere*, vol. 1:193–94).

109. In the appendix to chap. 3 published in the 1855 edition of *Osservazioni sulla morale cattolica*,, there is an interesting, long note on Machiavelli. The discussion in the appendix concerns the relation between utilitarianism and justice in morals. Below is an abridged translation of the note:

Among the writers who gave usefulness the supreme value in political matters, Machiavelli happened to earn the sad privilege of seeing a special version of that doctrine named after him, in several languages. [Machiavellism] came to mean exclusively the use of malice and of cruelty for the purpose of serving the advantage of one, of some, or many. The implicit judgment contained in the coinage of that word [Machiavellism] is only partially true. Machiavelli did not want injustice, either through shrewdness or violence, as the sole and primary means to achieve usefulness. He desired the latter and deemed it desirable either with or without justice, depending on the case. And we should not doubt that his soul preferred the first option. Without resorting to his behavior, both in his private and public life, we can infer his propensity for justice from his writings. For in praising or advising injustice, he is subtle; in condemning it, he is eloquent and sometimes affectionate when recommending a course opposite to injustice. A beautiful example is in chap. 10 of book I of the *Discorsi sulle Deche di T. Livio*. . . . Farthest removed from truth, in every respect, is the opinion that Machiavelli gave unjust advice only in one work, *The Prince*, and in order to acquit him of the charge of immorality, many say that he gave that bad advice to precipitate the ruin of the rulers of his state. . . . [Manzoni finds this an absurd argument for moral acquittal.] On the other hand, it is not hard to discover praises or recommendations of injustice in the *Discorsi*. . . . Such an ugly mixture [of the praises of virtue and fraud alike] in the writings of such a great mind [*grande ingegno*] originated in having posited usefulness instead of justice as the supreme value. And how many admirable thoughts are made inconspicuous by their bad companions in those writings! How much wisdom in connecting causes and effects, *in detecting the coincidence or the disparity between the intentions of men and the strength of things!* How much *nobly prudent advice*, how many generous intents in those writings, whenever justice is preached or simply understood! (*Osservazioni*, vol. 2:401–3)

In *Carmagnola* Manzoni reflects on the received opinion on Machiavelli and Machiavellism, as well as on the "nobly prudent advice" that Machiavelli gave in his writings.

110. The dismembered eye occurs in act I, scene iii, when it is resolved that the count will be under the scrutinizing eye of the State's spies; echoing Mark's words in I.iii, Marino uses the juxtaposition of eye and heart to make Mark confess to his divided loyalty between the state and the count: " . . . I shall tell you, since / Your heart was much less tranquil than the eye / Which followed you" (IV.i). A few lines earlier Marino evokes the state's ever-waking eye in the image of a veil falling from in front the senators' eyes: "The veil that obfuscated every eye / Has fallen" (IV.i).

111. Marino's metaphor could also be a reference to the Venetian register "called the 'Golden Book' in which were inscribed the names of all those who had sat in the grand council" and which "established the right to be elected in the State's posts" Sismondi, *History of the Italian Republics*, 119.

112. Martelli brings a passage from Pascal's *Pensées* to bear on the psychological moralism of the Manzonian tragic heroes: "The inner war between reason and passions has led many who desire peace to choose either of two parties: some have wanted to renounce passions, and *to become gods;* other have wanted to renounce reason and to become brutes. But neither party can succeed. Reason is bound to stay, it is always there to accuse the low iniquity of passions and disturb the quiet of those who dally in them; and the passions are always alive in those who wanted to renounce them" (Pascal, quoted in Martelli, introduction, li–lii).

113. As I have demonstrated through textual comparisons in Deigan, "General's Heart," the heart-opening and soul-transparency metaphors in *Carmagnola* derive from images in Shakespeare's *Othello.* The first of the two most important generative images is in Iago's famous monologue in act I (the French version eliminates the sleeve and the doves): "*Allez, quand mon action visible sera l'image naïve de ma pensée, quand mon extérieur fera voir le fond de mon âme, attendez vous à me voir aussi* porter mon coeur nud sur ma main, *pour l'offrir en proie* aux yeux *des méchants et des sots. Non, je ne suis point ce que je parois être*" [Come on, when my visible action is the naïve image of my thought, when my external aspect shows the depths of my soul, expect to see me carrying *my naked heart upon my hand* to offer it as a *prey to the eyes* of evil, stupid ones. No, I am not at all what I seem to be] (Le Tourneur, *Shakespeare*, vol. 1:6–7).

The imagery in the dialogue between Mark and Marino, in in *Carmagnola*, act IV, scene I, reveals Manzoni's use of Iago's heart metaphors with a view to depicting Mark as a parody of Shakespeare's famous villain. A second generative image is in Desdemona's description of her love for the Moor that she voluntarily offers to the practical-minded Venetian senators. In her speech in the senate she uses the famous image: "I saw Othello's visage in his mind" (I.iii.253). Although the literal implication here is simply that the lady did not care for the external look of her husband but rather only saw his spiritual qualities, the wording makes us envision the mythical transparence of the flesh that may let us see the inside of a man's mind: "en regardant Othello je ne vis que son âme; *et j'ai consacré la mienne à ses vertus guerrières, et mon sort à la gloire*" [In looking at Othello, *I have seen but his soul;* and I have consecrated mine to his warlike virtues, and my lot to glory] (Le Tourneur, *Shakespeare*, vol. 1:40). Desdemona's daring declaration suggests, in both its attitude and wording, the count's unrequested display of his feelings in front of the senate, in act I, scene ii ("Let me first speak to you about myself, / *Open to you a heart* that only yearns / to be utterly known"), as well as of Antoinette's love protestation (see n. 105, above). The wording of Mark's manifesto of utopian heart-opening, in act I, scene iv, is even more reminiscent of Desdemona's words: "If there is mortal man / I ever envied, it is but that man who / Lived in times and places in which he could / *Openly show his soul upon his face,* / And prove his mettle only in ordeals / Requiring force, not shrewdness. . . . "

114. In his novel Manzoni illustrates how even for the best of purposes one should not bend the rules, the moral precepts. For example: is it legitimate to eavesdrop? No, it is not. So even if that act is performed by a servant of the villain, Don Rodrigo, with the good intent to disrupt the abduction of the heroine, Lucia, eavesdropping cannot give any fruit. The novelist acting as creator in the secondary universe of the novel indicates the dead-end encountered by any breach of the moral rules, even when the breach is dictated by good intentions. Lucia escapes the kidnapping not because of the information the servant provides to her protector, Father Cristoforo, but rather thanks to her love toward her betrothed Renzo, which makes her overcome her initial disgust for imposition—Renzo tries to force their priest to marry them—and leads her out of the house in a timely manner. That first attempted marriage will not succeed either (see chap. 6 and 7 of *The Betrothed*).

115. Lonardi noticed that in *Carmagnola* the heart was juxtaposed to reason, and in particular the openness of the heart was opposed to verbs such as "to see," "to watch," to the invisible actions of the state, in the same way as the chivalric faith was opposed to Machiavellian foxes, light to darkness, and the direct line to the twisted ways of the Venetian oligarchy (Lonardi, "Il *Carmagnola*," 28). In line with the essay's spirit (the title translates as "*Carmagnola*, Venice, and the unjust rule"), Lonardi interprets the first terms in the above-listed juxtapositions as the representative of the innocent, righteous man, while the second terms are associated to the vicious ways of Venice. These simplistic dualisms, though, are utterly foreign to Manzoni's refined psychological moralism.

116. For historical plays on Napoleon from the 1820s onward, as well as for useful remarks on romantic historical drama, see Howarth, "Bonaparte on Stage." Manzoni's, Byron's, and Hugo's dramas under discussion here merely alluded to Napoleon through some traits of their characters.

117. The composition of this ode was prompted by the news of Napoleon's death that Manzoni read in the *Gazzetta di Milano* on 18 Jul. 1821, while he was at his countryside villa. He interrupted his work on his second tragedy, *Adelchis*. "Napoleon's death shook me so deeply, as if an essential element had suddenly left the world. I was seized by an urge to talk about it and I had to jot down that ode, the only one I improvised, one could say, in less than three days" (Parenti, *Immagini della vita,* 111) Fifteen-year-old Manzoni had seen Napoleon during a gala evening in honor of the then First Consul at the theater La Scala. "Young Alessandro was seated in the same balcony with Countess Cicognara, an open foe of Napoleon's, and as the man would insistently turn to stare at her in a challenging way, the poet could clearly see his eyes. He remained fascinated by them and that lasting impression helped Manzoni to immortalize them, 'those darting eyes,' in his commemorative ode that enjoyed immense popularity all over Europe" (ibid., 44 and 113).

118. For a thorough discussion of the influence of the historian Augustin Thierry on Manzoni see Cesare de Lollis, *Alessandro Manzoni.* Thierry (in articles published or prepared during Manzoni's stay in Paris in 1820) postulated that the Gallo-Romans preserved the legacy of the Roman civilization throughout the domination of the Germanic Franks, until the spirit of freedom, which the conquered had silently kept alive in their constructive cultural and economic activities, blossomed in the civilization of the Municipalities. Later, the same racial group formed the "third state" that promoted the French Revolution, thus dislodging from power the clergy and the nobility. De Lollis remarks that Manzoni had in common with Thierry the fascination for the silent

multitudes that formed the greater part of a nation; Manzoni followed Thierry in postulating the absolute separation of the races for the Italians under the Lombards, but he did not take the next step of ascribing the flourishing of the Municipality civilization in Italy to the surviving descendants of the Romans. Manzoni rather postulated the fusion between Franks and Lombards after Charles's conquest of Italy. De Lollis thinks that Manzoni was more interested in defending the role of the popes as helpers of the oppressed. However, de Lollis does not take into consideration the other focus of the *Discorso*, as well as the focus of the tragedy, the "moral superiority" that kingship requires, and Manzoni's quest for relative, if not absolute, political justice.

119. In his letter to Fauriel dated 17 Oct. 1820, Manzoni gives his friend an update on the historical research he is conducting in preparation for the tragedy: "In order to form a more complete vision on this point [the lack of fusion between conquerors such as the Turks, and the conquered, such as the Greek], I have plunged into the chronicles of the collection *Rerum Italicarum*, and I am even consulting some of the nineteen large volumes by Mr. Thyerri [*sic*] which I need not only for the history of Charlemagne in relation to the Lombards but also to capture suggestions on the establishment of barbaric domination, all instances of which look alike" (*Tutte le lettere*, vol. 1:216).

120. Manzoni, *Discorso sopra alcuni punti*, 2037.

121. Manzoni, many have argued, might have been envisioning a neo-guelph solution to the Italian unification problem: the formation of an Italian federation of states under the presidency of the pope. Neo-guelphism, or national guelphism, became a political movement at midcentury, but Manzoni was never part of it. For the question of Manzoni's neo-guelphism as emerging from his tragedies, see Cro, "L'idealismo neo-guelfo," and Belotti, "L'ostinato silenzio sul Giobert." Bollati, *L'italiano*, 80–93, praises everything in Manzoni's historical tragedies and the accompanying historical research, except for the "neo-guelph" conclusion concerning the positive role of the Popes in Italian history. On the other hand, di Nepi, "Manzoni e il principe pentito," rules out that Manzoni ever had a neo-guelph position, since from various sources he can prove that Manzoni judged the temporal power of the Church to be "impure": "Just because one judges a situation as positive relatively to the given historical circumstances, one can then legitimately maintain that as circumstances change, that situation will need to be re-evaluated accordingly" (ibid., 521). Dionisotti thinks Manzoni always believed that the French would eventually help the cause of Italy's unification, ultimately renouncing their traditional (and convenient) role of defenders of the pope's temporal power, and that came in fact to pass in 1859 ("Manzoni fra Italia," 509). The bottom line is that Manzoni agreed to be a senator of the newly founded Italian state at a time when the Church was recommending that people not take part in its public life.

Most clearly, Manzoni showed with his deeds his belief in both the Italian unity, as it originated from the political revolution of 1859–60, and the necessity of dismantling the temporal power of the Church of Rome. In April 1860 he accepted King Victor Emmanuel's appointment to the Senate of the newly founded Kingdom of Italy (see Manzoni to Cavour, *Tutte le lettere*, vol 3: 205–6), and in June of that year he traveled to the then Italian capital, Turin, to be sworn in. The following year he went again to Turin to participate in the opening session of the Italian parliament with the proclamation of the King Victor Emmanuel as king of Italy. With these gestures of active participation in his new senatorial duties, Manzoni was defying the pope's order to Catholics not to take part in the civic and political life of the new Italian state. At the end of 1864, on the eve of his ninetieth birthday, he traveled again to Turin in order to cast his vote in favor of transferring the Italian capital from Turin to Florence, a transfer which he perceived as an intermediary step on the way to proclaiming Rome as capital of Italy. Two years after Rome had been indeed conquered and had become the capital of the Italian state, in 1872, the Roman city council wanted to give Manzoni the honorary citizenship, and Manzoni promptly and warmly accepted, although only by letter (see Manzoni to the Mayor of Rome, *Tutte le lettere*, vol 3: 412). When the author died the following year, many obituaries in the Catholic press, such as those in Milan's daily *Osservatore Cattolico*, did not fail to tinge their inevitable praises of the writer with bitter criticism of those that were perceived as Manzoni's deplorable acts of participation in the life the new secular Italy (see Scherillo, "Manzoni e Roma laica").

122. Manzoni, *Discorso sopra alcuni punti*, 2060.

123. Parts of this section and its notes were published in Italian as Deigan, "Il re e la vittima."

124. Arnaldo Di Benedetto, in "La Storia,"advocates continuity between the content and the author's views in the historical tract and in the tragedy; accordingly, he refutes the quietistic reading that many give to the tragedy on the basis of the hero's Christian resignation in accepting his death. On the other hand, Vito Grasso, in "Il Manzoni tra l'*Adelchi*," thinks that Adelchis is the hero of the tragedy and Charles is the hero of the *Discorso*, and he denies any interdependence between the two works. Mario Petrini, in "L'*Adelchi*," thinks that the positive portrait of Charles does not appear in the tragedy and that in *Adelchis* Manzoni finally overcomes the conceptual need for the great man who resolves historical impasses and that he starts to concentrate instead on the masses, his truly deep interest, as the choruses show. I agree wholeheartedly with Di Benedetto.

125. Quoted by de Michelis, "Le tragedie," 121. The whole dialogue on *Adelchis* between Manzoni and his stepson, Stefano Stampa, as reported by De Michelis reads: "Stampa asked 'why the author did not resolve to tip the scales on one side,' in the fight between Desiderius and Charles; Manzoni answered: 'Because I wanted to describe historical truth with impartiality, and to show that in this world righteousness is never all on one side.'"

126. The overwhelming majority of critics deem Charles a negative character: a cold, heartless politician, greedy for power. Only a few critics have recognized in Charles a not altogether negative character: first and foremost, Ruggero Ruggieri, in *Storia poetica*, who argued that Manzoni based his Charlemagne on the tradition of the *Chanson de Roland*. The hero of that epic poem, Roland, is featured in *Adelchis* (with the name of "Rutlando") in a brief but meaningful scene, act II, scene v. Ruggieri thinks that Manzoni would have never contradicted the belief in Charlemagne as a king carrying out a plan willed by God (*Gesta Dei per Francos*, title of the twelfth-century history of the first crusade by Guibert de Nogent), a traditional and popular wisdom incorporated in the epic, in the chronicles, and in the legends featuring the Frankish kings since Clovis. In support of this thesis, see in *Adelchis* the intervention of a religious man of the indigenous race (a Latin), Martinus, also in act II, who discloses the route through the Alps to bypass the Lombards defensive line; Charles's comment on Martinus's tale: "Only an impious mind would not see *here* / *The arm* of the Almighty God!" (II.ii). Paolo Bellezza, in "Note manzoniane," compares Charles's comment on Martinus's tale to Shakespeare's Henry V commenting on his victory at Agincourt: "O God, *thy arm* was *here*; / And not to us, but to *thy arm* alone / Ascribe we all!" says the king in thanking God (*Henry V,* IV.viii.108–10).

127. Manzoni, *Discorso sopra alcuni punti*, 2069; a "moral superiority without peers" is being ascribed to Charles.

128. Ibid., 2068.

129. *"Chi vuol sapere appuntino cosa significasse la parola 're' nei secoli barbari, non si cerchi in istituzioni che, non esistevano, o non erano compite, né rassodate, ma nell'azione e nel carattere di ognuno di quei re: si vedrà allora che questa parola aveva in ogni caso un significato diverso. La corona* era un cerchio *di metallo, che valeva quanto* il capo che n'era cinto" (ibid.).

130. Le Tourneur, *Shakespeare*, vol. 8:104. The intertextual link between the *Discorso* and *Richard II* is all the more significant because Manzoni could read twice in the text the association of the crown with the circle and the head, a repetition often occurring in Shakespeare when crucial notions are involved. Richard's words about mortality and kingship respond implicitly to the admonition and prophecy of his dying uncle John of Gaunt at the beginning of the play: Richard's crown, he warned, has the same diameter as his head. Gaunt sees how Richard is being a foolish king and is blindly heading toward his own demise. The king seizes the nobleman's assets because he is short of money to wage a war on Ireland. He thus deprives Gaunt's son, Bolingbroke, whom he has unjustly banished, of his righteous inheritance. These two actions are instrumental in turning the tide against Richard's rule, leading directly to his deposition by Bolingbroke, who will become, at the play's end, Henry IV. In his pensive mood engendered by the times of troubles, Richard seems to remember vaguely his uncle's words about the crown and the circle and the head, but only when it is too late to make any practical use of them. He can now be only a philosopher and teach others, including the new king, about true prosperity, not only through his negative example—his past as an inept king—but also by the dignity with which he faces his fall. Richard's philosophizing is what lends the historical drama its vague reminiscence of a morality play.

131. Manzoni calls Richard's fall "such a natural and at once unexpected development": "The spectator had already met this stunning character and had had the impression of having fully understood him. However, there was some profound and hidden trait in him that had not manifested itself in times of prosperity, and that only the downfall could bring out. The main traits of his character are still the same: [he is wrathful, haughty], pride is still there. But during his time in power, his pride was expressed in levity . . . once he is deprived of power, his pride becomes grave and serious, solemn and contained" (*Scritti letterari*, 116).

132. Richard goes about his philosophical teaching as an experienced actor would. He knows the eyes of the world will watch him fall. He knows that in the script he is cast in the part of the victim, now. In the deposition scene, he twice associates himself to Christ, first directly: *"'Ne furent-ils pas mes Sujets: ne m'ont-ils pas dit plusieurs fois: hommage et respect au Roi. C'est ainsi que Judas salua Jesus-Christ. Mais lui dans douze Disciples, n'en trouva qu'un de perfide, et moi, dans deux mille Sujets, je ne trouve pas un seul ami"* [Were these not my subjects? Have not they said to me several times: 'Homage and respect to the King.' In this way Judas greeted Jesus Christ. But He, among twelve disciples, found only one who was malicious, while I, among two thousand subjects, cannot find a single friend] (Le Tourneur, *Shakespeare*, vol. 8:141)

In the following lines, Richard accuses the noblemen who sit passively watching the anointed king while he is being deposed but show compassion for him: they are hypocrites like Pilate. These New Testament quotations of Richard's must be compared to the usurper's symmetrical mentions of the Old Testament's archetypal murder scene. In the first act, Bolingbroke compares to Abel the duke whose murder Richard secretly ordered; in the last scene of the play, he calls "Cain" the courtier who took it upon himself to murder Richard in prison, obeying Henry's desire to live free from fear, a desire repeatedly, although ambiguously, voiced in public by the new king. The quotations from the sacrificial scenes of the scriptures seem geared to convey, in their ironic deployment, some message on traitorous killing. Although he has not refrained from political murder himself, Richard, in the face of his deposition, claims to be a new Jesus, and calls his subjects Judas and his courtiers Pilate. Bolingbroke, who seemed to be preoccupied with an innocent victim, the duke (Abel), was in fact intimidating the king by letting him know that he knew who had sent the duke's killers. In the end, Henry too proves hypocritical when he calls "Cain" the murderer of the deposed king, whose potential return he feared. Scriptural quotations can be used, Shakespeare is saying, for the rhetoric instrumental in conquering and retaining political power. Thus, we need not take at face value Richard II's self-identification with Christ, as many critics have done.

Lonardi was the first scholar who indicated Richard II's self-identification with Christ betrayed by Judas, quoted above, as the model for dying Adelchis's invocation: "...O King of kings, betrayed by one companion, / By all others forsaken, to your peace / I come: accept this weary soul" (V.x). With the validation of such an intertextual comparison between Manzoni's and Shakespeare's historical characters Lonardi, in *Ermengarda e il pirata*, 112, brought to perfection a theory that had been vaguely but persistently sketched since the mid-twentieth century: that the Manzonian tragic hero is a Christ figure. "The Manzonian hero is a modern hero: he delivers to his words and to his intellect what is denied to him in terms of deeds.... With the death of Christ, the death of the hero has become, for the entire epic-Christian area of Western theater, the death of the witness, of the martyr. And the martyr speaks because he wants to bring testimony" (ibid., 107–9). In his most recent essay on the topic, *Manzoni e l'esperienza del tragico*, Lonardi expresses more clearly what he thinks the Manzonian tragic hero as a martyr has to say when he gives his life to bear witness to a truth: "Adelchis understands, in the end, that between being king not being king, it is better not to be king. It is better to leave one's class if one's class is stained with blood and tainted by injustice and violence. Violence generates law, and as such law does not have real dignity" (20–21). It is hardly necessary to point out how far from Manzoni's views are Lonardi's own generalizations on law, on morals, on kingship, based on the last lines uttered by Adelchis in the tragedy. We have to remember that Manzoni conceived the chorus to voice his own opinion, so Adelchis's philosophizing represents the character's views, not the dramatist's. Moreover, the Christological interpretation advocated by Lonardi for Adelchis (and its relation to Shakespeare's Richard II) is not consistent with the Manzonian dramatic theory. Manzoni wanted indeed his spectators to be "judges," not "accomplices," of the tragic heroes, and Lonardi has rightly compared this aspect of Manzoni's poetics with that of Brecht's epic theater (see above). But how are we supposed not to sympathize with, and rather judge, a Christlike innocent victim, a character who practices the *imitatio Christi* in witnessing to the Christian truth?

If we posit instead that Manzoni wants to portray human beings as they are in life, not as Christian heroes, and if we posit that he imitates the whole Shakespearean strategy of scriptural quotations by his kings as we have seen it at work in *Richard II*, then the effect of "estrangement" in the spectator toward the tragic hero will indeed follow. The quotations by which Adelchis's vicissitudes are associated to Christ's story are only apparently meant to elicit our pity. Upon reflection, they rather elicit our negative judgment: the tragic hero is so blinded by pride that he thinks he has become like God. He thinks he is like Christ, but he is being blasphemous and blind to his true responsibilities. For Lonardi's forerunners and followers in announcing the Christological or

martyrological thesis in *Adelchis*, see, among others, Gaglio, *Lettura dell'Adelchi*; Gassman, "Lo spettacolo del Tpi"; Petrocchi, *Manzoni*; Mirri, *"Adelchi*, dramma"; Giordano, introduction; Bene and
di Leva, *Adelchi*; Annoni, "Un'interpretazione"; Nigro," "Storia e poesia"; Barberi Squarotti, "Tre
casi"; Mazziotti di Celsio, *"Adelchi* tragedia sacra"; Portinari, *"Il Conte"*; and Annoni, *Lo spettacolo*.

133. On Shakespeare's strategy of scriptural quotations in *Richard II*, see above, n. 132.

134. Annoni, in *Lo spettacolo*, 118–20, has rightly indicated the chorus's speeches in Shakespeare's
Henry V, as well as in *Winter's Tale*, as sources of important concepts for Manzoni's theoretical writings on drama.

135. Manzoni, *Discorso sopra alcuni punti*, 2066.

136. In a letter to Victor Cousin, dated 21 Feb. 1821, Manzoni writes, with a possible pun on the
word "poorly"(*poveramente*, in the original, maybe in the sense of "simply," "down-to-earth"): " I
am enthused in the composition of a tragedy where I have Charlemagne speak like neither Ariosto's
chief of the paladins, nor the saint of some ecclesiastical authors, nor the legislator of some grand
writers, nor the learned sage of some university professors, nor the scoundrel of some philoso-
phers, nor the hero of those who received a pension from his cadet brother; and that might turn
out to be, after all, a very *poorly* conceived character" (*Tutte le lettere*, vol. 1:231).

137. Some instances are extremely clear, as intertextual comparisons demonstrate (see Deigan,
"Il re e la vittima," for more complete intertextual comparisons): both Charles and Henry V are
shown among the soldiers' tents demonstrating their paternal solicitude toward their troops
(*Adelchis* II.i; *Henry V*, chorus in act 4). Both Charles and Henry V are remorseful for the innocent
victims they made while reinforcing their political power (Charles's nocturnal monologue in
Adelchis II.iv compares to *Henry V*, IV.i.93–109, and also to *Henry IV, part II*, III.i.45–79). Both
Charles and Henry are shown to promise mercy while they deal with the closed gates of an enemy
city under siege (*Adelchis* V.iv; *Henry V*, III.iii.1–43). The Frankish king's torment for his greatest sin,
the repudiation of his Lombard wife, Ermengarde, wells up on the eve of the decisive battle at the
Alpine Gates, in act II, scene iv. In the moment when victory and defeat are balanced on the scales
of history, Charles remembers his victim, Ermengarde, Adelchis's sister, just as Henry recalls
Richard II, the victim of his family's climb to power, before the battle that can, if won, enor-
mously increase his power.

It is important to remember that Manzoni the historian considers Charles's repudiation of
Ermengarde in the *Discorso* as an unmotivated and grave act. The marriage between Charles and
Ermengarde was concocted by his mother Bertrada and Desiderius with the aim of reinforcing
the chances of peace between the Franks and the Lombards. Charles repudiates Ermengarde while
the relationship with the Lombards becomes strained, and he falls in love with the Swabian Hildegarde. In chap. 1 of the *Discorso*, devoted to clarifying the historical notes to the tragedy, Manzoni
sternly labels as royal flatterers the historians who maintained that Charles repudiated Ermengarde
because she was sterile. Instead, he reports the story of one of Charles's brothers who retired to
a monastery and became monk to atone for the king's mortal sin. When, in the next paragraph,
Manzoni relates Desiderius's attempt to have one of Gerberga's sons, Charles's nephews, anointed
as king of the Franks, the historian also tells us that if Desiderius' scheme had succeeded, Charles
would have been victim of a wrongful usurpation. In these two adjacent paragraphs of the *Discorso*, we see Manzoni's objectivity at work: in one he tells us that Charles has committed a terrible sin by repudiating without motive Ermengarde; in the next one he tells us that Desiderius's

scheming against Charles was a downright attempt to usurp a legitimate king. For a similarly mixed moral record, Charles resembles Henry V, who was a great king for the English nation, but one who had grave family guilt on his conscience.

138. Le Tourneur, *Shakespeare*, vol. II: 130. Incidentally, we must notice here that no ghost (*l'horrible spectre*) is mentioned in the original English: "the wretched slave . . . never sees horrid night, the child of hell." We can then surmise that Manzoni found in the French "*l'horrible spectre de la nuit*" a precedent for the ghostly apparition of Ermengarde to sleepless King Charles in his nocturnal monologue on the eve of his attack on Italy: "*Larva, cresciuta nel silenzio e nell'ombra . . .*" ("O apparition, grown in silence and shadow . . . "II.iv).

139. Exemplary is the eulogy of the king in the chorus of act IV of *Henry V*:

> *Sur son noble visage, on ne voit nulle trace, nul sentiment de l'armée formidable dont il est environné; nulle impression de pâleur n'annonce ses veilles et la fatigue de la nuit passée sans sommeil. Son teint est frais et coloré, une douce majesté, une sérénité gaie brillent dans ses yeux; et le soldat, pâle et aupauravant abattu, dès qu'il le voit, puise dans ses regards l'esperance et la force. Ainsi que le soleil, son oeil généreux et bienfaisant verse dans tous les coeurs une douce influence qui les rechauffe et dissout les glaces de la crainte."*

> One cannot see, on his noble visage, any trace, any trepidation for the formidable army that surrounds him, no pale hue betrays the hours he spent waking, the exhaustion of a sleepless night. His complexion is fresh and flushed, a sweet majesty, a bright serenity shine in his eyes, and the soldier, pale and dejected, upon seeing the king, draws hope and strength from his gaze. *Like to the sun, his generous and beneficial eye* pours in every heart a sweet effect that *warms* them up and *melt* the ice of fear. (Le Tourneur, *Shakespeare*, vol. II:131)

140. Here is the whole passage: "in the conflict between those two opponents [popes and Lombard kings] the lot of *some million people* was at stake. Which of the two forces represented more faithfully the will and the rights of that *multitude of living beings*, which one aimed at diminishing their *sufferings*, to put *a little justice* in this world? This is, in our view, the true point at stake in this discussion" (Manzoni, *Discorso sopra alcuni punti*, 2060). The emphasized phrases echo Henry V's words of warning to the ecclesiastics who warmly recommend that he wage war against France (*Henry V*, I.ii.19–33).

141. Discussing the sun metaphor in *Adelchis*'s second chorus, Lonardi finds a perfect symmetry and similarity of destinies, determined by sun / king, between the woman / flower and the people / animal (with reference to the yoke metaphorically imposed onto the people with no name in the first chorus): both the woman and the people are "historical victims," and we have to supplement what the scholar does not bring his pen to write: that the Frankish king is the persecutor (*Ermengarda e il pirata*, 116). One rare mention of the Frankish king in the same essay ambiguously hints at Charles's "political realism" (ibid., 114) with, I assume, an implicitly negative judgment. But Adelchis has a calculating spirit, and is full of political realism himself: for example, when he sequester Charles's legate from contact with the potentially treacherous Lombard Dukes (I.viii).

142. Getto thinks that the description of Renzo's vineyard left uncultivated, in *The Betrothed*, chap. 33, echoes this passage in *Henry V* ("Manzoni e Shakespeare," 228).

143. To alert us to Adelchis's moral confusion at this stage of his development, Manzoni uses a cross-quotation from his own work. In the lines immediately preceding this famous heart metaphor, Adelchis echoes Mark's final monologue: "Thus I walk my way, dragged *along a route / I did not choose*, an obscure path to nowhere." (III.i.86–88)

144. Foscolo's novel *Last Letters of Jacopo Ortis* is replete with self-identification of the autobiographical protagonist with Christ, and Manzoni might have intended to provide in Adelchis, among other things, a veritable parody of the Foscolian romantic hero. For views that reinforce my thesis, see the comparison between Foscolo's and Manzoni's poetics in Ciccarelli, *Manzoni e la coscienza*, chap 1.

145. Le Tourneur, *Shakespeare*, vol. 8: 94.

146. Ibid., 138–39. *Champ du sang* is emphasized in Le Tourneur's text.

147. In Shakespeare the bishop alludes to the Passion of Christ; while Le Tourneur was probably thinking of Acts 1:19, where the death of Judas is described: the betrayer "purchased a field with the reward of iniquity; and falling headlong, he burst asunder in the midst, and all his bowels gushed out . . . the field is called . . . the field of blood." In perceiving this echo in Le Tourneur's version and making it his own, therefore, Manzoni makes Adelchis so clear-minded about the reasons of the fall of the Lombard kingdom that their last king metaphorically compares his own people, the Lombards, to Judas. The metaphorical Christ would then be the Latins or Romans, the inhabitants of Italy.

148. Carlo Torchio, in "Linguaggio scritturale," sees a biblical reference to Hosea 10:13 in Adelchis' final metaphor of land cultivation (a reference already detected by Lonardi,); Egidi, in his notes to these lines, refers to another passage, in Hosea 4:1.

149. Quoted by Collison-Morley, *Shakespeare in Italy*, 114.

150. Bellezza, "Note manzoniane," and Reforgiato, *Shakespeare e Manzoni.* The two scholars propose the following comparisons: both Katharine and Ermengarde are foreign queens. From Aragon the former came to England to marry into the English royal family (Arthur, and then Henry), and from Italy the latter came to France to marry Charles. Both express regret for having migrated to the foreign land, and both would like to be buried with the ensigns of queen, even if their kings have divorced them.

151. Bellezza compares Katharine's simile to describe her own fall from royal status (she is like the lily that "was once mistress of the field") with the parched grass blades to which Ermengarde is compared in *Adelchis*'s second chorus (ibid.).

152. The stage directions for act IV, scene ii, after line 82, in *Henry VIII* read as follows: "The vision. Enter . . . six personages clad in white robes, wearing on their heads *garlands* of bay . . . They first congee unto [Katharine], then dance . . . the first two hold *a spare garland* over her head, at which the other four make reverend curtsies. Then the two that held the *garland* deliver the same to the other next two, who observe the same order in their changes . . . they deliver the same *garland* to the last two . . . at which she [Katharine] makes (in her sleep) signs of rejoicing and holdeth up her hands to heaven; and so in their dancing vanish carrying the *garland* with them. The [sad and solemn] music continues. Upon awakening, Katharine speaks:

> . . . *Saw you not even now a blessed troop*
> *Invite me to a banquet, whose bright faces*
> *Cast thousand beams upon me, like the sun?*
> *They promis'd me eternal happiness*
> *And brought me garlands, Griffith, which I feel*
> *I am not worthy to wear. I shall, assuredly.*

Katharine's vision, which Shakespeare meant to be visible only to Katharine and the spectators (the other characters are supposed to be unaware of the angels) marks the crowning of the queen's preparation to a peaceful death, free of bitterness and resentment. In Le Tourneur, the English "garland" is rendered in French with *guirland* (Le Tourneur, *Shakespeare*, vol. 13:187ff).

153. It is not by chance that Manzoni marks the moment of Ermengarde's moral fallacy—her proud concealment even to herself of the love passion she harbors for Charles—by a startling quotation from Dante, meant to cast the heroine and her father in a bad moral light. In a discrete note to his essay "Ermengarda," 24, Francesco d'Ovidio recognized with disappointment the words that a lover addresses to Thaïs, the prostitute in *Inferno* XVIII, 134–35 (*"Ho io grazie / grandi* appo te?"), in Ermengarde's wording of her request for permission from her father to leave the Lombard court and retire in the monastery (*"Trova il mio prego /* Grazia appo te?" [Are you then willing to grant my request? literally: Does my request find favor with you?]). D'Ovidio cannot bring himself to utter the word "prostitute" and reproaches Manzoni for his neglectfulness in having resorted to those words, so clearly recognizable to any reader. D'Ovidio implies that such a hint could expose poor Ermengarde to the readers' mockery by associating her somehow with Dante's prostitute.

In this essay, d'Ovidio gives a very sympathetic interpretation of Ermengarde, and this is why he attributes Manzoni's wording to negligence. But the maddening scrupulousness with which Manzoni worded all of his works, even the bulky novel and his essays, driving the printer crazy in the printing process, is well known. No negligence on the author's part, then, but rather consistency in "estranging" us from the heroine, as he does with Adelchis's blasphemous self-identification with Christ. And there must be a deep reason for such a red flag. I propose that the reason is in pinpointing the origin of Ermengarde's error—not the love passion, but rather the repression of her passion, which begins with her stoic attempt to retire into a nunnery. It would seem a decent, praiseworthy thing to do, and Desiderius in fact approves, thinking solely of the family's honor. Ermengarde, in his view, should not show her face publicly until the dishonor of the repudiation has been washed away by the offender's blood. Ermengarde puts, like her father, her family honor ahead of her personal well-being and sanity. But her offended pride leads her in the wrong direction. She does not want to be a nun when she asks to retire to the monastery, and there she will continue to think obsessively of the past, until the passion consumes her. This is why we are not supposed to sympathize with her fully, as she commits that act of concealment and repression, out of pride. We have to pass a moral judgment on her for her hypocrisy, hence the heavy-handed, but recognizable, puzzling, and startling reference to the Dante's prostitute of the ancient world and her lover. It is, as often is the case in Manzoni, a question of refined psychological moralism in his literary creations.

The Count of Carmagnola

A Tragedy

IL CONTE.
O Dio pietoso, tu le involi a questo
Crudel momento; io ti ringrazio. Amico,
Tu le soccorri, a questo infausto loco
Le togli; e quando rivedran la luce
Di lor... che nulla da temer più resta.
Scena V.

To Mr. Charles-Claude Fauriel,

as testimony

of the author's

cordial and reverent

friendship.

.

Preface

Although this work of the imagination does not respond to the canons of taste most commonly accepted in Italy and most strictly sanctioned by custom, I do not deem it necessary to bore the reader by expounding at length the inspirational principles of this present work. Recently published writings contain such new, truthful, and wide-ranging ideas on dramatic poetry in which one can easily find the reason for the present dramatic work, which, while departing from the norms prescribed by the ancient scholars, is nonetheless carefully conceived. Moreover, every work of art provides its reader with all the necessary elements with which to judge it. In my view, these elements are: the author's intent; whether this intent was reasonable; whether the author has achieved his intent. To judge a work of art without such an examination and only by means of rules whose universality and certainty is controversial is tantamount to misjudging the work of art—which is, anyway, one of the smallest evils that can happen in this world.

Among the various expedients that men have devised to deceive themselves, one of the most ingenious is to hold as equally infallible two opposite maxims in every domain. In the small affairs of poetry, men tell to its makers: be original and do nothing for which the great poets have not already left you a model. These precepts not only make art even more difficult than it already is but also deprive an author of any hope of ever being able to account for his poetical choices, in case he was not already kept from doing so by the ridicule invariably incurred by those who praise their own verse.

But since the question of the two unities of time and place can be discussed in an abstract manner, without any reference either to this or to other tragedies; and since many still consider these unities indispensable conditions in a dramatic work, despite arguments that are overwhelming, in my view, brought by others against them; for all these reasons, I deem it useful to resume such a debate. In so doing, I will attempt to produce a small appendix to that debate rather than to repeat arguments already made by others.

I. The unity of place and the so-called unity of time have not been deduced from art's principles, nor are they connatural with dramatic poetry. They come to us from an ill-conceived authority and from arbitrary principles. This will be clearly seen in the manner of their origin. The unity of space stemmed from the observation that most Greek tragedies imitate an action that happens in one place and from the idea that the Greek theater should be held as a perpetual and exclusive model of dramatic perfection. The unity of time was derived from a passage in Aristotle,[1] which in fact, as Mr. Schlegel rightly observed,[2] does not contain a precept but simply reports a fact; that is, the widespread practice of Greek drama. For, if Aristotle had indeed wanted to dictate a norm for art, that sentence of his would have the double disadvantage of neither expressing a precise idea nor being corroborated by any reasoning.

Subsequently, when some, in utter disregard for authority, demanded the reasons for such rules, their advocates could not find but one; that is, because the spectator watches in his flesh and bones the performance of an action, it becomes nonverisimilar that that action might develop in different places and last for a long time, while the spectator knows that he did not leave his place and that only a few hours have elapsed since he began watching the action. But this reason clearly rests on a false premise; that is, that the spectator is there as part of the action, whereas he is, so to speak, a mind contemplating from the outside. Verisimilitude should not be engendered in the spectator by the action's relations to his actual way of being, rather by the mutual relations among the various parts of the action with each other. If one considers the spectator outside the action, the argument in favor of the unities vanishes into thin air.

II. These rules are not at all in line with other principles of art accepted by those same people who deem them necessary. Many things are in fact admitted as verisimilar in a tragedy that would not be such if one applied to them the principle on which the unities rest, that is, the principle that the only verisimilar facts in a play are those that accommodate the presence of the spectator within the play itself, so that those facts may appear to him verisimilar. One might say, for example: the two characters speaking among themselves about their secrets, as if they believed that they are actually alone, destroy every illu-

1. "While the Epic is metrically simple, narrative, and lengthy, Tragedy aims at confining itself within one daily course of the sun, or to go slightly beyond that time measure; but the Epic is without a measure of time and in this it differs from Tragedy." Castelvetro's translation. [Lodovico Castelvetro (1505–1571) produced a famous Italian translation of Aristotle's *Poetics*, with commentary.]

2. *Course on Dramatic Literature*, Lesson 10.

sion because I clearly feel that I am visibly present to them, and I see them exposed to the eyes of a crowd. This is the same type of objection moved by the critics who find fault with tragedies that breach the unities. The same reply should be made to both: the audience does not enter into the play. Conversely, if one inquired why the false principle has not been extended to such cases as the one above, why another yoke has not been imposed on art, the only reason he would find would be that there was no sentence in Aristotle regarding those cases.

III. Experience testifies most clearly to the uselessness of these rules for achieving dramatic illusion. Every day, in every place where theatrical performances devoid of dramatic unities are given, the populace find themselves in the mental state of illusion created by art. Let the populace be the best judge in this matter, for, since they know neither the distinction between different kinds of illusion nor the theory of the verisimilitude in art as defined by some thinkers, no abstract idea, no preconceived judgment could make them receive an impression of verisimilitude from things that do not themselves produce one. If changes of scene could destroy illusion, then this would more readily happen with a popular audience than with a learned one, since a learned person's imagination is more pliable to the artist's intentions.

If, leaving now the popular theaters, we pause to consider the respect paid to the unities in the learned theaters of several nations, we will first find that never were they sanctioned by precepts in the Greek theater and were breached every time the subject so required; we will then find that the most celebrated English and Spanish dramatic poets, those regarded as the national poets, were not acquainted with those rules or never cared to apply them; and that the Germans have refused them upon reflection. The unities were introduced into the French theater with great difficulty; the actors objected to the unity of place, in particular, when Mairet applied the rule in his *Sofonisba*, which is said to be the first regular French tragedy. It seems almost destiny that tragic regularity invariably begins with a boring *Sofonisba*. [Manzoni alludes to the first "regular" Italian tragedy, by Giangiorgio Trissino (1478–1550).] In Italy, these rules have been followed as if they were laws, without discussion and, as far as I know, probably without examination.

IV. The most bizarre thing of all is that those who proclaimed their acceptance of these rules have in fact refrained from strictly respecting them. For, without now mentioning episodic breaches of the unity of place in some Italian and French tragedies, among the so-called regular type, it is a well-known fact that the unity of time is not respected or expected *strictu sensu*, that is, in the coincidence between the fictional time of the dramatic action and the real time of its performance. Among all the French tragedies there are but three or four that comply with this stricture. In the words of a French critic, "Since it is very rare to find subjects that can be confined within such narrow limits, the rule has been enlarged, by extending it to twenty-four hours."[3] By so compromising the meaning of the rule, the authors of tracts on the dramatic art have done nothing but admit how unreasonable the rule is. They have cornered themselves into a position that precludes any defense. For one can have a serious discussion with those convinced that the time of the dramatic action should not go beyond the time of the performance, but how will he who abandoned this point then justify the limit so arbitrarily defined for the dramatic action? What can one say to a critic who is arguing that it is possible to render rules less strict? As is often the case in many other affairs, it so happens here that it is more reasonable to demand the greatest rather than the least thing. There are more than enough reasons to forgo the rules completely, but there is not a single one to facilitate the way to those who want to follow them. As put by another critic: "It would be then desirable that the action's fictive time coincide with the length of the show. However, imposing laws that the arts cannot possibly follow is tantamount to declaring oneself enemy of the arts and of the pleasure they procure, without renouncing their most fertile resources and most rare beauties. There are happy licenses tacitly acknowledged by the Public and the Poets alike, on condition that the Poets employ them with the aim of pleasing and moving the Public. The fictive, imagined extension of the real time of the dramatic action belongs to this number of happy licenses."[4] "Happy licenses" are meaningless words in literature. This is one of those expressions that conveys a clear idea in its proper and common sense but holds a contradiction when used metaphorically. Ordinarily, a license is what is done against the rules prescribed by men. In this sense, there are happy licenses because the rules can be, and often are, more general than is actually required by the nature of things. This expression is used in the

3. "*Comme il est très rare de trouver des sujets qui puissent être reserrés dans des bornes si étroites, on a elargi la règle, et on l'a étendue jusqu'a vingt-quatre heures.*" Batteux, *Principes de la litérature*, Traité 5, ch. 4. [The Abbé Charles Batteux (1713–1780) was a contributor to Diderot and d'Alembert's *Encyclopedie*, as well as a commentator on Aristotle's *Poetics*. His entries on literature were later published as a five-volume book entitled *Principles of Literature*.]

4. "*Il serait donc à souhaiter que la durée fictive de l'action pût se borner au temps du spectacle; mais c'est être ennemi des arts, et du plaisir qu'ils causent, que de leur imposer des lois qu'ils ne peuvent suivre, sans se priver de leurs ressources les plus fécondes, et de leurs plus rares beautés. Il est de licences heureuses, dont le Public convient tacitement avec les poètes à condition qu'ils les employent à lui plaire et à le toucher; et de ce nombre est l'extension feinte et supposée du temps réel de l'action théâtrale.*" Marmontel, *Elements de litérature*, article on "Unity." [Jean-François Marmontel (1723–1799), tragedian and literary scholar.]

domain of grammar and there it is apt; because grammar rules are conventional, and therefore alterable, if a writer breaches one of these rules he can better explain himself, but in the inmost rules of aesthetics, things stand otherwise.

The rules of art must be based on nature; they must be necessary, immutable, independent from the critics' will; they must be found, not made. Therefore, their violation cannot but be unhappy. Why all of these reflections on just two words? Because in those two words lies the error. When a twisted opinion is embraced, one uses it mostly to expound ambiguous and metaphorical phrases, which are true in one sense and false in another; this is because a clear sentence would let one see the contradiction. And if one wants to reveal the error in the opinion, one needs to point out where the equivocation is.

V. Finally, these rules bar many beauties and yield many inconveniences.

I will not enter into a demonstration of the first half of this proposition, which has already been done, and with excellence. The preferable choice is so evident, from even the most shallow examination of some English or German tragedies, that the very supporters of the rules are obliged to admit it. They confess that going beyond the strict limits of real time and space allows imitation in a greatly more varied and intense manner; they do not deny the beauties obtained through the violation of the rules, but they assert that one must renounce those beauties because, in order to obtain them, one must fall into inverisimilitude. Now, if we admit the objection, it is clear that the feared lack of verisimilitude would become evident only at the time of the stage performance. Therefore, the tragedy meant for the stage would be inherently incapable of that degree of perfection that tragedy can attain when it is conceived but as a poem in dialogues, destined to be read like the narrative or epic poem. If this is the case, whoever wants to obtain the most that poetry can yield should always prefer this second type of tragedy. Given the option of having to sacrifice either the material performance or the essence of poetic beauty, who would linger in doubt? Certainly not the critics who think that Greek tragedies have never been surpassed by the moderns and that those tragedies produce the highest poetic effect, notwithstanding the fact that they are no longer suited to anything but reading. I mean not to admit that dramatic works devoid of unities prove nonverisimilar on stage; I only mean to expose the principle behind the line of reasoning in favor of the unities.

The inconveniences stemming from strictly respecting the two unities, and especially the unity of place, are also openly admitted by the critics. Nay, it seems incredible that the lack of verisimilitude in plays abiding by the rules might be so well tolerated by those who support the rules with the aim of obtaining verisimilitude. I will quote but an example of this tolerance: "In the tragedy *Cinna* it is necessary that the conspiracy take place in Emily's room, and that Augustus come in this same room to confuse Cinna and forgive him: this is not very natural." The inconvenience is rightly pointed out and sincerely admitted. But the justification for it is indeed bizarre: "However, it needs be so."[5]

Perhaps we have discussed at length a question that has already been excellently resolved and that can appear to many a frivolous one. I will remind those many of what a famous writer said in a similar case: "To make a mistake at all in such regard does not cause a great damage; however, to make no mistake is even better, if that is possible."[6] And, after all, I believe that this question includes an important element. Only the error may be deemed merely trivial. Nonetheless, all that concerns the arts of the word and the different ways of influencing men's ideas and affections is intimately linked with the gravest objects. Dramatic art is found in the culture of all civilized peoples. Some consider it a powerful means of amelioration, and others deem it a powerful means of corruption; nobody judges it as neutral. It is therefore certain that all who aim to lead this art closer to or farther from its own type of truth and perfection must perforce alter, direct, increase, or diminish its influence.

The above considerations naturally lead us to a much-debated, old question, one that is nowadays almost forgotten but which I believe is far from having been resolved: whether the dramatic art is useful or harmful. I am aware that the doubts over this question may seem pedantic because in all civilized nations the Audience has deliberated in favor of the theater. Nonetheless, it seems to me very daring that one can agree, without reflection, with a deliberation protested by Nicole, Bossuet, and J. J. Rousseau, whose name, joined to the preceding ones, comes here to wield a peculiar authority. They were all unanimous on two points: first, all the theatrical plays they knew and analyzed were immoral; and second, any play must be so, in order not to appear passionless and therefore flawed according to art's criteria. As a consequence, dramatic poetry is something that must be renounced, even if it procures pleasure, because it is harmful. Although I entirely agree with the judgment passed by these writers on the vices of the

---

5. "*Dans* Cinna *il faut que la conjuration se fasse dans le cabinet d'Émilie, et qu'Auguste vienne dans ce même cabinet confondre Cinna et lui pardonner: cela est peu naturel. Cependant il le faut.*" Batteux, *Principes de la littérature,* Traité 5, ch. 4. [Cinna, *or the Clemency of Augustus* is a tragedy by Pierre Corneille (1606–1684).]

6. "*Il n'y a pas grand mal à se tromper en tout cela: mais il vaut encore mieux ne s'y point tromper, s'il est possible.*" Fleury, *Mœurs des Israelites,* ch.10. [The Abbé Claude Fleury (1640–1723), historian, was the author of the *Manners of the Ancient Israelites.*]

dramatic system they examined, I dare to believe that it is not legitimate to extend that same judgment to dramatic poetry in general. It seems to me that those writers were led into error by the assumption that no other dramatic system was possible than the one adopted in France. There can be, however, and in fact there is, another system with the highest degree of interest and devoid of the inconveniences of the other, because it promotes a moral aim, far from being opposed to it. My initial intent was to accompany the present essay in dramatic art with a speech on this topic, but certain circumstances have forced me to postpone such a work. Nonetheless, I wish and dare to announce it at this point because I deem it unbecoming to express an opinion contrary to the well-pondered judgment of highly intelligent men without submitting one's reasons or at least promising to do so.[7]

One thing remains to be done here; to account for the Chorus featured once in the present tragedy. Because no characters are indicated as members of the Chorus, this can appear as an oddity, or inexplicable. I cannot better explain my intention regarding the Chorus than by reporting some of what Mr. Schlegel said about the Greek Choruses:

> The Chorus must be regarded as the personification of the moral thoughts inspired by the dramatic action, as the organ of the poet's sentiments speaking on behalf of all humankind. . . . The Greek intended the Chorus in each drama to be, first of all, the representation of the national spirit and, secondly, the defender of the human cause. In sum, the Chorus was the ideal spectator, which would temper the most violent and painful impressions of a dramatic action oftentimes too close to reality; and by mirroring back its own emotions to the real spectator, it would sweeten them by the beauty and harmony of lyrics and it would lead thus the spectator into the more tranquil field of contemplation.[8]

7. Other circumstances did not allow the author to keep this promise. And he says so without precaution, knowing that these kinds of unfulfilled vows, far from depriving an author of his gentleman's title, often earn him instead the title of benefactor. After all, the issue has been partly discussed in the "Lettre à Monsieur Ch. sur l'unité de temps et de lieu dans la tragédie." And as far as the general question is concerned, it will perhaps suffice to remark that the arguments of those authors were based on the assumption that a dramatic work cannot be interesting unless it communicates to the spectator the passions depicted in it. This assumption stemmed from their having taken as a universal and natural condition of drama what was in fact a special peculiarity of the plays they examined. Of all this, the immortal plays of Shakespeare are the most clear and magnificent refutation.

8. *Course on Dramatic Literature,* Lesson III.

It seems to me that even if the Greek Choruses cannot be combined with the modern tragic system, one can nonetheless achieve their purpose and revive their spirit by inserting lyrical pieces composed with the idea of those Choruses in mind. If, on one hand, the independence of the modern Choruses from the dramatic action and characters deprives them of the effect they produced in the Greek drama, then, on the other hand, that same independence can make them more lyrical, more varied, and more inventive. Moreover, unlike the ancient Choruses, the modern ones have the advantage of being without inconveniences: because they are not intertwined with the plot of the drama, it will never have to be altered or upset in order to accommodate them. Finally, the Choruses present another artistic advantage, in that, as they provide the poet with a corner where he can speak with his own voice, they diminish the poet's temptations to intrude upon the action and lend to his characters his own sentiments, a well-known defect of dramatic writers. Without entering into the dispute about whether these choruses can ever be somehow adapted for the stage, I simply propose that, in general, they be meant for reading, independently from the essay here presented, because it seems to me that the literary project of the chorus might lend art more importance and perfection by providing it with a more direct, certain, and determined means of moral influence.

The tragedy is preceded by some historical notes on the character and the events that form its subject. I conceived such a premise thinking that whoever resolves to read a work resulting from the mixture of historical truth and fiction may like to be able, without lengthy inquiries, to discern what was preserved in it of the real facts.

HISTORICAL NOTES

Francesco Bartolomeo Bussone, a peasant, was born in Carmagnola [a town in Piedmont]. This toponym became his battle name, by which he has been known throughout history. The year of his birth is uncertain. His biographer, Tenivelli (*Biografia Piemontese*), believes that he was born around 1390. When he was still in his youth, while he was shepherding, a mercenary soldier noticed his fiery countenance and invited him to join in the war trade. He gladly followed the soldier and went to serve in the army of Facino Cane, a famous general.

From this point forward, the story of Carmagnola is intertwined with the history of his time. I will touch on but the main events, particularly those that are hinted at or represented in the tragedy. Some of these facts are recounted so differently by different historians that it is impossible to form and report a sound opinion on the basis of their tales. Having to sort out several, sometimes conflicting, versions, I have selected either those that seemed to me the most verisimilar or those on which there was a general agreement among historians.

When Giovanni Maria Visconti, duke of Milan, died (1412), his brother Philip Maria, count of Pavia, was heir to the dukedom. But the state of Milan, which had been greatly expanded by their father, Giovanni Galeazzo, had since decayed miserably. The reasons behind this deterioration were, first, Giovanni Maria's minority and a very bad regency and, later, Giovanni Maria's cruel and weak government. Among the cities belonging to the State of Milan, many had rebelled, and some had fallen back into the hands of their former lords. Some other cities were conquered by the very captains in charge of Duke Giovanni's army. Facino Cane was one of these captains: out of the territories of Tortona, Vercelli, and other cities, he formed for himself a small dukedom. Facino died in Pavia on the same day in which Giovanni Maria was murdered by conspirators in Milan. Philip married Beatrice Tenda, Facino's widow, and by this move he found himself lord over the cities formerly belonging to that general and his officers.

Among the latter was Carmagnola, already in charge of an entire army. This army Carmagnola led against Milan, in a joint mission with the newly created Duke Philip. They managed to oust the natural son of Bernabò Visconti, Astorre, who had seized Milan in the meantime. He was forced to retreat into Monza, where he was killed during the siege. So brilliant was Carmagnola's military conduct during the conquest of Milan that the duke appointed him general.

Historians are unanimous in considering Carmagnola the maker of Philip's political power. In a short time, Carmagnola won back for him Piacenza, Brescia, Bergamo, and other cities. Some cities were simply returned to the dukedom, either by sale or by the surrender of those who had seized them. Behind these rapid transactions was probably the terror inspired by the new general's fame. Carmagnola was also the conqueror of Genoa, which he returned to the dukedom's territory. This is how by 1424 Philip, who in 1412 was powerless and almost a prisoner in Pavia, had become lord over twenty cities, acquired, in Pietro Verri's words, "by means of the marriage to the unhappy duchess[9] and by the loyalty and military valor of Count Francesco." Upon Carmagnola, the duke bestowed the title of count of Castelnovo and gave him in marriage a kinswoman (the

9. Philip had her beheaded for having been found guilty of adultery, committed with Michele Orombelli. Most historians believe she was innocent. [The story of this "unhappy Duchess" became famous through Vincenzo Bellini's opera *Beatrice di Tenda* (1833).]

degree of kinship to the duke is unknown), Antoinette Visconti. Carmagnola then built in Milan a palace for his family, which is to this day called the Palazzo del Broletto.

The vast renown of the excellent general, the enthusiastic reverence that his soldiers showed him, his firm and haughty character, and perhaps the very overwhelming usefulness of his services—all these things alienated him from Philip's love. The count's enemies (among whom Bigli, a contemporary historian, mentions Zanino Riccio e Oldrado Lampugnano) nurtured their lord's suspicions and aversion. The count was sent to Genoa as governor and was relieved of the supreme command of the army. He maintained command over only three hundred horsemen. By letter, the duke demanded that he yield this last command as well. In reply, the count begged him to refrain from despoiling of arms a man who had grown up among them. Bigli[10] says that the count was aware that the advice of his own enemies was behind the duke's order. These men hoped to be left masters of everything once the count had been reduced to the status of a private citizen.

When he obtained no reply to his complaint, nor to his request to be exonerated from the service, Carmagnola decided to go and speak to the duke in person. The duke resided then at Abbiategrasso [in the province of Milan]. At the castle gate, to his surprise, Carmagnola was told to wait. He had himself announced to the duke, but the duke sent word that he was occupied and that the count should speak instead to Riccio. Carmagnola insisted upon seeing the duke, saying that he had just a few things to communicate but those few were only for the duke to hear. But the same reply came back again. At this point, Carmagnola took to addressing the duke, who was watching him from the slit of a tower: he reproached him for his ungratefulness and malice and swore that he would soon be missed by those who would not hear him. He then turned his horse and left with the few companions he had brought, vainly pursued by Oldrado, who thought, in Bigli's account, that it was better not to reach him.

Carmagnola headed for Piedmont, where he met with Amedeo, duke of Savoy, lord of his native land, making every possible effort to turn him into an enemy of Philip's. The count then traveled across Savoy, Switzerland, and Tirol to Treviso, while Philip confiscated all of his substantial assets in Milan.[11]

10. "History of Milan" by Andrea Bigli, book 4, *Rer. it.*, vol. 19:72. [*Rer. it.* stands for *Rerum italicarum scriptores*, a twenty-five volume collection edited by historian Ludovico Antonio Muratori (1672–1750).]

11. All of this tale is based on Bigli.

Carmagnola arrived in Venice on February 23, 1425, and there was received with honors. He was given lodging at the Patriarcato's expense, and the license to bear arms was granted to him and his retinue. After two days, the Republic hired him and entrusted him with a troop of three hundred men armed with spears.[12]

The Florentines, who were engaged in an unsuccessful war against Duke Philip, demanded Venice's alliance, while the duke pressured the Venetians to remain in peace with him. In the meantime, a man named Giovanni Liprando, who had been banished from Milan, made a pact with the duke: he promised to kill Carmagnola in exchange for permission to return home. This plot was uncovered in such a well-timed fashion to have the effect of erasing any suspicion in the Venetians' minds that the count might some day reconcile himself with Duke Philip. Bigli ascribes to the revealed plot the Venetians' decision to enter the war against Milan. The doge proposed to the senate that they hear Carmagnola's opinion on the war and Carmagnola advised them to wage it. The doge warmly pled the cause of the war, and thus the senate deliberated in favor of it. Venice announced that it would enter a league with Florence and other Italian states on January 27, 1426. On the eleventh of the following month, Carmagnola was made general captain of the Republic's landed forces. On the fifteenth, the doge publicly gave him the wand and banner of general captain at Saint Mark's altar.

I will cursorily review the course of the war, which was interrupted by two peace treaties, and I will linger to narrate only those facts that constitute the subject of the present tragedy.

The main battlefields of the war were in Lombardy. Carmagnola led the campaign impeccably and in a few months conquered many of the duke's cities, including Brescia, to the admiration of the contemporaries who deemed that city impregnable.[13] Pope Martin V intervened in the conflict, and a peace was negotiated by the end of the same year. Philip had to yield Brescia and its territory to the Venetians.

In the second war (1427), Carmagnola employed for the first time a fortification system he had devised for the military camp. It consisted of a double gird of carriages, with three crossbowmen standing on each carriage. After many minor incidents and after having conquered small cities, the count camped his troops outside the castle of Maclodio [a town in the province of Brescia], which was defended by one of the ducal garrisons.

12. Marin Sanuto, "Lives of Venetian Doges," *Rer. it.*, vol. 12:978.
13. Machiavelli, *History of Florence*, book 4.

Four distinguished captains were in charge of the duke's army: Angelo della Pergola, Guido Torello, Francesco Sforza, and Niccolò Piccinino.[14] Because a dispute arose among them, the duke sent in Carlo Malatesti, from a renowned family of Pesarese nobility, with the supreme command. But, Bigli remarks, nobility lacked talent. The historian reports that Malatesta's supreme command did not suffice to eliminate the rivalry among the captains. Conversely, in the Venetian camp, all willingly obeyed Carmagnola, despite the fact that among his officers were famous captains and princes such as Giovanfrancesco Gonzaga, lord of Mantua; Antonio Manfredi, lord of Faenza; and Giovanni Varano, lord of Camerino.

Carmagnola became acquainted with the character of the enemy general and was able to take advantage of this. He attacked Maclodio, near which the ducal garrison was stationed. The two armies found themselves on opposite sides of a boggy terrain, cut in the middle by an elevated road, similar to an embankment. Among the marshes were patches of firm land covered with thicket. The count deployed ambushes on each of these patches and then started to provoke the enemy. In the duke's camp, there were various opinions, and likewise the historians' tales on this point differ. But the most accredited hypothesis is that Pergola and Torello, who suspected the ambushes, advised against the battle, while Sforza and Piccinino wanted it at all costs. Malatesta sided with the latter; he engaged in the battle and was overwhelmingly defeated. As soon as his army attacked the enemy in front, the men in the ambushes assaulted it from left and right and took five thousand, some say eight thousand, prisoners from among the Milanese troops. The general himself was made captive, while the other four captains managed to escape in one way or another. Among the prisoners was a son of Pergola.

The night following the battle, the victorious soldiers set free almost all of the prisoners. The Venetian commissioners charged with supervising the military operations complained about this to the count. The count asked an officer what had happened to the war prisoners, and when the reply came that all but four hundred men had been set free, the count ordered that these latter too be released, in compliance with an old custom.[15]

There is but one historian of that period, to my knowledge, who, having per-

14. In order to satisfy metrical needs, the name of this character has been changed to "Fortebraccio." History itself suggested the change, since Piccino was nephew of Braccio Fortebracci, and, after his uncle's death, was the leader of the Braccian faction.

15. "He ordered that those, too, be released, according to the customary rule." Bigli, book 6.

sonally fought in those wars, took pains to explain the true reason behind this military custom. He ascribes it to the soldiers' fear of seeing a hasty conclusion of the wars, so that the people would have screamed at them: "Back to the hoe, soldiers!"[16]

The commissioners were offended by the count's conduct in the matter of the war prisoners and took to mistrusting him, but with no good reason. Upon hiring a military captain, they should have expected him to conduct the war according to the commonly accepted rules of war. By demanding from the count that he oppose a custom so useful and dear to the soldiers, they were in fact asking him to run the risk of becoming abhorred by his soldiers and remaining therefore without support. They were right in demanding from him loyalty and zeal but not an unlimited devotion: this would be in keeping only with a cause embraced for duty's sake or enthusiastically. I find, however, no other reports of further complaints that the Republic might have expressed to the count, after those first remarks by the commissioners. On the contrary, there are only mentions of honors and awards granted to him.

In April 1428, the Venetians and the duke signed another of those inconclusive peace treaties, after which the war was resumed in 1431. This time, however, unlike the previous two, the outcome for the count was unfavorable from the start.

The deputy governor for the duke in the castle of Soncino [province of Cremona] pretended to be willing to secretly betray the place to the count. The count went there with part of his army and was caught in an ambush. Bigli reports that six hundred of the count's horsemen and numerous foot-soldiers were made captive. The count himself was barely able to escape.

A few days after this episode, Nicola Trevisani, captain of the Venetian fleet on the Po River, came to confront the duke's ships. Piccinino and Sforza pretended to be about to attack the count, thus preventing him from lending succor to the Venetian fleet. In the meantime, the duke's captains sent the majority of their infantry onto the ships. When Carmagnola realized that he had been duped and rushed to help his fellow soldiers, the battle was taking place on the opposite shore. The Venetian fleet was defeated and its captain fled on a small boat.

For this, the Venetian historians accuse Carmagnola of treason. The historians who refrain at least from the sad task of justifying his murderers accuse him of no less than having let himself be deceived by a stratagem. It seems certain

---

16. *"Ad ligonem stipendiarii."* "Chronicle of Treviso," *Rer. it.,* vol. 19:864. [*ligo*=mattock, tillage; *stipendiarius*=soldier receiving pay.]

that Trevisani's conduct was imprudent from the start and irresolute during the battle.[17] The Republic punished that captain with banishment and seized all his assets; "the senate wrote letters of light censure to the general (Carmagnola), for not having provided his aid to the fleet."[18]

On October 18, Carmagnola ordered one of his officers, Cavalcabò, to take the city of Cremona by surprise. The captain managed to occupy a part of the city but the alarm bells having awoken all the citizens, he had to abandon the deed and return to the camp.

Carmagnola deemed it useless to support Cavalcabò with the bulk of his army, and it seems strange to me that Venice charged him with treason for this decision. The probably unforeseen resistance of the populace with which he was to meet in the city amply explains why the general did not persist in fighting in a city that he was hoping to take by surprise and without combat. Treason, on the contrary, hardly explains anything, for there are no reasons why Carmagnola should have ordered an enterprise, the negative outcome of which would have brought no advantage to the enemy.

But the Republic was, in the words of the historian Navagero, resolved to get rid of Carmagnola and sought a way of having him in their hands despoiled of his arms. They could not devise a safer and prompter way than that of inviting him to Venice under the pretense of wanting to consult with him on the peace negotiations. The count went to Venice suspecting nothing and along the way he and Gonzaga, who was accompanying him, were paid extraordinary homage. All historians, even the Venetian ones, agree that this procedure was deceitful—nay, it seems that they tell about this procedure with a certain complacency, as a point of merit in what was elsewhere called prudence and political virtue. When the count arrived at Venice, "he was met by eight noblemen who, before he could call at his house, accompanied him to Saint Mark."[19] Once inside the Ducal Palace, his men were dismissed with the pretext that the count would remain with the doge at length. The count was arrested in the Palace and led to prison. A body that the Navagero calls a "Secret Court" examined him and sen-

17. "On the thirteenth of July, having summoned Nicola Trevisano, the former captain of the fleet on the Po, and since he failed to respond to the summons, the Municipal Advocates asked the Prosecutors to proceed against him for having let himself be defeated on the Po river by the Milanese Duke's ships on June 21, thus offending the Signoria, and for not having discharged his duty, for his coward conduct, and because he told all around him that they should flee." Sanuto, · *Rer. it.,* vol. 22:1017.

18. "Venetian History," Navagero, *Rer. it.,* vol. 23:1096.

19. Sanuto, *Rer. it.,* vol. 22:1028.

tenced him to death. On May 5, 1432, the count was brought to the two columns of the Piazzetta, with bars in his mouth, and beheaded. The count's wife and their daughter (two daughters in some accounts) were then in Venice.

Nothing certain is known about the innocence or the guilt of this great man. One could expect that the Venetian historians, if they wanted to keep writing and living undisturbed, would find him guilty. They express this fact as a matter of course, with that nonchalance that comes natural to those who speak in favor of the strongest. Without wasting time in formulating hypotheses, they relate that Carmagnola was convicted by torture, by witnesses, and by his own letters. Of the three types of evidence, only the first was indisputably used, the most infamous, the one that cannot prove anything.

But besides the absolute lack of direct historical testimony that might confirm that Carmagnola was in fact guilty, many reasons make his guilt seem unlikely. Never did the Venetians reveal the supposed conditions for betrayal that the count bargained with the duke; nor did anybody ever learn anything of such a pact. This accusation stands isolated in history. Nothing supports it, but for some unsuccessful war enterprises, which can be fully explained without resorting to the idea of treason. It would be a bizarre, not less than an atrocious, rule to ascribe to the general's malice every military failure. On the other hand, one must mention a series of facts that speak to the possible innocence of the count. He unhesitatingly went to Venice when invited, without precautions. The Republic always kept this fact secret, notwithstanding the accusations of ungratefulness and injustice launched against her by many throughout Italy. The Venetians took the cruel precaution of putting bars in the count's mouth while conducting him to his execution, a precaution all the more remarkable because, being a foreigner, the count was not a person who could have supporters among the populace. Finally, one has to consider the well-known temperaments of the count and the duke. Both must have been completely averse to such a bargain between them. A secret reconciliation with a man who had been horribly ungrateful to him, and who had tried to have him murdered; a pact to conduct the war on the Venetians' behalf in a lax way, nay, in such a way as to let himself be beaten— these things do not suit Carmagnola's character: impulsive, active, greedy for glory. The duke was not a man who could forgive, and Carmagnola, who knew him better than anyone, never could have believed in a stable and secure reconciliation with such a man. The idea of returning to Philip when the duke had been offended could never cross the mind of the man who had tasted Philip's retributions when the duke had been served well.

I researched other histories of the time, to see if other historians had at least hinted at a public opinion different from the one that the Republic managed to make prevalent. Here is what I could collect.

The author of a Bolognese chronicle, having narrated the end of Carmagnola, adds: "They said that they had done so because he was not fighting loyally on their behalf in the war against the duke, as he should have, and that he had a pact with the duke. Others say that, as they saw their State in the hands of the count, captain of such a vast army, and having conceived that they were in great danger, not knowing what was the best way to dismiss him, they found motives for treason against him. God forbid that they have not acted wisely because it seems that, because of this, the Signoria has seen her own might greatly diminished and that of the duke augmented."[20]

And Poggio: "Some say that he deserved death through no crime of any sort, rather that his death had been caused by his pride, offensive for the Venetian citizens, abhorred by all."[21]

A historian of a slightly later period, Corio, asserts: "They took away from him the value of more than three hundred thousand *ducati*, which were the cause of his death more than anything else."

While the last of these three hypotheses is not worthy of much attention, it seems to me that the other two, that is, fear and offended honor, suffice, for that epoch, to provide a probable explanation, more likely, at any rate, than treason, which was in all things contrary to the nature and the interest of the man indicted.

Among all modern historians who, refraining from blindly adopting the ancient traditions, examined them with an unbiased judgment, there is only one, to my knowledge, who showed himself persuaded that the sentence passed on Carmagnola was just. This historian is Count Verri. But as soon as one reads a passage in his history concerning this event, one can see clearly that his opinion stems from his refusal to consider the facts on which that opinion should have been built. Here are his words:

Whether he was averse, owing to a repugnance in his soul, to bringing such a defeat to a prince from whom he had once received high honors and under whom he had achieved a wide renown; whether he still trusted that, once humiliated, the duke would propose to him a reconciliation, sacrificing to him the mean foes who had dared harm him, that is, those very cowardly courtiers of his; or for another reason, the Count Francesco Carmagnola, notwithstanding the grave dissent of the Vene-

20. "Bolognese Chronicle," *Rer. it.*, vol. 8:645.
21. Poggio Bracciolini, *History of the Florentine People*, book 6.

tian commissioners, decided to send all the captains and the numerous soldiers made captive after the victory on October 11, 1427, deprived of their weapons but free—to send them back to the duke. . . . The sequel of his actions made his intents clearer and clearer. He missed all good occasions and by progressing at a slow pace always gave time to the duke's men to recover and stay in combat. In sum, the bad faith of the count of Carmagnola became so evident that, after a formal trial, he was beheaded in Venice for having been found guilty of high treason.

It is amazing that a historian profoundly engaged in informing his readers about the injustice of the secret judicial procedure takes it, in this case, as valid evidence proving a man's guilt. As far as the question of the war prisoners is concerned, each can see the mistakes of the above-quoted report. The count of Carmagnola did not free all the prisoners but only four hundred of them. He did not send back the duke's captains because none of them were apprehended, except for Malatesti, who stayed captive. Moreover, it is not exactly correct to say that the soldiers were sent back to the duke. Rather, they were set free. I do not see why one must surmise reasons to explain Carmagnola's conduct in this matter, other than the motive, which history records, of a common military custom.

The news of Carmagnola's end produced sensation all over Italy. It seems that the Piedmontese people in particular resented it more keenly and kept the memory of the fact alive, as the following anecdote told by Denina indicates.

The first suspicion about the formation of the league of Cambrai came to the Venetians through the report of one of their agents in Milan, who had learned that "a certain Carlo Giuffredo Piemontese, a secretary of state in the services of King Louis, was heard repeatedly to welcome the forthcoming occasion to finally avenge a fellow countryman of his, the Count Francesco Carmagnola."[22]

I did not quote this passage to applaud a desire for vengeance or a sentiment of municipal patriotism, but rather as a clue to the attention commanded by the case of that great captain in the public opinion of that noble and warlike region of Italy that considered him more especially theirs.

The chronological order and the essential circumstances of the events chosen for the present tragedy have been preserved, with the exception of the attempt on Carmagnola's life, which is here set in Venice but actually took place in Treviso.

22. Carlo Denina, *Jtalian Revolutions*, book 20, ch. 1. [The League of Cambrai was a powerful anti-Venetian alliance secretly formed in 1508 by Pope Julius II, Hapsburg emperor Maximilian I, France, Spain, and the cities of Ferrara and Mantova.]

List of Characters

❧ Act I ❧

Scene I

[*Senate hall in Venice;* THE DOGE *and* SENATORS, *seated*]

THE DOGE

  The day you set for the deliberation,
  Which must to long debating put an end,
  Has come at last, O noblemen. Today
  We shall resolve the question of the League
  In which, with ardent prayers, Florence
  Solicits us to join against Milan.
  But before we proceed, you must be acquainted,
  If some of you have not heard yet the rumors,
  With a most somber fact that has occurred
  In this same Venice, unintruded haven
  Of peace and justice, before our eyes.
  And 'tis vital that all know about it,
  Because it bears on our deliberation.
  A stranger tried today to take the life
  Of count of Carmagnola, but he failed,
  And he's in fetters now. He did confess
  The name of those who sent him and this is . . .
  That same duke of Milan whose envoys are
  Still here to invoke peace, secure our friendship,
  Which is, in their speech, most precious to them.
  In the meantime such is the pledge he gives
  Of friendly love for us. I will not tarry
  To utter words about the villainy

Of such scheming, about the grave affront
Against our State, for such we must consider
The offense made to a soldier of ours,
But solely remark two simple facts:
The duke abhors the count, and every venue
Of reconciliation is closed forever
Between them. They sealed with blood a compact
Of eternal enmity. The duke loathes
The count and fears him because he knows how
That same hand that put him on the throne once
Can easily remove him from it now.
As he dreads that we will not linger long
In this inglorious, imprudent, vile peace,
He senses what this man can mean for us:
He is the best among the best of warriors
In Italy and, what perchance matters
Even more, he is deeply familiar
With the duke's army as well as with his wiles.
This is the man who will inflict on him
A mortal blow because he knows indeed
His weakest spot. This weapon he did drop
In our lap. Let us use it at once.
Whence can we derive more thoughtful counsel
Than from the trusted count? I invited him.
Would you hear him? [*gestures of assent*] Introduce the count.

Scene II

[*enter* THE COUNT]

THE DOGE

Count of Carmagnola, the Republic
Has today occasion, for the first time,
To avail itself of your service and show
To you the high esteem in which we hold you.
For a most serious matter, we are in need
Of most serious advice. The while I voice
To you the joy of our entire senate

For your escape from that nefarious peril,
The insult was made to us. Over your head
Now more than ever stretches our shield,
A shield of protection and of vengeance.

THE COUNT

Most serene doge, till this day I could
Do nothing but pronounce most solemn vows
To this fair land that warmly welcomed me
And that I dare to name my fatherland.
O, that I might at last make this life shine,
Which was just saved from most villainous plots
And flows in silence, adding day to day,
Mirroring itself in itself sadly:
May I spend it for you in such a way
That people might one day remark how worthy
Was the recipient of your courtesy.

THE DOGE

We surely expect grand things from you,
When needed. For the time being, your counsel
Will suffice. Florence has long requested
Our armed succor against the viscount.
Your say will throw no little weight upon
The scales that we now balance before us.

THE COUNT

My arm and my mind, and all I am,
Are a thing in your possession. I could not
Hope in a better case to offer you
Useful advice than this, and I will. But
Let me first speak to you about myself,
Open to you a heart that only yearns
To be utterly known.

THE DOGE

                        Speak freely, pray:
Something dear to your heart cannot but be
Of consequence for this whole assembly.

THE COUNT

Most serene doge, senators, I am
At a point where I cannot be to you
Loyal and grateful, unless I become
Enemy of the man who was my lord.
If I believed myself still bound to him
By the thinnest constraint, my will would be
To flee even the shadow of ensigns,
Which the whole world acknowledges and honors;
I would prefer to live in idle darkness
Rather than to emerge and come to light
To vilify myself in my own eyes.
My heart harbors no doubt about the course
I took, for it is just and honorable.
But I fear that the world will pass a judgment
Upon myself. Happy is he to whom
Fortune presents a crossroad where he can
Neatly distinguish the road of honor
From that of shame, so that he securely
Proceeds to obtain the world's commendation
And avoid steps that a foe's intent eye
Will regard as evil. But I must run
A course that will perchance earn me the name
—One needs admit it—of ungratefulness,
The insufferable fame of a betrayer.
I know it is the politicians' custom
To avail themselves of means that they judge evil,
And to bestow rewards as well as scorn
Upon the doer. I know it, but I
Was not born for this. The sole and loftiest
Reward that I expect is your esteem,
The high esteem of every courteous man.
I dare to say: I think that I deserve it.
I call on your wise judgment, senators,
To witness that I here divest myself
Of every obligation to the duke.
If one would reckon all the benefits
That we exchanged, all the world knows who would

Prove the debtor between us. But enough
Of this: I was faithful to him as long
As I was with him; I did not leave him
But when my lord himself forced me to it.
He took from me the rank that I had earned
By shedding my own blood; to no avail
I complained to my lord. My rivals barred
My access to the throne and I saw how
My very life was in danger. No time
Did I allow for their plan, for I am
Willing to offer my life, but in battle,
For a noble cause, and with honor, not
Treacherously caught in dastards' traps.
Thus I left him and asked you for shelter
And even here he contrived an ambush.
And now I am no more obliged to him;
I am his open foe as he is mine.
I shall serve your ends, but I shall be frank,
And determined in my resolve, like one
Who is certain in the justice of his deed.

THE DOGE

Such does this senate deem you. Of the dispute
Between you and the duke, all Italy
Is judge: he freed your faith and gave it back
To you intact, as it was when you swore
Allegiance to him on the first day.
That faith is ours now; we shall hold it
In due esteem. May it please you to give us,
As a first pledge, your sincere opinion.

THE COUNT

I shall most gladly and firmly give you advice.
I deem this war most urgent and if ever
It was allowed to man to see beyond
The present time with certainty, the outcome
Of the war at hand appears most certain,
More so if you will have less hesitation.

What is the duke's current predicament?
He half won Florence, but the winner is
Tired, bleeding: his treasure is depleted;
Vexed by terror and taxes, the citizens
Entreat from Heaven on their very arms
Desertions and defeats. I know them all:
In many a mind one memory is lasting,
The ancient, glorious life of the commune.
Restless and shameful in their present state,
They send forth gazes full of longing toward
Whatever ray of hope that may appear.
He knows about these minds, and that is why
You hear him speak to you in meekest terms,
And demand time from you, so that he may
At leisure tear apart the prey he holds
Tightly in his talons and devour it.
Let us imagine that you grant him time:
How utterly the face of things would change!
He would in time undoubtedly subdue Florence,
And with the booty fully sate his troops.
They will be ready then for further conquests.
What prince would at that point refuse to enter
An alliance with him? Happy the first one
Whom he will call his friend! He would then think
Of when and how he may best undertake
A war against your isolated land.
He does not know that kind of wrath that doubles
The courage in the valiant man who has
Suffered a defeat. His wrath is manifest
But when things prosper and bode well for him.
Impatiently he pursues all easy deeds,
Eager to go wherever success smiles,
But fearfully unresolved before dangers.
Always unseen by soldiers in the brawl,
He claims the prey after the fight is ended.
The present time he is spending undoubtedly
In his castle or in his country villas,
Chattering about hunting and banquets,

Or tremblingly consulting a soothsayer.
This is the time to vanquish him: seize it,
For daring may prove now the prudent course.

THE DOGE

The senate will duly ponder now, count,
Your earnest advice, and whether it shall
Take it or not, it is grateful for it
And does perceive in it your most wise mind
As well as your affection toward us.
[*exit* THE COUNT]

Scene III

THE DOGE

No one may reasonably expect my mind
To differ from such noble words. Because,
When the most lavish counsel is the safest,
Who could remain in doubt? Let us offer
Our hand to the brother who entreats us.
A sacred knot constrains the two Republics;
They share the same hopes and the same dangers;
At their foundations they are all shaken
When one of them collapses. And why now
Is the duke asking us for peace, he who
Provokes the weak and is sworn enemy
Of whoever is not fully his slave?
Only because he wants to choose the time
When to wage war on us, and time is not
Ripe yet for his advantage. This time
Is ours, if only we can see it,
And have courage. He wants divided foes;
Let us unite against him. O, this would
Indeed be the first time that the Lion
Remains dormant, assuaged by the sweet sound
Of flatteries. No, he will have tried in vain.
I here propose that we do form the league,
That we declare at once war on the duke,

And that the count have the supreme command
Of our forces in the land campaign.

MARINO

    I shall not rise to speak against a war
That is indeed urgent and just. One thing
I ask: that we think how we can ensure
Success. Half of the whole enterprise lies
In the general we choose. I know well
That the count has many friends among us.
But I am also confident that none
Among us loves him with a greater love
Than the one due to our fatherland.
When there's at stake the lot of our State
I do not pay respect to any man.
And as I speak, I do regret that I
Must stand opposed to your advice, today,
Most serene doge, but this man is not
A military chief such as requires
The seriousness and honor of this State.
I will not question why he left the duke,
He was the party offended, this is true,
And I concede that such the offense has been
That covenants between them cannot be.
I do believe his words. But these same words
We must carefully heed, because in them
He painted his whole self. And to govern
Such a susceptible pride, such a violent
And yet sensitive nature, is a task
Not less worrisome than to wage the war.
Till the present day our major efforts
Were devoted to exacting from our subjects
Their most complete obeisance. But instead
We should now pursue ways in which we can
Best revere him. Once we have placed our sword
Into his hand, how shall we rest assured
That we created an obedient servant?
Shall each of us have to take care to please

This man? If a difference arises,
Shall it be fit that our will prevail
Over the opinion of such a famous chief,
A most deft master in the art of war?
If he errs and we pay the price for it—
For invincible I do not deem him—
Shall it be licit to complain about it,
And if we reap, for it, insults and shame,
What shall we do? Suffer them patiently?
I cannot think that you would be content
With such a feeble course. Could we then show
Our anger? And give him thus a motive
To disdainfully, abruptly abandon us,
In the middle of things, in dire straits,
To go and offer to the first who wants it,
Maybe to our enemy—his arm,
Revealing all he knows about ourselves,
Exaggerating our ungratefulness,
Artfully pitted against his grand merits?

THE DOGE

The count forsook a prince, but do consider
That this was the sole ruler of the State,
Which means the count has never held himself
Of less stature than him; a prince encircled
By few, and these few, cowards; he was timid,
He did not know the right counsel to gather
From his own fear, to hide it in his heart
And remain wary. So foolish was he
That he showed the dagger before the blow.
Such is the lord who made the count his foe.
But, Heaven be praised, I do not see like
Faults in Venice. If a steed did bolt once
During a race and unsaddled a foolish,
Wrathful man, throwing him into the mud,
A cautious and frank rider would not shun
For that reason the occasion to mount it.

MARINO

> Since the doge is so certain of this man,
> I will no more object, and I ask him
> Only this: is he willing to answer
> For the count's actions?

THE DOGE

> A precise request
> Demands precise reply: I shall never
> Answer for the count's nor for any man's
> Actions. Nay, I shall answer solely
> For my actions, my advice. It suffices
> That men in our service be trustworthy.
> Did I propose to exempt the count from watching,
> To leave our State's guidance in his hands?
> He will act honestly, as I can foresee.
> But if he takes a wry course, do we lack
> An eye that might soon alert us to his ways,
> And an arm that might invisibly reach him?

MARK

> Why do we sadden thus the very outset
> Of such a handsome feat and devise now
> Terrors and punishments when one will need
> But high praises and thanks? I shall not mention
> That one way only leads to his advantage,
> To side with us; but how can I not name
> The thing that above all should inspire us
> With the utmost and serene trust in the man?
> Glory, that he already earned, and glory
> His proud, generous soul still hopes to gain.
> It is indeed absurd that he might wish
> To descend from his lofty thoughts into
> The vile crowd of the pusillanimous.
> Now, for prudence's sake, let the eye watch,
> But may the heart repose in utter trust.
> And since God sent us such a gift for this
> Just and grave cause, let us accept it gladly,

With such a brow and heart that fully become
The recipient of it.

MANY SENATORS

Let us vote!

THE DOGE

I order that the votes be now collected.
Let each of you remember the mandate
That not a word of this debate escape
The precincts of this assembly, nor hints
By which our intentions he might surmise.
Few men in our State have betrayed secrets
And no one among them remained unpunished.

Scene IV

[THE COUNT's *house*]

THE COUNT

To be a fugitive, or a captain:
Whether to live like an old warrior who
Must spend his days in idleness, reliving
His bygone glory, being ever ready
To offer thanks and prayers for the protection
By someone else's arm, which might tire,
One day, and forsake him—or to return
To battles, to plunge in life, to salute
My fortune, to awake at the bracing sound
Of trumpets, to command. This is the time
To resolve this question. Alas, if Venice
Remains in peace, must I keep here in hiding,
Confined in this haven, like a murderer
In church? So, one who made a kingdom live
Shall not have might to rule over his life?
Shall I not find one prince among the many
Who govern this divided Italy,
One prince, who dares to envy the fair crown

That makes the unworthy head of Philip glisten?
One prince who still recalls that it was I
Who won it, snatched it from the tight clutches
Of ten tyrants and put it on that brow?
And now I seek but to despoil the ingrate
Of that same crown and bestow it on those
Who shall benefit gladly from my arm.

Scene V

[*enter* MARK]

THE COUNT

Hail, sweet friend, what news do you bring me?

MARK

War is declared and you shall be the general.

THE COUNT

Never with bigger heart than this did I
Look forward to an enterprise before:
You placed much faith in me, and I shall be
Most worthy of it, I swear. This day seals
My destiny, and since this noble land
Receives me in her ancient, glorious bosom,
Bestowing upon me the name of son,
Such do I wish to be to her forever:
This sword of mine I consecrate forever
To her defense, to her magnificence.

MARK

O, your vows are sweet! May Heaven forbid
That fortune ever breach them, or yourself.

THE COUNT

And pray how could I leave them unfulfilled?

MARK

Perchance like all generous people, who
While benefiting others harmed themselves;
Who overcame all the harshest ordeals,
Then miserably failed in the one that
The least mortal would have easily passed.
Believe a man who loves you: most noblemen
Are your friends, but not every one is.
More I cannot tell, 'tis not permitted,
Perchance too much was said already. But
In my friend's trusted ear may my word be
As in the temple of my heart, imprisoned.

THE COUNT

Do I perhaps ignore this? Do I not
Know, one by one, my enemies?

MARK

                                                    And know
You who made them such? Mostly your being
So greater than them, and also the disdain
That you openly and always showed for them.
No one has harmed you so far, but who may not
Do it in time? You do not think of them
Except when sighting them as you proceed,
But they do think of you more than you imagine.
The great man is haughty yet oblivious,
But the base man derives his joy from hatred.
Beware not to kindle it; nay, appease it.
Perchance you shall succeed in this. I shall
Refrain from giving you sordid advice
That I myself revile, nor could you ever
Expect such advice from me. But between
Haughtiness and servile caution does lie
A middle course, a kind of prudence that
Becomes even the modest, noblest hearts,
An art by which one charms the vulgar souls

Without debasing oneself to their station.
This art you may find, if you so will,
In your wisdom.

THE COUNT
                         Most truthful is your counsel.
I gave it to myself a thousand times,
But it faded from my spirit always
When I most needed it. Always I learnt
At my expense that whenever wrath
Casts its seeds, repentance is the harvest.
O harsh and pointless schooling! So tired
Was I to hold myself to laws I would
Transgress, that I determined to surrender
To my own destiny: if it must needs be
That I am caught in such entangled knots,
Let that virtue that I lack—if virtue
'Tis indeed—resolve them once and for all,
If such is my destiny, that I be
One day trapped in those knots and perish there.
'Tis better to go encounter such a lot
Without posing resistance any more.
I appeal to you, my friend: were good men
Ever without adversaries? You yourself
Must have some, and I readily swear that
No one among them is worthy, I will
Not say of your soothing words, but even
Of your marks of disdain. Pray answer me.

MARK
It is most true. If there is mortal man
I ever envied, it is but that man who
Lived in times and places in which he could
Openly show his soul upon his face
And prove his mettle only in ordeals
Requiring force, not shrewdness. Therefore,
Marvel not if I am far from versed
In the art of feigning. Consider how

A failure in that art is more promptly
Pardoned in me than it would be in you;
And how few ways could an enemy's dagger
Find to wound my breast; how I am shielded
From private hatred by the public function;
How the same robe is donned by myself and
By those who can decide my lot. But you,
A foreigner, you, a captain of troops
Laboring in the service of gowned lords,
You whom the State entrusts with many swords
So that it may be saved, but with no weapons
To save yourself . . . I pray you, let your friends
Hear always but high praises about you,
Charge them not with the miserable care
To exculpate you. Think that we cannot be
Happy unless you are. What more shall I say?
I shall, if you will, touch a cord that deeper
Resonates in your heart: think of your wife,
Your daughter, whose sole hope you are; Heaven
Gave them a soul to sense the joy, a soul
That freely breathes in serene days but that
Cannot act to win them. That you can do,
And you will. Do not say that your destiny
Rules over you, because when the strong man
Says "I will," he feels himself the master
Of himself, more than he thought beforehand.

THE COUNT

How righteous is your speech! Heaven indeed
Is looking after me if such a friend
It sends me. Listen: success in war shall,
I hope, placate those who dislike me, and
All will end well. In the meantime, if you
Hear something displeasing about myself
Ascribe it, I beg you, to my nature,
To a sudden impulse of mine, never to
My neglect for your words.

MARK

> Now my joy
> Is complete: go, win, and return—O how
> Shall I await the messenger announcing
> With your glory conjoined the salvation
> Of my fatherland!

 Act II

Scene I

[THE DUKE's *camp with tents;* MALATESTI *and* PERGOLA]

PERGOLA

> As you demanded, my lord, the cohorts
> Are arrayed in battling order. To you
> The duke entrusted the supreme command;
> I have obeyed you, though with deep regret.
> I still beseech you: let us not engage
> In this present battle, over this field.

MALATESTI

> Your years and fame, O Pergola, confer
> Upon your words so much authority;
> The burden of your judgment I do feel,
> And yet I cannot change my own resolve.
> You see how Carmagnola every day
> Harasses us; to provoke us, before
> Our eyes, he laid siege to Maclodio,
> Leaving us but two choices: remove him
> From hence or abandon the city, which
> Would be utter dishonor and mere loss.

PERGOLA

> To a few men, the great ones, it is given
> To doubt again after they said: "'tis so."
> If I speak now, 'tis that I deem you such.
> Since the barbarians came down from the Alps,
> Italy had not seen two stronger armies

Confronting each other on its land.
But ours is Duke Philip's last endeavor.
In every war, who will deny that fortune
Has its part? But when all is committed
To fortune, O lord, it is not good
To give to it more than it will demand.
This army, which would make any feat possible,
Once lost, shall never be mustered again
In such numbers. Therefore it should not be
Cast like a die, blindly; we should not
Venture it upon such a small field,
And what is more, an ill-known field to us,
Well known to our enemies. The count
Has dragged us here: a winding embankment
Divides the armed arrays; on the two sides
Are boggy lands and over them are scattered
His cohorts. But for our encampments,
We do not hold a yard of this terrain.
Believe a man who knows his ruses well,
Who fought at his side: here is an ambush.
Perchance a better way to fight this man
Would be to hold him at bay, to take time,
So that some of his officers would tire
Of his haughty ways and the tight bundle
That he now holds in his hand would slacken . .
But if we must engage in battle, then
Let us move from hence; let us choose the field
Ourselves and drag the foe to it: there,
Without their lead, at least, be it decided.

MALATESTI

Two vast armies today confront each other;
Their clash shall be huge: this is the battle
That Philip now needs. Procrastination
Led to this day's juncture, and you propose
Now further delay. To escape from all this
We must confide in the opposite choice:
Delay is the true danger, and changing

Field would mean certain defeat. Who could say
What loss in number as well as courage
Might our army suffer while we move
The field? In this present hour the army
Is such as a captain might wish it be.
All things can be attempted with it.

Scene II

[*enter* SFORZA *and* FORTEBRACCIO]

MALATESTI

                                  You come
In good time, Sforza and Fortebraccio.
Pray tell us how you judge the battlefield,
What can be expected of it?

SFORZA

                             All good things.
When the troops heard the orders, when it seemed
The battle's preparation had begun,
I heard a most fierce cheer. They came rejoicing
To the summons, beckoning to each other
With a smile. And when I ran through the ranks
Each cohort loudly cheered, each soldier fixed
His eyes on mine as if to say: "Aye, sir."

FORTEBRACCIO

They all are in that mood: when I came to
My cohorts, all the soldiers ran to me.
One asked me: "When shall we hear the trumpets?"
Another said: "We are tired of being mocked,"
And all with one voice asked for the battle,
And seemed sure they would obtain it, doubtful
But of the time. I asked in turn: "Comrades,
If the signal is soon heard, do you promise
That you shall win with me?" They gave assent
With universal cry, and on their spears

Their helmets were hoisted. I still rejoice
For this. How could anyone ask that we
Order these soldiers to retreat; could we
Command these hands, already at their swords,
Waiting only to unsheathe them, that they move
Our tents away? Who could bear to face
These soldiers with such orders?

PERGOLA

                        I am learning
Today new rules of warfare: that soldiers
Are in command and captains obey them.

FORTEBRACCIO

The soldiers I lead, Pergola, are such
As my own father Braccio disciplined.
His name inspires still marvel and terror,
His soldiers do not suffer mockeries
From their adversary.

PERGOLA

                  I lead soldiers
Who are disciplined just by my humble self,
And they are wont to await the orders from
Their leader, and trust in him completely.

MALATESTI

Pray let us not forget that our time
Is precious, none is left for vain disputes.

Scene III

[*enter* TORELLO]

SFORZA

How now, Torello, did you change your mind?
You saw the ardent spirit of the troops.

TORELLO

I saw it. I heard the cries of ardor,
Of assurance, indeed the cries of courage.
My visage then I turned the other way,
So that none of those brave soldiers might read
The thought that was depicted there, even
Against my will: the thought of how that joy
Was false, short-lived, the thought of wasted valor.
I rode along the front line to its end;
I forced my gaze to reach the longest distance;
I saw once more those scattered spots around
The marshy terrain flanking the whole field.
Those are the ambushes, I would swear on it.
That double girdle of armed carriages
That surround the camp of the enemy
I then saw once again, and I thought that,
If they cannot withstand the first assault,
They have a safe retreat where to escape,
To get ready for the second charge. It's
A new invention of this man, making
His soldiers fully oblivious to the first
Of thoughts that comes to the defeated: flight.
To vanquish him, two major blows are needed,
While he can defeat us with one. Because
—'Tis better to aver what we see clearly—
These are no more those wars in which the soldier
Would fight for his own children, for his women,
And for his fatherland, and for its laws,
Which make a land more dear to people's hearts;
Wars where the captain would assign a place
To the soldier willing to die in combat.
Over mercenary men we hold command,
Among whom furor rather than ardor
Is much more promptly found; they gladly run
At first to meet victory in battle, but,
If she is late to come, none too doubtful
Is their own choice between swift flight and death.
This is the outcome that we should foresee,

More than anything else! O, craven times,
When the hardships of command increase
As glory wanes. I do repeat it now:
This is not a battlefield for us.

MALATESTI

                           What

Then?

TORELLO

    Let us change our plan. Our forces
Are unevenly matched with the enemy's.
Let us move where we can indeed win.

MALATESTI

Shall we deliver Maclodio to him,
Then, like a gift? The valiant men within
Will not resist more than two days.

TORELLO

                         I know.

But here the stake is neither a stronghold,
Nor a single city: it is the State.

SFORZA

And what is it, a State, if not the cities
That it comprehends? How many cities
Have we already left him? Casal, Bina,
Quinzano.... Pray continue the tally,
If it so pleases you; it grieves me much.
This precious cape that the duke confided
To us, shall we suffer to see it torn,
Piece by piece, as we hold it; shall we suffer
That our message to him will announce
A retreat? The while our foe becomes prouder
And prouder, and boldly insults our delays.

TORELLO

These are marks of his will to engage in battle.

SFORZA

And what more could he wish than chasing us,
As our swords remain in our sheaths?

PERGOLA

What more could he wish? I will tell you: that
We venture our army into a field
Where he has shrewdly secured all the lead.
Let us save the army, for cities are
Easy to recover if you have armies.

FORTEBRACCIO

Which armies? Not those that we instructed
To move the camp when the enemy appears,
To avoid the confrontation, to abandon
Comrades in anguish; rather those such as
We have now in hand, kindled with ire,
Eager to fight. With these we shall redeem
Our losses and win. Why are we waiting?
Why let sharp swords rust?

SFORZA

                         Torello, you fear
Ambushes, and I will tell you, in faith,
What I do fear. These are no longer wars
In which small cohorts would advance alone
With intent gaze, beware of every tree,
Every turn; now an entire army
Will clash with an entire army. And
Such a horde you can but win by fighting,
Not by surrounding; such a mass of men
Sweeps every hurdle that it finds ahead,
As long as it proceeds like to one man.
At all times, no matter where, any place
Is its terrain.

FORTEBRACCIO [*to* PERGOLA *and* TORELLO]
    Are you convinced?

TORELLO

                You will . . .

MALATESTI [*responding to* FORTEBRACCIO]
I am. Each word would be empty by now.
I expect that all of you shall in concord
Lead the troops, more united than you have been
In this debate. Since either choice entails
Great perils, let us select the one that
Has more glory. We shall engage in battle.
I will be at the forefront with my troops;
Sforza will be behind in the vanguard;
Fortebraccio will hold the middle. We'll try
To force and attack the foe's encampment
To break through it and reach Maclodio.
To you, Torello and Pergola, to whom
This day seems most uncertain, I entrust
The mission to save it. You keep the rear,
Following at a distance. Fortune helps
Her valiant men, and we shall trounce the foe;
You will then plunge upon the fugitives.
But if you see us enter into a place
Whence we cannot exit on our own,
You come to lend us help, to sustain friends
In danger. However it may happen,
You shall not see us retreat toward you.

FORTEBRACCIO
Nay, you shall not.

SFORZA

               Nay, you can swear on it.
Heaven be praised, we will combat at last.
Never befell to a captain such a thing,
That I recall: to endure all this debate,
So that he simply might discharge his duty.

PERGOLA

O Carmagnola, you did calculate
That youthful anger would today prevail
Upon the elder's prudence; you were right.

FORTEBRACCIO

Aye, prudence is indeed the elder's virtue,
And it so grows in years till it becomes . . .

PERGOLA

Speak freely, pray.

FORTEBRACCIO

Fear, as you must hear it.

MALATESTI

Fortebraccio!

PERGOLA

You said it. To a soldier
Who had already fought and won oft times
Before you ever saw a flag, you first
Today uttered this . . .

MALATESTI

Carmagnola is
On that far side, there where Maclodio lies.
I warn you all: whoever among us
Might think today to have another foe
Than him, that one would be a traitor.

PERGOLA

I will recant the word I gave beforehand.
I will stand for the battle. It shall end
As I then foresaw, but let no one mind.
It could have been avoided then, but now
I am the first to demand it. I stand
For the battle.

MALATESTI

I do accept your pledge,
But not your omen: may Heaven shift it
Onto the enemy's head.

PERGOLA

Fortebraccio,
You offended me.

MALATESTI

Pray now . . .

FORTEBRACCIO

If you think so,
Let it be so. You will not expect that
Since it displeased you, or any other,
I will retract a word my mouth uttered.

MALATESTI [*hints at departing*]
Whoever remains loyal to Duke Philip
Follow me now.

PERGOLA

I promise that we shall engage in battle
And no one will be missing at the summons.
O Fortebraccio, do not add shame to shame.
I repeat it, you offended me. Listen:
I offer you a way to give me back
My honor, while keeping yours intact.

FORTEBRACCIO

What
Do you ask?

PERGOLA

Your place in battle. You may
Fight anywhere, for all know well that you
Wanted the battle. But I . . . I must perforce
Fight in a place where both my friends and foes

Shall clearly see that I did not . . . , well, you
Understand me.

FORTEBRACCIO

                I will gladly consent.
You shall have that place you covet so.
O brave man, hear me: 'tis sweet to tell you:
I did not, in truth, intend to offend you.
You fear above all else our lord's ruin;
This is what I meant. But you intended
The fear that buds in the heart of those men
Who love their life above honor, the fear
That promptly dies in the heart of the brave
Upon the first peril he faces, never
To rise again. O valiant man . . .

PERGOLA

                      Nothing
Did I mean. You speak as the generous
Man that you are. [*to* MALATESTI] Sir, will you consent that we
Trade places in the forthcoming battle?

MALATESTI

I will, and I am glad to see much wrath
Thrown back at the enemy.

TORELLO[*to* SFORZA]

                   Sir, I sided
With Pergola beforehand, therefore
It will not seem unjust to you that I . . .

SFORZA

I understand you. Be with Pergola
In the army's vanguard. Either first or last,
We shall all combat, little matters where.

MALATESTI

Let us pause no more. Godspeed to the brave.
[*exeunt*]

Scene IV

[*Venetian camp*, THE COUNT'S *tent;* THE COUNT, *then a* SOLDIER]

SOLDIER
> My Lord, the enemy's troops are astir.
> The vanguard is on the embankment, advancing.

THE COUNT
> Where are the officers?

SOLDIER
> All here, outside
> Your tent, awaiting your word.

THE COUNT
> Let them in.
> [*exit the* SOLDIER]
> Here comes at last the hour I so craved.
> Only now can I recollect with joy
> The day he denied me a hearing, when
> In vain I begged, for every access was barred.
> Amidst general mockery I departed,
> For an unknown destination. I said:
> "You shall repent, you shall see me again,
> At the head of troops fighting against you,
> Ungrateful one!" When I uttered these words,
> It seemed but a dream, engendered by anger.
> But now 'tis true: I face him, here we are,
> My heart is leaping, I sense the battle
> Coming, and if . . . but no, victory is mine.

Scene V

[*enter* GONZAGA, ORSINI, TOLENTINO, *and other* OFFICERS]

THE COUNT
> Comrades, you heard the good news: the enemy
> Did what I wanted, so you will as well.

The sun that rises now, to each of us
Shall bring the fairest day, I swear on it.
No one among you will fight this battle
To acquire renown, I know. But by sunset
Our names will be more glorious, and the word
Most welcome to our ears will be Maclodio.
—Orsini, are your men ready?

ORSINI

They are.

THE COUNT

You will rush to the ambushes on the right
Of the embankment; rejoin those who are there
And assume their command. You do the same
On the left, Tolentino. Do not move
From those positions till the clash begins.
Then close in the enemy from behind.
You both listen: if they perceive the ambushes
And try retreating, assault them at once,
As soon as they turn their face from you, and
I shall promptly join you. Whether they flee
Or provoke us, they must be won today.

ORSINI

They shall be.
[*exits*]

TOLENTINO

We shall obey you unfailingly.
[*exit*]

THE COUNT [*to the others*]

Gonzaga, you shall be at my own side;
I shall assign the places on the field
To all the others. Let us go, comrades.
Let us resist to the first fierce assault,
The rest is certain.

CHORUS

On the right, sudden sound of shrill trumpets;
From the left quickly a flourish replies.
From both sides the earth rumbles with footsteps
Of the infantry and cavalry charging.
Here emerges in view one ensign;
There another advances unfolded;
Yond appears a whole cohort arrayed,
And another against it attacks.

The terrain in the middle is swallowed,
And already the swords strike on swords;
On both sides chests are wounded and bleed,
And the battle's vehemence redoubles.
Who are they? To this beautiful country
Who is the stranger that came to bring war;
Who is the native that swore to defend
His own land from the assault, or to die?

All these fighters belong to one land,
They all speak the same language, and "brothers"
Is the name that the foreigner gives them;
The same traits appear on all faces,
The same land has nurtured them all,
This land that their blood now submerges,
And that nature from others divided
By the girth of the seas and the Alps.

Who was first among them to unsheathe
The sacrilegious sword to kill brothers?
For what blameworthy cause did they start
Such a blameworthy war, such a terror?
No one knows. Without ire they came here
To give death or receive it: they sold
Their young vigor to a captain who is paid,
And for him they now fight without question.

Dire event! Do these men not have wives,
Sisters, mothers, these foolish combatants?

All the women should come to the field,
Put an end to such infamous battle.
And the old men, whose wise minds contemplate
The chaste thoughts of the grave, should address
This murderous throng and placate them
By the force of their prudent, sage words.

Like the peasant, who sits on the threshold
Of his tranquil abode and points surely
To the rain cloud that threatens to come
And destroy his unharvested crop,
So by watching the armies approaching
Every man can predict by the thousands
All the victims this battle will cause,
Tell the pity of cities laid waste.

You can see there: some children are learning
From the mouth of their mothers the nicknames
To distinguish in mockery people
Whom one day they shall combat and slaughter.
There you see women pompously wearing
In the mournful, dim light of death vigils
Golden medals, and belts that their husbands
Or their lovers brought back as their booty.

What a dire, most dire event!
All the land is now covered with corpses;
The vast plain is now dripping with blood;
The cry roars and the furor redoubles,
But the ranks are depleting, disbanded,
One array is now yielding, is broken.
Lust for life rises up in the hearts
Of the people who know they will lose.

Like the wheat when it's tossed in the air
By the winnowing fan all around,
So the vanquished are scattered all over;
They are dispersed on the ample terrain.
But then suddenly terrible bands

On the path are confronting the fugitives;
Others hear, just behind their own shoulders,
A steed galloping in dreadful pursuit.

At the foot of their foes they drop trembling
And their weapons surrender; they are captives.
And the clamor of those who have won
Suffocates the laments of the dying.
On his horse jumps the herald; he takes
A parchment, secures it, and goes.
Whipping, spurring, he devours the way
Every town quickly awakes at his passage.

And you all, from the houses, the fields,
Why now rush to the well-trodden highway?
Every man asks his neighbor with fervor:
"What glad news did the herald bring to us?"
You all know, wretched people, the place
Whence he comes, and you hope that he will
Announce joy.... "Brothers murdered their brothers,
This the horrid announcement I bring."

All around I now hear festive cries,
They are adorning the church, and they sing,
And there rise from those murderous hearts
Hymns and thanks that offend God in Heaven.
From beyond the tall crown of the Alps
Most intently the stranger is looking,
Sees the strongest now biting the dust,
Counts the dead with most cruel content.

Make haste, O, be ready in the ranks,
Interrupt merry games and the triumphs,
And return to your banners of war;
For the stranger is coming, he is here,
Is victorious! Weak and scant are your troops?
That is why he is coming to challenge,
And he is waiting for you on those fields
Where the brothers have murdered their brothers.

Fated land, that appeared all too narrow
To your children and never could nourish
Your issue in peace, welcome the strangers.
This ordeal is beginning for you:
Here an enemy comes that you never
Offended; he sits down at your table.
[*swears; partitions the spoils of the foolish*]
All your kings he despoils of the sword.

No less foolish the stranger! Was a people
Ever saved by its murders, its insults?
To the vanquished no troubles befall,
While the joy of the impious turns sour.
Oftentimes God's vengeance is silent,
Does not strike man as proudly he treads on
His ephemeral way, but she marks him:
When he gives his last breath, then she appears.

We are all made in the image of One,
We are all children of a sole Redemption,
And no matter in what epoch, in what region,
We all pass through this ether of life,
We are brothers, we are tied by one pact.
Cursed be those who infringe such a pact,
Those who rise by trampling the weak,
Those who sadden an immortal spirit.

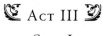 ## Act III

Scene I

[THE COUNT *and the* FIRST COMMISSIONER]

THE COUNT
  Are you satisfied?

FIRST COMMISSIONER
                    To hear the triumph
  Of the fatherland, to see it, to be

The first to hail victory, which now crowns
Our State, to announce the good tidings;
And to witness the flight of our foes
While we have yet their threats in our ear;
To see the glory of the fatherland
Come out of danger brighter than ever,
Like to a sun that from behind the clouds
Returns to shine more freely, more serene;
Is this a joy, I ask, that words can tell?
You can see it: be it a measure of
Our gratefulness. Too laggard seem to us
These thanks that we now give you on behalf
Of others, this message from the senate
About their gladness, about your reward,
Which shall be as great as your merit is.

THE COUNT

I hold already my reward. Venice
Is saved; I thus fulfilled in part my promise;
I revived memories about myself,
Things people had forgotten. I have won.

FIRST COMMISSIONER

Now is the time when one wants to secure
The fruit of victory.

THE COUNT

'Twill be my care.

FIRST COMMISSIONER

Now that your sword has cleared the way, we expect
That you shall go with no hesitation forward,
Nor shall we rest except when we have come
To the enemy's throne.

THE COUNT

All in due time.

FIRST COMMISSIONER
What do you mean by this? Do you not have
A mind to chase the fugitives?

THE COUNT
                                    Not now.

FIRST COMMISSIONER
But the senate expects this.... So certain
Were we of your zeal to complete the conquest,
Which you began with such a glorious triumph,
That we reported ...

THE COUNT
                                    You were too hasty.

FIRST COMMISSIONER
When they learn that we are still stationed here,
What shall they say?

THE COUNT
                              That they trust in the one
Who already gave them one great victory.

FIRST COMMISSIONER
But what is your scheme?

THE COUNT
                                    I would have told you
More gladly but a few moments ago.
But 'tis meet that I tell you. I do not
Want to leave this territory until
I conquer the citadels around us.
I must deal with but one enemy, and
That one must be in front of me.

FIRST COMMISSIONER
                                    Why, then,
Our words ...

THE COUNT

          . . . have been more daring than my sword,
More swift than my horses . . . and I . . . this is
The first time that someone hastens me so.

FIRST COMMISSIONER

Have you given enough thought to this scheme?

THE COUNT

What? Is this perchance the first victory
I have achieved? You think this new joy baffles
So my heart that I can't reason clearly
On what remains to be done?

Scene II

[*enter* SECOND COMMISSIONER]

SECOND COMMISSIONER

          General,
If you don't intervene immediately,
A bold act of depravity will make
Utterly vain our victory. Already
It did so, in part.

THE COUNT

          How?

SECOND COMMISSIONER

          The prisoners
Are swarming out of the camp in large numbers,
Officers and soldiers are now vying
To set them free. Nothing but your order
Can stop them.

THE COUNT

          An order of mine, you say?

SECOND COMMISSIONER
> Would you refuse to give it?

THE COUNT
>   You know that
> This is an ancient custom of the warriors.
> 'Tis sweet to pardon after victory!
> And wrath is changed to friendship in those hearts
> That beat under the armor. Do not spoil,
> I beg you, such a noble gift to those
> Who for you endangered their lives, and are
> Generous now, for they were brave before.

SECOND COMMISSIONER
> Let the one who for himself combats be
> As lavish as he likes, sir. But these soldiers
> —and I think they should hold it an honor—
> Receive our pay, and prisoners are ours.

THE COUNT
> You may yet believe so, but those who saw
> The adversary in the face, who did receive
> His blows upon their flesh, who with an effort
> Did lay their bloodied hands on him, they
> Will not think so as easily as you do.

FIRST COMMISSIONER
> Is this perchance a joust for your own merriment?
> And is Venice not winning to preserve
> What is conquered? Victory shall be then
> But a vain outcome?

THE COUNT
>   Again I hear
> These words: they come to harass me
> Like an annoying insect that returns
> To buzz around my visage many times.
> Victory is vain? A field covered with corpses,

The living frightened and disbanded: nothing
Remains of the most mighty army, with which,
If it were whole yet, and in my possession,
I would now rush to conquer Italy.
The foe's scheme has been disrupted, even
The thought of an attack has been dispelled;
Barely have the four captains escaped
Capture. They were happy to flee, these who,
Till yesterday, were dreaded opponents,
But to resist to whom 'was a great merit.
Their vast renown is thus by half diminished,
Courage redoubled in our soldiers,
While it waned in theirs. We can control now
The outcome of the war, ours are the cities
They abandoned . . . and you call this nothing?
Do you think that those captives will go
To the duke, that they love him, they care
More for him than for you? They fought for him?
They fought because the man behind a banner
Heeds an imperious voice within his heart
That says: fight, and win. They lost, they return
To freedom and will sell themselves—for such
Is the soldier, these days—to the first buyer.
If you can buy them, they will be yours, too.

FIRST COMMISSIONER

We thought we bought them long ago already,
When we did pay the one who would fight them.

SECOND COMMISSIONER

Venice confides in you, in you she sees
A son, expecting that you do all things
That will bring to her profit and glory.

THE COUNT

All things within my power . . .

SECOND COMMISSIONER
                                    What is out
Of your power in such business?

THE COUNT
                                         Just this
That you ask of me: 'tis an old custom
I will not breach, a rule dear to the soldiers.

SECOND COMMISSIONER
You, whom no one dares to confront, whom all
Promptly follow, so that one cannot tell
If they are moved by love or rather fear,
You cannot form a law for such a business
And then enforce it?

THE COUNT
                        I said awhile that
I cannot, but now I shall say better:
I will not. Enough with words. When I can
Satisfy my friends' righteous requests,
I do it at once, and gladly as well,
But I deny the unjust ones openly.
Soldiers, oh!

SECOND COMMISSIONER
            What do you intend to do?

THE COUNT
You shall see. [*to a* SOLDIER *who enters*] How many captives are
    still
In the camp?

SOLDIER
            Four hundred, I believe, sir.

THE COUNT
Summon the most distinguished, the first whom
You can find, send them here presently. [*exit* SOLDIER] Aye,

I could for sure: if I gave such an order,
You would not hear replies among my men.
But could I thus betray my sons, my mates
In perils and in joys, those who trust me,
Who think they follow a leader willing to
Defend the honor and the privilege
Of the armed men. Their lot would be made
More servile than it is, more reviled.
Sirs, I am trustful and so are my soldiers.
But if you now demand from me a thing
That will estrange my mates' love toward me
If you will isolate me from them and
Reduce me in such a state that I no more
Enjoy their love and friendship, so that I
Depend but on yours—I say this almost
Against my will—, you do force me to doubt . . .

SECOND COMMISSIONER

How now, sir, what daring words are these!

Scene III

[*enter* PRISONERS, *among whom is* PERGOLA'S SON]

THE COUNT

You who were brave for nothing, wretched men!
Will fortune be most cruel but with you,
The only ones bound to captivity?

A PRISONER

Such was not our expectation, Sir,
When we were summoned into your presence.
We thought to hear at last the messenger
Of our freedom. All those who fell captive
To the other captains under your command
Had already recovered their freedom . . .

THE COUNT

And you, whose prisoners are you?

THE PRISONER

                                          We were
The very last to surrender our arms.
All were in flight or prisoners erstwhile,
But the day's outcome did remain for us
Suspended. Then you beckoned your cohort
To encircle us—we were not vanquished, but
What was left of the vanquished.

THE COUNT

                                        So you are
Those ones! I am most glad to see you again,
And I can testify that you fought bravely.
If so much valor had not been betrayed
And you had had a chief equal to you,
It would not have been pleasant to combat
Against you.

THE PRISONER

                            Will it be our misfortune
Not to have surrendered but to you, sir?
And those, conversely, who were vanquished by
A less glorious one will have been treated
More liberally? In vain did we beseech
Your officers to set us free: no one
Dares decide our lot without your leave,
But every one promised we would have it.
O, if only you could speak to the count,
They said, he would not further aggravate
The lot of the defeated, he will not
Neglect an ancient courtesy of war,
For his deeds are such as he seems the first
Who invented it.

THE COUNT [*to* THE COMMISSIONERS]
                          O sirs, you heard these men.
What can you say, what would you do in my place?
[*to* THE PRISONERS] Heaven forbid that anyone may think

More highly of me than my own self. —Friends,
You are unbound, farewell, follow your fortune,
And if it brings you again behind the banner
Of a foe of mine, we will meet again . . .
[*exeunt* PRISONERS *with gestures and sounds of joy;* THE COUNT
 gazes at PERGOLA'S SON *and stops him*]
Young man, you belong not to the populace;
Your attire and, even more, your visage
Tell me this. Why then do you remain mixed
With the rest, silent?

PERGOLA'S SON

      O captain, which words
Can a defeated man utter?

THE COUNT

       You bear
Your present lot in such a way that shows
How you are worthy of a better one.

PERGOLA'S SON

I bear a name whose worth cannot be increased,
A name that does impose upon its bearer
A great duty. Pergola is my name.

THE COUNT

Are you the son of that most valiant man?

PERGOLA'S SON

I am.

THE COUNT

    Then come and embrace the old friend
Of your father. I was as young as you
When I first met him. You remind me of
The happy days, the days of hope. And you,
Lift up your heart. Fortune did grant to me
Happy beginnings, but for the brave ones

She keeps in store her promises, and sooner
Or later she fulfills them. Greet for me
Your father, young man, and tell him that,
Without asking, I knew most certainly
That he cast not his vote for this battle.

PERGOLA'S SON
Certainly not, but his words were wasted.

THE COUNT
Do not grieve. Upon the general falls
The shame of the defeat. 'Tis good start
To fight valiantly in one's assigned place.
I want to show you to the officers
And give you back your sword, come! [*to* THE
    COMMISSIONERS] Farewell, sirs.
I shall never have mercy on your foes
But until after I have vanquished them.
[*exeunt* THE COUNT *and* PERGOLA'S SON]

Scene IV

[*after some time of silence*]

SECOND COMMISSIONER
Will you still say that I am too eager
To foretell dangers? That it is the words
Of his opponents, my ancient suspicions,
Perchance my hatred, that make me unjust
Against this man? That he is haughty, fiery,
And yet loyal? That one should not expect
From him homage, rather services?
That, in case we dictate our strong will
To him, it is a dream to doubt that he
Refuse to carry it out?

FIRST COMMISSIONER
                    'Tis even worse.
I told him about the senate's desire

That the defeated foe be further chased,
And he refused.

SECOND COMMISSIONER
>   What motives did he give?

FIRST COMMISSIONER
> He wants first to secure citadels,
> He fears . . .

SECOND COMMISSIONER
>   All of a sudden, he became
> Most cautious, and after a victory.

FIRST COMMISSIONER
> He could barely bring himself to utter
> His reply, as if it were the answer
> To a harassing man seeking to know
> A secret that does not affect his life.

SECOND COMMISSIONER
> Did he unveil his secret when he spoke,
> After all? The motive that he gave you
> To satisfy you, does it seem to you
> His real and sole motive, the true one?

FIRST COMMISSIONER
> I do not know, because I had time but
> For few thoughts: that I had before me
> A reckless fellow, that I was hearing
> Words ever unheard by a peer of ours.

SECOND COMMISSIONER
> Perchance he wants to inflict more terror than
> Damage to his old master, the first from
> Whose hand he obtained the highest honors,
> To the towering creature of his sword.
> To demonstrate the importance of his arms,

The perils that they pose being hostile,
To prove such a powerful enemy
To him, that he will want to be his friend
Once more. The count perchance cannot distract
His mind from the throne that he lifted
From the dust. He was second in command
But to one man, sitting upon that throne.
The duke may seem to him a sweeter master,
For he's eager to conquer but unable
To bear the armor's weight and needs therefore
A hand as well as counsels for his wars.
The master will thus ask for counsels to
The very man to whom he then will order
The same things that those counsels inspired.
One master must appear better than many,
Who are circumspect, who seek but to preserve
Their lands rather than acquiring new ones,
And willing above all to command truly.

FIRST COMMISSIONER

I now believe him capable of all.

SECOND COMMISSIONER

Let us keep our suspicion secret.
His actions as well as our conduct
Shall in short prove if it is true, or else
Shall lead us to some other conclusions.
'Tis certain that he is hatching some plot.
His very speech reveals in him the man
Who, being so sure of his plot's good outcome,
Unwittingly speaks boldly about it.
The man who insults his master to his face
Already has in his heart another master,
Or thinks that he himself can become master.
His ties with the duke are not yet severed;
He is not stranger to the house from whom
He had a wife. Too dear must be the knot

That bound one day his life to such a bride,
And his daughter, forever present in his thoughts,
Is she not perhaps a living vessel
Where his blood and the Viscontis' mingle?

FIRST COMMISSIONER

The manner of his speech, the rapid passage
From wrath to indifference; the placid pride
With which he disobeyed! Are we in the camp
Of Venice, are we her envoys? And were
Those ones the vanquished we made prisoners?
Their gaze was more self-confident than ours,
We, who are the witness to his might,
To the high esteem in which he holds us,
To our conquests, scattered to the winds
To these joys, these graces, these embraces!
No, this cannot last!—What is your idea?

SECOND COMMISSIONER

There is no doubt. To be patient, to feign,
To complain of an offense that he knows
We cannot forget, meanwhile paving him
The way to mend it of his own making,
To thank him for it, to ask of him but
What we are sure to obtain, to oppose him only
On occasions, to make the rest appear,
On our part, true acquiescence.
We shall not force him to confess; instead
We shall watch and then write to the Ten Sages
About all this and await their orders.

FIRST COMMISSIONER

How can we live like this in the meantime?
What would all say in Venice about us,
Who were given in trust such a high mission,
Amidst the universal envy, and now,
What has it become?

SECOND COMMISSIONER

'Tis always glorious
The occupation that can be of service
To the fatherland, to her own intents.
The count elicits reverence from all;
Soldiers and officers, all admire him,
There's not a soul that envies him.
To obey him is a mark of high honor;
The sole contest among his men consists
In vying to be his lieutenant. Therefore,
If such an honored voice will ever say
That word that lingers in each heart—revolt,
How pithy would that exhortation be,
After today's pronouncements! It would spell
For us dire events. He indeed topples
All thoughts in all minds, of his men as well
As of his enemies.

FIRST COMMISSIONER

But shall our scheme
Be timely? He may yet be suspicious.

SECOND COMMISSIONER

Yes, we still have time. These men of arms are
Lavish with their lives, do not fear danger,
Nay, they love it, and in their deeds look but
For hope. If they were not more than men
On the battlefield, yet children in all the rest,
If they did not as lightly lay aside
Suspicions as they form them, if flattering
Words, friendly gestures were not enough
To turn them into things easy to use
By those who know how to handle them,
Where would we be? Would we be the masters,
Would the sword still obey our commands?

FIRST COMMISSIONER

It is resolved. Whether it will succeed
Or fail, this is the sole course to pursue.

🜲 ACT IV 🜲

Scene I

[the hall of the Council of the Ten's chiefs, in Venice; MARK *and* MARINO*]*

MARK

> I am come, obedient to the summons
> Of the chiefs of the Ten Sages' Council.

MARINO

> I speak on their behalf. A most grave mission
> Will be entrusted to you, away from Venice.
> Your conscience will suggest to you how secret
> One should keep this matter.

MARK

> My conscience says
> The fatherland does well to entrust me
> Such a mission, if not for my merits
> And my wit, then surely for my loyalty
> And my heart.

MARINO

> Fatherland! 'Tis a sweet name
> For those who love her above all else and
> Devote to her their life. Yet 'tis a name
> That should be uttered not without trembling
> By those who do remain friends with her foes.

MARK

> And I, pray . . .

MARINO

> For whom did you speak today
> In the senate? For the fatherland?
> For her you expressed your fears, your deep concerns,
> Which made your plea so warm? Whose endangerment?
> Whom did you defend with your lonely stance?

MARK

I know the power before whom I stand.
My life is in your hand but not my will:
The judge of it can only be my heart.
My will's guilt, therefore, can only be
To have lied before such an authority,
In which case, I shall respond for it.

MARINO

All that can endanger the fatherland,
Or hinder her high aims, or raise suspicions,
We firmly hold in our hand; and why
This is your place also at this hour
You shall hear shortly, if you do not know,
If the show of ignorance best suits you.
It is about today we want to speak,
And examine, of your entire life,
But one day.

MARK

Why, what else can be ascribed
To me? I cannot fear for anything,
My conduct . . .

MARINO

. . . is better known to us than
To yourself. Time has perchance erased much
From your memory, but our book leaves
Nothing to oblivion.

MARK

I can account
For each thing.

MARINO

You shall give explanation
But when 'tis requested from you, no more.
—When the senate bestowed on Carmagnola

The supreme command, many did not trust
His faith, yet to others it seemed secure,
And it might well have seemed such at that time.
But now he frees the captives and openly
Insults our envoys, our own peers.
He won, yet dissipates the victory
In calculated idleness. By now
The veil that obfuscated every eye
Has fallen. Confiding in his succor,
The Trevisan upstream did thrust his ships
On the Po River, to engage the enemy.
Outnumbered by the foe, he requested
Help from Carmagnola, who refused it.
The senate is in anguish, yet a few
Still dare speak in his defense. Cremona
Would have been easily seized if only
He had rushed there: he refused. The senate
Heard this news today. But one defender
Is left to the count, one yet most ardent,
Who deems the man devoid of guilt and worthy,
Not of reproach, but of praises; mishaps
Are only bad fortune's fate, or ours.
It is not justice that accuses him,
It is but private hatred, but base pride
Of unforgiving souls who are envious of
The magnanimous man. He remains silent,
And lets his actions scream: I am greater
Than you all—accents unheard by the fathers,
Who yet heard them today, in their senate.
Mutely they turned around to see the speaker,
Whether it was a stranger or a foe,
Daring to take a senatorial seat.
The count is clearly shown to be a traitor,
And every means by which he can attack
Must be removed from him. But his cunning
And his audacity are so great that
He has acquired a most dreadful power
Over his masters; he has become strong

With the very strength we entrusted him.
He owns the soldiers' hearts, so our arms,
When he wants, shall be his, to fight against
Ourselves, and he will. It is a folly
To idly await his next move. All agreed
That he must be arrested presently.
'Twould be most dangerous to attempt this deed
In an overt manner. Shall we stand for this?
Shall we permit him to remain unpunished
For the most serious of all his offenses?
Justice has but one method to secure him,
The art of deceiving the deceiver:
He forced us to tread such a way, and so
We will. This is the deliberation.
What was the stance that the man's friend took?
You do not recall? I shall tell you, since
Your heart was much less tranquil than the eye
That followed you. You lost every restraint;
You passed that mark which a remnant of prudence
Had until then prescribed to your own zeal.
Forgetful of your promise to yourself,
You then let the less watchful senators
See your entire self, without concealment.
They deemed utterly novel what for many,
The most attentive, was already known.
Then every man did think that in the senate
There is no place for such a senator,
That the secret of the State must be saved.

MARK

Sir, all is licit to you. Before you
I do not know any longer who I am.
Yet I do not forget that I am noble.
Can I omit to mention the insult
Made to myself by such a doubt? I am
One of you; the cause of the State is also
My cause; the secrets of the State import
· To me no less than to others.

MARINO

> You wish
> Indeed to know who you are in this place?
> You are a man that the State fears and deems
> A hurdle for the attainment of its aims.
> Pray, show us that you are not such—'tis a great
> Mark of clemency that you are given
> This occasion to prove yourself.

MARK

> I am
> The count's friend. This is the accusation.
> I will not deny this, I am his friend.
> And I thank Heaven that grants me the strength
> To confess it in this hour. But if
> He is a foe of the fatherland, and
> This is to me proven, he is my foe.
> What is imputed to him? That he freed
> Captives? But did not the victorious soldier
> Deliver them? The general was begged
> In vain to restrain this act, he willed not.
> Yet perchance he could not. —But he himself
> Delivered them. Yet was he not constrained
> To follow an ancient use of war? The senate
> Did acknowledge such a custom and lavished
> On him many tributes. —He denied
> Succor to the Trevisan. Was it not
> More dangerous to grant it? That deed was
> Undertaken unbeknownst to the count;
> His help was not requested in due time.
> The sentence that exiled the Trevisan
> To that man alone ascribed the blame.
> And Cremona? Who thought of seizing it,
> Who gave the order to attempt the conquest?
> The count. But he and his meager forces
> Were met by the rabble in revolt, so
> They were unable to withstand the brunt
> Of such unexpected attack. The count

Returned to the camp without losses.
The judgment of the general was against
Venturing such uncalculated risk.
He forsook the conquest and yes, it is
A failed attempt among the many deeds
That were achieved. Does this prove his betrayal?
You say his speech has been for a long time
Brimming with pride and insolence, and that
Our protracted patience has tainted
Our honor. Shall a ruse reclaim it?
Since such a knot, which was so dear once,
Can no longer tie Venice and the count,
Who bars us from dissolving it? A friendship
That began so nobly should also end
On the same note of nobility. How now?
Is even this perceived as a danger?
We fear the count's great genius, his renown,
His soldiers' love for him. If we find fault
With thorough explanations of the truth,
If 'tis not licit to object to terror
By advocating the count's loyalty,
May our sense of honor chase away
That terror, let us have of ourselves
A higher concept, let us not think that
Venice might have come to such a point where
One man's actions can imperil her.
Let us relinquish such cares to tyrants:
They must dread military valor, for
The wand is in one hand, and 'tis enough
That just one warrior seize it who will say:
"More worthy am I to hold it," and who will
Persuade a few companions to such deed.
But what could the count ever attempt?
Some say he could return to the ancient master,
Lead the troops with him in his desertion.
But how can he return to a man well known
To never forgive insults or great service,

To the man whose throne he erected, then shook,
Who disliked the count while he was his general.
How can the duke befriend him again now
That he defeated him! How can the count
Approach again that hand that paid a murderer
To have him killed in this very haven?
Only hatred can lead us to believe this.
Whatever be the reason why I am
In front of this most dreaded council now,
It will be a motive of honor for me
If I can voice the truth once again.
I harbor in my heart the flattering thought
That I shall not have spoken in vain. Yes,
Only blind hatred could achieve this goal,
That such a suspicion might be proposed,
And tolerated on the senate's floor.
The count has many enemies, and I
Do not inquire why they are: they are.
When I unveiled private abhorrence hidden
Behind the shadow of public enmity,
When I asked that the welfare of the State
Should be pursued as well as justice,
I was not speaking as the count's best friend,
But as a loyal patrician. Nonetheless,
I do not justify my hasty speech:
When I heard the proposal that the count
Be recalled in Venice under pretense
Of consultations, and that more honors
Than ever be paid to him, to entice him
Into a snare . . . then, I do not deny . . .

MARINO

You thought but of your friend.

MARK

                                                  Aye, in that moment.
I will not feign: I did feel my soul's powers

Rebel against a scheme . . . which was accepted!
And yet I did have more than one thought, then:
The honor of the fatherland, which I
Saw diminished; the cry of foes as well
As of posterity; the sense of horror
That betrayal must provoke in a man
Who can prevent it or be part of it.
And if the pity for a valiant soul
Did mingle with so many affections,
How could I hush it? I rest accused
Of having deemed most useful what honors
Our fatherland. Venice can still be saved
Without becoming . . .

MARINO

                  No more. If I listened
So far it was because the council's chiefs
Wanted to know you fully, to await you
At your second thoughts, to see if riper
Meditations could lead your mind to wisdom
And civic sense. But since their hopes were vain
Do you think that I will engage with you
In the defense of a senate's decree?
Your lot is at stake here, and you must care
For yourself, not for the fatherland.
Her fate is safely held in strong, pure hands,
And to her heart it is indeed the same
Whether you will approve or not; her will
Must be fulfilled, and she will vanquish
Even the thought of an impediment.
We will watch and ensure this end is met.
Thus I demand from you but one answer:
The senate has decided this man's lot
And will proceed to see that it be such
As was determined. What are your thoughts?

MARK

How now, sir, what an inquiry!

MARINO

You know
What the senate will do, and in your heart
You wish that it shall not be accomplished.
Is it not so?

MARK

What matters what I wish
To the State? From facts it knows that the guide
Of my actions will be not my wish, rather
My duty.

MARINO

What pledge do we have from you
That you will do as you say? In this moment,
On behalf of the Court, I ask you a pledge.
The Court shall deem you a traitor if you refuse.
And you know what is in store for traitors.

MARK

I . . . What do you ask of me?

MARINO

Admit that
Your daring heart made you prefer one time
A stranger to your fatherland. She is
Reluctant and tardy to lay her hand
Over her sons; she consents to lose some
Just when they can no longer be redeemed.
She is willing to forgive every error
In you and paves your way to repentance.

MARK

Repentance? What is the way?

MARINO

The Muslim
Has a scheme to assault Thessalonica,

And there you are dispatched. You shall know shortly
What your office shall be. The ship is ready,
Today you shall depart.

MARK

                              I will obey.

MARINO

  Another pledge of your good faith is needed.
  You must now swear on what you hold most sacred
  That nothing of today's deliberations
  Shall be manifested by you in words
  Or gestures. This is the oath. [*produces a sheet*] You must sign.

MARK

  How now, sir, is it not enough . . . ?

MARINO

                              Be acquainted
  With what follows: The messenger who must
  Recall the count is on his way already.
  If he will obey promptly and come here,
  He shall find justice, perchance clemency.
  But if he balks or tarries or displays
  Any suspicions—this is highly secret,
  Keep it to yourself—it is so ordained
  That he be killed at once. The traitor
  Who dares give him a hint, that shall kill him
  And shall himself be lost. I will not hear
  Your voice any more. Sign, or else . . .

MARK

                              I sign.

MARINO

  All is consigned to oblivion. Your loyalty
  Has accomplished much, and duty prevailed.
  Prudence will now finish the deed. This virtue

You cannot lack, if you keep in mind that
Two lives are now committed to your hand.
[*exit*]

MARK

It is decided thus: I am a coward!
My ordeal came and what did I do?
Before this day I did not know myself.
O what a secret did I learn today!
My friend I could abandon in the snare!
I see an assassin from behind attacking,
I see the dagger lowered on his back,
Yet I cry not: "Beware!" and I could have,
I did once.... No longer can I save him.
Heaven I called as witness to my oath
Of shameful cowardice. I undersigned
His death sentence; my hand is now besmeared
with his own blood. What did I do? Alas,
I let myself feel fear for my own life.
Sometimes one cannot save one's life without
Committing some crime. Knew I not this? Why
Did I swear? For whom did I tremble then?
For myself? For this dishonored head?
Or for my friend? Far from thwarting it,
My refusal would have sped the blow home.
—Almighty God, who can discern all things,
Reveal my heart to me, that I may see
In what abyss I fell, what I have been,
More of a fool, a coward, or ill-starred—
O Carmagnola, you shall come indeed!
Most certainly he will, even if he
Might harbor some suspicions of these foxes,
He shall think that Mark sits in the senate,
That the invitation comes from me as well.
He shall then chase away all his doubts and
Regret of having ever harbored them.
I am the one who sends him to his ruin.
Perhaps ... that knave did mention clemency.

Yet can the mighty grant some clemency
To the man they ambushed, the man they indict,
The man they want to find guilty? Clemency
For an innocent! O, I am the coward
Who wished to believe it. He mentioned it
On purpose, for he knew that fear would not
Be enough to corrupt me, the evil fear
That he slowly distilled upon my soul.
He saw that I required a noble pretext,
And he gave me one. Shrewd people, traitors!
How they artfully arranged this performance!
One had the role of smiling; the other had
A dagger; this one threatened . . . and myself?
My part was to perform deceit and weakness.
And I did take the part! I despised them,
And now I am baser than they are. For
They are not his friends. I wished his friendship;
I should not have sought it. I was conquered
By his noble nature, by his great renown.
Why did I not think first of what a burden
Is a friendship with a man who towers
Over all? Why did I not let him run
Alone his splendid path, if I could not
Follow in his footsteps? My hand I gave
To him and courteously he took it.
Now while he's sleeping and the foe attacks,
I take my hand away: he awakes abruptly,
Looks for me, and I am not there, I fled.
He shall despise me, and die. I cannot
Bear such a thought. O, What have I done?
Nay, what I did is nothing so far.
I undersigned a paper, nothing more.
If such an oath was a crime, it shall be
Virtuous to breach it. I am on the verge
Of the precipice still, I can see this.
I can recede, can I find some means? . . . Yet
If I kill him? Perchance 'twas a pretense
To frighten me. And what if he meant it?

O impious men, O what a loathsome snare
You wove for me. I have no noble choice.
'Twill be a sin whichever way I choose.
Atrocious doubt! —Yet I must thank them all;
They chose my destiny, they thrust me
Along a way, and I shall run it all.
That I myself did not choose such a way
Must be all my solace. I nothing choose;
All I do is someone else's will.
—City, where I was born, farewell forever,
I hope to die away from you, before
I learn anything new about your fate.
'Tis Heaven's mercy that dispatches me
Among perils. I will not die for you.
What do I care that you be grand and glorious?
I too had too grand treasures, my virtue
And a friend—you did deprive me of both.
[*exit*]

Scene III

[THE COUNT'*s tent;* THE COUNT *and* GONZAGA]

THE COUNT
What is it that you gathered at last?

GONZAGA
                                    I spoke,
As you asked me, with the commissioners.
To them I demonstrated that the blame
For the shameful defeat of those ships lies
With the inept captain and his faulty art;
And that his enterprise was doomed because
He undertook it without you; that he
Requested your succor too late, when you
Could not undo your mission to go serve
Another enterprise; that Venice's arms
Would at all times be led by you to triumph

If the war were entirely committed
To the wisdom and will of one sole captain.

THE COUNT

What did they say?

GONZAGA

They seemed persuaded by
The things I said. At first they replied that
They did not wish to conceal how bitter
Was the thought of those ravaged ships and of
The failure in Cremona, but that they
Were happy to learn 'twas not your fault, yet,
No matter whose fault it was, 'tis from you
That they expect repair.

THE COUNT

You see, Gonzaga,
To listen to the popular advice,
These men of State should be carefully treated,
With utmost reverence and with practiced art.
Yet I have been with them the same as usual.
When I refused their most unjust requests,
I then made them descend from the high seat
Where sits the one who is used but to the sight
Of slavish men. I then showed them the marks
That those who are my masters should not pass.
And they did not exceed those limits since,
They have been wise and courteous with me always.

GONZAGA

Yet I would not advise to keep such course
To any living soul. You have been wooed,
For a long time, by fortune and by glory.
You are useful, indeed indispensable,
And dear to them, even dreadful perchance.
And therefore you won the confrontation,
If one can say that it is over yet.

THE COUNT
 What are your doubts?

GONZAGA
                     What are your certainties?
 Sweet visages I see, I hear sweet words,
 The marks of love. But are there other marks
 For frightened hate?

THE COUNT
                     Nay, I do not fear this.
 They are well versed in the art of ruling
 And know 'tis better not to ask untimely
 The lesser thing from him who can produce
 A greater one if he is granted time.
 Believe me, I have observed them closely:
 Their somber art, their twisted snares of lies,
 Their shows of silence, feigning, calculation,
 For which the world extols and condemns them,
 —All this is less than it seems to the world.

GONZAGA
 Unless such was a token of their feigning,
 To seem artless to you.

THE COUNT
                     Nay, you still look
 At them through the world's eyes. When you will look
 With your own eye, your mind shall change.
 There are many a good and sincere man,
 And there are some who do possess within
 A lofty soul, never tainted by thoughts
 Less than kind, a sweet soul, and proud, which
 You cannot read unless you are yourself
 Full of love, awe, desire to be their peers.
 Pray do not fear; they're not displeased with me,
 Or else I would soon know.

GONZAGA

Heaven forbid
That you be deceived.

THE COUNT

Another matter
Vexes me. I am tired of a war
That I cannot conduct the way I wish.
—When I was but a simple soldier, hidden
And lost among the thousands, when I sensed
That the low rank was not the place God meant
For me, when I breathed the heavy air
Of obscurity, when I strongly yearned
For the supreme command, which seemed to me
So full of beauty, who would have told me
That I would one day achieve it, that I
Would be the chief of glorious officers,
Of so many trusted and brave soldiers,
And yet that I would not be happier for it. . . .
[*enter* A SOLDIER]
What is it that you bring?

SOLDIER

A letter from
Venice.
[*gives letter, exit*]

THE COUNT

Let us see. [*reads*] Did I not tell you?
Never were they more friendly toward me.
The duke has asked for peace, therefore they wish
To confer with me. Will you follow me?

GONZAGA

I will.

THE COUNT

What do you say of this peace?

GONZAGA
> You ask this to a soldier?

THE COUNT
>   'Tis true. But
> Is this war? — O my spouse, O beloved daughter,
> I shall soon see you again; I shall embrace
> My friends, and this certainly is good. And yet
> I cannot be content entirely.
> Who could tell me with certainty if I
> Shall again see such a handsome battlefield?

❧ Act V ❧

Scene I

[night, the hall of the Council of the Ten, lighted;
THE DOGE, THE TEN COUNCILORS, THE COUNT, *seated]*

THE DOGE [*to* THE COUNT]
> Such is the peace the duke offers to us,
> The council wants to hear your thoughts on it.

THE COUNT
> I gave you once, sirs, different advice.
> I promised much to you, and you did like it.
> I fulfilled only in part what I had promised;
> Deeds are still far from words, but not for this
> Do I wish that my words fall into oblivion.
> 'Twas not the boldness of a reckless soldier
> That made me speak. Now that you ask me again
> I cannot but repeat my previous thought.
> If you decide a resolute, fierce war,
> You are in time; it is still the best course.
> In the peace treaty he yields Bergamo
> And Brescia to you, but are they not yours
> Already? Arms had made those cities yours,
> And he cannot offer you as much as
> You can hope to take from him. And yet—

Since you wish not to hear but the pure truth
From the warrior who swore you loyalty—
Accept his offer if you will not change
The way this war is made.

THE DOGE

                  By many hints
Your speech seems to say much yet explains nothing.
We here demand of you a clearer thought.

THE COUNT

Nay, listen: appoint one general, then
Trust in him; let him attempt all things and
Let nothing be attempted without him.
Concede to him large powers, and demand
Precise account of all. I do not ask
To be that one; I only say that you
Cannot hope much from one who is not such.

MARINO

Were you not such when you resolved to give
The captives freedom? They gained it, and yet
The war did not become more resolute,
Nor more certain. If you had been a general,
Indeed you would have not conceded that.

THE COUNT

I would have done much more: those most brave men
Would have joined in the fight behind my banners,
And Philip's throne would be empty by now,
Another would be seated there.

THE DOGE

                       Your scheme
Is indeed vast.

THE COUNT

            The will to carry it out
Is yours. If it is not fulfilled as yet

The reason lies in the ties hindering
A hand that should have a complete freedom.

MARINO

Another reason was given to us:
That the duke moved you to pity, and that
The hate you bore for your ancient master
You then turned all against your present ones.

THE COUNT

Was this told to you? 'Tis the misfortune
Of the head of States to hear with peacefulness
The boldest lie, nay, the repulsive dreams
Of a coward to whom a private man
Would never lend an ear.

MARINO

                   'Tis your misfortune
That such report be mirrored in your deeds,
That your foul words confirm it, disclose more.

THE COUNT

I revere in you your rank, which by chance
You came to share with these generous men;
And I remain comforted that they show
They think highly of me, since they bestowed
Upon me such an unmerited honor,
When they invited me to hear you now.

THE DOGE

We all have the same thought.

THE COUNT

                Which?

THE DOGE

                      You heard it.

THE COUNT

   Is that which I heard the council's judgment?

THE DOGE

   You can believe the doge.

THE COUNT

                    Such a doubt . . .

THE DOGE

   'Tis no longer a doubt.

THE COUNT

              You summoned me
For this then, and kept silent till now?

THE DOGE

                       Aye,
To punish you for treason, and prevent
Further moves of yours.

THE COUNT

                 A traitor, you say?
I do begin to understand you, at last.
Why did I not believe others' wise words?
Myself, a traitor? This shameful name
Cannot reach me, it is not mine; those who
Deserved it can keep it to themselves.
Yet call me foolish and I will bear it,
Because I do deserve this name, this place
Which among you I occupy today,
Which I would not, at any rate, exchange
With any of you, for mine is the worthiest.
—If I look back and consider the time
Spent at your service as your warrior,
I see but a way adorned with flowers.
When did I seem a traitor to you all?
Point to just one day not full of praises,

Of promises, of graces. . . . Why should I
Say other useless words? Here I am, now,
And when I came to this that seemed to me
A high honor, when louder in my heart
Spoke trust, and love, gratitude and zeal . . . nay,
The man who is invited among friends
Thinks not of trust . . . but I came into a snare!
Yes, I was beguiled. But I thank Heaven
That you have dropped the visage of feigned smiles,
For now we are in a field that I too know.
It is your turn to speak, mine to respond.
Say, then, which are my acts of treason?

THE DOGE

You soon shall hear them from the Secret Council.

THE COUNT

I oppose this, for all I did for you
I did under the sun. I do not want
To account for it in darkness and deception.
The warrior's judge should only be the warrior.
Before impartial eyes must I defend
My honor? I will the world hear all . . .

THE DOGE

Gone is the time to will . . .

THE COUNT

                              You force my hand?
Come, my guards, O! [*raising his voice and walking away*]

THE DOGE

                              Nay, they are far from here.
Soldiers! [*enter armed people*]
                    These are your guards.

THE COUNT

                              I am betrayed!

THE DOGE

> It was most wise then to dispatch your guards.
> Little did we think that, when caught plotting,
> The traitor could become even a rebel.

THE COUNT

> A rebel . . . Aye, you can say what you will.

THE DOGE

> Bring him away to the Secret Council.

THE COUNT

> Listen first, a brief word: you have decreed,
> I can see it, my death sentence. Thus you
> At once condemned yourself to eternal shame.
> The ensigns bearing the Lion now do fly
> Upon towers beyond the ancient border,
> And Europe knows 'twas I who infixed them there.
> No one will say this here, yet all around you,
> Beyond the silence of your reign of terror,
> Someone will ponder this and chronicle
> The deed and its reward in lasting words.
> Think of your annals, think of the future.
> You shall presently need another warrior,
> But who will be yours? You alarm the men of arms.
> I am now at your mercy, it is true.
> And yet whence I come you should remember,
> I was born among warlike, guileless people,
> Accustomed to consider as their own
> The glory of each fellow citizen.
> They will not gladly take such an offense.
> Some enemy of yours and of myself
> Dragged you by means of deceit to this point.
> You cannot believe that I betrayed you.
> There is still time.

THE DOGE

>   There is indeed no time.
> When you conceived the crime and attacked boldly

The people who were bound to punish you,
That was the time for prudent forethought.

THE COUNT

O unworthy man, you have restored me now
To my true self. You thought that I was begging
For your mercy. Indeed you dared to think
That a brave man was trembling for his life!
O, you shall see how nobly one can die.
When in your coward bed death finds you at last,
You will not meet it bearing such a brow
As I bear now in facing this base death
To which you are dragging me.
[*exit* THE COUNT *among* SOLDIERS]

Scene II

[THE COUNT's *house;* ANTOINETTE *and* MATILDA]

ANTOINETTE

'Tis still unknown to you, who are so young,
But I can tell that happy events come late,
After long yearning, to the end uncertain.
But barely and confusedly foreseen,
Misfortune plunges most swiftly on us.
O daughter, past is the night, the hours
Belong no more to painful longing, but
To joy, just moments away. 'Tis almost time.
This long delay bodes well, I think, because
If they protracted so their consultations,
It was undoubtedly to undersign the peace.
He shall be ours and for a long time.

MATILDA

I hope that it is so, mother. We spent
Many a night weeping, many a day musing,
'Tis time for us to ban all fears at last.
No more trembling at each popular whisper,

No more that thought, constantly returning
To our troubled minds: perchance the one
Whom you so wish to see is dying now.

ANTOINETTE

O evil thought! 'Tis far from us now, daughter.
Yes, every joy must needs be paid with pain.
Do you recall the day when your great father,
Carried in triumph, brought to the temple
The enemy's ensigns and was there welcomed
Among the great men of the State?

MATILDA

That day!

ANTOINETTE

All men looked smaller next to him.
The air resounded with his name. And we,
Apart from the populace, from above
Did watch the man by all beheld,
Repeating with an inebriated heart:
We are his.

MATILDA

O, bliss!

ANTOINETTE

How did we deserve
Them? Heaven did choose us among many,
Such a name Heaven wrote on your fair brow,
Such a gift it was, that any man to whom
You will bring it shall be most proud of it.
Envy besieges our lot, these pains
Are our atonement for it.

MATILDA

No more anguish . .
Listen! I hear oars on the water, near,
Closer . . . ceasing now. Gates are flung open,

It must be him. I see a man in armor.
'Tis him.

ANTOINETTE

Who else could it be otherwise?
O dearest husband . . .

Scene III

[*enter* GONZAGA]

ANTOINETTE

Gonzaga! Where is
My husband? You do not answer? Heaven,
Your countenance is herald of misfortune!

GONZAGA

Alas, it is most truthful, then.

MATILDA

Whose misfortune do you come to announce?

GONZAGA

O women! Why is such heavy burden
Imposed on myself?

ANTOINETTE

You wish to be kind
Yet you are cruel. Pray do not keep us
Trembling. For God's sake, speak: where is the count?

GONZAGA

May Heaven give you strength to hear what follows .

ANTOINETTE

Did he have to return to the war?

GONZAGA

    Alas, there he shall return never more!
He fell in disgrace with the lords, and now
He is kept prisoner.

ANTOINETTE

                In prison! Why?

GONZAGA

    He stands accused of treason.

ANTOINETTE

                   Him a traitor?

MATILDA

    O father!

ANTOINETTE

           Pray proceed. We are ready
To hear the rest. What will they do to him?

GONZAGA

    You shall not hear this from my lips.

ANTOINETTE

                      Alas,
They killed him!

GONZAGA

             He lives, but he is condemned.

ANTOINETTE

    He lives, you hear, O daughter? Do not cry,
'Tis time to act. Gonzaga, pity us,
Do not become impatient with our woe:
Heaven entrusts you with two wretched women.
He was your friend; pray lead us to the judges.
And you, poor guiltless thing, will come with me;

There must be pity still on this earth, come!
Those too are husbands, those too are fathers!
While they were writing that impious sentence,
They did not think he's father and husband.
When they see that a word their mouths uttered
Is the cause of such great sorrow for us,
They shall tremble with horror, with pity.
There's no doubt, they will annul the sentence.
Sorrow's sight is to men unbearable.
Perhaps that valiant man has been too proud,
He did not care at all to excuse himself,
He did not mention all the services
He performed for them. We will remind them.
Most certainly he did not beg, but we,
We will beg. [*gesture to walk away*]

GONZAGA

                O Heaven, why can I not
Leave this hope of yours intact? No begging
Will be accepted; those judges are most deaf,
And pitiless, their names unknown to all.
Down strikes the lightning bolt, hidden remains
Among the clouds the hand that sent it forth.
They will grant you the solace to see him,
And this sad solace I now bring to you.
But we must haste, and may your heart be strong.
This ordeal shall be terrible and yet
God, who never forsakes His wretched souls,
Will be with you.

MATILDA

              No hope then?

ANTOINETTE

                        O daughter!

[*exeunt*]

Scene IV

[*prison;* THE COUNT]

THE COUNT

They must know all, by now. O why at least
Can I not die far away from them?
The news would be terrible for them, but
The most sorrowful hour would be past.
And now it looms before us, and together,
In slow sips, we shall taste of it. —Alas,
The open fields, the shining sun, the clangor
Of weapons, the thrill of perils, the trumpets,
The warriors' cries, my steed. . . . To die amidst
All this would have indeed been beautiful.
Instead I go to meet my death disgusted,
Like a criminal, dragged by violent hands,
Scattering to the wind vain lamentations,
Impotent vows . . . —Mark too betrayed me. . .
What a base suspicion, tormenting doubt!
I wish I could discard it before dying.
But 'tis all vain! To what avail should I
Turn back and consider my life, to look
Where I cannot direct my step? —And Philip,
You will enjoy my fall. But no matter!
Unholy joys like those I myself felt,
I now know how little worth they have.
Alas, to see my women, hear their wails,
To hear the last farewell from those voices!
To be in their arms and then to let them go,
Forever! They come! God, send upon them
Your merciful gaze!

Scene V

[*enter* ANTOINETTE, MATILDA, GONZAGA]

ANTOINETTE

O husband!

MATILDA

Father!
Is this the way you are returned to us,
Is this the moment we coveted so? . . .

THE COUNT

O forlorn women, Heaven knows how dire
It is for me, because of your suffering.
I have been long accustomed to the thought
Of death, to expect it. But for you my strength
Might fail me, and you, my dears, cannot wish
To take it all away from me. When God
Lets misery fall upon good people
He gives also a big heart to bear it.
Alas, may yours be now as vast as this
Present tragedy. Now let us take joy
From this embrace; this too is but a gift
From Heaven. O do not weep, my daughter!
And you, my wife, before I married you,
Your days would go by peaceful and serene.
I elected you my mate in this sad lot,
And this thought embitters my last moments.
Pray do not let me see how wretched you are
Because of me!

ANTOINETTE

Love of my happy days,
You who are their maker, gaze at my heart.
I am dying of sorrow, yet cannot
But desire to be yours.

THE COUNT

                    Wife, I knew well
What was my loss in losing you, but now
Let me not feel too much my going hence.

MATILDA

    Alas, murderers!

THE COUNT

              My sweet Matilda,
Do not let revenge's evil cry rise
In your pure soul; do not let rancor spoil
These last moments together, they are sacred.
The wrong is great, yet forgive, and you shall see
A high joy arising amidst the evils.
O, what is death? The cruelest enemy
Can only speed the course that leads to it.
Nay, men did not invent death; it would be
Full of rage, unbearable. From Heaven
Death comes to us, and Heaven sends with it
Such solace that men cannot give or take.
O wife, daughter, listen to my last words:
They shall sound bitter to your heart, I know,
And yet one day it will be sweet for you
To remember them in conversation.
You, my beloved wife, live, conquer sorrow,
And live, that this our daughter might not be
Wholly deserted; flee from this land, at once.
Bring her to your house; she is their own blood,
And you were once by them so much cherished,
Less so when you married a foe of theirs.
Wrathful questions of State pitted against
Each other Visconti and Carmagnola,
But you return dejected to their threshold,
The wretched cause of hatred is removed,
Death is a great peacemaker. You, daughter,
Tender flower that used to come and cheer
My spirit midst the arms, you bow your head,

Alas, the storm is roaring over you—
You tremble; your breast can no longer
Contain your sobs; I feel your burning tears
Fall on my chest, and yet cannot wipe them.
You seem to entreat some pity from me,
Matilda, yet nothing can your father
Do for you. For the deserted ones, though,
A Heavenly Father is there, you know.
Trust in Him and live your tranquil if not
Happy days, for He for certain destines
You to this. Alas, why would He otherwise
Have poured a stream of anguish on your youth
If not to keep His pity for later?
Live and comfort your afflicted mother;
May she one day wed you to a worthy
Bridegroom. —Gonzaga, I give you this hand,
Which you often took before a battle,
When it was doubtful whether we would meet
Again at night. Will you take it once more,
And swear that you shall be the trusted escort
Of these two women till they are returned
To their kinsfolk?

GONZAGA

        I swear.

THE COUNT

            This comforts me.
If you ever go back to the battlefield,
Greet my companions for me; tell them that
I am condemned though I am innocent.
You were the witness to my deeds, you know,
You heard my thoughts. Tell them I did not taint
The sword with shameful treason, I did not,
I am betrayed. —And when the trumpet sounds,
When banners fly in the wind, think of me,
Your old friend. And when, after the battle,
The priest walks on the field, among the dead,

With lifted hands, with somber chanting,
To sacrifice to Heaven for their souls,
Remember me, and how I too thought that
I would die on a battlefield.

ANTOINETTE

                              O God,
Have mercy on us!

THE COUNT

                         Wife, Matilda, my hour
Is near, we must part, farewell.

MATILDA

                              No, father . . .

THE COUNT

Once more come to these arms. —For pity's sake,
Now leave.

ANTOINETTE

                    No, by force they must part us.
[*a clangor of armed soldiers is heard*]

MATILDA

O that din . . .

ANTOINETTE

                    God help us!
[*enter* THE SOLDIERS; THE CHIEF goes to THE COUNT; THE
    WOMEN *swoon*]

THE COUNT

                         Merciful God,
I thank You that You spared them this cruel time.
Friend, assist them, from this unhappy place
Lead them away. When they open their eyes,
Tell them that nothing is left to be feared.

END OF THE TRAGEDY

Adelchis

A Tragedy

To his beloved and adored wife,

Enrichetta Luigia Blondel,

who through her life

of affectionate spouse and wise mother

retained intact her soul's maidenhood,

this Adelchis is consecrated

by the author,

who sadly regrets that he cannot

entrust to a more splendid and lasting monument

her dear name and the memory of her great virtues.

Historical Notes

Facts Preceding the Tragedy's Action

In the year 568, the Lombard people left the Pannonia region, surrendering it to the Avars, and headed for Italy, which was then under the rule of the Greek emperors. Twenty thousand Saxons and men of other northern nations joined the Lombards in their descent toward Italy, under the guidance of King Alboin. The Lombards occupied that part of Italy that was named after them and there founded a kingdom, with the city of Pavia as royal residence.[1] As time went by, the Lombards increased their possessions in Italy, either by conquering lands beyond the borders of their kingdom or by establishing dukedoms that were more or less subject to the Lombard king's central authority. By the end of the eighth century, the Italian peninsula belonged to them, except: some Venetian inland possessions; the Byzantine exarchate, with Ravenna as capital; and some maritime cities in the Magna Grecia. Rome and its dukedom also belonged, in principle, to the emperors, but their power there was progressively eroding, while the Popes' authority grew stronger each day.[2] The Lombards made forays into the Roman lands on several occasions and even tried to acquire them permanently.

754

The Lombard king Haistulf invaded some of these lands and threatened to invade the rest. Pope Stephen II went to Paris and asked Pepin for succor, anoint-

---

1. *The Deeds of the Lombards*, book 2, by Paul the Deacon.

2. A more detailed description of the division of the Italian territory in Lombard times would lead us into complicated and irrelevant questions. See Ludovico Muratori, *Antiquitates italicae*, second dissertation. [This work is hereafter abbreviated *Antiq. It.*; Muratori was also the editor of the twenty-five volumes of *Rerum Italicarum Scriptores*, abbreviated in *Rer. it*, which was also consulted for *Carmagnola*. Manzoni indicates, and sometimes comments on, the various sources, such

ing him king of the Franks. Pepin descended into Italy, chased Haistulf back into Pavia, and laid siege to the city. Thanks to the Pope's intercession, Pepin granted a peace covenant to Haistulf, in which this latter swore to free the lands he had occupied.

755

As soon as the Franks left, Haistulf not only breached the pact but also went to lay siege to Rome and burn down its surroundings. Stephen again summoned Pepin to his aid, and again Pepin came. Haistulf rushed to the Alps' Gates [le Chiuse dell'Alpi, see below], but Pepin passed them and drove Haistulf into Pavia. When he was near his city, two legates from the Greek emperor Constantine Copronime came to beseech Pepin, with promises and gifts, to give back the recovered cities of the exarchate to the emperor. Pepin replied that he had fought neither to serve nor to please men, but rather for his devotion to Saint Peter and for the atonement of his sins. He said that he would never take away from Saint Peter what he had once given Him, not even in exchange for all the world's gold.[3] Thus, facts terminated abruptly a curious question that is still widely debated to this day in its legal terms, for the human mind seems to derive pleasure in disputing at length an ill-conceived problem. Once cornered in Pavia, Haistulf yielded and renewed his old promises. Pepin traveled back to France and sent a written act of donation to the Pope.

756

Haistulf died. Desiderius, nobleman from Brescia[4] and Lombard duke, longed to be king. He convened with all the Lombards of Tuscany, where Haistulf[5] had

---

as chronicles and annals by secretaries, bishops, monks, letters, articles of law, etc. that he found in this collection of "writers of Italian affairs" and elsewhere. I will indicate in quote these miscellaneous sources.]

3. " . . . affirming also under oath that he did not engage in battle with the aim of winning anyone's favor, but rather for love of the Blessed Peter and for the forgiveness of his own sins. He also asserted that no sum of money, no matter how large, would persuade him to take away from Peter what he had once given to Peter." "Bibliotheca Anastasii," *Rer. it.*, vol. 3:171.

4. "Of which city [Brescia, Latin "Brixia"] this Desiderius was a nobleman." "History of the Secretary Ridolphus" (eleventh century), [Gianmaria] Biemmi's *History of Brescia* [1742]. "History by Bishop Sicardus," *Rer. it.*, vol. 7:577; confirmed by other sources.

5. "Anastasius," 172.

sent him, and they elected him king. Ratchis, Haistulf's brother who had been king before him and had then retired into a monastery, sought to be king again. He left the cloister, gathered some men and moved against Desiderius. The latter asked for the Pope's support. The Pope made Desiderius promise to return the cities that Haistulf had conquered and still occupied; the Pope then intervened in the conflict in his favor. The Pope advised Ratchis to return to Montecassino,[6] and he obeyed. Thus, Desiderius became king of the Lombards.

It is not precisely known what year Desiderius and his wife Ansa founded the monastery of San Salvatore in Brescia, but it was definitely one of the first years of Desiderius's reign. The monastery was later named after Saint Giulia, and its first abbess was Desiderius's daughter Ansberga, or Anselperga.[7]

758

Liutprand, duke of Benevento, and Alboin, duke of Spoleto, rebelled against Desiderius, seeking Pepin's protection. Desiderius attacked them, defeated them, made Alboin captive, and forced Liutprand to flee.[8] In this or the following year, Desiderius's son, was elevated to sharing the kingship with his father. In the chronicles and in the Popes' letters, he went by the names "Adelgisus," "Atalgisus," and "Algisus," but he signed public documents as "Adelchis."

In the year 768, Pepin died and the Franks' kingdom was divided between his two sons, Charles and Carloman. In their letters to Pepin, Stephen II's successors, Paul I and Stephen III, complained strongly about Desiderius, who was not only refusing to return the cities as promised but was also occupying other lands.

770

Pepin's widow, Bertrada, eager to promote friendship between her own house and that of Desiderius, came to Italy and proposed two marriages: one between

6. "[Desiderius] made a promise under oath that he would return the other cities—Faenza, Imola, Ferrara—with their surrounding territories, to the Blessed Peter." "Letter of Stephen to Pipinus," *Codex Carolingium*, 8.

7. "Anselperga was consecrated to Gods as abbess of the monastery of Saint Salvatore which was built in the city of Brescia, whose monuments Lord Desiderius, excellent king, and his wife Ansa, her parents, built from their foundations." Document of the year 761, *Antiq. It.*, dissertation 66, vol. 5:499.

8. "Letter of Bishop Paul to Pepin," *Codex Carolingium*, 15.

Desiderata, or Ermengarde,[9] and one of his sons, and another between her daughter Gisla and Adelchis. Stephen III wrote then to the Frankish king a celebrated letter, trying to dissuade him from entering such a kinship.[10] Notwithstanding the Pope's advice, Bertrada led Ermengarde back to France with her, and Charles, later called the Great, married her.[11] The marriage between Adelchis and Gisla was never celebrated.

771

For uncertain reasons, Charles repudiated Ermengarde and married the Swabian Hildegarde.[12] Charles's mother, Bertrada, disapproved of the divorce, and this was, in fact, the only dissension they ever had.[13] Carloman died. Charles rushed to Carbonac, in the forest of the Ardennes, which marked the border between the two kingdoms. There he obtained the electors' votes and was appointed king in stead of his brother. He thus reunited the states that had been divided at Pepin's death. Gerberga, Carloman's widow, fled with her two sons and some barons, seeking shelter with Desiderius. Charles was profoundly offended by this.[14]

772

Hadrian succeeded to Stephen III. Desiderius sent envoys demanding his friendship. The new Pope replied that, while he certainly wished to remain in peace with him as with all the Christian kings, he could not see how he could trust a

9. Chronicles record different names, if at all mentioning her.

10. Letter in *Codex Carolingium*, 45.

11. "Berta took the Lombard king's daughter to France with her." "Annals by Nazarius," for that year; *Rerum Francicarum*, vol. 5:11. [This work—abbreviated by Manzoni as "Rer. Fr."—is most likely the collection of historical documents relating France's history from the earliest days, and entitled *Rerum Gallicarum et Francicarum scriptores*, by the Benedictine monk Martin Bouquet, who prepared the first five volumes (chronicling French history up to the year 987) and saw them published by 1754. The work was continued by other monks and finally edited in twenty-five volumes by Leopolde Delisle in 1869. In a letter to Gaetaneo Cattaneo, who was lending him history books for his novel, Manzoni reminds him that some of his volumes are still with him from earlier times. This list includes a work abbreviated as "*Rer. Gallic.* T. 1, 2, 3, 5, 6" (*Tutte le lettere*, vol 1:235).]

12. "Having, upon exhortation of his mother, married the daughter of Desiderius, king of the Lombards, he repudiated her after one year, for cause unknown, and took as wife a noble woman of the Swabian people, Hildegarde." *Life of Charles*, by Einhard (a contemporary writer), 18.

13. "So that no dissension ever arose between them , except over the divorce from the daughter of King Desiderius whom he had married upon his mother's recommendaion." Ibid.

14. "The king bore with impatience their useless actions." *Annals*, by Einhard for that year.

man who had never fulfilled the promise, indeed the sworn oath, of returning to the Church what belonged to it. Desiderius kept invading lands that Pepin's donation act had assigned to the Pope.[15]

Facts included in the Tragedy's action

772–774

While Charles was engaged in combat against the Saxons, from whom he took Ehresburg or, some say, Stadtberg in Westphalia,[16] Desiderius conceived a plan to take revenge against the Frankish king and at the same time mar his relations with the Pope. He wanted the latter to consecrate Gerberga's sons as kings of the Franks, and for this purpose pressured the Pontiff to meet with him. Given the barbarian spirit of the times, the barbarous king's stratagem was not without merit. But Hadrian, aware of his duty, proved adamantly opposed to such a plan.[17] He said he would willingly meet with the king wherever he wished, but not until the Church had been returned the occupied lands. Desiderius invaded more lands and laid them waste.[18] Full of anguish, after having sent other envoys to beg and admonish him, Hadrian finally sent a legate to ask for Charles's succor.[19] After a time, three legates from the Frankish king came to Rome: Charles's personal adviser, Alcuin Albinus,[20] the bishop Georgius, and the abbot Wolfar. They had to ascertain whether Desiderius had in fact withdrawn from the Papal lands, as went the reports that the Lombard king had been spreading in France. When Charles's legates departed, Hadrian sent another envoy to Desiderius in a last attempt to obtain the lands. At this point, as he was no longer able to deceive anyone, the Lombard king openly refused to make any restitution.[21] With this reply, the Franks went back to their king, who was stationed at Thionville for the winter retreat. Hadrian's legate Peter also went there to meet with Charles.[22]

At the same time, the Frankish king probably received an equally authoritative message, secretly sent by some of the Lombard dukes. They exhorted Charles

---

15. "Anastasius," 180.

16. *History of Charlemagne*, by Hegevisch, translated from German into French.

17. "Anastasius," 181.

18. Ibid., 182.

19. Ibid., 183.

20. "Albinus was very dear to the king." Ibid., 184.

21. "He said that he would not return anything at all." Ibid.

22. "Annals" by Tilianus, Loiselianus, "Chronica Moissiacensis," and other sources in the vol. 5 of *Rerum Francicarum*. In those centuries that we generally call barbarian, the writers of annals

to descend into Italy and conquer the Lombard kingdom, promising the delivery into his hands of Desiderius and his riches.[23]

Charles summoned the kingdom's general assembly, or sinodus, in Geneva, and this ratified the war.[24] The Frankish king moved with his army toward the Alps' Gates [*chiuse*=dams, gates]. This was a line of walls fortified with large watchtowers and turrets, blocking the outlet of the Susa Valley in the point that still preserves the toponym "Chiusa." Desiderius, who had previously restored and reinforced these walls,[25] rushed then to their defense. The resistance opposed to Charles was much stronger than that once met by Pepin.[26] The monk of the Novalesa region, previously quoted, reports that Adelchis, a robust man and valiant, accustomed to bearing an iron club in battle, would ambush the Franks near the Gates and massacre them in great numbers by taking them by surprise.[27] Charles despaired of ever being able to pass the Gates and, without suspecting the existence of another route to Italy, decided to return to France.[28] But a deacon called Martinus, sent by Leo, Ravenna's archbishop, arrived at the Franks' camp[29] and informed Charles of a mountain pass that led to Italy. Martinus later succeeded to Leo as archbishop of Ravenna.

---

were as deft as we are today in copying from each others trivial facts; and they all showed the same predisposition to omit what we really would like to know.

23. "However the Lombards, animated by unjust greed, made agreements among themselves, and sent a certain group of nobles to King Charles, with the message that he should come with a strong army, and he would get the Kingdom of Italy whenever he asked, and that they would deliver into his hands the tyrant Desiderius and many riches, etc. . . . Having learned these things, King Charles headed to Italy in great haste with a large army." "Anonymous Chronicle from Salerno," ch. 9, *Rer. it.*, vol. 2 of part II:180. This chronicle dates from the tenth century.

24. See annals quoted above and Einhard's *Annals* for the year 773.

25. "Anastasius," 184; "Chronica Novalicensis," 1.3, ch. 9, *Rer. it.* vol. 1, part II:717. Muratori surmises that the anonymous monk who wrote this chronicle lived in mid-eleventh century.

26. "Securing with strong works the borders of the kingdom, [Desiderius] prevented the Franks from entering it." "Letter by Frodoardus," *Rerum Francicarum*, vol. 5:463. Frodoardus, parson of Rheims, lived in the tenth century.

27. "Desiderius had a son called Algisus, full of manly vigor since his youth. In times of war he used to carry an iron staff while riding. When this young man, being on his watch day and night, would see that the Franks were asleep, he would attack them with his men from right and left, arriving suddenly upon them, and he would produce a massacre among them." "Chronica Novalicensis," 1.3, chapter 10.

28. "Having been pushed back at the Gates, they meditate a quick return into their kingdom. Only one night's darkness, as it happened, caused a delay in their return." "Frodoardus," 463. " . . . In the daytime the French want to return to their kingdom." "Anastasius," 184.

29. "[Leo] first showed the way to Italy to the French thanks to his deacon Martinus, who after

Charles sent a chosen troop along the craggy pass. Arriving at the Lombards' back, the Franks could attack them from the side they had left unguarded.[30] Owing to this surprise attack, as well as to the betrayal of some dukes, the Lombards were disbanded and Charles was able to overcome the abandoned Gates with the rest of his army. Desiderius took refuge in Pavia with a group of the dukes who had remained faithful to him, while Adelchis retreated into Verona, bringing with him Gerberga and her sons.[31] Many other disbanded Lombards went back to their cities. Some surrendered to Charles; others prepared to withstand the siege. Among the latter was Brescia, over which Desiderius's nephew, Potus, was duke. In this tragedy, his name has been changed to "Baudus," with a slight alteration in line with the variants of German spelling. Aided by his brother Answald, bishop of the city, Baudus opposed a staunch resistance to Ismundus, the Frankish count whom Charles had sent to conquer Brescia. But later, the citizens, frightened by the atrocities suffered by those captured by Ismundus, obliged the two brothers to surrender.[32]

Charles laid siege to Pavia and led his new wife Hildegarde to the camp. Because he could see that the siege would last a long time, he went with a retinue of bishops, counts, and warriors to visit the Apostles' tombs in Rome. Hadrian welcomed him as a son and a benefactor.[33] The siege of Pavia lasted for part of 773 and into the following year. It is impossible to establish the timeline with greater precision without incurring contradictions among the chronicles and getting into possibly unanswerable questions that are, at any rate, irrelevant to the present goal. When Charles returned to the camp outside Pavia, the Lombards, tired of the long siege, opened the city's gates to him.[34] Desiderius was delivered into Charles's hands by his Faithful [see below][35] and led captive to France. There

---

this held a quarter of the government of the Church, and King Charles came to Italy when invited by him." "Agnellus," *Rer. it.*, vol. 2:177. Agnellus wrote in the first half of the ninth century and met Martinus, whom he describes as a tall and athletic man. Ibid., 182.

30. "[Charles] then sent a chosen body of excellent fighters through the difficult mountain pass. Once they had overcome the mountain, they put in flight the Lombards with their King. The king Carles then entered with his army through the open Gates." "Chronica Moissiacensis," *Rerum Francicarum*, vol. 5:69. This chronicle of uncertain author ends at the year 818.

31. "Anastasius," 184.

32. "History of the Secretary Ridolfus," Biemmi's *History of Brescia.*

33. "Anastasius," 185 and following.

34. "The Lombards, exhausted with the siege of the city, went out to encounter the king [Charles] with King Desiderius." "Annals" by Lambecus, *Rerum Francicarum*, vol. 5:64.

35. "In fact Desiderius, as we said, was cunningly betrayed by his Faithful." "Anonymous Chronicle from Salerno," 179.

he was confined in the monastery of Corbie,[36] where he spent the rest of his life in a saintly fashion. The Lombards rushed from everywhere to pay homage to Charles as their new king.[37] It is uncertain when Charles reached Verona. As he drew near, Gerberga emerged from the city to meet him and remit herself and her sons into Charles's hands. Adelchis abandoned Verona, and the city surrendered. Adelchis sought shelter in Constantinople, where he was honorably received. Some years after, he obtained a command over some Greek troops and, with these, landed in Italy,[38] engaged in battle with the Franks, and was killed.[39]

In the tragedy, the death of Adelchis has been transposed to the time he departed from Verona. This anachronism, together with the other of having anticipated Ansa's death to the year preceding the beginning of the tragedy's action (while in reality she was led captive with her husband to France, where she died)— these two anachronisms are the sole alterations of the ascertained historical facts. As far as the moral part is concerned, the characters' speeches have been invented with a view to their actions and to the circumstances under which they are known to have acted. Only one character, Adelchis, utterly lacks historical foundation. His plans, his judgments on the events, his inclinations—in brief, his entire character—was entirely invented afresh. His fictive presence intrudes on the historical characters in such an unhappy fashion that even the most demanding and ill-disposed of my readers will not resent him as much as the author does.

Notes on Some Lombard Customs Hinted at in the Tragedy

I.ii.149: The sign of election to kingship among the Lombards was to put a rod into their hand.[40]

   I.iii.212: Young women had their hair cut upon being married. Unmarried women were called "long-haired."[41] Muratori adds, though without evidence,

36. *Rerum Francicarum*, vol. 5:385.

37. "And as the Lombards of all Italian cities came here from everywhere, they submitted themselves to the rule and government of the glorious king Charles." "Chronica Moissiacensis," *Rerum Francicarum*, vol. 5:70.

38. "Letter of Hadrian to Charles," *Codex Carolingium* 88 and 90.

39. "Chronica Sigiberti," *Rerum Francicarum*, vol. 5:377.

40. "According to the custom, they delivered [to Hildeprandus] the rod." Paul the Deacon, I.6, ch. 55.

41. "If a Lombard man has given some daughters in marriage, and he has other daughters with long hair left in his house . . . " "Law of Liutprand," book I, 1.2.

that they were also called "unshorn" [*intonse*] and infers that the word *tosa*, still found in some Lombard dialects, could derive from this custom.[42]

I.v.335: All Lombards able to bear arms and possessing a horse were obliged to join the military service. A judge could exempt but a few of them.[43]

III.i.78: In the Germanic tribes, as early as the times described by Tacitus, it was a sought-after mark of distinction[44] to be at the personal service of princes. In the Middle Ages, this form of service included domestic as well as military assistance and was a mixture of honorable subjection and affectionate devotion. Among the Lombards, this type of servant was known as *gasindi*, but later the term *domicellus* became widespread, from which we have *donzello* in the historically attested language. This type of noble servant, utterly distinguished from the ordinary servants, is similar to that found in the "heroic age," and represents one of several similarities between those times and that which Vico called "the second part of the barbarian age." Having killed Anfidamantes' son in a brawl, young Patroclus was sent by his father to take refuge in Peleus' household. "Knight" Peleus raised Patroclus and later put him at the service of his own son, Achilles.[45]

III.iv.212: The Franks paid homage by kneeling and putting their hands into those of their new lord.[46]

IV.ii.221: One of the formalities of swearing an oath was to put one's hands on the weapons previously blessed by a priest.[47]

Chorus of act IV, stanza 7: Like all Franks, Charles was versed in hunting.[48] An anonymous poet, contemporary of the king and a connoisseur and imitator of Virgil (as much as a poet could be in the ninth century), described at length Charles hunting while the women and the royal family watched from a knoll.[49]

---

42. See note to quoted passage, *Rer. it.* vol. 1, part II:51.

43. "All the judges should draft only those men who have a horse, so that in the army they will not find themselves wanting one because of much walking . . . " "Law of Liutprand," book 6, 29.

44. "Noble birth or great merits of their fathers can earn the chief's approval even to very young men, who are thus grouped together with more mature men and with those who have already been approved; and you will not see any shameful blushing over this on the face of the chief's companions." Tacitus, *Germania*, 13.

45. Homer, *Iliad*, 1.23, line 90.

46. "The chief of the Bajoari committed himself in service by putting his hands in the hands of the king, according to the French custom," "Annals," by Einhard, *Rerum Francicarum*, vol. 5:198.

47. "He should swear on consecrated weapons." "Law of Rotharis," 364, *Antiq. It.*, dissertation 38.

48. "He oftentimes exerted himself in horse-riding and hunting, which was typical of his people." Einhard, *Life of Charles*, 22

49. *Rerum Francicarum*, vol. 5:388.

The king also enjoyed bathing in natural warm springs, which is why he built the palace at Aix-la-Chapelle.[50]

Recurring in this tragedy is the word "Faithful" [*Fedele*], always employed with the same meaning that it had in the barbarian age; that is, to signify the title of vassal. Because no suitable word could be found to replace it, and in order to avoid confusing it with the same word having today's meaning, we settled for distinguishing the two by capitalizing the initial letter. *Drudo*, the Germanic synonym of *fedele*,[51] would have sounded too strange for the peculiar meaning it has in today's language ["lover"]. In French, the barbarian *fidelis* became *féal*, and remained as such; the reasons for the different paths of these two words in Italian and French are to be sought in the history of the two nations. A sad resemblance, though, is found in their very different historical vicissitudes: the French have preserved the word in their idiom by shedding blood and tears; likewise, through blood and tears, the word has been erased from the Italian language. [*Fedele* has here been here translated as "vassal," "companion," or "faithful," depending on the context.]

50. "He also would amuse himself with the steam of the naturally warm springs. This was the reason he built the Palace at Aix-La-Chapelle." Einhard, *Life of Charles*, 22.

51. "Treu"=faithful.

List of Characters

The Lombards:
DESIDERIUS, king
ADELCHIS, his son, king
ERMENGARDE, DESIDERIUS's daughter
ANSBERGA, DESIDERIUS's daughter, abbess
VERMUNDUS, DESIDERIUS's squire
ANFRID, ADELCHIS's squire
TEUDI, ADELCHIS's squire
BAUDUS, duke of Brescia
GISELBERT, duke of Verona
ILDECHIS, INDULF, FARWALD, ERWIG, GUNTIGIS: dukes
AMRI, GUNTIGIS's squire
SVARTUS, soldier

The Franks:
CHARLES, king
ALCUIN, envoy
ROLAND, ARVINUS: counts

The Latins:
PETER, Pope Hadrian's legate
MARTINUS, deacon from Ravenna

LOMBARD DUKES, SQUIRES, SOLDIERS;
DAMSELS and NUNS in ANSBERGA's monastery;
FRANKISH COUNTS; a HERALD

🐚 ACT I 🐚

Scene I

[*Royal Palace in Pavia;* DESIDERIUS, ADELCHIS, VERMUNDUS]

VERMUNDUS

King Desiderius, and you, noble Adelchis,
Who jointly reign over the Lombard people,
I carried out the duty, lofty and sad,
That you committed to my loyal trust.
We stopped at the high wall that bars the way
To the valley of Susa and divides
The Lombard land from the Frankish realm.
Accompanied by damsels and by squires
Most noble Ermengarde there arrived.
She left behind the Frankish party and came
To put herself in our trusted escort.
Devout farewells uttered by those people
And tears badly concealed in every eye
Showed openly how worthy they all were
To have her as their queen forever,
How innocent in their thoughts they were
Of their king's cowardly repudiation;
How vanquished in their hearts all of them were,
All but one conquered by the royal bride.
Back to Pavia we traveled, and she is now
In the wood that surrounds the western moat.
I ran ahead to announce her return home.

DESIDERIUS

May Heaven's wrath and earth's utter abhorrence
Fall in one blow with the avenging sword
Onto the head of the disloyal one,
Who took my daughter from her mother's hands,
A maid handsome and pure, and now returns her
With the disgraceful brand of repudiation.
Shame on that Charles by whose nefarious deeds
The arrival home of a belovéd daughter
Becomes a dire event for her own father.
He shall have righteous payment for all this.
May he sink to the deepest depths, so that
Amidst the dust the humblest of his subjects
May approach him and tell him without fear:
"Coward! You betrayed an innocent!"

ADELCHIS

                                       Father,
Let me go and lead her in your presence.
How wretched she will be when she demands
In vain to see her mother! Mourn shall join
Sorrow, then, and memories will gather
To wound a soul that is already hurt.
That she may come prepared for this assault,
Let me bring her a loving word of comfort.

DESIDERIUS

My son, please stay. And you, faithful Vermundus,
Go back to Ermengarde and tell her this:
Her beloved ones to whom Heaven has granted
To remain longer in this earthly light
Are awaiting her, ready for the embrace.
Lead back that cherished countenance to us,
Her father and brother. As her escort
Two discreet damsels, Anfrid and yourself
Will be more than enough. In coming here
Follow the secret way and try to be
As unobserved as you can. Divide

The attendants in small groups and mind to enter
Within the city walls by diverse gates.
[*exit* VERMUNDUS]

Scene II

DESIDERIUS

How could you think to go to fetch your sister?
The city of Pavia would have convened
To watch our disgrace. As in a feast
The evil populace would have rejoiced.
You know that Rachi's partisans yet live
Who challenged my own right to wear the crown.
Overt enemies then, they are hiding now.
Secret revenge and solace they derive
From every source of our humiliation.

ADELCHIS

The crown levies indeed a bitter price,
If rulers should fare worse than their own subjects,
If we must guard ourselves from envious looks,
Conceal our brow for shame and refrain from
An open show of a familial grief.

DESIDERIUS

Not until vengeance has paid back the offense
And blood has washed away the spot of shame
Will Ermengarde come out from her retreat.
Her mourning garments gone, she will then lift
Her brow before the admiring crowd, adorned
With glory and vengeance, worthy daughter
And sister of kings. That day is not far.
A mighty weapon in my hands I hold,
A weapon Charles himself offered to me:
The embittered widow of his brother, whom
He had stripped of the crown. Gerberga has come
To put herself, together with her sons,
Under the shelter of the Lombard throne.

These sons we shall conduct to Rome; an army
They will have for their retinue. The Pope
We shall order to anoint these most pure heads
And consecrate them rulers of the Franks,
With proper prayers. Then we shall lead them
In the Franks' domain, where their father reigned.
There they retain many supporters,
And there the wrath for the usurpation
Silently rages still in many a breast.

ADELCHIS

The Pope's consent to this is most uncertain.
So many knots tie up his lot to Charles
That he does not address the Frankish king
Except to flatter, glorify, and bless.
For Charles the Pope entreats Saint Peter's favor,
Promising glorious rule, victory, triumph.
And while we speak, the Pope is welcoming
King Charles's envoys, with whom he will complain
Against us. The shrine and the whole city
Echo with his laments for the lost towns . . .

DESIDERIUS

If he denies our will, he shall become
Openly adverse to us. This sorry war
Made of unending wailing, messages,
And scheming, will then cease, and swords at last
Will start to speak, cutting the story short.
Ours will be the victory, no doubt,
Ours the day our fathers wished in vain:
Rome will be ours. Too late the Holy Father
Will see the fact and beg in vain for mercy.
Forever dispossessed of earthly swords,
To holy studies Hadrian shall return;
The king of prayers, the lord of sacrifice,
Will finally vacate the throne for us.

ADELCHIS

He won the Greek and terrorized the rebels,
He never returned home but as a victor,
And yet before the shrine of Peter Haistulf
Twice lowered the ensigns, obliged to flee,
Twice he refused to accept offers of peace
By the preceeding Pope, remaining deaf
To his defenseless cry. Beyond the Alps
'Twas heard: twice Pepin came to the pope's aid.
The Franks, whom we defeated more than once,
Dictated then the rules in our state.
From here I see the plain where stood the tents,
Where freely then the Frankish hooves did stamp.

DESIDERIUS

To what avail do you name these long-dead kings?
The earth by now holds Haistulf and Pepin;
Other men reign, who brandish other swords.
Changed circumstances dominate this hour . . .
Because the soldier who first climbed the wall,
Did fall and perish, shall the entire army
Abandon in despair the besieged city?
Is this the advice that comes from my own son?
Where is my proud Adelchis who, still a boy,
Saw ruin-bearing Spoleto come to attack
Like a young hawk plunging to seize its prey;
Adelchis then entered the bloody brawl
Without a thought, and shone amidst the crowd
Of the combatants like to a bridegroom
At the feast. He came back from the battle
Having vanquished the duke who had rebelled.
I asked him, on the field, to be my peer
In kingship: the crowd consented with cries
And ovations, and thus the royal rod
Was put in your right hand—powerful then.
Adelchis now can see nothing but hurdles
And dire events. Not even after news
Of a defeat should you dare speak like this.

If someone came to tell me that Charles's mind
Is preoccupied with the same kind of thoughts
That hover in the mind of my own son,
That messenger would fill my heart with joy.

ADELCHIS

Why can I not confront him, here and now,
In single combat? Am I not the brother
Of Ermengarde? Why can I not entrust
To my own sword the vengeance of the affront,
Before your person, by God's judgment?
I wish I could from you receive the admission
That from your lips a word too quickly escaped .

DESIDERIUS

This is the voice that becomes Adelchis.
My deeds are bringing near the day you covet.

ADELCHIS

The day I see approaching is indeed
Very unlike that one. Hadrian's cry is inept
And yet revered. Charles will soon answer it
And descend here with all of France to fight.
That day will mark Haistulf's children's combat
Against Pepin's son. Never forget
Over whom we rule. Among our subjects
Are some loyal people and some hostile.
The latter are more numerous perhaps;
Recall that at the sight of foreign ensigns
Every enemy turns into a traitor.
Father, my heart is up to dying, but
Victorious government is for the one
Who in harmony rules consenting people.
When I am forced to guard against the soldier
Who is fighting by my side, the spear becomes
A burden in my hand, and I loathe
The dawn harbinger of the battle day.

DESIDERIUS

> Who ever reigned indeed without opponents?
> This is no matter for the heart. Are we
> Then kings in jest, that we should keep our swords
> Sheathed, until all inner strife dies down,
> And stay the while in idleness to wait
> For the enemy who mercilessly strikes us
> As we stand gazing from our home's doorway?
> What other choice is left us but to dare?
> What is it that you propose instead?

ADELCHIS

> I propose what I would if I were king
> Of an unvanquished people, and loyal,
> In a victorious day: let us return
> The lands to the Romans; let us be friends
> With Hadrian: he too so wishes.

DESIDERIUS

> To die, to die either crowned or deposed,
> Would be better to me rather than yield
> In such a shameful way. Advice like this
> Should never pass your lips. Your father
> Bids you this.

Scene III

VERMUNDUS [*preceding* ERMENGARDE, DAMSELS *escorting her*]
> O kings, here comes Ermengarde.

DESIDERIUS

> Come, my child, be brave.

ADELCHIS

> You are in the arms
> Of your own brother, by your father's side,
> Amongst your faithful, oldest friends. You are,
> In the kings' palace, more revered and belovéd
> Than when you left.

ERMENGARDE

                              Blesséd voice of my blood!
May Heaven reward you for these kind words,
May Heaven always treat you as you treat me,
Bringing comfort to a forlorn kinswoman.
If ever a happy day could dawn for me,
It is this one in which I see you again.
—O sweet mother, here did I leave you, here
You died and I heard not your final words.
Certainly you now watch us from above.
Behold your Ermengarde, whom you adorned
That day with so much joy, with so much love,
Whose hair you trimmed with your own hands;
See now how she returns! Bless your dear ones
Who welcome this rejected woman!

ADELCHIS

                                        To us
The offense was made. Your woe is ours.

DESIDERIUS

    Ours is also the resolve to avenge it.

ERMENGARDE

    It is not vengeance that my sorrow claims.
    I only wish oblivion, and the world
    Easily grants it to the dejected.
    I do not wish my sorrow's perpetuation
    In others. I should have borne to all but
    Peace and friendship. Heaven willed otherwise.
    May it at least remain unsaid that I
    Brought with me, in every place where I went,
    Sadness and sorrow, I, who should have been
    To everyone the most pure gift of joy.

DESIDERIUS

    Would perhaps the undoing of the villain
    Cause more sorrow for you? Are you perchance
    In love still with that coward?

ERMENGARDE

Father,

Why do you search the bottom of this heart?
Nothing that can relieve you will come out
Of it, and I myself fear to question it.
Everything past is worthless to me—Father,
I ask you to grant me this last favor:
This court, where I grew to be adorned
With hopes, protected in my mother's bosom,
Cannot be my abode. What would I do,
here now? Garland briefly desired, worn
On the brow for sport on festive days
And soon thrown at the feet of passers-by.
Let me retire in that peaceful shelter,
That holy refuge where pity is bestowed,
Which your virtuous spouse, as in a vision
Of my present lot, once wished to build.
There my sweet sister took the vows and wedding
That Bridegroom who never casts us off.
My other wedlock bars my aspiration
To such pure nuptials, but I could spend
Unseen and peaceful there my final days.

ADELCHIS

Let the wind dissipate this sad omen:
You shall live. Heaven did not deliver
Supreme control of the best people's lives
To the will of the evil ones. It is not
In their power to lay waste every hope,
To ban every joy from the whole world.

ERMENGARDE

I wish Bertrada had never seen the shores
Of the Ticino and willed a Lombard
As her daughter-in-law. Had she never
Rested her eyes upon me. . . .

DESIDERIUS

O vengeance,
Never too quickly will your blow strike!

ERMENGARDE

Are you then willing to grant my request?

DESIDERIUS

Sorrow often acts as a hasty helper
Lacking in wisdom. Time can bring along
Novel thoughts and unforeseen events.
If your resolve does not alter in time,
Nothing will I deny to my dear daughter.

Scene IV

[*enter* ANFRID]

ANFRID

Sire, an envoy is in the palace
And demands permission to be admitted
To see you.

DESIDERIUS

Whence does he come? Who sent him?

ANFRID

He comes from Rome, but a king sent him.

ERMENGARDE

Father, permit me to retire.

DESIDERIUS

Women,
Accompany my daughter to her rooms;
Attend to all her needs. She must be now
Given the title and honors of queen.
[*exeunt* ERMENGARDE *and* DAMSELS]

DESIDERIUS

    The envoy comes from a king, you said, Anfrid?
From Charles?

ANFRID

                O king, you yourself have said it.

DESIDERIUS

    What words can change by now the state of things
Between us? Whatever can link us now
Other than death?

ANFRID

              Of a great message
He says he is the bearer. To dukes and
To all he encounters in this palace,
He is speaking in a flattering manner.

DESIDERIUS

    I know too well Charles's arts.

ADELCHIS

                  Let us not give
His legate any time to practice them.

DESIDERIUS

    Anfrid, muster at once all my vassals
And let the man from Rome enter with them.
    [*exit* ANFRID]

DESIDERIUS

    The moment of the ordeal has come at last
Are you with me, my son?

ADELCHIS

             When did I give you
Any reason to ask me such a question?

DESIDERIUS

The day has come when our wills must be one.
Do we have perfect concord of hearts? How
Shall you act?

ADELCHIS

                    The answer to this question
Lies in past deeds. I will loyally obey
All your orders.

DESIDERIUS

                    Even against your will?

ADELCHIS

To our doorstep comes an enemy
And you ask me what I shall do? I am
Nothing more than a sword in your hand, father.
Here comes the envoy. My duty is inscribed
In your reply to him.

Scene V

[*enter* ALCUIN *and* Lombard COMPANIONS]

DESIDERIUS

                    Dukes, my companions,
Always the king draws profit from your being
His counselors as well as his warriors.—
What is it that you seek, ambassador?

ALCUIN

Charles, the God-chosen king of the Franks, sends
To the Lombard kings, through my mouth, these words:
Are you willing to abandon those lands that
Glorious Pepin once bestowed on Peter?

DESIDERIUS

O Lombard men! Before our people you
Shall be the witnesses of my reply.

If I received at all the emissary
Of a man I do not want to name,
If I did lend an ear to what he said,
It was only to faithfully discharge
The sacred duties of kingship. Now, stranger,
Listen: your request is most burdensome.
You ask that we reveal the secret will
Of kings. Know that this revelation
Is solely reserved to those whom you
See gathered around us, the princes of
This nation, from whom only we expect
Loyal advice. We have never revealed
To strangers our own will. Therefore
The worthiest answer to your question is
To give none.

ALCUIN

                    Then such a reply means war.
On Charles's behalf, I declare war against
Adelchis and Desiderius, 'gainst you,
Who laid your greedy hands on God's bequest
And anguished the Holy Father. My good lord
Is not a foe to this illustrious nation.
Yet he is God's champion: summoned by God,
To Him his arm he consecrates. In spite
Of his own will, that arm will strike those men
Who, staying at your side, will share your sin.

DESIDERIUS

Go back to your king and throw off the mantle
That makes you so bold. Take a sword and come
Here to see for yourself if God can ever
Choose a traitor as champion. Companions!
What shall we all answer to this man?

MANY COMPANIONS

                                    War!

ALCUIN

You shall have it, and soon, and here. God's angel,
Who leads and never stops to look behind,
Who twice guided and led Pepin's horse,
Is on his way already.

DESIDERIUS

                            Every duke
Deploy his ensigns, every judge affix
The war ban to muster troops at once.
Every man possessing a horse, ride it,
And make haste here to answer the entreaty
Of his kings. At the Alps will this combat
Be decided. [*to the* LEGATE] Report this invitation
To the Frankish king.

ADELCHIS

                            And tell him also
That every man's God, the God who hears
The vows made to the helpless and lends them
Surety either for fulfillment, or for
Avenging their breach; the God whose favor
Some boast to have who are by Him accursed;
That God sends often madness to the heart
Of the sinful, which drives him unaware
To his punishment. Tell him how ill-advised
Is he who comes defying Lombard swords,
Having offended a Lombard woman.
[*exeunt* THE KINGS, *with most of the* LOMBARDS, *and the* LEGATE,
   from opposite doors]

Scene VI

[DUKES *who have stayed*]

INDULF

War, he said!

FARWALD

The kingdom's fate depends on it.

INDULF

And ours.

ERWIG

Shall we then wait for it
In idleness?

ILDECHIS

Friends, this is no place for
Debate. Let us depart and convene, each one
Through diverse routes, at Svartus's house.

Scene VII

[SVARTUS *'s house*]

SVARTUS

That was a Frankish legate! Some big event
Impends, whatever will be. —My name lies
On the urn's bottom, buried by a thousand
Other names. If the urn is not shaken,
There it will stay forever, I will die
Obscure: nobody shall even suspect
I ever wished to be drawn out of it.—
I am nought. If the notable people,
Those who can safely counter the kings,
Sometimes do meet under this humble roof,
If they admit me to their secret meetings,
It is because I am nought. Who cares for Svartus?
Who wants to spy which foot crosses this threshold?
Who hates me? Who fears me? —O if daring
Could bestow preferment! If destiny
Ruled not from the beginning, if leadership
Were given by the sword, then you would see,
O haughty dukes, who would win the contest.

If the crafty could obtain the power!
I read the hearts of all of you, but mine
Is sealed. You would be amazed if you could see
In it only one wish, one hope, that tie
Myself to all of you: to be your peer, one day.
You think you can appease me with some gold.
To throw some gold at your inferior, that
Is life! But to be one among many
Who stretch their hands to seize it, like beggars
In helplessness and humiliation . . .

Scene VIII

[*enter* ILDECHIS *then others join*]

ILDECHIS

Heaven save you, Svartus. Has anyone
arrived yet?

SVARTUS

          No. What news at court?

ILDECHIS

                         Most grave.
The war against the Franks has been declared.
The knot becomes every hour more tangled,
And needs cutting by the sword, O Svartus.
The day is near, I hope, when every man
Receives at last his reward.

SVARTUS

                  Here I stand
At your service.

ILDECHIS [*to* FARWALD, *entering*]
          Is anyone else coming?

FARWALD
　Indulf is behind me.

ILDECHIS
　　　　　　　　　Here he comes.

INDULF
　Friends!

ILDECHIS [*welcoming more incoming persons*]
　　　　　　Vila! Erwig! Brothers! Now
　Is the moment that we were awaiting,
　As you can see. We will be the vanquished
　In this war, whichever is the winner,
　If grand, decisive action we don't take.
　As soon as fortune smiles upon one king,
　That king will despoil us. If Charles triumphs,
　What is the place that we shall occupy
　In his realm, newly conquered? We are forced
　To side with one, and only one, combatant.
　Do you believe these kings have in their hearts
　Any forgiveness toward those who wished
　To be the subjects of another sovereign?

INDULF
　No peace with them!

OTHER DUKES
　　　　　　　　　No peace!

ILDECHIS
　　　　　　　　　　　　We must perforce
　Become allied with Charles.

FARWALD
　　　　　　　　　　　To his legate . . .

ERWIG

We cannot speak to him. The kings' friends hold
Him amongst themselves. 'Twas Adelchis's thought.

ILDECHIS

One of us must go, then, to manifest
Our promises to Charles, bring back his vows,
Or return ours.

INDULF

Well said.

ILDECHIS

Who will be
The messenger?

SVARTUS

I will. Dukes, lend an ear
To me. If anyone of you is missing,
Eyes will start looking for him, suspicion
Will search his way and find him at last.
But if an ordinary knight, if Svartus
Is absent, the world will not take note more
Than if it saw a rabbit disappearing
In the woods. If in a roll-call anybody
Inquires upon my whereabouts, it is
Enough to say: "Svartus? I saw him riding
Along the Ticino. His horse bolted
All of a sudden and unsaddled him.
He fell into the river, and his armor
Kept him from floating; he drowned." Poor wretch,
They will say, and nobody will ever
Again mention my name. 'Tis not allowed
To you to go unobserved, but as for me,
Who will ever gaze at my face? Maybe
A Latin or two will turn around to watch
My horse approaching in the morning's quiet.
But those ones too will soon yield me the way.

ILDECHIS

I did not know that you were so courageous.

SVARTUS

Necessity sharpens the zeal to act.
And after all, nothing more than quickness
Is needed for delivering messages.

ILDECHIS [*to the* DUKES]

Shall Svartus go?

DUKES

He may.

ILDECHIS

At the dawn of
Tomorrow be ready, Svartus. By then
Our orders will also be ready.

Act II

Scene I

[*the Frankish camp in* Val di Susa; PETER, CHARLES]

PETER

Indomitable Charles, what do I hear?
You have not even put your foot within
The borders of that second realm that God
Reserves for you, and rumors of retreat
Are whispered all around your camp today!
May royal refutation hush at once
The unholy voice! Do not let posterity
Remember that King Charles did leave undone
A deed that God ordained for him to accomplish.
Do not let me go back to our father
To tell him how the sword God had you unsheathe
Was put away, and say: "Your great son
Willed for a moment only and then despaired."

CHARLES

O man of God, you saw how much I did
For the sake of the holy father's safety.
The whole world saw it and will so recount.
I cannot take advice from my desire
When necessity has shown me what to do.
The Almighty God is one. When first I heard
The anguished cry of our holy father,
I was trampling over the vanquished idols
That the perfidious Saxons left behind.
Their flight opened the way before me,
I was able to advance victoriously,
To bargain pacts where I would rule soon after.
The Frankish assembly met in Geneva
And every will was pliable to mine.
Resembling one man with one sole purpose,
The whole of France had but one cause to serve,
And with glad spirit headed for Italy,
As if to reclaim back its own lost land.
You can see for yourself where things stand now:
The Alps' pass is impervious. If men
Were the only obstacle between us and
The land to conquer, the king of the Franks
Would surely say: "Entrance can be obtained."
But nature itself fortified the field
For our enemy, dug chasms as moats,
And these high mountains our Lord erected
Are their bulwarks and watchtowers. Each pass,
Even the smallest, is secured by walls,
Whence ten men could hold off a thousand,
Nay, women could safely injure warriors.
—Too many brave ones did I lose already
In deeds where courage will never suffice.
Too much of Frankish blood Adelchis shed,
Safely defended in his coign of vantage.
As daring as a lion by his lair,
He swiftly attacks with deadliest blows.
When visiting the camp I often heard

His name uttered with horror by my soldiers,
As I stood still beside the tents, at night.
I shall not keep my people any more
In this sad state of fear. If we had faced
The foe in open field, certain victory
Would have smiled on us in brief time. Indeed
That victory could hardly have been called such
With respect to true honor and glory.
Yet Svartus, a deserter with no fame,
Would have shared that victory with me.
He came to enumerate so many foes
Who had submitted to my will already.
One day, one day only would have sufficed.
God denies it to me. So shall it be.

PETER

    O king, do not keep from humble begging
The servant of the one who elected you,
Placing the royal sign within your house.
Think in what hands you leave the one you call
Father. You have provoked his enemy
To war, you were ready to fight, and yet
The cruel old man, maddened by rage more than
By fear, ordered the Holy Shepherd
To give the Franks other kings—you know them.
Such the reply the Pope sent to the tyrant:
"May my hand be paralyzed for ever,
May the chrism desiccate on the altar,
Before I cast it as a seed of war
Against my own son." "Have your son then
Help you," was the response of that king.
"But if he fails you, one day, between us
Will the dispute be settled."

CHARLES

                  Why do you
Rekindle this pain? Why should I join you
In voicing fruitless queries? Or you think

That Charles needs any spurring on his flanks?
In danger Hadrian lies—does perhaps Charles
Need a warning from others? Within me
I can hear him, see him. No other mortal's
Sufferings can touch me more than the Pope's.
But overcome these fortifications
And fly to his succor, the Frankish king
Cannot. I said it now, and this word I
Do not willingly repeat. Until today
I was able to obtain all I desired
From my people because I asked from them
Only things grand and feasible. To one
Who watches from afar, the lightest things
Look burdensome, but he will deem most light
Those tasks that far exceed the human might.
The man who grapples with things and must obtain
What he wants through toil, that one only knows
The minutes that go to make the hours.
I offered peace in exchange for freeing
The Romans' lands. I offered gold for peace.
It was refused! Alas the shame! To mend it
I will go to fight on the Weser . . .

Scene II

[*enter* ARVINUS]

ARVINUS

  My Lord, a Latin man arrived and asks
  To see you.

PETER

          A Latin man?

CHARLES

                    Whence did he
  Come? How did he pass the Gates?

ARVINUS

                              Through unknown
Paths, circumventing them. He boasts to have
Precious advice for you.

CHARLES

                    Admit him here.
[*exit* ARVINUS]
You will hear him with me. I want to leave
Nothing untried in this attempt to rescue
Pope Hadrian. You will be witness to this.

Scene III

[*enter* MARTINUS, *preceded by* ARVINUS, *who then retires*]

CHARLES

    You are a Latin and you arrived at my camp,
    Unharmed and unobserved?

MARTINUS

                         Most noble hope
Of the herd and of the holy shepherd,
I see you now, and this is ample prize
For the dangers and pains I had to face.
But there will be another! To you who
Have been chosen to destroy the godless
I am coming to point the way.

CHARLES

                    Which way?

MARTINUS

    The one I traveled.

CHARLES

                    How did you come here?
And who are you? Whence did the daring thought
Come to you?

MARTINUS

                    I belong to the deacons'
Holy brotherhood. Ravenna gave me light,
And its shepherd, Leo, sends me to you.
"Do go, said he, to the savior of Rome,
Find him; God be with you; and if he will
Bestow on you such an honor, become
His trusted escort. Manifest to him
The lamentation of the Pope and Rome."

CHARLES

You can see here his legate.

PETER

                              O let me
Take your hand, brave fellow countryman,
To us you come as an angel of joy.

MARTINUS

I am just a mortal sinner. But joy
Is from Heaven and will not be in vain.

CHARLES

Magnanimous Latin, please recount
All that you saw along the way, the perils,
Your sufferings. Tell me all.

MARTINUS

                         As soon as
Leo beckoned me, I headed for your camp.
I traveled the fair region that the Lombard
Has as his lair, and after him is named.
The Latin people were the only dwellers
Of the cities and villages I saw.
Of the godless race, who is our enemy,
As well as yours, nobody is extant there,
But the disdainful brides of these oppressors,
Their mothers and the youth, training in arms;

They left tired old men to keep an eye
On the subjects, the slaves who till the land,
Too large a flock for so few and weak shepherds.
When I came to the Gates, I saw the horses,
The arms, an entire people gathered there
For you to destroy with one mighty blow.

CHARLES

    Could you look at their camp from a short distance?
What are they doing?

MARTINUS

                They feel so secure
From the Italian side, that no moat or fence
Is there, no troops are orderly arrayed.
They are thickly gathered only on this side,
Whence solely they fear that you may strike.
In vain I would have tried to cross their camp,
In an attempt to reach you from that side,
Because it is well girded, like a fortress.
My shaved chin and short hair, my face, my garments,
My Latin tongue, all would have easily
Given me away as foe amidst their crowd.
I would have met a sure, meaningless death.
But to return without having seen you
Would have been worse to me than dying thus.
Then the thought struck me that just a brief distance
Kept me from seeing the savior's countenance,
Charles's face. I resolved to look for the way,
And I found it.

CHARLES

             But how could this way be
Known to you, yet hidden to the enemy?

MARTINUS

    God blinded them, God guided me. I left
The camp unobserved, retracing my steps

On my way out. Then turning left I headed
To the north and I abandoned all
Well-trodden paths. I entered into a dark,
Narrow valley, but as I walked along
It became spacious, more and more airy.
There I saw roaming flocks and wretched sheds,
Resembling mankind's ultimate abodes
In a wasteland. A shepherd hosted me
For the night, and I slept on woolen hides.
When I awoke at dawn I asked the way
To France of the good shepherd, and he said:
"Beyond those mountains are other mountains
And others still, and then, but very far,
There is France. But there is no way to go.
There are thousands of mountains, steep and bare,
And dreadful. No one lives there but spirits;
No mortal man did ever pass them." "God's
ways are many," I replied, "many more
Than a mortal man has, and God sends me."
"Then may God guide you," he said; and out of
The loaves he kept in store he gave me many,
As many as a pilgrim can carry;
In a bag of coarse cloth he put them and
I shouldered it, as I prayed our God
To reward him. And then I set out.
I came to the valley's border and climbed
A slope, and trusting in God, passed the crest.
No human vestige was there, only woods
Of untouched fir trees, unknown rivers, and
Valleys not yet furrowed by paths; silence
Reigned supreme; only my footsteps echoed,
Sometimes splashing streams, or suddenly
The croaking of the hawk, the swoosh of wings,
Above me, of an eagle flying out
Of her impervious nest, early in the morning;
Late in the afternoon, the pine trees' cones
Would crackle as the sun parched them. Three days
This journey lasted; three times I rested

At night under big trees or in ravines.
The sun was my guide. I rose with him and
Followed his route, heading toward sunset.
Always uncertain I was of the way,
As from valley to valley I traveled;
For often, after ascending with ease
An accessible slope, I reached the peak,
More and higher mountains would appear.
Many were white with snow from foot to tip,
Like huge tents firmly infixed into the ground.
Others were naked, much like iron walls,
Impassable. At dusk on the third day
I saw a big mountain, topping all others:
Its slope all green, its summit crowned with plants.
Promptly I turned my feet in that direction.
It was the eastern side of this mountain,
This very mountain, O king, against which
Your camp leans, facing the setting sun.
As I was on its slope, night's darkness fell.
The dry and shining needles of fir-trees,
That covered all the ground with a thick layer,
Were my mattress, the ancient trunks my bed-posts.
A smiling hope awoke me at daybreak,
And full of renewed strength I climbed the slope.
As soon as I arrived on top, a humming,
As if from a far distance, hit my ear:
It was dim, unceasing. I paused to hear:
'Twas not the waters breaking on the rocks
Further down the slope; it was not the wind
Blowing with soughing sound across the forests.
It was indeed the noise of living souls,
A muffled sound of tongues speaking at once,
Of laboring hands, walking feet, swarming,
Huge crowds of people jostling. My heart gave
A jump, I sped my steps. On that far peak
That resembles a wedge from this viewpoint,
A sharp axe cutting the sky, lies a plain,
Wide and covered with grass that human feet

Had not yet touched. I crossed the plain along
The shortest line; at every step I took
The noise grew louder. With blissful spirit
I devoured the last tract of the way.
I came to the verge, glimpsed the valley
Below and saw . . . Yes, I did see the tents
Of Israel, the desired pavilions
Of Jacob. I lay on the ground, thanked God
And blessed those pavilions. Then I descended.

CHARLES

Only an impious mind would not see here
The arm of the Almighty God!

PETER

       Much more
Manifest will His arm be in that deed
God intended for you.

CHARLES

       I will do it.
[*to* MARTINUS] Think first, and then make answer to my
 question
With no misgivings: can my knights pass through
The way you traveled?

MARTINUS

      They can. For whom else
Would the Heavens have prepared such a path?
Why should an unknown mortal come and tell
All about it to the king of the Franks,
If this were but a wonder with no use?

CHARLES

Tonight you shall rest in my tent: at dawn
You shall guide a chosen band of warriors
Through that way. Consider, O brave man, that
Into your hands I put the best of France.

MARTINUS

    O, I shall be with them, and let my head
    Be surety for my promise, nothing less.

CHARLES

    If I can from these Alps depart at last,
    If I as victor can arrive at Peter's
    Holy shrine, if in the cherished arms of
    Father Hadrian I can be received, and
    If my plea can win his holy favor,
    You shall don the sacred vestment of bishop,
    Visible sign of the honor Charles pays
    To you.—Arvinus, [*to* ARVINUS, *entering*] summon the counts
        and
    The Priests.
    [*exit* ARVINUS]

CHARLES [*to the* LEGATE *and* MARTINUS]
              And you, raise your hands to Heaven
    So that your thanks to God will also be
    Our entreaty for His lasting grace.
    [*exeunt the* LEGATE *and* MARTINUS]

Scene IV

CHARLES

    This is the way, then, Charles returns to France:
    In front of him did loom the bitter scorn
    Of foes and of posterity alike,
    But he had sworn he would return to France.
    Who, among my men, my trusted counselors
    Would have dissuaded me from my resolve,
    Either by prayer or advice? And lo,
    A stranger comes along, a man of peace
    And he alone can bring me novel thoughts!
    But 'tis not he that gives me back my heart:
    The star that shone when I exited France
    And that was hidden for a time, now is

Back in the sky. 'Twas a deceitful ghost
That came to keep me out of Italy.
False was the voice that whispered in my heart:
"You will never be king over the land
Where Ermengarde was born"—And yet I
Am unstained by your blood; you are alive.
Why was your image then so unyielding
When it appeared to me, voiceless, and with
Reproachful brow, dejected, pale, as if
You had come out of your tomb? God condemned
Your house; should I then have remained allied
With it? If Hildegarde enticed my eyes,
Was it not in the highest interest
Of the kingdom that she enter my bed?
If your feminine heart is a lesser
Concern, what can I do? What can be achieved
By one who wants to foresee all the pains
Before he acts? A king cannot travel
His lofty route without crushing someone
Under his feet. O apparition, born
From shadow and silence, the sun is rising,
The trumpets have been sounded, leave me now.

Scene V

[*enter* COUNTS *and* BISHOPS]

CHARLES

My friends, I put you through a harsh ordeal,
Exposing you to many useless dangers,
And sufferings that seemed without a purpose.
But you had faith in your king; you obeyed
Him as on a day of battle. The end
Of this ordeal is by now near, and you
Will have a reward worthy of the Franks.
At dawn a band departs—and you, Eggihard,
Will lead them. They will seek out the enemy
And will reach him where they are least expected.

I will impart more clear commands, Eggihard.
I have some friends within the Lombard camp
And you will learn the sign by which to know
Them, and how to avail yourself of their help.
To oust the foes from there will be for you
A very simple mission. We will pass
The Gates without resistance; we will fight
At last in open field—O friends! No more
Swift arrows shot from high embattlements,
Accompanied by laughter from those who
Can wound, deride, and yet remain unpunished
Behind walls; no more attacks by surprise.
But freely will the flags fly in the wind,
And horse will smack with horse: people dispersed
Over the plain, their chests no farther from us
Than a spear's length. Tell this tonight
To my soldiers: tell them you saw the king
As happy as that time he did foretell
The victory at Ehresburg; command
That they prepare to fight, and we will speak
Of return to France when we have won and
Shared the booty. Three days from now, the battle
Shall be crowned with victory, and we shall
Enjoy our rest on Italy's fair soil,
On golden wheat fields, swaying in the wind,
In orchards full of fruit that were unknown
To our fathers, in time-honored temples
And mansions, in the land that songs make merry,
And that the sun over all others favors.
The land that guards within its ancient bosom
The emperors of the earth and God's martyrs.
The land where the holy shepherd's lifted hands
Will bless our emblems. The land inhabited
And ruled by a small nation, hostile to us,
Which inner strife divides among themselves,
And half of which already sides with me;
The same nation my father twice defeated,
An extinguished people. The rest is

All for us to conquer; all awaits us
—Let the enemy from their towers watch
Our camp move, let them rejoice as they
Dream of our departure, as they dream
That they will conquer Rome, enslave the Pope,
The common father, our friend; until
Eggihard comes, like an abrupt awakening.
—And you, holy men, priests, and bishops, order
That wakes of prayer be held around the camp,
Because to God we wish to consecrate
This enterprise that is in truth His own.
Just as my Franks, prostrating in the dust
Will bow their head before the King of kings,
So our foes will yield to us in battle.

 Act III

Scene I

[*Lombard camp, in front of* ADELCHIS's *tent;* ADELCHIS, ANFRID]

ANFRID [*while arriving*]
My lord!

ADELCHIS

Dearest Anfrid—any sign
That the Franks are about to leave for good?

ANFRID
No sign as yet. They are in the same spot
As they were when you saw them at dawn;
Three days elapsed without changes, since their
Retreat began. Along the moat I went
Observing; I climbed onto a tower
And watched: they were arrayed in tight, thick ranks,
Alert, unlike those willing to attack,
Rather like those who are fearful of assault,
All the more wary 'cause their troops are dwindling;

They intend no offense, they seem impatient
To withdraw, they await the occasion.

ADELCHIS

And so they will, I fear. The recreant knave
Who offended Ermengarde, the one who
Swore to extinguish our house, is fleeing;
I cannot pursue him with my horse,
Cannot seize him, and fight with him, until
I can lie down to rest on his armor.
No, I cannot! I cannot challenge him
In open field. Only here at the Gates
To me 'twas given to defend the kingdom
With the loyal few whom I appointed
As sentries to the camp, and with those warriors
Whom I chose to fight in rapid forays.
Thus I could keep the traitors off the fight,
At bay for a while. But in open field
They would abandon me and my faithful
In the hands of the Franks. Alas the rage!
When the messenger comes to give me news
Of Charles's departure, what a glad message
It will be! How can I rejoice when Charles
Is yet escaping from my sword?

ANFRID

                                    Sweet sire,
Let present glory suffice. Charles came to
Your kingdom with the thought of despoiling
An easy prey: he returns defeated.
Defeat was clearly admitted when he asked
For peace and offered gold. You rebuffed it;
Your father was elated, and the whole camp
Could not but talk about it; the faithful
Are made proud by this glory of yours, proud
That they can share it with you; and the knaves
Who vowed not to love you must fear you now
More than ever.

ADELCHIS

                Glory, you say? My lot
Is to seek glory and die before I can
Ever taste of it. No, this is not glory,
Anfrid. My foe departs unpunished,
Ready to accomplish more and more conquests.
He was won here; he will stalk victory
Elsewhere. And so he can because he reigns
Over a nation whose will is as firm
As the iron the king's sword is made of,
Cast solidly in one piece. As he handles
His sword nimbly in his hands, so does he
Handle, too, his own people. Against him,
Who wounded me most deeply in my heart,
And then, to atone for it, prepared to invade
My kingdom—against this one I cannot
Take my vengeance! Another enterprise
Must needs be done, that always was displeasing
To my thought, neither righteous nor glorious,
And this, of course, will be easy and successful.

ANFRID

    Is the king thinking of the old plans, then?

ADELCHIS

    Could you doubt it? Now that he is delivered
From the Frankish threat, he will promptly move
Against the holy prince. Thus we will lead
Lombardy to the Tiber, unanimous
And eager, against a helpless people.
And Lombardy will lightly move to fight
For such an easy booty! Is this war,
Is this a foe? We will heap ruins over
Existing ruins. This is our art,
You know, an ancient one: to set fire
To huts and palaces alike. We will
First kill the lords of the land, then all those

Who randomly shall fall under our axes.
The rest will be enslaved and distributed,
And the most feared, that is, the most disloyal
Lombards will have the booty's best share. —Alas,
That my destiny should come to this,
To be the leader of a band of thieves!
I thought Heaven would destine me to deeds
On this land other than to despoil it
Without peril or honor. —O dearest friend,
You who have been with me since the first years
Of my life, my companion in arms, games,
And dangers alike, my chosen brother—
With you only I can let my thoughts fly
Over my lips. My heart aches, O Anfrid.
It does command me lofty and noble deeds,
But fortune condemns me to unjust ones;
Thus I walk my way, dragged along a route
I did not choose, an obscure path to nowhere . . .
And my heart becomes dry, like to a seed
Cast onto a barren ground and blown away
By the wind.

ANDFRIDO

O most noble sufferer,
My royal friend! Your devout companion
Cannot but feel admiration and pity
For you. Although I cannot take away
Your splendid woe, I can share it with you.
To tell your heart to be content with pomp,
Authority, and gold that come with kingship
Would be to solace you with shameful peace,
That peace the pusillanimous men seek.
Can I tell this to you, and would I wish
To say these things to you, were I able?
It is your lot to suffer and be grand,
Till this hour. Suffer but hope. Your course
Has just begun. Who can tell now what works

Heaven reserves for you, what occasions?
That same Heaven that has made you king
And endowed you with such a noble heart.

Scene II

[*enter* DESIDERIUS *and exit* ANFRID]

DESIDERIUS

My dear son, as you are my peer in kingship
I cannot grant to you any more honors.
No mortal man can make you greater than
You are; the sole reward I can offer,
Which will be dear to you for my own sake,
Is my joy and fatherly high praises.
You saved a kingdom, and your glory has just
Begun to shine over an even larger
And smoother field. You once thwarted my plans
With doubts and fears that now your arm dispelled.
Your prowess in arms, your valor admit
No excuse you want to find for yourself.
Vanquisher of the Franks! I hail in you
The conqueror of Rome: with your conquest
You will append the last, most precious leaf
To that royal wreath that never, so far,
Was worn entire by Lombard kingly heads.

ADELCHIS

Obedient warrior I will always be,
O father, whichever the enterprise that
You order.

DESIDERIUS

Son, 'tis mere obedience, then,
That prompts you to pursue such noble conquests?

ADELCHIS

To obey you, father, is, in faith, an action
That solely depends upon myself.

Therefore obedience you shall have from me
As long as I can breathe.

DESIDERIUS

                  Would you obey
While disapproving?

ADELCHIS

             I would.

DESIDERIUS

                    O glory
And torment of my old age, thus you are
Your father's arm in battle and hindrance
In his thoughts. Will it always be so, that
You have to be dragged by force to victory?

Scene III

[*enter a* SQUIRE]

SQUIRE
The Franks! The Franks!

DESIDERIUS

               What are you raving, madman?

SQUIRE
The Franks, O king.

DESIDERIUS

            How, the Franks?
[*enter a crowd of* FUGITIVE LOMBARDS *and* BAUDUS]

ADELCHIS

                 What happened,
Baudus?

BAUDUS

      O woe! The camp is invaded
From all sides. The Franks suddenly struck at
Our back.

DESIDERIUS

      But what way did they arrive?

BAUDUS

Who knows?

ADELCHIS

      Let us act promptly. It must be
A disbanded cohort.

BAUDUS

      It is indeed
A whole army, and we are the disbanded.
All is lost.

DESIDERIUS

      All is lost?

ADELCHIS

      The Franks are here,
So, are we not here ourselves just for them?
What matters whence they came? Let us go now!
We do have our weapons to receive them.
Unsheathe your swords! The Franks already did
Taste of their blades. This is but another
Battle, 'tis nothing new for the warrior.
O Lombards, turn around, I say! Where are
You running to? For Heaven's sake, the way
You take is most shameful. The enemy is there.
All follow Adelchis! [*enter* ANFRID] Anfrid!

ANFRID

      I come
With you, O king.

ADELCHIS [*as he goes*]
                    Father, rush to the Gates
To guard them.
[*exit* ADELCHIS, *followed by* BAUDUS *and some* LOMBARDS]

DESIDERIUS [*to the* FUGITIVES *passing by*]
                    Wretched people! Come at least
To the Gates with me: if you value life
So dearly, then there stand towers and walls
For your protection.
[*other* FUGITIVE SOLDIERS *arrive from the direction toward which*
    ADELCHIS *left*]

A FUGITIVE SOLDIER
                    O king, why are you
Still here? Be gone!

DESIDERIUS
                    For shame! This is advice
To give to your king? Whom are you fleeing?
You want to leave the Gates unguarded, say?
What happened? Cowardice did rob you all
Of your wits.
[*the* SOLDIERS *keep fleeing;* DESIDERIUS *points his sword against the*
    chest of one of them, arresting him]
                    You heartless fellow, if iron
Makes you flee, this iron kills no less than
The Frankish one can do. Speak to the king:
Why are you abandoning the Gates?

SOLDIER
    The Franks suddenly attacked the unguarded side
    Of our camp. We saw all from the towers.
    Our warriors are disbanded.

DESIDERIUS
                    You lie.
My son did muster them and leads them now
Against the scanty enemy. Turn around!

SOLDIER

My Lord, in faith, no time is left for that.
Their numbers are not scanty, they are charging,
We are doomed. They are all tightly arrayed
While our troops are scattered here and there,
Deprived of weapons, in flight. Adelchis
Cannot muster them. We are betrayed.

DESIDERIUS

O cowards! Let us retreat to the Gates:
There we can defend ourselves.

ANOTHER SOLDIER

        The Gates
Are deserted. The Franks will pass them and
We are caught in-between at this hour.
Only a small passage remains for us to escape,
And that shall soon be gone.

DESIDERIUS

        Then let us die
Here, as valiant warriors.

ANOTHER SOLDIER

      We are betrayed.
They sold us as to the slaughterhouse.

ANOTHER SOLDIER

We want to die in a more righteous war,
As it becomes to warriors, not betrayed
And slain.

ANOTHER SOLDIER

  The Franks!

SEVERAL SOLDIERS

      Let us flee!

DESIDERIUS

Let us run,
Then, I will flee with you. Such is the lot
Of kings who reign over cowards. [*goes with the* FUGITIVES]

Scene IV

[*the camp abandoned by the* LOMBARDS, *at the* Gates; CHARLES *surrounded by
the* Frankish COUNTS, *and* SVARTUS]

CHARLES

We finally did pass these Gates. To God
Goes all the honor of this deed. O Italy,
In your bosom I infix this spear, sign
Of our conquest. 'Twas a victory indeed
Without a battle. Eggihard alone
Had already done all. [*to a* COUNT] Climb on that hill
And watch for his cohort. Come and warn me
When he arrives.
[*exit the* COUNT]

Scene V

[*enter* ROLAND]

CHARLES

How now, Roland, so soon
Do you return from the battle?

ROLAND

O king,
I pray you to be witness, with you all,
Counts, that today I have not unsheathed
My sword once. Let the one fight as he likes
Who wants to fight in such a shameful day.
I will not chase a frightened flock of sheep.

CHARLES

    Have you not met one who would show his brow?

ROLAND

    I saw a party coming toward me
    Headed by many dukes. I ran to charge,
    But they presently lowered their ensigns
    And displayed marks of peace and cried that they
    Were friends. How, friends? We were not such for sure
    When we clashed at the Gates. They asked to see
    The king. I then showed them my shoulders and
    Soon you yourself will see them. Had I known
    What kind of foe we were coming to fight,
    Certainly I would not have moved from France.

CHARLES

    Peace, my brave man. The conquest of a land
    Is still a worthy thing, whichever way
    We achieved it. All this will not last long,
    Do not fear to stay idle: Saxony
    Yet to be vanquished and conquered.
    [*enter the* COUNT *sent to watch on the hill*]

COUNT

    Eggihard is on the field, heading this way.
    He advances through the battle; the Lombards
    Are in disarray, fleeing left and right.
    The plain that divides us will soon be cleared.

CHARLES

    All according to plan.

COUNT

                  I saw a party
    Who surrendered to us. They were running
    This way.

ANOTHER COUNT

           They are here.

CHARLES

                    Svartus, are these
The ones you announced?

SVARTUS

                  They are. —Hail my comrades!

Scene VI

[*enter* ILDECHIS *and other* ᴌombard DUKES, JUDGES, SOLDIERS]

ILDECHIS

Hail Svartus! The king!

CHARLES

                  Aye, I am the king.

ILDECHIS [*kneeling and putting his hands in* CHARLES*'s*]
    O king of the Franks and our own!
    I pray, take our devout hand in yours,
    Which is victorious, and from the mouth
    Of the Lombards accept the homage
    That long ago was to you assured.

CHARLES

Svartus, count of Susa!

SVARTUS

               O king, this honor . . .

CHARLES

Pray tell me the names of these loyal men.

SVARTUS

    Ildechis, duke of Trento, Erwig
    of Cremona, Ermenegild of
    Milan, Vila of Piacenza, Indulf
    of Pisa; these other here are judges,
    these are warriors.

CHARLES
                                    Pray stand, my faithful people,
And listen: judges and dukes will remain
Each one in his rank, for the time being.
The first moments of rest that we shall have
I will devote to rewarding your merits.
This is a time for action. O brave men,
Go back now to your brothers and tell them
That, as a chief of warriors belonging
To the same race as theirs, I do not mean
To bring war to a kindred people.
I came to oust from the Lombard throne
A family that God has cast away,
Utterly unworthy of the crown. Simply,
Your kingdom will change king. Look at the sun.
Those who will come to render homage
Before the sun sets, either in my hand,
Or in that of the Frankish vassals, or
In yours, those shall become my faithful men,
And shall preserve their rank. To those who will
Bring to my presence the two former kings
I will consign a prize commensurate
With the greatness of their deed.
    [*exeunt* LOMBARDS]

CHARLES [*to* ROLAND, *aside*]
                                    Roland,
    Did I call these people "brave"?

ROLAND
                                    Alas, you did.

CHARLES
    Then the king's lip went wrong: that word I should
    Keep in store as a reward for my Franks.
    May every one forget that I said it!

Scene VII

[*as* CHARLES *is about to exit, enter two Frankish* SOLDIERS
carrying wounded ANFRID]

ROLAND
  Here is an enemy. Where is the battle?

A FRANKISH SOLDIER
  This was the only one who fought.

CHARLES
                                                    Alone?

FRANKISH SOLDIER
  Most of them simply put down their weapons
  And surrendered; others ran away in swarms.
  We saw this man alone, slowly retreating.
  His weapons manifested his high rank.
  Four of us set out to pursue him
  Full slack over the fields. As we chased him,
  He did not run, did not hasten his flight.
  When we reached him, he turned around. "Surrender,"
  We cry to him, but now he assaults us.
  His spear he throws against the closest one,
  Kills him, extracts the spear and kills another,
  But as he hit we struck him and he fell.
  As he lay on the ground, he stretched his arms
  Begging us to set aside all rancor
  And to carry him far from the turmoil,
  To a place where he could die in peace.
  Victorious Lord, a better thing to do
  We could not find: we yielded to his prayer.

CHARLES
  You did well. Preserve your wrath for those
  Who resist you. Svartus, do you know him?

SVARTUS

    This is Anfrid, Adelchis's squire.

CHARLES

    Anfrid, did you charge these warriors alone?

ANFRID

    Who needs companions in facing his death?

CHARLES

    Behold, Roland, a brave man at last.
    [*to* ANFRID] Why did you waste a worthy life, warrior?
    Did you not know that it would become ours,
    That surrendering would mean to be still
    A warrior, not a captive, of the king
    Of the Franks?

ANFRID

              How could I have ever been
    Your warrior, when I was given the occasion
    To die in Adelchis's service? To Heaven
    Adelchis is dear, O king. And Heaven
    Will take him, I hope, from this present shame
    To a better day. But remember these words:
    Whoever causes offense to Adelchis
    Either as he still reigns or is dethroned,
    That man offends God in his purest image.
    You surpass him in power and fortune,
    But no man ever had a greater soul.
    And this is the true word of one who dies.

CHARLES [*to the* COUNTS]

    This is the love a loyal man must harbor.
    [*to* ANFRID] You depart now accompanied by our
    Admiration. 'Tis the king of the Franks
    Who holds your hand as a mark of honor
    And true friendship. In the land of brave men,
    Anfrid, your name shall live. The Frankish

Women will hear it from us and with awe
And pity they will say it and pray for
Your eternal rest. —Fulrad, bestow
Upon this pious man the extreme unction.
[*to the* SOLDIERS *around*] Behold in him a true friend of the
    king.
My counts, let us go and meet Eggihard,
He amply deserves a solemn welcome.

Scene VIII

[*a solitary wood;* DESIDERIUS, VERMUNDUS,
and other fugitive LOMBARDS *in disarray*]

VERMUNDUS

    We are safe at last, my king. Sit you down
    And rest your old and venerable bones
    Upon this grass. Restore your tired spirit.
    We are far enough from the battle, far
    From the highway: we cannot even hear
    The baneful hum. You are safely surrounded
    By loyal men.

DESIDERIUS

              What happened to Adelchis?

VERMUNDUS

    He will soon join us, I hope. I did send
    More than one trusted man in search of him,
    To call him back from such a futile risk,
    And guide him to this loyal company,
    That he might be spared for worthier battles.

DESIDERIUS

    O Vermundus, the king is indeed tired,
    Exhausted—by the flight!

VERMUNDUS

                         Treacherous knaves!

DESIDERIUS

   O, those coward rogues! They dragged the white hair
Of their king into the mud; they forced him
To flee like a dastard. To flee! And hence
Will I not rise but to flee again, and
Whereto, to what end? My journey will be
But a quest for a tomb devoid of glory.
To what profit? Alas, that I should flee
Because of such base people! Those who seized
My kingdom may have my life as well, and,
Once underground, there is nothing that Charles
Shall have power enough to do to me.

VERMUNDUS

   O revered king, forever our king,
Please be comforted. You still have many
Loyal subjects whom the surprise attack
Scattered around. Honor will recall them
To you. You retain still many strongholds;
Adelchis is alive, I hope.

DESIDERIUS

                     Cursed be
The day when Alboin climbed the mountain
And, looking down, said: "This will be my land!"
An untrustworthy land, which would soon gape
Under his heirs' feet and swallow them all.
Cursed be the day when he led to this land
A people who prove to be so worthless
A guardian! Cursed be the day when he founded
On this land a kingdom, which should have come
To such a wretched end, amidst such shame.

VERMUNDUS

   The king is here!

DESIDERIUS
My son, is it you?

Scene IX

[*enter* ADELCHIS]

ADELCHIS
Father, I see you again.

DESIDERIUS
O, if only
I had listened to your words!

ADELCHIS
What good now
Is it to remember that? You live, father,
Then my life has still a worthy purpose:
I can still spend it in defending you.
O, sir, how can you bear this effort?

DESIDERIUS
For the first time I am feeling the burden
Of my years and of this plight. Other loads
I have carried, but not while fleeing
from the foe.

ADELCHIS [*to the* LOMBARDS]
Behold your king, O warriors,

A LOMBARD
We are ready to die for him!

MANY LOMBARDS
We are!

ADELCHIS
If you are so disposed, we can preserve
More than his life, perhaps. Do you still vow

Your allegiance to our cause, which is
Most uncertain but always sacred, and
Rife with obstacles but not lost yet?

A LOMBARD

Adelchis, do not demand a promise
From your warriors; they are not meet today
For Lombard lips. Vows would sound like perjury.
Instead, ask deeds of us: deeds only can
Be tokens of loyalty in this hour.

ADELCHIS

Yet I do hear some Lombard voices now!
Let us rush to Pavia, then, let us flee,
Let us save our life, for the time being,
To make its price more dear in future times.
It is unworthy to give it away
For the benefit of our betrayers.
We will gather as many dispersed Lombards
As we can while we proceed, and we shall
Mingle with them so as to win them back.
You, father, will stay and rest in Pavia,
Defending the city. The walls are intact;
There are plenty of weapons. Twice Haistulf
Took refuge in that city and remained
Crowned; I shall depart for Verona; now
Make choice of your lieutenant among these.

DESIDERIUS

The duke of Ivrea.

ADELCHIS [*to* GUNTIGIS, *who comes forward*]
                        O Guntigis,
I here entrust my father to your care.
Where is the duke of Verona?

GISELBERT [*coming forward*]
                              Among
The faithful.

ADELCHIS

You will come with me. Gerberga
We will conduct with us. 'Tis villainous
To forget the wretched in the hour
Of wretchedness! Baudus, you know your place.
Bar yourself in Brescia, in defense of
Your dukedom, and of Ermengarde. And you,
Alachi, Ansuldus, Cunbert, Ansprandus,
Ibba, [*pointing at them among the crowd*] go back to our camp.
    Today,
Alas, the Lombards can safely mingle with
The Franks. Examine closely dukes, counts, warriors.
Discern the guiltless from the betrayers.
To those who seem half ashamed to awake
In this present nightmare of cowardice,
Tell them there is still time, and that the kings
Are alive, that the war is not over,
That there remains a way to die with honor.
Conduct them to the fortified cities,
And they will be victorious, for the sword
Of repentant warriors is newly tempered
With a fatal strength. The time that goes by,
Our opponents' weaknesses, your heart—
These things will yield unexpected advice.
Time will bring salvation. Today our reign
Is besieged but not destroyed as yet.
[*exeunt those whom* ADELCHIS *designated*]

DESIDERIUS

O son, you gave me back my vital spirits.
Let us depart.

ADELCHIS

To these valorous people
I now entrust, father, your safety.
I will join you shortly.

DESIDERIUS

                Why so, my son?

ADELCHIS

I wish to wait for Anfrid. We parted,
And he followed me from afar, so as
To shield my rear-guard from any attacks.
I could not swerve his unbending will
From this risky mission he embraced
For loyalty's sake. And I could not stay
To await him when I had not found you yet.
But now that you are safe, I shall not leave
Till he comes.

DESIDERIUS

        I will wait with you.

ADELCHIS

                        Father . . .
[*to an oncoming* SOLDIER] Did you see Anfrid?

SOLDIER

                          King, do not ask this
Of me.

ADELCHIS

      For Heaven's sake, speak!

SOLDIER

                          I saw him
Fall, deadly wounded.

ADELCHIS

                  Such a death does put
A worthy end to a shameful, wrathful day!
Most dear brother, you died for me, you fought
While I . . . O cruel one, why did you want
To face a deadly danger without me?

This is not the pact we two had made. God,
You Who keep me still alive, and leave me
A ponderous duty, give me the strength
To fulfill it. Let us depart from here.

CHORUS

Within mossy mansions, among city ruins,
Within silent forests, in hot, noisy forges,
Among furrowed pastures by servants' sweat sprinkled,
A people's sparse remnants are suddenly astir.
They are raising their heads, they are pricking their ears
To the growing tumult, to the novel clangor.

Like to a sun ray that pierces thick clouds
The fathers' grand virtue still shines on those brows,
Beneath the pale cheeks, in those fearful eyes.
The offenses they suffered and their tattered pride
For their ancient glory appear in those eyes,
And patience and pride collide on those brows.

They eagerly gather, then tremble and part,
And through twisted paths, with wandering steps,
With fear and desire, advance and recede.
They watch their cruel masters for once fleeing cruelty:
The enemy swords are prompting their flight,
In disarrayed crowds, disheartened, confused.

And like savage beasts made prey to their fear,
Their reddish manes bristling for terror and fright,
They are running for shelter, to find their old lairs.
Their usual proud visage the women cast down,
No longer dismissive, nor haughty, but pale,
They pensively gaze at their pensive sons.

The warriors pursuing them are greedy for blood,
They run everywhere, unceasingly searching,
Like greyhounds unleashed to seek out their prey.
A newfound contentment pervades the bystanders,

Swift hope makes them see the outcome already:
They dream of deliverance from their heavy serfdom.

Yet listen! Those brave ones who won the day's battle
And kept your cruel tyrants from easy withdrawal,
Came here from afar, through craggy and rough paths.
They abandoned the joy of festive communal,
Abruptly awoke from lulling repose,
And ran to the summons of bellicose trumpets.

They left in the halls of their castles at home
Their women dejected, repeating, on parting,
Advice and prayers that sobbing would hush.
They loaded their foreheads with crested, bruised helmets,
They saddled their horses, their superb dark coursers,
And galloped away as the drawbridges rumbled.

They crossed many a land in numerous swarms,
They merrily sang, as they rode, their war songs,
Yet cherished in secret sweet thoughts of their castles.
Inside rocky valleys, on sloping ravines,
Their camp they protected in nights that were freezing,
As memory went to trusted love words.

The indefinite dangers of rugged encampments,
And rushes down chasms of difficult passage,
Harsh orders, stark hunger, all this did they bear.
They saw the spears flying, aimed straight at their chests,
And skimming their shields, and grazing their helmets;
They heard the keen arrows that whizzed past their heads.

Thus, how can you hope that, as their sole reward,
These brave ones intended to bring you deliverance,
To bring to an end the pains of some strangers?
Return to your ruins replenished with pride,
To the unmanly work of the hot, noisy forges,
To those furrows sprinkled with the sweat of slaves.

The brave ones will merge with the people they vanquished;
The masters of old will remain with the new ones;
They will steer together the plough that you pull.
They jointly will own all the cattle and the men.
They are taking possession of blood-drenched pastures,
Belonging to a people who have lost their name.

🦕 Act IV 🦕

Scene I

[*orchard in the monastery of San Salvatore, in Brescia;
enter* ERMENGARDE *supported by two* DAMSELS, *and* ANSBERGA]

ERMENGARDE
Here, under this linden tree. [*she sits on a bench*] How sweet is
The April sun! How gently its rays stroke
The budding leaves! Now I do comprehend
How the age-ridden man yearns for the sun,
As life escapes him. [*to the* DAMSELS] I dearly thank you,
Ladies, who supporting my diseased body,
Satisfied this desire that seized me today
To be immersed once more in this brisk air,
The same air I first breathed, here, along
The Mella; and under my native sky
To rest and look as far as my eyes reach.
Sweet sister, Mother to God consecrated,
Pitiful Ansberga!
[*offers her hand to* ANSBERGA; *exeunt* DAMSELS, ANSBERGA *sits
next to* ERMENGARDE]
                            Your cares will soon
Be ended, and my pains, too. O, how justly
God metes them. A tired peace invades me,
Heralding the grave. My tamed youth no longer
Combats the will of God, and my soul, after
Much dwelling with sorrow, loosens itself
At last from these constraints more gently than
I ever hoped. A last favor I ask
Of you: receive my last words, listen to

The vows of a dying woman, keep them
In your heart and give them back one day
To those I leave behind. Do not be, dear,
So distraught; do not look at me with such
Grieved eyes. 'Tis God's merciful will, you see.
Would you prefer that He let me on earth,
To see the day when Brescia falls, at last,
And such an enemy approaches this place?
He does not hold such an ineffable
Tribulation in store for me.

ANSBERGA

                              Sister,
Do not fear that: remote from us remains
The dire battle; against Verona,
Against Pavia, haven of the loyal
Lombards, that baneful man is employing
All his forces, and I pray God that they
Never suffice. All around Brescia's walls
The holy bishop Answald and our
Noble cousin, brave Baudus, have gathered
Warriors from the Benaco and the valleys.
Steadfast they stand, ready to give their life
In this defense. And even if Verona
And Pavia ever did fall, God forbid!
A long, new conflict . . .

ERMENGARDE

                              I shall not see it.
Free from every fear, from every earthly
Passion, delivered from sinful hoping,
I will be far. I shall pray for my father,
For beloved Adelchis, for you, for those
Who suffer, for those who make others suffer,
For all. And now I beg you to receive
My final words. Ansberga, tell our dear
Father and brother, when you do see them
—And may this joy be granted to you soon—

Tell them that as I was on death's threshold,
When all things fade from memory, I kept
A vivid remembrance, sweet and grateful,
Of that day, when, by a most courteous act,
They welcomed with no hesitation and
Much pity their trembling and confused
Kinswoman. Never were they ashamed to have
A rebuffed wife under their roof. Tell them
That I prayed warmly and unceasingly
To God Almighty for their victory.
And if He does not hear them, it will be
The deepest mercy of His supreme wisdom.
Tell them that upon dying I blessed them.
Then . . . pray do not refuse to do this:
Find a noble man, willing and able
To go to that fierce enemy of my people,
No matter when or where . . .

ANSBERGA

                              Charles!

ERMENGARDE

                                        You've named him.

The message must be so: Ermengarde
Died without rancor, no hated people
Did she leave behind. She will beseech
Our God not to demand atonement
From anyone for the suffering that
She bore on earth, since all things were by her
Accepted that came from the Lord's hands.
This should be said to him and . . . if the word
Doesn't sound too bitter to the haughty ear,
That I forgive him. Will you do it?

ANSBERGA

These final words of yours are as sacred
To me as my last words that I, on dying,
Will address to Heaven.

ERMENGARDE

                              My dear sister!
But there is more that I must ask of you:
As you attended with generous care
To this mortal spoil of mine while it hosted
The soul, so let it not be distasteful
To attend to its final care: compose
My body in the tomb in peaceful posture.
This ring that you see here on my left hand
Must accompany me into the grave.
It was given to me at the altar,
Before God. Although my burial place must
Be unadorned—since we all are but dust
And I, what glory can I boast? —yet I
Must have the emblems of a queen, because
I was made queen by a most sacred knot,
And nobody can steal God's gift, you know it.
In life and death alike it must be honored.

ANSBERGA

O pray renounce your painful memories!
Fulfill the sacrifice; listen: become
Consenting citizen of this haven
Where God led you as a pilgrim, and let
This be the house of your sleep. Take the robe
And the spirit that comes with it, oblivion
Of all that is human.

ERMENGARDE

                         Do you wish, then,
That I lie to God, Ansberga? That I
Present myself before Him as a bride,
A virgin bride, but married to a mortal?
No, you can be happy, all of you who
Offered a pure heart, unencumbered by
The past, to the King of kings, you who donned
The holy veil over your eyes before

You ever saw a man. I belong to
Another.

ANSBERGA

   O had you never been his!

ERMENGARDE

Were it so! But one needs to tread the way
God chose for us to the end, whichever
It may be. —Perhaps, upon hearing of
My death, his heart will be assaulted by
A novel thought of repentance and pity.
He might demand as his own my dead body,
To make late, yet sweet amends and have it
Buried in the royal tomb. —Oft the dead,
My Ansberga, are stronger than the living.

ANSBERGA

No, he will not do that.

ERMENGARDE

     How can you, who
Are so pious, impose such harsh a gauge
To God's goodness, which can touch every heart,
And rejoice in His justice to have
A wrong redressed by the one who caused it.

ANSBERGA

But he will not do it, poor soul, because
He cannot.

ERMENGARDE

   Why can he not?

ANSBERGA

     Do not ask
More, my dear, forget all that is past.

ERMENGARDE

Speak, I beseech you, that I descend not
To my grave laden with such a doubt.

ANSBERGA

That impious man committed the crime.

ERMENGARDE

Pray say more!

ANSBERGA

                        Chase him out of your heart
Completely. By entering a new marriage,
He became deadly sinful. Before men
And before God, this unabashéd man
Brings with him to the camp, as if in triumph,
This Hildegarde of his ... [ERMENGARDE *swoons*] But you
     grow pale!
Ermengarde! O Heaven! Sisters, help!
What did I do?
[*enter some* NUNS *and the two* DAMSELS]
                    Nobody can heal her.
See how her own sorrow kills her!

FIRST NUN

                                    Be brave,
She breathes.

SECOND NUN

                    Poor woman, so young, so noble,
And yet so afflicted!

A DAMSEL

                    My sweet lady!

FIRST NUN

Look, she opens her eyes.

ANSBERGA

O Heaven,
What strange eyes!

ERMENGARDE [*delirious*]

O squires! Chase away
That woman! Can you not see how she walks
Daringly and tries to seize the king's hand?

ANSBERGA

Awake! For God's sake do not say these things,
Come to your senses, drive away these ghosts,
Pray to His holy name.

ERMENGARDE [*delirious*]

Charles! Bear not this.
Send forth that stern look of yours. Presently
She will be in flight. I, your guiltless spouse,
Pure-hearted, cannot glimpse that look without
Trembling. What do I see, you smile at her!
Arrest this cruel mockery at once,
It destroys me, I cannot bear it. Charles!
If you can make me die from heartbreak,
Will it be glory for you? You yourself
Will be grieved by this, one day. —Tremendous
Is my love, you do not know it yet, for
I did not show it to you. You were mine,
And, secure in my joy, I kept silent.
Never would my coy lips have revealed wholly
The inebriation of my secret heart.
Pray send her away! See how I fear her!
Like a serpent, her gaze is killing me.
—I am frail and alone, and are you not
My only friend? If I was ever yours,
If you had any sweetness from me,
Do not make me beg in humiliation
Before this crowd who deride me. O Heaven!
He leaves! In his arms . . . I die! . . .

ANSBERGA

                             You will make
Me die with you!

ERMENGARDE [*delirious*]
              Where is Bertrada?
I want that sweet, pious lady. Bertrada!
Tell me, do you know it? You, whom I first
Loved in this house, do you know it? Speak to
This wretched one. I hate each human voice,
But in your gracious eyes and sweet embrace,
I can sense a life, a bitter joy that
Resembles love. Let me look at you,
Let me sit near you. Yes, I am tired.
I want to stay with you; I want to hide
My face in your lap and weep. With you
I can weep. O do not leave; promise me
You will not go, until I rise dizzy
From crying. You will not have to bear
With me for too long, and you loved me so.
How many happy days we spent together!
Remember how we passed mountains and forests
And rivers, and with every dawn the joy
Of awakening would grow. O what days! No,
Pray do not speak of them. Heaven knows if
I could deem a human heart capable
Of so much joy and so much grief alike.
You weep with me. You want to comfort me?
Then call me daughter. Upon hearing this,
I feel a plenitude of martyrdom
That invades my heart and plunges me
Into oblivion. [*she swoons again*]

ANSBERGA
              Thus in peace she died.

ERMENGARDE [*delirious*]
If this were but a dream! And dawn could melt
It into fog, if I could wake up panting,

Wet with tears, and Charles asked me the reason,
And gently scolded me for lack of trust . . . [*she falls back in
lethargy*]

ANSBERGA

O Virgin Mary, help this tormented soul!

FIRST NUN

Peace returns over her face; my hand can
No more feel her heart throbbing in tumult.

ANSBERGA

O sister! Ermengarde!

ERMENGARDE [*coming to her senses*]
Who calls me?

ANSBERGA

Look at me. This is your dear Ansberga.
Around you are your damsels, the good nuns
Praying for your peace.

ERMENGARDE

God bless you—your faces
Bespeak peace and friendship. I awake
From an evil dream.

ANSBERGA

O poor sister!
This somber quiet brought you torments rather
Than relief.

ERMENGARDE

'Tis true. All my breath is spent.
Support me, my dear, and you, courteous ladies,
Carry me to my bed. 'Tis the last effort

I impose on you. All help bestowed here
Is in Heaven reckoned. I die in peace.
Speak of God to me; I know He is coming.

CHORUS

Her soft braids on the throbbing breast
    Are eased, loosely spread,
Her hands' grip slackens, the dewy
    Paleness of the dead
Is on her mien: pious she lies,
    Her eyes seeking the sky.

Orisons rise at once from every lip,
    After long-lasting wail,
A hand with light touch lowers
    Gently the eyelid's veil,
Passing on the algid forehead,
    Over the azure eye.

Free, gentle soul, your anxious thoughts
    From earthly passion,
Lift to the Eternal your offer
    Of chaste meditation,
And die: beyond this life your grief
    Will find an ending.

Such was the lot of this sad one,
    On earth, immutable,
To beg oblivion, constantly,
    For her unattainable,
And to ascend to God at last,
    Purged by suffering.

Alas, the sleepless nights, lonely
    Pacing the cloister,
When you sang with the maidens,
    Praying at the altar,

Vivid the bygone days would come
      To your mind steadily.

You were still beloved, unaware
      Of your future pain,
Breathing sprightly the lively air
      Of the Franks' domain,
When amidst envious looks you joined
      The Salic family.

Your hair adorned with gems, you watched
      From a knoll down the plain
The bustling hunting company,
      The long-haired sovereign
Riding ahead, bent on the horse
      With bridles full-slack.

Behind, sweating bodies of steeds
      Furiously running,
Greyhounds swarming all around,
      Rapid and panting;
And from the shaken shrub there sprang
      The boar, fearing the attack.

When the blood of the beast slaughtered
      By the royal arrow,
Streaked the sandy dust, the lady
      Would turn, in sorrow,
To the damsels, as if filled with
      Sudden, charming fear.

O meandering Meuse! O sweet baths
      In many a lukewarm spring,
At Aix, where, to wipe off
      His noble sweat, the king,
Divesting his coarse coat of mail,
      Would wash in water clear.

As dew brings freshness to the tufts
 Of scorchéd grass,
And through those shriveled blades
 Makes new life pass,
So they turn green and rise again
 In the dawn's tepid air;

Such was a sweet, solacing word
 To the mind fatigued
By the impious love's cares:
 It spurred a heart besieged
Into wishing another love's
 Peaceful joy and cheer.

But like to the sun returning
 To climb the parchéd hill,
Warming with heat relentless
 The still air until
Again the newly risen blades
 Wilt and waste away;

Such would return the dormant love
 From frail forgetfulness,
To assault the saddened soul and bring
 Renewed wretchedness,
Sudden and forceful memories
 Of images kept at bay.

Free, gentle soul, your anxious thoughts
 From earthly passion,
Lift to the Eternal your offer
 Of chaste meditation,
And die: the earth that will receive
 Your mortal remnants

Already holds other ladies
 Sadly consumed by grief:

Brides widowed by the sword and maids
            Bereft of their brief
Betrothal, and mothers
            Of slaughtered infants.

You belong to an evil race
            Of savage oppressors,
Brave only when they were numerous,
            Brazen perpetrators
Of offenses, whose law was bloodshed,
            Whose glory violence.

Providential woe rendered you
            One of the oppressed.
Dearly mourned, you die and sleep now
            Among them, unvexed.
To your guiltless ashes, no one
            Will ever cause offense.

You die: may your fair brow in death
            Become as peaceful
As when, unaware of your lot,
            That turned so sorrowful,
Only virginal thoughts would paint
            On it hues most serene.

Likewise, from behind torn clouds,
            The setting sun reappears,
Purple light, beyond the mountain,
            To the West full of fears,
Harbinger to the pious peasant,
            Of a day more serene.

Scene II

[night; inside a watchtower along Pavia's walls;
armor lies in the middle ground; GUNTIGIS, AMRI]

GUNTIGIS

Amri, do you remember Spoleti?

AMRI

How could I ever forget him, my lord?

GUNTIGIS

After your master's death, you found yourself
Alone, encircled by raging Lombards,
Defenseless, one axe was already poised
Above your head when I stopped it. And you
Fell on your knees at my feet and shouted
That you were mine. What did you swear?

AMRI

                                      Faith and

Obedience until death; Have I ever
Betrayed my promise?

GUNTIGIS

                    No, but it is time
For you to prove it by a deed.

AMRI

                        Demand.

GUNTIGIS

Upon these consecrated weapons swear:
You will execute my orders and never
Reveal them under threat nor flattery.

AMRI [*putting his hands on the weapons*]
I swear. And if I ever lie, may I

Go roaming as a beggar, no more bear
A shield, and become slave to a Roman.

GUNTIGIS

    Listen, then: the safety of these walls lies
In my trust. Here I wield total command,
Second to none but to the king himself.
I put you on this bulwark as a sentry,
I kept every other warrior far from here.
Now prick your ear and send forth most intently
Your gaze under the moonlight: at midnight
You shall see an armed man stealthily approach
The walls: 'twill be Svartus. . . . Why do you look
So surprised? Yes, Svartus, who among us
Counted less than you, and who now, among
The Franks, has a high rank only because
He knew how to serve timely and in secret.
Be reassured, he comes in friendship to us.
He will rap lightly with his sword onto
His shield. Three times you will respond the like.
He will then lean a ladder 'gainst the walls,
And when it is in place, repeat the rap.
After he has climbed the walls, you will lead him
To this tower. Stay just outside to guard
The entrance. At the first hint of footsteps or
Breathing, enter and warn us.

AMRI

                    I shall do
As you order.

GUNTIGIS

           You will serve a great plan,
And great will be your reward.
[*exit* AMRI]

Scene III

GUNTIGIS

                                        Loyalty!
This word I leave it for the wretched friend
Of the fallen lord, for the man who was
Stubborn in hoping, or lacking in resolve,
And remained at his lord's side till the end,
Falling with him. "Loyalty! Loyalty!"
Let him cry, and let him thus be consoled.
What consoles is easily believed. But
When all can still be saved as well as lost,
When the victorious king, God-chosen lord
The anointed Charles sends me a messenger,
Wants me his friend, exhorts me not to die,
And to separate my lot from misfortune . . .
Why does this word then linger in my mind
Like an unwanted guest who will not leave?
Why does it throw itself amidst my thoughts
Disrupting their accordance?—Loyalty!
It is the seal of beauty on any life,
On any death. —Who says this? The lord who
Demands loyalty even if it costs death.
But the whole world seems unanimous,
Repeats the same refrain, and adds to it
That even when he's destitute of all,
Alone, the loyal man deserves more honors
Than the rich traitor surrounded by friends.
Is it so? Why is he then stripped of all
And forsaken, if he is so worthy?
Who is preventing those who admire him
From rushing to comfort and honor him,
So as to heal the wounds of unjust fortune?
Pray leave the side of those happy men whom
You despise and show yourself there, where honor
Resides: then will I gladly believe you.
If ever I should ask for your advice
I would certainly hear: reject the shameful

Offers, share with your kings their lot, whichever
It might prove to be—but why do you care
For my choice? Because if I fall, you shall
Pity me, but if I keep standing firm
Amidst ubiquitous ruin, and if I
Am seen riding next to the conqueror
As he smiles back at me, I shall be envied
By you, and you are more pleased to envision
Yourself as pitiful than envious. No,
This advice of yours is not pure—O, Charles,
Too, in his heart, will despise you—not at all.
Does he at all show any scorn for Svartus,
An obscure warrior whom he has promoted
To the highest ranks? When the king's visage
Bears the marks of honor on it, who will
Ever read in his heart? And does it matter?
I think you wish to smear with gall the rim
Of the chalice that is beyond your reach.
The truth is you rejoice to contemplate
The downfall of great men and to bemuse
The shadows of a past, extinguished fortune,
To reason on these facts and thus derive
Some comfort for your lack of glory and fame:
Such is the goal of your ambition.
A brighter one shines before mine, and you,
With all your clamor, shall not keep me from it.
If, to obtain your highest commendation,
It is enough to confront a danger
With steadfast mind, well, a terrible one
Is before me. One day you shall learn how
The ordeal at hand required of me more courage
Than a whole day of battle on the field.
For if the king, as he is wont to do,
Comes to visit the walls, and finds me here
With Svartus in confabulation, Svartus,
Whom he calls traitor and Charles calls faithful.
But this is not a time to glance behind.
'Tis fate that wills either of us be dead,

O ancient king, and I must act so as
Not to be that one.

Scene IV

[GUNTIGIS, SVARTUS *led by* AMRI]

SVARTUS

Guntigis!

GUNTIGIS

Svartus!
Did you see anyone, Amri?

AMRI

No one.

GUNTIGIS

Stay outside and watch this place most carefully.
[*exit* AMRI]

Scene V

[GUNTIGIS, SVARTUS]

SVARTUS

Guntigis, in coming here I commit
My head to your good faith.

GUNTIGIS

You have a pledge
For that, since we are both in mortal danger.

SVARTUS

'Tis in your power to gain a just reward
From this ordeal. You cannot wish to arrest
The grand career of a nation and yours.

GUNTIGIS

>   That Frankish prisoner they led within
>   Pavia asked me to speak in secret,
>   Revealed himself as Charles's envoy, and
>   Told me, on Charles's behalf, that the foe's wrath
>   Could most promptly be changed to royal favor,
>   That the king set much hope on me and would
>   Repair any damage I had suffered;
>   That you would be dispatched to deal with me,
>   And I agreed. He then demanded that
>   I give a pledge, and I sent forth at once
>   My son, in utmost secret, to the camp
>   Of the Franks, hostage and herald in one.
>   How can you cast doubt, then, on my resolve?
>   Is Charles as firm in his as I'm in mine?

SVARTUS

>   Can you have any doubts?

GUNTIGIS

>   I wish to know
>   What he wants and of what he makes promise.
>   He seized my city and gave it as a gift
>   To someone else, and so I hold now but
>   An empty title.

SVARTUS

>   'Twas meet that all saw
>   And believed your loss, thus judging King Charles
>   Implacable. Know this: the rank you held
>   You lost only to gain a higher one.
>   To your peers Charles does not make any promise,
>   He gives: you lost Ivrea, of Pavia
>   You are now the count. [*giving him a parchment*]

GUNTIGIS

>   From this hour I
>   Do take upon me this office. My lord

Shall know his faithful servant by his works.
Report now his commands, Svartus.

SVARTUS

                                        He wants
Pavia and the king, alive in his hands.
You must hasten this deed toward its outcome.
Verona's siege is still barely holding;
But for a few, all men want to come out
And surrender. Adelchis is their sole source
Of force. But if Charles arrives in that city
Having conquered Pavia, who will then dare
Pose any resistance? Other sieged cities
That still hope in delay, will forthwith fall
Like the dismembered limbs of a headless body.
Once the kings have fallen, the sense of honor
Will decline with them, for blindly stubborn
Faithfulness will lack any direction.
And once Charles reigns, there will be no more war.

GUNTIGIS

Certainly so. Pavia is due to him.
And he shall have it, even tomorrow.
Let him come to the Western gate and there,
With some cohorts, make pretense of attack.
Meanwhile the fronting gate I will keep poorly
Guarded, with a few of my faithful men.
When the brawl kindles at that gate, let him
Rush to this one, 'twill be opened for him.
Only one thing I do wish to be spared:
To hand the captive king to his very foe.
Charles cannot ask this of me, for I
Was Desiderius's vassal in happier days.
This act would smear my name with useless shame.
Once encircled from all sides, the wretched king
Will not escape.

SVARTUS

Happy harbinger I
Will be to Charles, with such a message! And
Happier must be you, who so much can do
To serve him. —But pray speak more and tell me
About people's opinions in Pavia.
Are many standing fast in the resolve
To save the crumbling king or die with him?
Are finally more and more people gazing
At the triumphal star of Charles rising
Over their heads? Will this final clash be
Easily won, as was the latest battle?

GUNTIGIS

Most are by now hopeless as well as tired,
By force of habit only they remain
Behind the old banner. Reason counsels
Them to leave the side of one whom God
Has long ago forsaken. But foremost
In their minds a word looms large that scares them:
Betrayal. A wiser word shall I whisper
Into their ears: the kingdom's salvation.
Thus they will be converted; indeed
They already are. Others who remain
Obdurate in their love, expect nothing
From Charles . . .

SVARTUS

You must promise to win them all
To Charles's cause.

GUNTIGIS

'Twould be an idle peril.
Let those who so wish die for their cause. All
Can be accomplished without them.

SVARTUS

Guntigis,
Pray do follow me: I speak to you now

As a vassal of the king of the Franks
But also as Lombard to fellow Lombard.
I do believe that Charles will keep his promise,
But is it not better for us to be
Surrounded by friends, the grateful people
Whom we saved from the fall?

GUNTIGIS

                        In faith, I want
To reply to you with like sincerity:
We must indeed dread the day when King Charles
Will reign without a sword against him brandished.
As long as foes remain at large, alive,
To keep the new-found kingdom under threat,
There is no risk that those who made it rise
Will be neglected.

SVARTUS

                    Your speech sounds most wise
And honest notes. Mark you now what I say:
We took the only way to achieve salvation,
But there are many hurdles all along,
And ambushes, you will see. To tread
That path in loneliness is harsh. And since
'Tis fate that joined us in this solemn hour,
Rendering us mates in this present venture,
In this hour of peril, lest we forget
This night, let us both pledge our own lives.
I promise to be heedful of you fortune,
I swear your foes will be mine.

GUNTIGIS

                        Your word, Svartus,
I do take and give you mine.

SVARTUS

                        In life and
Death alike, then.

GUNTIGIS

My right hand be my pledge. [*gives the right hand* SVARTUS *seizes it*]
Report my homage to the Frankish king,
My friend.

SVARTUS

Till tomorrow!

GUNTIGIS

Till tomorrow!
Amri! [*enter* AMRI] Is the walkway clear?

AMRI

It is. All is
silent around.

GUNTIGIS [*to* AMRI, *indicating* SVARTUS]
Lead him back now.

SVARTUS

Farewell!

🐚 Act V 🐚

Scene I

[*royal palace in Verona;* ADELCHIS, GISELBERT *duke of Verona*]

GISELBERT
The entire army sent me here, O king,
To announce their will: soldiers and dukes alike
Demand surrender. All know the news,
The attempt to hide the facts was all in vain:
To the Franks Pavia opened its gates,
The victorious king heads for Verona,
Alas, bringing with him the captive king.
Gerberga and her sons had gone already
Out of the city to encounter King Charles,

Trusting more in the pardon of the king,
Although embittered, than in the help of
A powerless friendship. Verona's strength
Is sapped by the long siege, deplete of soldiers,
Of food, incapable by now to endure
Even the siege, it will in brief succumb
Under the fresh onslaught of the enemy.
But for a few, O king, none, of those who
Defended the city so far, are willing
To face the risk of an uneven battle,
Of an assault most pitiless. As long
As they could hope in a reward to toil
And suffering, they did toil and suffer.
They gave what honor and duty demanded,
But now they invoke the end of fruitless pains.

ADELCHIS

Await outside. You shall soon hear my will.
[*exit* GISELBERT]

Scene II

ADELCHIS

Go, and live on, till a serene old age.
Remain among the first of your own people,
You deserve it. Go, do not fear, you shall
Be a vassal. The times are just in tune
With your ambition, with the aspirations
Of your peers—but, O, to be constrained
To hear the cowards' will dictate the law,
To take the cue of ruling from the fearful—
It is too much. They made a choice. 'Tis easy
For them, since they are cowards and therefore
Have a will; terror pushes them to daring;
Nor shall they suffer that their base fury
Be opposed by some, that one man worthy
Of this name remain among them. —O Heaven!
My father in Charles's talons! His last days

He shall live as a slave and have to obey
The beckoning of a hand that he would
Not have seized even in friendship; he shall
Eat the bread of the man who offended him,
Who had him for a price! And there's no way
To rescue him from this ditch, where he roars,
Betrayed, alone, calling in vain the one
Who cannot save him! No way! Brescia fell,
Loyal Baudus, generous man, him too,
Forced to open the gates by those unwilling
To die. O, truly fortunate are you,
Ermengarde! O, house of Desiderius!
It has come to this, envied is the one
Who died heartbroken! —O, it is too much!
Beyond these walls, the haughty man approaching
And soon, at my door, asking that I make
His triumph complete; inside, the cowards
Responding to him, daring to urge me.
Even when hope was lost, I had at least
Some works, each day had its tomorrow, and
Each crossroad imposed a choice. But if I
Failed to graft into those vile breasts a heart,
Shall the cowards forbid that the brave man
Die as brave? No, they cannot all be vile.
Someone will hear me, I shall find companions,
If I cry: "Let us confront these people,
Let us show them how it is not true that
Above all things the Lombards prize their life.
If nothing else, we shall die . . . " —No, this is
Unjust, to drag such brave men down with me
Into my fall. If nothing else is left
For me to do here, why not die alone?
My soul finds solace in this thought at last;
It smiles at me like to a friend whose face
Bears painted the good news on every trait.
To escape from this oppressive, shameful crowd,
To shun the laughter of a winning foe,
And to be free from this burden of wrath,

Of doubt, of pity. . . . You, my sword, that settled
Final scores for many a life, and you,
My swift hand, well used to handling it. . . . All
Would be quickly finished, in a moment.
All? Wretched me, that to myself I lie!
The whisper of these worms benumbs indeed
My mind, and the mere thought of confronting
A victor defeats fortitude in me.
The present anguish overwhelms me so,
That makes me cry: too much! But how could I
Face God, and tell Him: "Here I come, without
Awaiting your call, tired of tending
The place you allotted me, it was too harsh,
And I deserted it." Impious thought,
To flee and thus bequeath this memory
To my father to keep him company
Until his death, a legacy of despair!
Be gone, impious thought, and you, Adelchis,
Heal your soul, be a man. What do you want?
You only wish the end of every pain,
But can't you see that it's not in your hands?
The Greek empire offers you a shelter,
'Tis God that offers it to you, this way.
Let us gratefully accept; it is indeed
The sole wise move, the only worthy choice.
Preserve some hope for your father, that he
May at least dream of your return as victor,
Coming to unbind his fetters, rather than
Tainted with your own blood, shed in despair.
Perchance 'twill be no dream. From deeper depths
Did others rise before: fortune makes not
Eternal pacts with anyone; time gives
And takes; and friends, the successor makes them.
Teudi!

Scene III

[*enter* TEUDI]

TEUDI

    Aye, my king.

ADELCHIS

                    Are there still friends
  Loyal to the falling king?

TEUDI

                  Aye, those who
  Were Adelchis's friends.

ADELCHIS

              What is their resolve?

TEUDI

  To hear yours they await.

ADELCHIS

             Where are they now?

TEUDI

  Here in this palace, apart from those knaves
  Whose only wish is to be fully lost.

ADELCHIS

  It is bad, Teudi, when the seed of valor
  Is scattered among cowards! —I shall take
  Those friends along with me and leave at once.
  I can do but this, and there is nothing
  They can now do for me but follow me
  To Byzantium. Alas, if any among them
  Can conceive of a more noble course,
  Let those advise me, for pity's sake!
  From you, my Teudi, I shall ask instead

A more courageous deed, more trust-demanding:
I ask you to stay here and to relate
This message to my father: that I fled
Just for him, that I live to redeem him
From captivity, one day; and that he
Must not despair. Now come and embrace me,
Till better days. —To the duke of Verona
You shall say that the oath of loyalty
Toward myself is null. I rest upon
Your faith, O Teudi.

TEUDI

                May Heaven help me!

[*exeunt from opposite sides*]

Scene IV

[CHARLES*'s tent in the camp outside Verona's walls;* CHARLES,
a HERALD, ARVINUS, *and* OTHERS]

CHARLES

Herald, go hence into Verona, and tell
The duke and all his warriors these same words:
King Charles is here. If you open the gates,
He will enter the city with a mind
To granting his favors to all; if not,
His entrance is delayed but not less certain,
And treatment will be such as just one side
Dictates, and with an embittered spirit.

[*exit messenger*]

ARVINUS

The vanquished king wants to confer with you,
O king.

CHARLES

        His request?

ARVINUS

       He will not say, but
He begged most pitifully.

CHARLES

       Let him come. [*exit* ARVINUS]
Aye, let us meet the one who foreordained
The crown of Charles for someone else's brow.
[*to the* COUNTS] Go to the walls and double the watch there;
Each outlet must be guarded by armed men,
Nobody must escape.

Scene V

[*enter* DESIDERIUS]

CHARLES

       Why do you wish
To speak with me? What words can we exchange,
When Heaven has established our lot
And there is no room left for blabbering?
'Tis unbecoming for you, who were king,
To come here and complain, and weep before
The conqueror; nor is it meet that I
Give vent in sharp words to my old hatred;
Nor that I show on my visage my heart,
Full to the brim of a rejoicing pride,
That God might not wind up disdaining me,
Repent and desert me before the end.
Nor can you expect from me a vain comfort
Of words. How would I utter them? What saddens
You is my joy; there cannot be laments
Where there lacks the will to change the facts.
Such is the mortal lot: when there are two
In a battlefield, perforce one will leave
Weeping. You shall live. This is the only
Gift Charles has for you.

DESIDERIUS

King of my kingdom,
Destroyer of my issue, how can life
Be a gift to the dethroned king? You think
I could know no more joy, even in defeat?
Yet I could, blackening your triumph
With the poison in which my heart is drowning,
Just saying words you would acknowledge yours,
So I would die avenged, in part. But I
In you adore Heaven's just vengeance, and
I kneel before the one before whom God
Did bend my knees. I came here to invoke you,
As you shall hear. It is a mortal sin
To scorn the prayers of the dejected.

CHARLES

Speak.

DESIDERIUS

Did you unsheathe your sword against myself
In defense of Hadrian?

CHARLES

Why do you ask
What you already know?

DESIDERIUS

Learn that my self
Alone was the Pope's enemy; Adelchis—
And witness to my words be that God who
Abides by the tormented—Adelchis
Opposed my fury always, with his prayers,
With his advice, even with scolding,
As much as filial piety would allow.
But in vain!

CHARLES

Pray, your point.

DESIDERIUS

Your deed is done.
Your Roman ally has no extant foes.
He freely and fully enjoys his vengeance now,
And safety most complete, more than a weak
And wrathful heart would ever need. For this
Purpose you came, you said it. And thus you
Prescribed the limits of the war. You said
It was God's cause. It is won, nothing else
Does God demand from you.

CHARLES

So you would want
To impose the law to the conqueror?

DESIDERIUS

Law,
You say? Alas, do not invent a pride
That my words lack, so that you can more lightly
Scorn them. O Charles, Heaven gave you so much;
You see now your adversary at your feet,
You hear a prayer in whispers from his lips
And flattering remarks. You rule over
The land where he did fight you. Ah, do not
Wish for more, remember, Heaven abhors
Measureless desires.

CHARLES

Pray speak no more.

DESIDERIUS

No, you must listen. One day you might still
Savor dire fortune, and on that day
You may need a serene, comforting thought.
Then the memory of the present day's mercy
Would blissfully visit your sad spirit.
Remember that before the throne of God
You will await in tremor His response,

Either severe or merciful, as I
Await to hear from your lip in this hour.
Alas, perhaps they already sold my son
To you! Alas, that such an ardent spirit,
His indomitable soul, should perish
Languishing in chains! Think that he is not
Guilty, except for wanting to defend
His own father, and even this from him
Is taken now. What do you fear? No sword
Is fighting for us, and those who were once
Our vassals are yours, now. They shall not
Betray you: to the strongest all loyalty
Is due. Italy is yours, govern in peace.
Let one captive king suffice to you; let
My son flee to foreign lands . . .

CHARLES

                         Speak no more,
I say. You are asking me a favor
That not even Bertrada could obtain.

DESIDERIUS

O fool that I am, I was begging you!
I should have known from facts
Your true mettle. If you deny indeed
My request, may the treasure of vengeance
Gather on your head. And as you conquered
By deceit alone, so may your conquest
Render you proud and merciless. Aye, tread
Upon the dejected, and climb upward,
And displease God . . .

CHARLES

                    Be silent, you who are
Utterly vanquished. How now, till yesterday
You dreamt of my demise and now you ask
For favors as if from your dinner table
I were merrily rising to converse

With my nice host! And since my answer was
Not at all attuned with your desire,
With your prattle you come to pester me,
Like to a beggar who is denied alms.
But what you had prepared for me . . . Adelchis
Was with you . . . you do not say, so I will.
Gerberga was fleeing from me, her kinsman,
Bringing along her children, my brother's
Issue, and as she fled she filled the air
With screeching, like to a bird who has rescued
Her chicks from the hawk's talons. Her terror
Was a lie, true only the displeasure
Of not ruling. In the meantime she painted
My renown in somber hues, as if I
Were a monster, a devourer of children,
A parricide. I suffered all in silence.
You promptly welcomed that ill-advised woman
And readily made echo to her screeching.
Thus you played the hosts of Charles's nephews!
The champion of my blood against myself!
But Gerberga returned, if you don't know it:
She did come back to the one from whom she
Should have never escaped in the first place.
To this tremendous tutor she now leads
Her sons, to this hand she commits their lives.
But you had promised to give my own nephews
Gifts well beyond survival. You demanded
From the Holy Father, not without threats,
To pour mendacious oil onto those heads
Not yet accustomed to the weight of helmets.
You chose a dagger, whetted it, and put it
Into the hands of my most beloved friends,
That in due time they might transfix my heart.
While I would be on mission to defeat,
Between perilous Weser and wild Elba,
The enemies of God, you would have rushed
To France, to oppose ensign to ensign, chrism
To chrism. O crooked people! That was

The thorny bed you had reserved for me;
That was the happiest dream of yours. But God
Disposed otherwise. A bitter cup you
Had prepared for me, 'tis left for you now,
Empty it. You speak of God to me: but
If I did not fear Him, why would I bring
To France as a captive the evil one
I coveted so much to annihilate?
Pick the flower you have cultivated
And speak no more: misfortune breeds indeed
Unending blabber, but not unending
Is the patience of an offended victor.

Scene VI

[enter ARVINUS*]*

ARVINUS

Long live King Charles! Responding to your call
Ensigns are lowered from towers and walls,
The enemy's iron gates are all dropped open
In one chorus of clangor; all rush to
The open portals to pay you homage.

DESIDERIUS

Alas the sorrow, what have I to hear!
And what remains for me to be heard yet!

CHARLES

Has anyone escaped?

ARVINUS

No one. A few
Were seen departing, but when our men
Chased them and attacked them, most valiantly
They fought, although in vain. All of them died
Or are dying.

CHARLES

Who are they?

ARVINUS

One is here
Who would be aggrieved, if I said their names.

DESIDERIUS

Herald of death, I heard you.

CHARLES

Is Adelchis

Dead?

DESIDERIUS [*to* ARVINUS]
O cruel man, speak to his father.

ARVINUS

He still can see the light but not for long,
As he lies wounded by a mortal blow.
He demands his father and you, my lord.

DESIDERIUS

Will you deny this too?

CHARLES

No, unhappy man.
Let him be carried into my tent and
Tell him that he has foes no more, Arvinus.
[*exit* ARVINUS]

Scene VII

DESIDERIUS

O hand of God, you heavily descended
On my ancient head; you return to me
My son in this state! My son, my sole glory
I yearn to see you and yet tremble, as

I will see the mortal wound on your body,
I, whom you should have buried! O unhappy
Am I, indeed, I am the one who caused
You this: my blind love wished to make your throne
More gorgeous, instead I dug you a grave.
O, had you died on a victorious day,
Amidst the chanting warriors! Or had I
Closed your eyes in our palace, amidst
The heartfelt sobbing of your loyal people,
And still it would have been the harshest sorrow.
Dethroned you shall die now, by all forsaken,
In your foe's hands, with no one to mourn you
But your father, weeping before a man
Who, upon hearing this, will celebrate.

CHARLES

Old man, your sorrow is deceiving you.
Not joyfully but pensively I consider
The lot of a king. I was Adelchis's
Enemy and he was mine, and such that
I could not sit in peace on my own throne
As long as he remained alive, out of
My hands. Now he is in those of God, where
The enmity of a pious man abides not.

DESIDERIUS

Most somber gift is your mercy indeed
If never it alights but on those who
Have lost all hope, if only then you hold
Your striking arm, when there is no place left
To inflict new wounds.

Scene VIII

[*enter* ADELCHIS, *wounded and carried*]

DESIDERIUS

                    Alas, my poor son!

ADELCHIS

Heaven wills that I see you once more, father.
Come near and touch the hand of your own son.

DESIDERIUS

Horrid it is to see you in this state.

ADELCHIS

Many did fall like this in this last battle
By my own hand.

DESIDERIUS

Is this wound mortal then,
Dear son?

ADELCHIS

Mortal.

DESIDERIUS

Wretched me, cruel war,
Myself most cruel who willed it. It is I
Who killed you.

ADELCHIS

No, it was not you, nor he,
But our common Lord.

DESIDERIUS

O, how my eyes
Yearned to see you, how did I suffer far
Removed from you. One thought has kept me alive,
Among these pains: that I would recount them
One day, in a peaceful, serene hour.

ADELCHIS

That peaceful hour is for me this one,
So long as I do not leave you, father,
Overwhelmed by grief.

DESIDERIUS

                  O bold brow, serene,
Vigorous hand, O fright-inspiring eye!

ADELCHIS

  Pray, father, cease every lamentation,
For Heaven's sake. Has not my hour come
In due time? You, rather, who will live on
As captive, having been a king, listen:
Life is arcane and only upon dying
One comprehends. Of your kingdom you were
Despoiled: do not lament the loss, I say.
When to this same hour you will come near,
The happy memories that will visit
Your mind will only be the years in which
You will not have been king, in which no tears
Shall have been ascribed to you in Heaven,
Nor shall your name have ascended there
Accompanied by the victims' curses.
Have joy of not being king; have joy of not
Being able to act. There is no room
For guiltless action, 'tis only given
To either inflict wrongs or suffer them.
A fierce and dire force governs the world;
Men call it law! With blood-stained hands our
Forefathers cast the seeds of injustice;
Our fathers manured it with blood
And the land does not yield other harvest.
It is not sweet to rule over the unjust,
And you know it from facts, it's right that thus
It should all end. This happy man for whom
My death strengthens the throne he sits upon,
For whom everything smiles and shines, is but
A mortal man.

DESIDERIUS

               But who shall solace me
Who am losing you, my son?

ADELCHIS

That God who
Is the only solace for all. [*addressing* CHARLES] And you,
My proud enemy . . .

CHARLES

Do not deem me such,
Adelchis, not any more. I was once
But enmity is evil and impious
Before the grave. It dwells not, believe me,
In Charles's heart.

ADELCHIS

My speech will be the like,
Friendly and humble, and will shun all hints
Of memories that are bitter for both.
And this dying hand of mine I put in yours
To ask of you to grant my last request.
I shall not ask that you give freedom back
To such important prey, for I can see
How I as well as every mortal man
Would beg for that effect to no avail.
Your wisdom does not budge and to that limit
Your pardon does not stretch. What you cannot
Deny without being cruel I demand:
That the captivity of this old man
Be mild and devoid of offenses, just
Such as you would wish for your own father,
If Heaven had destined you to the pain
Of leaving him at someone else's mercy.
From every insult defend this ancient head,
Many a strong man will gladly attack the loser.
May he not suffer to be in view of
His former vassals.

CHARLES

This glad certainty
You can bring with you to the grave. Adelchis,

May Heaven be my witness, your request
Is Charles's word.

ADELCHIS

Your enemy does pray
For you in this last hour.

Scene IX

[*enter* ARVINUS]

ARVINUS

Impatiently,
Unvanquished king, warriors and dukes do ask
To be in your presence.

ADELCHIS

Charles!

CHARLES

No one dare
Come near this tent. Adelchis is ruler
Here, his father and a minister of
Divine pardon can here abide.
[*exit* CHARLES *with* ARVINUS]

Scene X

DESIDERIUS

Alas,
My belovéd son!

ADELCHIS

Light flees from these eyes,
O father.

DESIDERIUS

No, do not leave me, Adelchis!

ADELCHIS

O King of kings, betrayed by one companion,
By all others forsaken, to your peace
I come: accept this weary soul.

DESIDERIUS

He hears
Your prayer. O Heaven, you breathe your last!
Alone, in bondage, I remain to mourn you.

END OF THE TRAGEDY

Bibliography

PRIMARY SOURCES AND NINETEENTH-CENTURY CRITICISM
ON MANZONI'S TRAGEDIES

Alighieri, Dante. *La Divina Commedia.* Ed. G. Giacalone. 3 vols. Rome: Signorelli, 1977.

———. *Vita Nuova.* Ed. G. Petrocchi and M. Ciccuto. Milan: BUR, 1994.

Avitabile, Grazia. *The Controversy on Romanticism in Italy.* New York: Vanni, 1959.

Battistella, Antonio. *Il Conte di Carmagnola: studio storico con documenti inediti.* Genoa: Annuario generale d'Italia, 1889.

Bellezza, Paolo. "Note manzoniane." *Giornale storico della letteratura italiana* 31 (1898): 251–90.

Bognetti, Gian Piero. "La genesi dell'*Adelchi* e del *Discorso* e il pensiero storico-politico del Manzoni fino al 1821." *Adelchi. Dai Longobardi ai Carolingi,* 14–45. Milan: Electa, 1984.

Bonghi, Ruggero, Giuseppe Borri, and Niccolò Tommaseo. *Colloqui col Manzoni.* Ed. A. Briganti. Rome: Editori Riuniti, 1985.

Branca, Vittore, ed. *Il Conciliatore. Foglio scientifico-letterario.* 3 vols. Florence: Le Monnier, 1954.

Brand, Charles Peter. *Italy and the English Romantics.* Cambridge: Cambridge UP, 1957.

Byron, George Gordon. *The Works of Lord Byron.* Ed. Th. Moore. 4 vols. Philadelphia: Lippincott, 1898.

Carducci, Giosuè. "A proposito di alcuni giudizi su Alessandro Manzoni" (1873–83). *Opere Scelte.* Ed. M. Saccenti, vol. 2:399–430. Turin: UTET, 1993.

Carini, Isidoro. "Relazione inedita sull'arresto e sulla morte del conte di Carmagnola." *Il Muratori* 2 (1893): 77–102.

Chauvet, Vincent. "*Le Comte de Carmagnola,* tragédie, par M. Alexandre Manzoni. Milan, 1820." *Lycée Français* 4 (1820): 61–76.

Commentari dell'Ateneo di Brescia. Per l'anno 1820; Per l'anno 1823. Brescia: Bettoni, 1823, 63–84, and 1824, 14–18. Reprinted in *Bulletin* no. 18 of the Centro Studi Manzoniani.

Constant, Benjamin. "Quelques réflexions sur le théâtre allemand." *Wallstein, tragédie en cinq actes et en verse,* v–lii. Geneva: J. J. Paschoud, 1809.

Corbett, Martin. *Byron and Tragedy.* New York: St. Martin's, 1988.

Crivellari, Domenico. *Venice.* Trans. H. Evans. Milan: Electa, 1993.

De Simone, Joseph Francis. *Alessandro Manzoni: Esthetics and Literary Criticism.* New York: Vanni, 1946.

Dionisotti, Carlo. "Manzoni e la cultura inglese." *Annali manzoniani*, vol. 7:251–64. Milan: Casa del Manzoni, 1977.

———. "Manzoni fra Italia e Francia." *Forme e vicende per Giovanni Pozzi*. Ed. O. Besomi, 497–511. Padua: Antenore, 1988.

Ellet, Elizabeth F. "Specimens of the Italian Tragedians. Alexandro Manzoni." *American Monthly Magazine*, Jan. 1834, 289–96.

Foscolo, Ugo. "Della nuova scuola drammatica italiana." *Edizione nazionale delle opere di Ugo Foscolo*, vol. 9, pt. 2:559–618. Florence: Le Monnier, 1958. .

Ginzburg, Natalia. *La famiglia Manzoni*. Turin: Einaudi, 1994.

Goethe, Wolfgang. "Gli scritti critici di Goethe sul Manzoni." Trans. E. Michelson and E. Blauth. Appendix in *La Lucia del Manzoni e altre note critiche*, by P. Fossi, 219–78. Florence: Sansoni, 1937.

Gozzoli, Maria Cristina, and Fernando Mazzocca. *Hayez*. Milan: Electa, 1983.

Guiccioli, Teresa. *My Recollections of Lord Byron and Those of Other Witnesses of His Life*. Trans. H. E. H. Jerningham. New York: Harper, 1869.

Hayez, Francesco. *Le mie memorie*. Ed. F. Mazzocca. Vicenza: Neri-Pozzi, 1995.

Howarth, W. D. "Bonaparte on Stage: The Napoleonic Legend in Nineteenth-Century French Drama." *Historical Drama*. Ed. J. Redmond. Cambridge: Cambridge UP, 1986.

Le Tourneur, Pierre. *Shakespeare traduit de l'anglois*, vol. 1: *Othello;* vol. 8: *Richard II;* vol. 9: *Henry IV*, Parts I and II; vol.11: *Henry V;* vol.13: *Henry VIII*. Paris: L'advocat, 1776.

Manzoni, Alessandro. *Discorso sopra alcuni punti della storia longobardica in Italia. Tutte le opere*. Ed. M. Martelli, vol. 2: 1981–2070. Florence: Sansoni, 1973.

———. *I promessi sposi*. Ed. G. Giacalone. Rome: Signorelli, 1972.

———. *Opere inedite o rare*. Ed. R. Bonghi. 7 vols. Milan: Rechiedei, 1889.

———. *Opere varie*. Milan: Redaelli, 1845.

———. *Osservazioni sulla morale cattolica*. Ed. R. Amerio. 3 vols. Naples: Ricciardi, 1965.

———. *Poesie e tragedie*. Ed. S. Blazina and P. Gibellini. Milan: Garzanti, 1990.

———. *Scritti letterari*. Ed. C. Riccardi and B. Travi. *Tutte le opere*, vol. 5, pt. 3. Milan: Mondadori, 1991.

———. *Tutte le lettere*. Ed. C. Arieti. 3 vols. Milan: Adelphi, 1986.

Mazzocca, Fernando. "La sfortuna visiva dell'*Adelchi* e dei fatti di storia longobarda nella cultura figurativa della Restaurazione." *Adelchi. Dai Longobardi ai Carolingi*. Milan: Electa, 1984.

Milman, H. H. "Article III.1. *Il Conte di Carmagnola: Tragedia*, di Alessandro Manzoni. Milano, 1820; 2. *Ricciarda: Tragedia*, di Ugo Foscolo. Londra, 1820; 3. *Francesca da Rimini: Tragedia*, di Silvio Pellico. Milano, 1818." *The Quarterly Review* (London: John Murray, 1809–), Oct. 1820, 72–102.

Parenti, Marino. *Immagini della vita e dei tempi di Alessandro Manzoni*. Florence: Sansoni, 1973.

Paul the Deacon. *History of the Langobards*. Trans. W. D. Foulke. New York: Longmans, Green & Co.: 1907.

Pellico, Silvio. *Opere scelte*. Ed. C. Curto. Turin: UTET, 1954.

Reforgiato, Vincenzo. *Shakespeare e Manzoni*. Catania: Galati, 1898.

Rovani, Giuseppe. *La mente di Alessandro Manzoni*. 1873. Reprint, Milan: Scheiwiller, 1984.

Sainte-Beuve, Charles Augustin. *Portrait Contemporains*. Paris, 1846. Reprint, as *Fauriel e Manzoni. Leopardi*. Florence: Sansoni, 1895.

Scalvini, Giovita. "Dalla *Biblioteca italiana.*" 1820. Reprint, in *Foscolo Manzoni Goethe.* Ed. M. Marcazzan, 195–205. Turin: Einaudi, 1948.

Scarano, Nicola. "Amleto e Adelchi." *Nuova Antologia* 3rd ser., 41 (1892): 324–34.

Scherillo, Michele. "Il decennio dell'operosità poetica di Alessandro Manzoni." Introduction to *Le tragedie, gli Inni Sacri e le odi di Alessandro Manzoni,* xi–clxxiv. Milan: Hoepli, 1907.

———. "Manzoni e Roma laica," *Corriere della Sera,* 4 April 1911.

———. "La prima tragedia del Manzoni." *Annuario Scolastico dell'Accademia Scientifico-Letteraria,* 13–60. Milan: Tipografia Raimondi, 1895.

Schlegel, von August. *Course of Lectures on Dramatic Art and Literature.* Trans. J. Black. London: Henry G. Bohn, 1846.

Shakespeare, William. *The Complete Works.* New York: Barnes & Noble, 1994.

Sismondi, Sismonde de (J. C. L). *A History of the Italian Republics.* Abridged ed. Trans. W. K. Ferguson. New York: Anchor Books, 1966.

———. *Storia delle repubbliche italiane del Medio Evo.* Trans. L. Toccagni. 5 vols. Milan: Scotti, 1852.

Stendhal. *Rome, Naples et Florence.* Ed. D. Muller. 2 vols. Paris: Champion, 1968.

Tommaseo, Niccolò. "Alessandro Manzoni." *Ispirazione e arte, o lo scrittore educato dalla società e educatore,* 313–435. Florence: Le Monnier, 1858.

Vigorelli, Giancarlo, ed. *Manzoni: il suo e il nostro tempo.* Milan: Electa, 1985.

Watkins, Daniel. "The Dramas of Lord Byron: *Manfred* and *Marino Faliero.*" *Byron: A Critical Reader.* Ed. J. Stabler, 52–65. London: Longman, 1998.

Zajotti, Paride. "*Adelchi,* tragedia di Alessandro Manzoni, con un discorso su alcuni punti della storia longobardica in Italia. Milano, 1822, per Vincenzo Ferrario, in ottavo." 1825. Reprint, in *Polemiche Letterarie.* Ed. R. Turchi, 57–164. Padua: Liviana, 1982.

Zardo, Antonio. "Due tragedie veneziane." *Nuova antologia* 41 (1892): 102–24.

SELECTED AND ANNOTATED BIBLIOGRAPHY OF TWENTIETH-CENTURY
CRITICISM ON MANZONI'S TRAGEDIES

Accame Bobbio, Aurelia. *La crisi manzoniana del 1817.* Florence: Le Monnier, 1960. Historical-biographical reconstruction of Manzoni's religious crisis, supposedly taking place during the composition of his first tragedy and leading him to doubt the positive role of the Church in history.

———. *Storia dell'Adelchi.* Florence: Le Monnier, 1963. Historical-biographical reconstruction of Manzoni's evolution into an increasingly painstaking historian of the Lombard rule in Italy. Manzoni's discovery of the plight of the Latin population in those centuries caused the changes from the first to the second version of the tragedy.

———. Introduction. *Liriche e tragedie,* by Alessandro Manzoni. Rome: Signorelli, 1965. Review of major critical appraisals of Manzoni's poetry and tragedies (De Sanctis, D'Ovidio, Momigliano, Croce, Russo).

Alonge, Roberto. "Un eroe forse non troppo 'solare.'" Piccolo Teatro di Milano / Teatro d'Europa / Teatro Studio. Milan, Season 1989/90. Performance booklet of *Il Conte di Carmagnola,* by Alessandro Manzoni, directed by L. Puggelli, 13–14. Points out that Carmagnola is a strongly egotistical character, engaged primarily in a personal war. Even if Manzoni deemed him innocent, he portrayed him in such a way as to make us aware of his unconscious will to betray Venice, since the count is prey to a love-hate relationship with the duke.

Annoni, Carlo. "Un'interpretazione dell'*Adelchi*." *Manzoni tra due secoli*. Ed. F. Mattesini, 49–75. Milan: Vita e pensiero, 1986.

——. *Lo spettacolo dell'uomo interiore*. Milan: Vita e Pensiero, 1997. Most chapters of the book are concerned with Manzoni's theoretical writings (comparison between first and definitive draft of the *Lettre*) and their possible sources. The chapter "Dall'Adelchi al Natale del '33" is a revised version of the 1986 essay cited above, interpreting Adelchis as a *figura Christi*. The last chapter proposes Medieval Christian sources such as the *Stabat mater* as subtext of some passages in the tragedies.

Azzolini, Paola. "Note per una lettura anti-hegeliana del *Carmagnola*." *Manzoni e l'idea di letteratura*, 77–90. Turin: Assesorato Cultura Piemonte, 1985. The drama is in the hero's sufferings, but, unlike the Schillerian pathos of the suffering great man of action, Manzoni's hero has at his disposal Christian meditation on death to accept his defeat, which is a common element with the baroque drama as defined by Walter Benjamin. Intertextual references with one of Manzoni's *Inni sacri*, "La passione," lead to the identification of Carmagnola with Christ betrayed and crucified.

——. "L'ascesa della montagna: aspetti del dantismo manzoniano." *Romanische Forschungen* 3–4 (1986): 324–40. The realistic description of Martinus's ascent of the Alps separating him from Charlemagne (act II of *Adelchis*) includes numerous symbolic elements, mainly borrowed from Dante's ascent of Mount Purgatory. The convincing intertextual examples lead to an unclear conclusion about the function of Martinus's tale in the tragedy: between the Lombards and the Franks, the real winner is supposedly the humble man who made himself a docile tool of God's will.

——. Postfazione. *Il Conte di Carmagnola*, by Alessandro Manzoni. Ed. G. Lonardi and P. Azzolini, 229–43. Venice: Marsilio, 1989. Revision of the 1985 essay cited above.

——. Postfazione. *Adelchi*, by Alessandro Manzoni. Ed. G. Lonardi and P. Azzolini, 257–74. Venice: Marsilio, 1992. Martinus, the docile tool of God's will, is instrumental to Charles's victory. The Frankish king is not altogether negative: his positive traits in the tragedy reflect Manzoni's appreciative comments on Charles's iron will in the historical tract, and his character could be a portrait in disguise of Napoleon (see Scherillo, "Il decennio," above), more than of Murat or Carlo Alberto. Even Svartus and Guntigis, although they are the betrayers, express deeply human tension, which Manzoni paints in Shakespearean hues (*King Lear*'s Edmund is suggested as model for Svartus's monologue in the first act). The words of the dying Anfrid (see Petrocchi) and of the dying Adelchis clarify the tragic hero as a figure of Christ. Likewise, Ermengarde, even if the subtext points to Racine's *Phèdre* (see Trompeo) and Dante's Francesca (see D'Ovidio), also is a sacrificial character.

Banti, Alberto. *La nazione del Risorgimento. Parentela, santità e onore alle origini dell'Italia unita*. Turin: Einaudi, 2000. *Carmagnola* and *Adelchis* are among the literary works that the author considers fundamental to the spirit of nationhood during the Risorgimento. The author takes at face value Manzoni's complex use of Christ references as he includes these in the systematic analysis of religious imagery employed by many writers to foster the cult of the *patria*.

Banti, Anna. "Ermengarda e Gertrude." *Paragone* 5, no. 52 (1954): 23–30. Negative evaluation of Manzoni's fictive reconstruction of the historical Lombard princess.

Barberi Squarotti, Giorgio. "Tre casi di ricostruzione linguistica tra lirica e romanzo." *Teorie e prove dello stile del Manzoni*, 57–69. Milan: Silva, 1965. In *Adelchis* there is a tension between the chorus addressed to Ermengarde and the scene of her madness and death. In the first we have the structuring moral imperatives; in the latter we have the details, the small gestures of the heroine. The unresolved contrast and ambiguity is embodied by the oxymoron "provida sventura."

———. "La storia impraticabile: le tragedie del Manzoni." *Manzoni: le delusioni della letteratura*, 125–56. Rovito: Marra, 1988–90.. The function of the tragedy in history is to proclaim the truth of the vexed and spiritually noble victim. Such is Carmagnola and such are Adelchis and Ermengarde. Adelchis, unlike Carmagnola, addresses Christ in his final invocation because Christ is the model of historical suffering pointing beyond history itself. Manzoni abandons the tragic genre because he wants to portray the sacrifice and *imitatio Christi* by humble people, not by kings and nobles. The tragedy can redress the injustice suffered in history by noble victims, while the novel can better render the lot of the humble victims.

Bardazzi, Giovanni. Introduction. *Il Conte di Carmagnola*, by Alessandro Manzoni. Ed. G. Bardazzi, xi–ciii. Milan: Fondazione Mondadori, 1985.Raises the central question of the motives leading Manzoni to change dramatically the first and second acts of his first tragedy. The major alterations were eliminating the themes of familial affections (the count's father) and of the Venetian populace excluded from political power rewriting of act II with an exclusively military subject.

Barricelli, Gian Piero. "Provident Ill-Fortune." *Alessandro Manzoni*, 55–83. Boston: Twayne, 1976. Sees Carmagnola as a Christian romantic hero whose fate is like the Napoleon of the ode, "purified of the need for earthly conquest and glory." Mark is a "more tragic figure" than the count. Manzoni's first tragedy is "acceptable but not an exceptional tragedy," as it lacks "warmth and intensity." Adelchis is "a solitary hero in the Shakespearean tradition, but a representative hero, imbued with religiosity," with "the realization of Christian renunciation." He represents the "apogee of Christian fatalism in the theatre." Guntigis and Svartus should have been developed more because they have Shakespearean vigor, as the poet Carducci had remarked. Manzoni's theater appears profoundly marked by Jansenistic determinism.

Beaumont, Jean F. "Manzoni and Goethe." *Italian Studies* (1939): 129–40. Biographical reconstruction of the mutual appreciation of the two authors throughout the years of Manzoni's prolific creativity.

Becherucci, Isabella. Introduction. *Adelchi*, by Alessandro Manzoni. Ed. I. Becherucci, vii–cxlvi. Florence: Accademia della Crusca, 1998. For Manzoni's major changes from the first to the second version of the tragedy, the conclusions in Accame Bobbio, *Storia dell'Adelchi*, are reported and corroborated.

———. "'Una storia così bella . . .': suggestioni per l'*Adelchi*." *Annali manzoniani* new series, 3 (1999): 95–114. Surmises a direct influence of Angelo Maria Ricci's *Italiade* on Manzoni's second tragedy. The intertextual evidence presented, however, is liable to the objection that Ricci might have read Shakespeare too.

Belotti, Giuseppe. "L'ostinato silenzio sul Gioberti." *Il messaggio politico-sociale di Alessandro Manzoni*, 55–88. Zanichelli: Bologna, 1966. Reconstructs the relationship between Manzoni and Vincenzo Gioberti, whose book *Primato morale e civile degli Italiani* (1843) was an important source of inspiration of the neo-guelph movement during the Risorgimento.

Bene, Carmelo, and Giuseppe Di Leva. *Adelchi, o della volgarità del politico*. Milan: Longanesi, 1984. A reading enhancing Adelchis's qualities as illuminated political hero and victim of paternal authority; many comparisons with the "misery" of contemporary Italian politics. Furthermore, Adelchis is seen as a Christ figure, as opposed to his father who would represent the first person of the Christian Trinity.

Beronesi, Patrizia. "Il prologo storico di Manzoni." *Il teatro del personaggio. Shakespeare sulla scena italiana dell'Ottocento*. Ed. L. Caretti, 19–63. Rome: Bulzoni, 1979. From the first to the second draft of *Carmagnola*, Manzoni loses what the author calls the Shakespearean dramatic structure, which should include scenes featuring ordinary people. The author agrees with De Sanctis's judgment about the lack of drama in Manzoni's characters. Even if the overall Shakespearean structure is lost in the realization of the creative works (not in his theoretical writings), Shakespeare's influence is apparent in situations and characters of Manzoni's theater (the well-known comparison between Ermengarde and Katharine is proposed; see Bellezza, D'Ovidio, Reforgiato).

Bermann, Sandra. Introduction. *On the Historical Novel*, translation of *Sul romanzo storico* by Alessandro Manzoni. Lincoln: University of Nebraska Press, 1984. The introduction proposes many interesting parallels between Manzoni's 1845 essay on historical fiction and twentieth-century literary theory.

Blasucci, Luigi. "Interpretazioni dell'*Adelchi*." *Manzoni vivo*, 9–30. Bari: Levante, 1987. A useful review of the most influential interpretations by De Sanctis, Croce, and Russo, with a final invitation to give back to this tragedy the critical attention it deserves.

Bollati, Giulio. Introduction. *Tragedie*, by Alessandro Manzoni, vii–xxxvi. 1965. Reprint, Turin: Einaudi, 1973. In line with Croce's reasoning, Adelchi is seen as an exile among his own people because of his moral stature and refined mind, which bring him to perplexity and inaction. In this respect he is, with *Carmagnola*'s Mark, a figure of the modern intellectual with a paralyzed will, incapacitated to be active in history.

———. "Un carattere per gli italiani. Alessandro Manzoni." *L'italiano. Il carattere nazionale come storia e come invenzione*, 80–93. Turin: Einaudi, 1983. *Carmagnola* embodies the first stage of Manzoni's thought on history, Italian history in particular. Where Sismondi saw vital competition among principates and exalted pride and courage, Manzoni saw senseless anarchy and lack of unity. Manzoni condemned stupid presumptuousness and fierceness. In the historical tract on the Lombard domination, a further stage consists in identifying the victims of historical violence with the Italians. The author approves of the tract, but for the "neoguelph" conclusion on the positive role of the Pope in Italian history.

Borsellino, Nino. "Nota bibliografica." *Quaderni del Teatro popolare italiano. Alessandro Manzoni. Adelchi*. Ed. L. Codignola, 143–49. Turin: Einaudi, 1960. A very useful review of criticism of Manzoni's tragedies from Manzoni's contemporaries onward.

Bosisio, Paolo. "Le tragedie." *Manzoni: il suo e il nostro tempo*, 106–8. Milan: Electa, 1985. Recalling the fervid romantic milieu in which Manzoni's tragedies were born (romantic faith in the theater as a direct means of communications with the audience; see also Santangelo, "Socialità"), the author asserts the profound novelty of Manzoni's tragedy, whichwas and stillis misunderstood by critics. After a reconstruction of the history of Manzoni's tragedies on the Italian stage (see also Franzi, Mangini), the author demonstrates that the tragedies were indeed composed with a view to their potential stage rendition, contrary to the received opinion, popularized by Manzoni's modest remarks on his own works. Visual poetry of the narrative parts, vividly evoking the scene of the narrated events, detailed captions, and realistic dialogue are evidence that Manzoni conceived his tragedies for the stage.

————. "*Il Conte di Carmgnola* e la tecnica teatrale di Manzoni" and "Il Manzoni drammaturgo dal *Carmagnola* all'*Adelchi*." *La parola e la scena. Studi sul teatro italiano tra Settecento e Novecento,* 271–365. Rome: Bulzoni, 1987. The first essay develops and expands the essay cited above. In the second essay, the author notes that in his second tragedy Manzoni reintroduces the coup de theatre, transition scenes, and numerous entrances that he eliminated in his first, more compact tragedy. The more complex content of the second tragedy requires a more complex structure, and Manzoni was able to master the technical means to achieve it. The soliloquies can be functional (e.g., Svartus at the end of act I), but above all they allow to finely develop the characters' psychology. Their slow tempo is wisely contrasted with adjacent scenes of action. The choruses are perfectly integrated into the dramatic fabric. The high number and the quality of the captions suggest again that Manzoni had the scene in mind while writing his tragedies. With *Adelchis*, despite some defects in theatrical suitability, Manzoni carries out his dramatic project to renew the genre.

————. "Una tragedia 'sperimentale.'" Piccolo Teatro di Milano / Teatro d'Europa / Teatro Studio. Milan, Season 1989/90. Performance booklet of *Il Conte di Carmagnola,* by Alessandro Manzoni, directed by L. Puggelli, 7–10. Condensed rewriting of Bosisio, "*Conte di Carmagnola*."

————. Introduction. *Il Conte di Carmagnola,* by Alessandro Manzoni, v–xvi. Turin: Einaudi, 1990. The author sees a confirmation of his ideas on the theatrical potential of Manzoni's tragedies in Puggelli's then recent stage rendition of *Carmagnola* for the Piccolo Teatro, in 1989–90, the first performance since 1828. Act II proves very interesting on stage, while the critics always deemed it redundant. Mark's character on stage is static and almost redundant—again a refutation of much criticism exalting Mark as the real tragic hero of Manzoni's first drama. From the philological point of view, the author decides to present the 1845 edition with Manzoni's latest linguistic corrections, arguing against the choice of Bollati, Bardazzi, and Lonardi who consider the 1820 edition as princeps.

Bottoni, Luciano. *Drammaturgia romantica.* 2 vols. Pisa: Pacini, 1984. Vol. 1, *I paradigmi culturali,* illustrates the romantic dramatic theories of Kant, Herder, Goethe, Schelling, A. W. Schlegel, Schiller, and their reception in France. Vol. II, *Il sistema letterario manzoniano,* shows the influence of the above-mentioned authors on Manzoni's conception of theater (see also Carlson; Derla; Di Benedetto; Puppo; Santangelo, "Socialità").

Branca, Vittore. "Manzoni librettista." *Corriere della Sera,* 23 Mar. 1973. Argues that Manzoni's choruses had an influence on Verdi's operas.

————, ed. *Manzoni, Venezia e il Veneto*. Florence: Olschki, 1976.

Brandalise, Adone. "Dalla tragedia al romanzo. A proposito del frammento VII dei *Materiali Estetici*." *Tra illuminismo e romanticismo*, 533–53. Florence: Olschki, 1986. Manzoni's tragedies are interpreted through Benjamin's definition of *Trauerspiel* (sacrifice of bodies and passions to intellectual abstraction) and through Nietzschean and post-Nietzschehan conceptions of tragedy as manifestation of man's perception of God's absence from the world. For its intrinsic nature, the tragedy could not satisfy Manzoni's demand of historicism (see also De Castris), whereas the novel responds better to Manzoni's need for a detailed tale of causes and effects. The passage from the tragedies to the novel could be seen also as evidence of a Hegelian awareness of the end of the tragic genre, as well as of the end of the vitality of the social pact. Carmagnola and Adelchis are tragic only because of their inability to act, and this decrees the failure of tragedy itself. Somewhat contradicting his view of Manzoni's tragedies as allegorical, the author concludes that Manzoni probably perceived the great men as inadequate mirrors of history.

Brusamolino Isella, Silvia. *Bibliografia manzoniana 1949–73*. Milan: il Polifilo, 1974.

Caesar, Michael. "Manzoni's Poetry and the Witnessing of Events." *Comparative Criticism: A Yearbook*, vol. 3: 207–220. Cambridge: Cambridge UP, 1981. Through the device of the eye-witnessing of events (e.g., the Latins, bystanders in the first chorus of *Adelchis*), Manzoni posits the following aesthetical relationship within the tragedies: "The reader is the 'knowledge' to the protagonists' 'action'" and makes historical drama "a way of knowing ourselves as fully as possible." In *The Betrothed* the hero will be allowed to acquire knowledge as well. (See Lonardi, *Esperienza stilistica*, on "theatre within the theatre" conveyed by verb "to see" and other visual verbs.)

Caretti, Lanfranco. *Ideologia e stile*. Turin: Einaudi 1972. "Teleological" vision of Manzoni's career as a writer and as an intellectual. He was bound toward the ideology of historicism and the style of realism since his Jacobin youthful beginnings. In the tragedies he confronts for the first time the problem of the masses, which will be the novel's main concern.

Carlson, Marvin. *The Italian Stage*. Jefferson, N.C.: McFarland & Co., 1981

————. *The Italian Shakespearians*. Washington, D. C.: Folger Shakespeare Library, 1985

————. "Nationalism and the Romantic Drama in Europe" and "The Italian Romantic Drama in its European Context." *Romantic Drama*. Ed. G. Gillespie, 139–52 and 223–48. Amsterdam: John Benjamins, 1994. The author has the rare merit to assess Manzoni's art in the context of European romantic theater.

Carpentari Messina, Simone. "Manzoni dramaturge et la France." *Mélange à la memoire de Franco Simone*, 251–76. Geneva: Slatkine, 1984. Manzoni's tragedies, with their refusal to employ dramatic unities and their inclusion of history, are seen as exemplary romantic deconstruction of the tragic genre, its "epicization."

Caserta, Ernesto G. "The Tragedies." *Manzoni's Christian Realism*, 85–129. Florence: Olschki, 1977. Manzoni's tragedies are seen as the unsatisfactory achievement of the author's period of religious pessimism. The novel will fulfill Manzoni's aspiration to Christian realism.

————. "Un decennio di studi manzoniani in America." *Annali di Italianistica* 3 (1985): 44–63.

Cavallini, Giorgio. *Lettura dell'Adelchi*. Rome: Bulzoni, 1984.

————. "Politica e giustizia." *Annali d'italianistica* (1985): 114–22. The discovery of an unpublished article Manzoni wrote in 1848 reinforces the view that political justice was one of his central concerns.

———. "Il dilemma di Adelchi." *Tra illuminismo e romanticismo*, 521–31. Florence: Olschki, 1986. Manzoni's pessimistic vision of history is compensated by the Christian sense of duty and responsibility. Adelchis's greatness is in the "universal awareness" he achieves and articulates in the end—negation of the philosophical validity of Machiavelli's *Prince* and liberation offered by the inner life (see Bollati, Croce, Spinazzola).

———. "Nota sulle liriche e sulle tragedie." *Un filo per giungere al vero. Studi e note sul Manzoni*, 19–43. Florence: D'Anna, 1993. Discussion of the most important critical views on Manzoni's theater, concluding with the inevitability of a "teleological" vision of Manzoni's career, since his final choice of the democratic genre—the novel—responds not to a passing fad but to a deeply-felt artistic and moral need, as well as to long-held convictions (see Caretti, De Castris).

Cazzato, Carmelo. *Appunti sul "Conte di Carmagnola" del Manzoni*. Rome: Società Editrice Dante Alighieri, 1907. Interesting textual comparisons of Manzoni's first tragedy with Shakespeare's *Coriolanus*. The author hints at the notion that the Manzonian tragic heroes might not be "admirable models," although clad in greatness. There is extensive discussion of the function of the chorus in Manzonian tragedy.

Chandler, Bernard S. "*Adelchi* and *La pentecoste*." *Alessandro Manzoni: The Story of a Spiritual Quest*, 55–68. Edinburgh: Edinburgh UP, 1974. The tragedy embodies Adelchis's spiritual progress toward the following disillusionment: God is the universal consoler but only after death. In his final hour, Adelchis transcends his political concerns and views life in the eternal light. His acceptance of death marks the cathartic sacrifice of the Christian hero rather than the defeat of the romantic victim.

Chiari, Alberto. "Qualche osservazione sul manzoniano *Conte di Carmagnola*." *Otto/Novecento* 3 (1979): 173–91. If not a masterpiece, the tragedy is a fully accomplished work of art. In particular, it maintains a historical precision, harmoniously fused with the moral truth (refutation of Foscolo's opinin). Carmagnola was probably modeled on Giocchino Murat (see also Scherillo, above section).

Chiesa, Mario. "Qualche aggiunta sulle reminiscenze bibliche dell'*Adelchi*." *Giornale storico della letteratura italiana* 155 (1978): 439–42. The brief note is meant to supplement Torchio's article on the same subject. The author detects very important Biblical references in Charles's nocturnal monologue in act II. This philological discovery is not used to reverse or mitigate the negative judgment on this character; on the contrary, Manzoni is thought to be condemning through Charles his hypocritical contemporaries who professed to be religious but were in fact oppressors.

Chiusano, Italo A. "La tragedia cristiana e Claudel." *Altre lune*, 375–84. Milan: A. Mondadori, 1987. Within the general argument that the Christian tragedy is indeed the tragedy par excellence, Manzoni's *Adelchis* is defined "one of the most vivid and, at the same time, subtle Christian tragedies, with its historical failure witnessed by a silent God."

Ciccarelli, Andrea. *Manzoni e la coscienza della letteratura*. Rome: Bulzoni, 1996. By contrasting Manzoni's poetics and works with those of Foscolo, Alfieri, and Leopardi, the author shows the profound implications that the Christian conversion had for Manzoni's art. The *Inni sacri* were an innovative poetic attempt, not only within the Italian lyric tradition, but also with respect to the previous production of Manzoni. The final rejection on his part of the blank verse (endecasillabo sciolto), traditionally deemed the loftiest meter of poetic expression, mirrors Manzoni's changed attitude toward the role of the poet, a shift away from elitist art toward popular, morally meaningful poetic communication. The author also discusses Manzoni's vision of war and violent revolt in the framework of the then ongoing national revolution of Risorgimento (see also Jacomuzzi).

Collison-Morley, Lacy. "Shakespeare in Italy during the Romantic Movement." *Shakespeare in Italy,* 98–133. Stratford-upon-Avon: Shakespeare Head Press, 1916. Reports the numerous and unconditional praises Manzoni tributed to Shakespeare in his writings. The author states that the characters' monologues are all obviously modeled on Shakespeare and refers to Bellezza for textual comparisons.

Colombo, Umberto. *Alessandro Manzoni.* Rome: Edizioni Paoline, 1985. In chaps. 5 and 6 the author refutes Francesco Ruffini's (who has written extensively on Manzoni's religious life) thesis of Manzoni's Jansenism and asserts that *Carmagnola* does not present us with a somber image of God. The author reports on Goethe's positive judgment of the drama and provides an appreciative evaluation, especially of the chorus of act V. The chorus develops, as it proceeds, from civic poetry into a sacred hymn; act V conveys with lofty poetry the resignation of the count and his Christian pathos. *Adelchis's* first chorus was certainly meant to allegorize and mourn the Italian vicissitudes between the Napoleonic regime and the Holy Alliance. The meaning of Manzoni's tragedies is in the overcoming of earthly passions, in the harmonious composure of events, in the detection in history of something beyond contingencies.

Cordié, Carlo. "Alessandro Manzoni tra Schiller e Constant." *Ideali e figure d'Europa,* 181–200. Pisa: Nsitri-Lischi, 1954. The author argues that Constant's translation and abridgement of Schiller's *Wallenstein* influenced Manzoni's *Carmagnola,* especially the historical notes (see also Mazzucchetti).

Cro, Stelio. "Manzoni and the Lombard Question." *The Reasonable Romantic: Essays on Alessandro Manzoni.* Ed. S. Matteo and L. H. Peer, 161–77. New York: Peter Lang, 1986. Rebutting De Sanctis's thesis that there is a lack of historical content in *Adelchis,* the author demonstrates that in his second tragedy, Manzoni describes the historical moment in which the Italian people had a glimpse of the necessity of national unification. Manzoni forgoes historical accuracy somewhat in portraying Adelchis only "in order to make Italians aware of current historical events." On these bases, the author shares Croce's positive evaluation of *Adelchis.*

———. "L'idealismo neo-guelfo e il teatro nazionale in Alessandro Manzoni." *Teatro contemporaneo* 8, no. 18 (1988): 215–37. Elaborating further on his previous article, the author states that Manzoni is the founder of Italian national theater, since his plays express a deeply historical awareness of the Risorgimento. The tragedies can be read as social and political allegories: Carmagnola is the idealistic politician juxtaposed against the Machiavellian cynical politician, mirroring historical figures of the Risorgimento such as Mazzini and Garibaldi. Adelchis could foreshadow Carlo Alberto as the Hamletic king (see Bognetti). The positive role Manzoni assigned to the Church in protecting the Italians makes him into a neo-guelph in politics (see also Di Nepi, Bollati).

Croce, Benedetto. "Alessandro Manzoni" and "Adelchi." *Alessandro Manzoni: Saggi e discussioni*, 7–31 and 103–10. Bari: Laterza, 1969. The first essay was originally published in the 1921 book *Poesia e non poesia* and argues that critics should devote more attention to Manzoni's works prior to the novel. The second essay, first published in 1946, opens with the assertion that *"Adelchis* is Manzoni's most poetically robust work" and presents Adelchis as a highly refined and noble spirit endowed with moral strength, someone who happened to live in miserable historical conditions the logic of which escaped him.

De Castris, Arcangelo Leone. "Il bisogno di storia" and "La poetica storica." *L'impegno del Manzoni*, 3–113. Florence: Sansoni, 1965.

———. "La scommessa della poetica storica." *Il problema Manzoni*, 21–42. Palermo: Palumbo, 1990. The most recent book is a slightly more pensive, condensed rewriting of the first one. The main thesis is unchanged: the tragedies were a failed attempt to fulfill Manzoni's deeply felt "need for history," which only another genre, the novel, would eventually satisfy (see the "teleological" thesis in De Sanctis). The tragedy cannot achieve the unity between the following dichotomies: "the facts and their evaluation; the plot provided by history and the author's idealistic compensation; the action and the choruses."

Deigan, Federica Brunori. "Il re e la vittima: un modello shakespeariano per l'*Adelchi* di Alessandro Manzoni." *Filologia e critica* 25, no. 2–3 (2000): 457–75.

———. "The General, the Heart, and the State: Manzoni's *Carmagnola* and Shakespeare's *Othello*." *Italian Culture* 19, no. 1 (2001): 15–39.

De Lollis, Cesare. "A. Thierry e la teoria della razza" and "Manzoni e il terzo stato." *Alessandro Manzoni e gli storici liberali francesi della Restaurazione*, 5–44 and 65–82. Bari: Laterza, 1926. Surmises that at the time he conceived *Adelchis* and the novel, Augustin Thierry's theories on conquering and conquered races had a profound influence on Manzoni, one mediated by his friend Fauriel and by Jansenistic French authors. However, unlike Thierry, who saw in the German-subjugated Gallic-Romans the caretakers of the national spirit that would surface victoriously at the time of the revolution promoted by the "third state," Manzoni does not show much compassion for the vanquished Romans in the first chorus of *Adelchis*, perhaps because he was frustrated by the slow pace of the contemporary process of national unification.

De Michelis, Eurialo. "Le tragedie." *Studi sul Manzoni*, 102–73. Milan: Feltrinelli, 1962. *Carmagnola* seems to be inspired by the same central concern of the canzone "April 1814," that is, the legitimacy of Machiavellian strategies in human behavior. The last acts of the tragedy, composed after Manzoni took a break to write a tract on Catholic morals, have a totally different inspiration, which causes the unbalance we feel in the aesthetics of the work. The elimination of a unifying theme, such as Adelchis's national project for Italy, from the definitive draft of the second tragedy entails the even greater centrifugal nature of this work. The three focuses of dramatic action—the conquerors, the victims, and Providence—remain unrelated. Although he emphasizes Manzoni's quotation about his impartiality in portraying the historical figures in order to demonstrate that right is never all on one side only, the author deems Charles an "inconsistent" character. By contrast, Adelchis's character is flawed for his faithfulness to an inconclusive idealism, and the bitter words uttered at his death lack Christian resignation. Ermengarde, a creature between the Dantean and Metastasian feminine figures, seems more manly in resignation than her brother.

Derla, Luigi. "Manzoni, o la riforma del classicismo." *Otto / novecento* 19, no. 3–4 (1995): 5–40. Discussion of Manzoni's philosophical ideas with a view to illustrating his reform in drama.

De Sanctis, Francesco. *Manzoni*. Turin: Einaudi, 1955. The volume contains the lectures on Manzoni delivered by the author at the University of Naples in the 1860s and 1870s. His famous judgments on Manzoni's tragedies have influenced subsequent criticism of these works. He argued that the tragedies fail to incarnate the ideal into the real; the characters are not at all dramatic, only lyrical. The synthesis between the real and ideal will take place in Manzoni's novel (the so-called teleological vision of Manzoni's career, in which the novel represents the greatest achievement after a ten-year crescendo).

Di Benedetto, Arnaldo. "La storia, le passioni, la vera natura umana (La teoria tragica di Manzoni)" and "Il discorso sulla dominazione longobardica." *Dante e Manzoni. Studi e letture*, 63–87 and 89–109. Salerno: Laveglia, 1987. The first essay analyzes Manzoni's dramatic writings in the light of European romantic drama. In the second essay, the author advocates the continuity between the content of the historical tract and Manzoni's second tragedy; accordingly, he refutes Manzoni's quietism in the tragedies.

Di Nepi, Piero. "Manzoni e il principe pentito." *Il veltro* 30, no. 5–6 (1986): 520–24. Consideration of Manzoni's political stance on the temporal power of the Church (he rules out neo-guelphism, compare Cro, "Idealismo neo-guelfo"); on the legitimacy of political action; on possible sources in Italian religious dramas of late 1500s, by della Valle and others (see also Gorra), as well as in A. M. Ricci's *Italiade* (see Becherucci); and on the romantic theme of the just man such as Adelchis atoning the sins of the world.

Doglio, Federico. Introduction. "Dal romanticismo al Risorgimento." *Il teatro tragico italiano. Storia e testi del teatro tragico in Italia*, cxxxix–clxiv. Parma: Guanda, 1960. *Adelchis* is seen as the apogee of the Italian tragedy. For its Christian theme coupled with the tragic form, *Adelchis* resembles the fourteenth-century *Ecerinis* (*Ezzelinide*) by Albertino Mussato. Manzoni is a refined mind and his tragedies, although moral, shun the simpler didacticism of Alfieri's and Foscolo's dramas.

D'Ovidio, Francesco. "Ermengarda." *Nuovi studi manzoniani*, 3–188. Milan: Hoepli, 1908. After considerations on how Manzoni addressed the theme of love in his works, the author surmises that his first inspiration might have been a tragedy about Ermengarde, modeled on Shakespeare's Catherine in *Henry VIII*. He defends the dramatic nature of Ermengarde, her drama being in her conflicting inner life. In this, the author takes issue with De Sanctis who had found her lyrical. Also arguing against De Sanctis's remarks on the chorus (that it is realistic, recited by the nuns around the dying Ermengarde), the author defends it as a legitimate subjective expression of the poet. Ermengarde's elegiac tragedy is well integrated into the tragedy as a whole.

Egidi, Pietro. Introduction. *Tragedie*, by Alessandro Manzoni, vii–xxxiv. Turin: UTET, 1921. *Carmagnola* is seen as a preparation for *Adelchis*. In Manzoni's second tragedy the hero is endowed with a great soul and surrounded by iniquity and misery. (These serve to illustrate Adelchis's greatness, as the critic quotes from the drama's first draft.) The choruses are better integrated in the second tragedy than in *Carmagnola*. After the tragedies,

Manzoni chose to write a novel rather than a third tragedy on Spartacus because he could better portray the masses and, above all, because the seventeenth-century heroes were closer to himself than Spartacus was in feeling the consolation of the Christian religion.

Faitrop-Porta, Anne-Christine. *I promessi sposi. Riduzioni teatrali.* Florence: Olschki, 2001. The author reconstructs the theatrical works based on Manzoni's novel (nine in the nineteenth century, ten in the twentieth century, up to 1985).

Forti, Fiorenzo. "Il primo getto del *Carmagnola.*" *Fra le carte dei poeti,* 190–214. Naples: Ricciardi 1965. Philological study opposing Sanesi and Ghisalberti's theory of continuity between successive drafts. The author would like to see Acts I and II (with scenes of the populace scenes and the count's father) neatly separated in an appendix, as those scenes were not even part of a first definitive draft.

Foster, Kenelm. "*Pentecost* and other poems. By Alessandro Manzoni. Translated by Kenelm Foster." *Comparative Criticism: A Yearbook,* vol. 3:200–206. Cambridge: Cambridge UP, 1981. Includes a prose translation of the first chorus of *Adelchis.*

Frosini, Vittorio. "Del teatro politico di Alessandro Manzoni." *Il pensiero politico* 7 (1974): 91–98. Carmagnola was based on Gioacchino Murat, Charles on Napoleon; the political nature of Manzoni's theater would focus on the shipwreck of a man in politics in the first tragedy and a denunciation of Machiavellism in the second (see also Scherillo, above section; Bognetti).

Frugoni, Arsenio. "La 'colpa' di Francesco Bussoni, detto il Carmagnola." *Humanitas* 10 (1955): 38–46. Careful reconstruction of the career of the historical Carmagnola, concluding that if the count did not betray Venice for Milan, he did betray her for himself. His aim was to be lord of Milan in competition with the rising star of Francesco Sforza, a military captain like himself. The author thinks that Manzoni should not have believed the numerous protestations of the count's innocence published by Renaissance historians. However, the historical details revealed in his article coincide precisely with Manzoni's portrayal of the count as vain and proud, fighting for himself more than for any master (for historical studies, see also Battistella, Carini, both in above section).

Gaglio, Antonietta. *Lettura dell'Adelchi.* Palermo: Manfredi, 1955. The fundamental opposition in the tragedy is between Adelchis and Charles. The first is the man defeated on earth but faithful to a superior justice; the second is victorious on earth, the champion of God, but unworthy of such a role for his moral misery. Leopardi would have had his tragic hero deny God in the moment of utter despair following the downfall. Instead, Manzoni has Adelchis associate himself with Christ, as a redeemer of humanity.

Galletti, Alfredo. "Manzoni, Shakespeare e Bossuet." *Saggi e studi,* 3–139. Bologna: Zanichelli, 1915. Illustrates the influence of Bossuet's *Oraisons funèbres* on Manzoni's dramatic works. Manzoni's Christianity ultimately makes his characters weak because they are devoid of a real, instinctual drive to live, unlike most Shakespearean characters but similar to Hamlet.

Gassman, Vittorio. "Lo spettacolo del Tpi. Appunti per la regia." *Quaderni del teatro popolare italiano. Alessandro Manzoni. Adelchi.* Ed. L. Codignola, 119–27. Turin: Einaudi, 1960. The Cross is the central symbol of the director's stage production, especially to emphasize "the heroes' death" and "the [spiritual] death from which the Italian people seem unable to wake up." Adelchis is given speeches from the first draft of the tragedy (where he features as a king with a mission to unify Lombards and Romans as one people) and recites both choruses.

Getto, Giovanni. "Manzoni e Shakespeare." *Lettere italiane* (1967): 187–236. Reprint in *Manzoni europeo*, 229–98. Milan: Mursia, 1971. Seminal study establishing the philological practice of referring to Pierre Le Tourneur's 1776 French version of Shakespeare's plays for textual comparison. The author convincingly shows Shakespearean references in the historical novel.

———. "Prospettive sul *Conte di Carmagnola.*" *Lettere Italiane* (1971): 332–80. Reprint in *Tre studi sul teatro*, 86–164. Rome: Sciascia, 1976. Excellent structural study of the play; it highlights how Manzoni, although he eliminates the traditional dramatic unities, organized space in a coherent, meaningful manner, accomplishing a perfect work of art. However, in the final part, the scholar defines the tragedy as "a martyrologic drama."

Ghisalberti, Fausto. *Critica manzoniana di un decennio.* Milan: Casa del Manzoni, 1949.

———. Introduction. *Tragedie*, by Alessandro Manzoni, 5–18. Milan: Rizzoli, 1954. Reiterates, from a different angle, Goethe's critique of the uselessness of distinguishing between historical and fictive characters. The author's analysis of *Adelchis* closely reflects Russo's distinction between characters illuminated by Grace—Adelchis, Ermengarde, Anfrid—and those damned by political power—Charles, Desiderius (although Desiderius later undergoes an evolution toward Christian conversion). The overall aesthetic evaluation, in contrast to Russo's opinion, is very positive.

———. "Spartaco, terzo eroe tragico manzoniano." *Convivium* 31(1963): 151–59. Analysis of the extant manuscripts of sketches for a third tragedy. The author concludes with De Lollis that after *Adelchis* the problem of the oppressed people became a priority in Manzoni's creative enterprises.

Giannantonio, Pompeo. "Valore europeo del teatro di Alessandro Manzoni." *Alla scuola del Manzoni.* Turin: Genesi, 1989. 101–17. The author traces the various factors influencing Manzoni's tragedies: they mirror the French and German literary debate around the theater, Manzoni's first-hand reading of Shakespeare, as well as the political turmoil immediately preceding their composition that prompted the poet to reassert a popular and pedagogical form of art. That Manzoni's intention was to penetrate in the heart of history can be seen in the greater vividness of the historical backdrop as we proceed from *Carmagnola* to *Adelchis.*

Giordano, Alberto. Introduction. *Adelchi*, by Alessandro Manzoni, 5–39. 1976. Reprint, Milan: BUR, 1982. Adelchis is a lacerated hero, torn between desire and action, and this is an "energetic dilemma in his conscience." His Christian pessimism is "great"; it is "the ethical denial of the logic of power, a denunciation of the tears and blood that temper any whatsoever form of power," "a denunciation of the limits of political action in a reality which is impervious to ethical values." Adelchis's final words are a message of greatness, suffering and lucid protest not far from some of Leopardi's poems and thoughts. Adelchis is a *figura Christi*, as revealed not only by his final invocation, but also by Anfrid's words (see Petrocchi), and this is the central theme of the play.

Goffredo De Robertis, Mariella. *Bibliografia manzoniana, 1980–1995*. Milan: Biblioteca Nazionale Braidense, 1998. The most recent comprehensive bibliography on Manzoni.

Gorra, Marcella. "Conobbe il Manzoni il teatro di Federigo della Valle?" *Belfagor* 11 (1956): 89–96. This essay proposes interesting intertextual references between Manzoni and the sixteenth-century tragedian della Valle.

——. "Ermengarda." *Manzoni: un discorso che continua*, 65–79. Milan: Ceschina, 1975. Analyzes the second chorus of *Adelchis*. Ermengarda dies of love pains, the amorous passion vividly described, but on dying she reestablishes her virginal purity, which is compared to Eden in the last stanza.

Gramsci, Antonio. "Critica letteraria." *Dante e Manzoni*, 80–86. Rome: Editori Riuniti 1992. Compares Manzoni with Tolstoy, Verga, and Shakespeare. Manzoni gives a too paternalistic portrayal of the low classes because of his "aristocratic Catholicism."

Grasso, Vito. "Il Manzoni tra l'*Adelchi* e il *Discorso storico*." *Italian Filolojisi* 5, no. 6 (1973): 127–32. After reporting and endorsing the studies of the definitive draft of *Adelchis* by Margiotta and Accame Bobbio, the author concludes that one has to acknowledge that if Adelchis is the hero of the tragedy, Charles is the hero of the *Discorso*. But the tragedy and the historical tract are concomitant, not necessarily interdependent, works.

Jacomuzzi, Stefano. "'Insegne aperte al vento': eserciti e battaglie nella poesia del Manzoni." *Omaggio a Alessandro Manzoni nel bicentenario della nascita*, 169–182. Assisi: Accademia Properziana del Subasio, 1986.

——. "La guerra tra epica e sarcasmo" and "Ermengarda: un'eroina improvvida." *Le insegne della poesia. Studi su Dante e sul Manzoni*, 77–93. Turin: SEI, 1996. Isolating the theme of war in Manzoni's tragedies, the critic notices an apparently contradictory attitude in the poet: on the one hand, violence and conquest are strongly condemned; on the other, Manzoni shows admiration for certain beautiful spectacles such as the banners flying in the wind. Manzoni treats war in both an epic manner and with sarcasm. Ermengarde typifies the tragic hero in which lack of self-awareness and innocence coincide. God sacrifices her and her brother in his providential plan for salvation.

Jeronimidis, Elena D., and Keith Wren. "A One-Way Ticket to Heaven: History, Politics, and Religion in the Theatre of Manzoni and Hugo." *Neophilologus* 66, no. 1 (1982): 66–91. Excellent comparative study concluding that the interaction of history and poetry, Providence and free will, is more successful in Manzoni's tragedies than in Hugo's historical dramas, where events seem to stem exclusively and mechanically from God's design.

Kennard, Joseph S. "Minor Dramatists." *The Italian Theatre*, vol. 2:231–36. 1932. Reprint, New York: Blom, 1964. After a summary of the tragedies' plots, the author gives a negative evaluation: "In Manzoni's tragedies there are beautiful episodes, but theatrical art demands unity of design and vitality, and this is lacking in *Adelchis*."

Kostka, Edmund. *Schiller in Italy*. New York: Peter Lang, 1997. A brief chapter early in the book summarizes the importance of Manzoni and his theater in the Italian literary and artistic scene.

Leri, Clara. Introduction and notes. *Inni sacri e altri inni cristiani*. Florence: Olschki, 1991. This annotated edition of Manzoni's *Inni sacri* highlights, among other things, Manzoni's metrical choices with special emphasis on the influence of Metastasio's poetic art.

Lonardi, Gilberto. *L'esperienza stilistica del Manzoni tragico*. Florence: Olschki, 1965. Stylistic analysis of

Manzoni's tragedies, highlighting the reformatory rather than revolutionary character of his innovations. *Adelchis* is more fully modeled on the "Shakespearean system" than *Carmagnola* is. There is an epic development that deemphasizes dialogue and revolves around "the identification of the tragic hero with the wise, defeated hero of the European Christian tradition."

———. "Il *Carmagnola*, Venezia e il 'potere ingiusto.'" *Manzoni, Venezia e il Veneto*. Ed. V. Branca, 19–40. Florence: Olschki, 1976. Not afraid of falling into a stereotype, Manzoni decided to present Venice as an oppressive state, master in intrigue and deceit. After eliminating from the first draft the physical images of the Venetian street crowded with people, the tragedy presents Venice as symbol of unjust power.

———. Introduction. *Il Conte di Carmagnola*, by Alessandro Manzoni. Ed. G. Lonardi and P. Azzolini, 9–66. Venice: Marsilio, 1989.

———. *Ermengarda e il pirata*. Bologna: il Mulino, 1991. Essays include Manzoni's influence on opera libretto. In "Allontanare Dioniso"—a rewriting of the Marsilio introductions to the two tragedies edited by the author—the Manzonian tragic hero is seen as a figura Christi. In this respect, Adelchis is modeled on Shakespeare's Richard II.

———. Introduction. *Adelchi*, by Alessandro Manzoni. Ed. G. Lonardi and P. Azzolini. Venice: Marsilio, 1992.

———. Introduction. *Tutte le poesie*, by Alessandro Manzoni. Ed. G. Lonardi and P. Azzolini. Venice: Marsilio, 1992.

———. *Manzoni e l'esperienza del tragico*. Modena: Mucchi, 1995. Text of a lecture focusing on Manzoni's trascendent, rather than immanent, tragic mode, with reference—besides the two tragedies—to the 1833 version of "Il natale" (from the *Inni sacri*), revised on the day Manzoni's first wife, Enrichetta, died.

Low, Murray R. "Manzoni in the American 1830s: Poet, Dramatist, or Novelist?" *The Reasonable Romantic: Essays on Alessandro Manzoni*, 49–72. Ed. S. Matteo and L. H. Peer. New York: Peter Lang, 1986. Seminal study reconstructing Manzoni's fortune in the United States, with particular focus on his tragic and poetic works.

Lukàcs, Georg. *The Historical Novel*. 1937. Trans. H. and S. Mitchell. Boston: Beacon Press, 1963. In the chapter devoted to the romantic historical drama, Manzoni is recognized as the most important author in this genre, and his theoretical notions are applied in the analysis of the drama of the period.

Mancini, Franco. "Tradizione scritturale e mistico-liturgica dagli *Inni Sacri* ai cori tragici." *Omaggio a Alessandro Manzoni nel bicentenario della nascita*, 107–28. Assisi: Accademia Properziana del Subasio, 1986. The author detects references to the Bible and to Catholic liturgical and religious texts in Manzoni's choruses and poetry with a view to highlighting Manzoni's conception of history as a meaningful chain of events.

Mangini, Nicola. "Manzoni e il teatro." *Manzoni, Venezia e il Veneto*. Ed. V. Branca, 377–85. Florence: Olschki, 1976. The author deals with the scarce scenic fortune of Manzoni's tragedies, endorsing the evaluation of the actor Gusatavo Modena, who thought that however innovative Manzoni's tragedies were, they remained in between classicism and artistic freedom, and were therefore far from successful.

Margiotta, Giacinto. *Dalla prima alla seconda stesura dell'Adelchi*. Florence: Le Monnier, 1956. A philological and critical study comparing the first draft and the definitive version of Manzoni's second tragedy and showing how Ermengarde was conceived as she is from the beginning, while Charles is a "complex figure," thoughtfully developed.

Marrapodi, Michele. "Carmagnola e Coriolano." *Nuovi annali della facoltà di Magistero dell'Università di Messina*, 504–45. Rome: Herder, 1985. Bases the resemblance of Carmagnola with Shakespeare's Coriolanus on thematic evidence. Both represent the ironically bitter adventure of a man who cannot adapt in a world devoid of moral values. Both tragic heroes are crushed by the arts of dissimulation, by immoral and corrupted politics (see Cazzato for more convincing arguments).

Martelli, Mario. Introduction. *Tutte le opere*, by Alessandro Manzoni. 2 vols. Ed. M. Martelli, vol. 1:xli–lxiii. Florence: Sansoni, 1973. *The Count of Carmagnola* occasions a concise and cogent discussion of Manzoni's tragic conception, as well as its defense. The author thinks that Manzoni shows the count's tragedy to readers so that they might avoid their sad lots. The author also convingly discards the hypothesis that Manzoni had a religious crisis in 1816–17.

Matteo, Sante and Larry H. Peer. *The Reasonable Romantic: Essays on Alessandro Manzoni.* New York: Peter Lang, 1986. This book has had the rare merit of reviving Manzonian scholarship in the American academy, with useful insights and groundbreaking research.

Mazziotti di Celso D'Ambrosio, Anna Maria. "*Adelchi* tragedia sacra e il 'core' romantico." *Humanitas* 45, no. 2 (1990): 191–212. Stylistic study, focusing on the recurrent image of the heart in the words of Adelchis, Anfrid, and Ermengarde; these characters represent the soul's rights in a world that ignores the spiritual dimension; this is why the tragedy is sacred, not because Charles carries out a God-ordained enterprise. Charles's victory is burdened, in the tragedy, with too many negative and antiheroic traits to be in line with the positive vision of the papal request for Frankish help, outlined in Manzoni's historical tract. Adelchi's final identification with Christ is part of the traditional, edifying role of the dying martyr.

Mazzucchetti, Lavinia. "Federico Schiller e Alessandro Manzoni." *Schiller in Italia*, 193–298. Milan: Hoepli, 1913. Shows the influence of Schiller's *Wallenstein*, via Benjamin Constant's *Wallstein*, on *Carmagnola*.

Mirri, Francesco Saverio. "*Adelchi*, dramma e lirismo in una tragedia mancata." *Saggi di varia letteratura*, 55–73. Florence: Sandron, 1974. The author follows De Sanctis and Russo in criticizing the tragedies. Ermengarde is the only viable tragic character. The Christian spirit chokes the dramatic potential of the historical material.

Molinari, Cesare. "La (s)fortuna teatrale di Manzoni." *Biblioteca teatrale* 2d ser., 1 (1986): 77–93. Reports on Manzoni's negative attitude toward staging his tragedies, as well as on the nineteenth-century stagings of *Carmagnola* and *Adelchis*, with their unsuccessful outcome. The author also reviews stage adaptations of *The Betrothed*, which were possible because of the intrinsic theatricality of the novel.

———. "Manzoni, il dramma storico e il *Carmagnola*." Piccolo Teatro di Milano / Teatro d'Europa / Teatro Studio, Season 1989/90. Performance booklet of *Il Conte di Carmagnola*, by Alessandro Manzoni, directed by L. Puggelli, 12–13. Unlike other works of romantic theater that take into account the importance of a colorful and realistic scenarios (e.g., Schiller's), Manzoni's tragedy is bare. The conflict is among abstract forces, so much so that the Alfierian neoclassical model could have easily been followed. *Carma-*

gnola portrays the maneuvers of powerful people to hold on to political power at the expenses of the powerless people (similar to Brecht's rendition of Marlowe's *Edward II*). These people are therefore necessarily excluded from the scene, except for the chorus, meaningfully placed in the center of the tragedy.

Momigliano, Attilio. "Le tragedie e le liriche." *Alessandro Manzoni*, 175–94. Milan: Principato, 1952. The hero of *Carmagnola* is split in two halves unrelated to each other. Mark is a more profound character than the count, but the tragedy as a whole is "weak." *Adelchi* is "sublime" for its hero's "Christian fatalism," but the artistic value remains concentrated in a few intensely poetic points: the choruses, the passion of the queen, and the viciousness of Svartus and Guntigis, who, being potential Iagos, should have been developed more.

Montano, Rocco. "Manzoni in America." *Annali manzoniani* 7 (1977): 267–84. Traces the fortune of Manzoni's novel in the United States.

Nava, Giuseppe. "Manzoni e *L'Histoire des républiques italiennes* del Sismondi." *Studi letterari della serie "Studia Ghisleriana,"* 143–72. Pavia: Tipografia del libro, 1967. After comparing the many points Sismondi and Manzoni, the historian of the *Discorso,* have in common, the author concludes that there remains a great difference. Manzoni was deeply averse to moral relativism and to historicism. He would not pass a less stern judgment on the Lombard for their unjust behavior in view of their lesser degree of development in the history of civilization. Justice is eternal and its precepts should be followed by every man under all skies. This fundamental difference led Manzoni to write works of art, where he could express, better than in the description of history, his moral and religious vision.

Nigro, Salvatore. "Storia e poesia, 'eros' e 'thanatos': la *Lettre à Monsieur Chauvet,* l'*Adelchi* e il *Discorso sur alcuni punti dell storia longobardica.*" *Manzoni*, 64–102. Bari: Laterza, 1988. The martyrs of Manzoni's Christian tragedy *Adelchis* are the Latins portrayed in the first chorus (in line with the conclusion of the historical tract) and the hero and his sister, "the innocents who atone, by means of their martyrdom, the ancestral guilt of wielding political power." The final words of Adelchis are a "denunciation of the immorality of Power in an unjust society opposed in everything to Christian values" (see Lonardi, *Manzoni e l'esperienza del tragico,* for a similar thesis).

Petrini, Mario. "L'*Adelchi* e il *Discorso* sulla storia longobardica." *Rivoluzioni manzoniane.* Messina: D'Anna, 1974. The tragedy is not in line with the historical tract: the positive portrait of Charlemagne in this history does not appear in the drama. In *Adelchis* the author finally overcomes the need for the great man, the tragic hero, and starts considering the masses, his real interest, as it is manifest in the choruses.

Petrocchi, Giorgio. "Il momento letterario del *Carmagnola*." and "Preludio e morte di Anfrido." *Manzoni. Letteratura e vita,* 59–95. Milan: Rizzoli, 1971. The author believes that Manzoni experienced a deep crisis in 1816–17, as demonstrated by the somber and hopeless religious dimension of his works in those years. By 1819 Manzoni's situation was totally different, as can be seen in the words full of hope Carmagnola utters upon dying, words composed together with the new version of the *Pentecost*. Anfrid's death is a poetic prelude to the more sublime and fully Christian death of the two Lombard siblings.

———. "Realismo e forma poetica nel *Carmagnola*." *Manzoniana e altre cose dell'Ottocento,* 9–27.

Rome: Sciascia, 1987. The tragedies are the works where Manzoni experiments in psychological and ethical realism, creating dilemmatic characters. This was a necessary step for the artist before tackling the novel.

Portinari, Folco. "*Il Conte di Carmagnola e la Lettre à Monsieur Chauvet.*" and "*L'Adelchi.*" *Storia della civiltà letteraria italiana*, ed. G. Barberi Squarotti, vol. 4:686–784. Turin: UTET, 1990–92. Adelchis is a martyr like those of old described by Jacopo da Varagine, that is, the kind of anti-tragic Christian hero that supplanted the classical precedent.

Pozzi, Emilio. "Manzoni precede Brecht?" *Sipario* 324 (1973): 12–13. This is an interview with Giuseppe Testori, who sees preaching and moralism as the common element between the two artists.

Puggelli, Lamberto. "*Il Conte di Carmagnola:* note per la messa in scena." Piccolo Teatro di Milano / Teatro d'Europa / Teatro Studio, Season 1989/90. Performance booklet of *Il Conte di Carmagnola*, by Alessandro Manzoni, directed by L. Puggelli, 4–6. The chorus contains the deepest meaning of the tragedy and must be the climax of the performance. It is recited twice: at the end of the first part of the performance by the whole company, literally in a chorus, and at the beginning of the second part by an actor in bourgeois attire. The members of the audience in the first row are invited to wear the red robes of Venetian senators to create a bridge between the two sides of the curtain.

Puppo, Mario. *Romanticismo italiano e romanticismo europeo.* Milan: Istituto di propaganda libraria, 1985. The essay on A. W. Schlegel's fortune among the Italian romantics analyzes the influence of the German author on Manzoni's *Lettre.*

Radcliff-Umstead, Douglas. "The Transcendence of Human Space in Manzonian tragedy." *Studies in Romanticism* 13 (1974): 25–46. Manzoni wanted to show the vanity of man's temporal struggle for territorial possession and therefore depicted the territorial sphere in the two plays not as a space of love and happiness but as one of hatred and combat. In *Carmagnola* a claustrophobic atmosphere reigns, and in the chorus Italy is not the beloved and happy land that men defend against invasions but instead an arena for greedy battles. In *Adelchis* the conception of space is less centripetal. The land features as a site for hardships and struggles. Manzoni's aim was to lift the spectator into the lofty sphere of Christian contemplation (for treatment of space in *Carmagnola*, see also Getto, "Prospettive").

Raimondi, Ezio. "Alessandro Manzoni e il Romanticismo." *Il Romanticismo*, 180–92. Budapest: Akademiai Kiado, 1968. Shakespeare was a catalytic element in Manzoni's poetics from the *Inni sacri* to the tragedies and to the novel. For the tragedies, through Guizot's *Vie de Shakespeare*, Manzoni could project the contemporary problem of the utopian but irresolute intellectuals onto Hamletic characters, and he could find in Shakespeare the inquiry over the antinomy between morals and political power. When unsatisfied with the inner-life conflicts and the "Romanesque," Manzoni developed the Shakespearean element he had left aside—the comic—for his realistic, historical novel.

———. "Il dramma, il comico, il tragico." *Il romanzo senza idillio*, 79–124. Turin: Einaudi, 1974. Discusses Manzoni's rejection, in the *Lettre*, of Schlegel's advice to dramatists to mix the tragic and the comic after the Shakespearean drama. After reading *Vie de Shakespeare*, Manzoni must have changed his mind and turned to the tragicomic mixture. Manzoni's tragedies contain a narrative tendency, and the novel in turn inherits from them a theatrical structure.

———. "Il dramma, la storia." *Romanticismo italiano e romanticismo europeo*, 97–114. Milan: Mondadori, 1997. Considers adherence to historical facts as an absolute value in Manzoni's art. Shakespeare is his model because he produced works of art in which human feelings are always portrayed against the backdrop of history and society, allowing tragicomic portrayal of characters as well.

Repanaj, Ferruccio. "Adelchi, personaggio biblico?" *Proc. Congresso Nazionale di Studi Manzoniani* 5 (1961): 85–95. Makes a compelling case for similarities in the plot of *Adelchis* and the first book of Kings, the end of Saul's kingdom, which Alfieri had dealt with in his tragedy *Saul*.

Ruggieri, Ruggero. *Storia poetica e poesia storica:tradizione e attualità nell'Adelchi*. Milan: Centro nazionale di studi manzoniani, 1975. Suggests the possible influence of the *Chanson de Roland* on the tragedy's portrait of the Franks, especially for the common theme of betrayal. A rare positive appreciation of Charlemagne's character derives from the consideration that Manzoni would have never contradicted the commonly held belief that God was acting through the Frankish victory (*gesta Dei per francos*), which is also apparent in the historical tract.

Russo, Luigi. "Parere sull'*Adelchi* (1935)." *Ritratti e disegni storici. Dal Manzoni al De Sanctis*, 39–108. 1946. Reprint, Florence: Sansoni, 1965. In this famous essay, the author considers *Adelchis* the product of Manzoni's 1817 Jansenistic crisis. The theological Janseninsm of the tragedies will yield to a moral Jansenism in the novel. In the tragedies, God's grace descends only to the chosen (Adelchis, Ermengarde, Anfrid); the political characters (Charles, Svartus, Guntigis) are excluded from it. Desiderius is seen as a character in transition from politician to one of the chosen. Adelchis is a representative of the romantic culture, and the tragedy as a whole is artistically weak.

Sala di Felice, Elena. "Ermengarda come Henriette." *Filologia e letteratura* 15 (1969): 410–46. Convincingly traces some traits of Ermengarde to the two Henriettes of Bossuet's *Oraisons Funèbres* (see Galletti). By extending Ermengarde's status of innocent victim to Adelchis, however, the author has to postulate Manzoni's quietism, that is, Manzoni's belief that the good life and justice are achievable only in the afterlife.

Sanesi, Ireneo. Introduction. *Le tragedie secondo i manoscritti e le prime stampe*, by Alessandro Manzoni, ix–cci. Florence: Sansoni, 1958. Important philological, biographical, and critical study.

Santangelo, Giorgio. "La 'socialità' del teatro nella teoria e nella prassi della drammaturgia romantica." *Saggi di letteratura italiana in onore di Gaetano Trombatore*, 411–449. Milan: Istituto editoriale cisalpino-La goliardica, 1973. Considers Manzoni's *Lettre à Monsieur Chauvet* in the framework of European writing on drama: Lessing, Schlegel, and the Italians Pellico and Visconti.

———. "Le prime polemiche intorno al *Conte di Carmagnola*." *Omaggio a Alessandro Manzoni nel bicentenario della nascita*, 169–182. Assisi: Accademia Properziana del Subasio, 1986. Describes the early fortune of *Carmagnola*.

Santini, Emilio. "Le idee del Manzoni sulla tragedia e l'*Adelchi*." *Giornale Storico della letteratura italiana* (1928): 233–66. Underlines Manzoni's closeness to Aristotle's *Poetics* on the relationship between history and poetry; only Manzoni's "providential woe" alters the concept of catharsis and the aims of dramatic poetry. In *Adelchis* the author sees a successful artistic elaboration of Manzoni's ideas on tragedy. Unlike his novel, Manzoni's tragedies paint human passions such as the will to power, erotic love, and desire for glory with a Shakespearean touch, and Manzoni's own moral judgment on those passions seems uncertain (on the greater freedom of characters in tragedies with respect to the novel, see also Lonardi, Introduction to *Carmagnola*).

———. *Il teatro di Alessandro Manzoni.* Palermo: Palumbo, 1940. Thoughtful and convincing comparison between Manzoni's tragedies and Greek tragedies, especially Sophocles (see also Chiusano on Christian tragedy). The author also makes a comparison with Alfieri's tragedies, *Carmagnola* being more Alfierian than *Adelchis. Adelchis* is a great tragedy because the protagonist is highly dramatic, presenting us with the deep-seated conflicts of a Christian soul coping with events.

Scarpati, Claudio. "Pietà e terrore nell'*Adelchi.*" *Manzoni tra due secoli,* 77–99. Ed. F. Mattesini. Milan: Vita e pensiero, 1986. After a philological reconstruction of the composition stages of *Adelchis,* the author examines the changed role of the Greek *phobos* and *eleos* in Manzoni's tragedies. The victim is the happy beneficiary of superior salvation.

Scelfo, Maria Luisa. *Le teorie drammatiche nel Romanticismo.* Catania: CUECM, 1996. The author reprises Trompeo's line of inquiry and demonstrates, by intertextual comparisons, the dependence of French romantic writing on drama from the Italian romantic debate, including Manzoni's preface to *Carmagnola.*

Spera, Francesco. "La necessità del tradimento: le tragedie del Manzoni." *Metamorfosi del linguaggio tragico. Dalla tragedia classica al dramma romantico,* 87–125. Rovito: Marra, 1990. Manzoni's tragedies hinge on the theme of betrayal and represent the final evolution of classic tragedy into Christological drama.

Spinazzola, Vittorio. Introduction. *Inni sacri. Tragedie di Alessandro Manzoni,* vii–xxxvii. Milan: Garzanti, 1984. Carmagnola is the superior man of action with an upright heart, a character of Schillerian ascendancy, victim of the deceits that make the very fabric of history. The harsh law regulating human affairs—the necessity of deceit—can be overcome by the religious feeling, the only means to make man master of himself in his inner life. The same is true for Adelchis, who symbolizes the "eternal martyrdom of the just men, whom the world blindly judges anti-heroes." The novel element in the later tragedy is a well-articulated psychology of the tragic hero (see Cavallini) faced with a dilemma between justice and obedience to the father. Charles embodies the harsh political reality, but he has a "complex inner life, not totally absorbed by practical concerns." Manzoni's pessimistic conception of history is tempered by the choruses, which try to draw a lesson from history in view of the process of national unification.

Timpanaro, Sebastiano. "Antileopardiani e neomoderati nella sinistra italiana." *Belfagor* 30 (1975): 129–56. Positive evaluation of *Adelchis* paradoxically based on Manzoni's pessimism, which reaches its peak in the work. In the tragedy there is a "bitterly heroic tension" that will be lost in the novel, that comes from acting in a world "devoid of Providence, governed by the fierce rule of either inflicting or suffering wrongs."

Torchio, Carlo. "Linguaggio scritturale e reminiscenze bibliche nell'*Adelchi.*" *Rivista di storia e letteratura religiosa* 11 (1975): 24–65. Seminal study on Biblical references in *Adelchis,* factual and

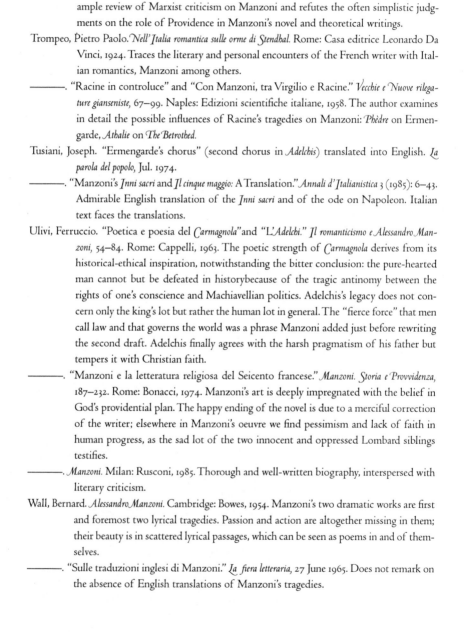

devoid of evaluations, except for a remark on Charles's "mixture of sincere religious piety and utilitarianism" in the Biblical quotations he employs.

———. "Cinque saggi sulla lingua dell'*Adelchi*." *Tra romanticismo e decadenza*. Turin: Tirrenia Stampatori, 1995.

Triolo, Franco. "Manzoni and Providence." *The Reasonable Romantic: Essays on Alessandro Manzoni*. Ed. S. Matteo and L. H. Peer, 245–57. New York: Peter Lang, 1986. The author gives an ample review of Marxist criticism on Manzoni and refutes the often simplistic judgments on the role of Providence in Manzoni's novel and theoretical writings.

Trompeo, Pietro Paolo. *Nell'Italia romantica sulle orme di Stendhal*. Rome: Casa editrice Leonardo Da Vinci, 1924. Traces the literary and personal encounters of the French writer with Italian romantics, Manzoni among others.

———. "Racine in controluce" and "Con Manzoni, tra Virgilio e Racine." *Vecchie e Nuove rilegature gianseniste*, 67–99. Naples: Edizioni scientifiche italiane, 1958. The author examines in detail the possible influences of Racine's tragedies on Manzoni: *Phèdre* on Ermengarde, *Athalie* on *The Betrothed*.

Tusiani, Joseph. "Ermengarde's chorus" (second chorus in *Adelchis*) translated into English. *La parola del popolo*, Jul. 1974.

———. "Manzoni's *Inni sacri* and *Il cinque maggio*: A Translation." *Annali d'Italianistica* 3 (1985): 6–43. Admirable English translation of the *Inni sacri* and of the ode on Napoleon. Italian text faces the translations.

Ulivi, Ferruccio. "Poetica e poesia del *Carmagnola*" and "L'*Adelchi*." *Il romanticismo e Alessandro Manzoni*, 54–84. Rome: Cappelli, 1963. The poetic strength of *Carmagnola* derives from its historical-ethical inspiration, notwithstanding the bitter conclusion: the pure-hearted man cannot but be defeated in history because of the tragic antinomy between the rights of one's conscience and Machiavellian politics. Adelchis's legacy does not concern only the king's lot but rather the human lot in general. The "fierce force" that men call law and that governs the world was a phrase Manzoni added just before rewriting the second draft. Adelchis finally agrees with the harsh pragmatism of his father but tempers it with Christian faith.

———. "Manzoni e la letteratura religiosa del Seicento francese." *Manzoni. Storia e Provvidenza*, 187–232. Rome: Bonacci, 1974. Manzoni's art is deeply impregnated with the belief in God's providential plan. The happy ending of the novel is due to a merciful correction of the writer; elsewhere in Manzoni's oeuvre we find pessimism and lack of faith in human progress, as the sad lot of the two innocent and oppressed Lombard siblings testifies.

———. *Manzoni*. Milan: Rusconi, 1985. Thorough and well-written biography, interspersed with literary criticism.

Wall, Bernard. *Alessandro Manzoni*. Cambridge: Bowes, 1954. Manzoni's two dramatic works are first and foremost two lyrical tragedies. Passion and action are altogether missing in them; their beauty is in scattered lyrical passages, which can be seen as poems in and of themselves.

———. "Sulle traduzioni inglesi di Manzoni." *La fiera letteraria*, 27 June 1965. Does not remark on the absence of English translations of Manzoni's tragedies.

Zumbini, Bonaventura. "L'*Egmont* del Goethe e il *Conte di Carmagnola* del Manzoni." *Studi di critica e letteratura comparata*, 63–78. 1907. Reprint, Rome: Archivio Guido Izzi, 1996.

SELECTED REVIEWS OF TWENTIETH-CENTURY PERFORMANCES
OF MANZONI'S TRAGEDIES

Almansi, Guido. "Ma che tragedia!" *Panorama*, 29 Mar. 1992. Negative review of Tiezzi's *Adelchis*. The author thinks that the nineteenth-century posturing and costumes do not work. However, he appreciated Ermengarde's death scene, set in war hospital, in line with the setting of the Risorgimento wars.

Annaloro, Nino. "Scene di una tragedia." *Theatre Design*, 5 Jun. 1992. Descriptive and appreciative review of Tiezzi's *Adelchis*, focusing on the lighting techniques the director adopted.

Bandettini, Anna. "Capitano di sventura." *La repubblica*, 26 Oct. 1989, suppl. Positive and descriptive review of Puggelli's *Carmagnola*.

Bernardelli, Francesco. "Per le rappresentazioni dell'*Adelchi* in Boboli." *La Stampa*, 4 June 1940. Positive review of Simoni's stage production of *Adelchis* in the Garden of Boboli in Florence. In the reviewer's words, the performance managed to minimize the fragmentary and cerebral nature of Manzoni's text.

Bertani, Odoardo. "La sfida del *Carmagnola*" *Avvenire*, 29 Oct. 1989. Very positive, scholarly review of Puggelli's *Carmagnola*.

Blasich, Gottardo. "L'*Adelchi* di Carmelo Bene." *Teatro* (May 1984): 433–35. Negative review of Bene's 1984 *Adelchis*, criticizing the too emphatic delivery of the lines by an actor who seems to demand the spectators' attention to himself rather than to the work. The music by Luporini is deemed out of tune with the text. Only the choruses obtained an adequate reading.

———. "*Adelchi* di Alesandro Manzoni." *Letture* 47, no. 490 (1992): 729–30. Negative review of Tiezzi's *Adelchis*. Important Manzonian themes are effaced in the performance. It compares unfavorably with Puggelli's *Carmagnola*. Director Puggelli had to start from a more challenging text and admirably solved the challenges, unlike Tiezzi, who was had an easier text to deal with and failed.

Boggio, Maricla. "Manzoni e Adelchi: l'autore, il mito, la storia." *Primafila*, Nov. 1997. Positive review of Bene's 1997 *Adelchis*, judged a "ritual or sacred performance" with sublime accents for Adelchis and beloved Anfrid and pragmatic coldness for Charles. Manzoni's tragedy has been rescued from the mortifying reading forced on students in classrooms.

Bonanni, Francesca. "Dopo un lunghissimo silenzio." *Il tempo*, 30 Oct. 1989. Fairly positive, scholarly review of Puggelli's *Carmagnola*.

Borsoni, Renato. "Quell'elitario di un Manzoni." *Brescia sera*, 14 Sept 1997. The writer complains that the municipal council of Brescia canceled the project of a yearly stage production of *Adelchis*. Other supposedly more modern authors such as Hugo and Von Hoffmansthal have been preferred to Manzoni, on account of the Italian author's elitist attitude.

Bruni, Flavia. "Manzoni da scoprire." *Il Secolo d'Italia*, 4 Oct. 1997. Positive presentation of Bene's then-forthcoming 1997 *Adelchis* and an interview with Renzo Tian, chair of the Italian

Theater Agency, who praises the nontraditional performance by Bene as the sole possible rendition of Manzoni's difficult tragedy.

Cappa, Felice. "Gli eroi di *Adelchi* come sculture in un itinerario tra archeologia e spettacolo." *La notte*, 20 Jul. 1994. Descriptive review of Mezzadri's *Adelchis* set among Brescia's monuments. Ermengarde's death scene was not effective owing to the mediation of a gigantic television screen. The recital of the choruses was too emphatic.

Caruso, Roberto. "Una tragedia della storia." *Cittadella cristiana*, 15 Feb 1990. Fairly positive review of Puggelli's *Carmagnola*.

Cavallazzi, Maria Paola. "Risorge Carmagnola 170 anni dopo." *L'Unità*, 26 Oct. 1989. Positive and descriptive review of Puggelli's *Carmagnola*.

Cauti, Andrea. "Manzoni, gusto antico." *Momento sera*, 28 Mar. 1992. Positive review of Tiezzi's *Adelchis* but negative judgment on Manzoni's text.

Chinzari, Stefania. "Il mio Adelchi, eroe solitario sulle montagne russe della poesia." *L'Unità*, 16 Feb. 1992. Neutral review of Tiezzi's *Adelchis* and interview with director.

Cornara, Franco. "Il Conte Carmagnola ritorna dopo 150 anni." *La provincia pavese*, 27 Oct. 1989. Positive scholarly review of Puggelli's *Carmagnola*.

Cuminetti, Benvenuto. "*L'eco di Bergamo*, 29 Nov. 1989. Positive and scholarly review of Puggelli's *Carmagnola*.

———. "Quel Manzoni travolto da inatteso . . . Ermengarda nel monastero di San Salvatore." *L'Eco di Bergamo*, 6 Jul. 1995. Very positive review of Garella's *Adelchis* in Brescia.

Degradi, Annalisa. "Un *Conte di Carmagnola* autorevole e espressivo." *Il cittadino*, 28 Nov. 1989. Positive and descriptive review of Puggelli's *Carmagnola*.

Distefano, Giuseppe. "*Adelchi* come melodramma." *Città nuova*, 25 Apr. 1992. Moderately negative review of Tiezzi's *Adelchis*. Defects were the obtrusive music and mediocre performances (with the exception of Patrizia Zappa Mulas as Ermengarde). Praises for Manzoni's text, a masterpiece not yet adequately rendered on stage.

Fagioli, Andrea. "Carmelo Bene dà voce all'*Adelchi*." *Toscana oggi*, 9 Dec. 1984. Fairly positive review of Bene's 1984 *Adelchis*, with the remark that much of the text is lost for the use of excessive microphone amplification, which makes the human voice vie for attention with Luporini's music and Striano's drums.

Falvo, Angelo. "S'ode lo squillo del *Carmagnola*." *Corriere della sera*, 26 Oct. 1989. Positive and descriptive review of Puggelli's *Carmagnola*.

Franzi, Tullia. "Le tragedie del Manzoni sul teatro." *Nuova antologia* 275 (1931): 57–74. History of peformances in the nineteenth century.

Gregori, Maria Grazia. "Manzoni, che disgrzia la storia!" *L'Unità*, 29 Oct. 1989. Fairly positive scholarly review of Puggelli's *Carmagnola*.

Guardamagna, Dante. "Mille anni dopo." *Radiocorriere* 12 Apr. 1992. Positive review of Tiezzi's *Adelchis*. Desiderius-Foà's delivery of the first chorus is praised in particular.

Guerrieri, Osvaldo. "Carmagnola d'acqua e d'onore." *La stampa*, 29 Oct. 1989. Positive, descriptive and scholarly review of Puggelli's *Carmagnola*.

Jattarelli, Leonardo. "All'Argentina la poesia di *Adelchi*." *Il messaggero* 16 Feb. 1992. Positive review of Tiezzi's *Adelchis*.

Lanzone, Giovanna. "'Sola e debol son io', geme la donna-Ottocento." *Cinema nuovo* (Apr. 1983): 42–48. Ermengarde's destiny is exemplary of all the female protagonists in nineteenth-century theater. Their lot is to be passive objects of men's choices, never subjects entitled to happiness.

Longo, Piero. "*Adelchi*, che gran melodramma." *Giornale di Sicilia*, 22 Feb. 1992. Interview with Tiezzi. Adelchis is a wonderfully modern character because of his complex inner life.

Lucchesini, Paolo. "Manzoni popolare." *La nazione*, 10 Mar. 1992. Positive review of Tiezzi's *Adelchis*.

Manciotti, Mauro. "Ma questo Manzoni sembra Verdi!" *Il secolo XX*, 10 Mar. 1992. Negative and insightful review of Tiezzi's *Adelchis*. Adelchis should not be seen as a victim but just as a forerunner of an existential malaise. Instead of superimposing Verdi and the bourgeois melodrama on Manzoni's tragedy, it would have been better to emphasize the Shakespearean reminiscences. The Risorgimento setting is totally inappropriate.

Manin, Giuseppina. "S'ode uno squillo di tromba." *Corriere della sera*, 25 Oct. 1989. Positive and descriptive review of Puggelli's *Carmagnola*.

Manini, Licia. "Eroi del Risorgimento." *L'Adige*, 17 Mar. 1992. Positive review of Tiezzi's *Adelchis*.

Manzini, Giorgio. "Pure gli eroi hanno un inconscio." *Paese sera*, 29 Oct. 1989. Positive and descriptive review of Puggelli's *Carmagnola*.

Manzoni, Franco. "*Adelchi*, mille anni dopo." *Corriere della sera*, 7 Apr. 1992. Neutral review of Tiezzi's *Adelchis*. Manzoni's tragedy is deemed pessimistic. Ermengarde dies tormented because of the state affairs; Adelchis, who hates war, can find peace only in death.

Mele, Rino. "Vita e morte del *Carmagnola*." *Il giornale d'Italia*, 7 Nov. 1989. The then forthcoming Puggelli's *Carmagnola* occasions a scholarly essay on what is deemed a tragedy that reveals the presence of the divinity.

Paganini, Paolo A. "Manzoni gran drammaturgo grazie a Puggelli." *La notte*, 28 Oct. 1989. Positive, scholarly, and descriptive review of Puggelli's *Carmagnola*.

Palazzi, Renato. "Un Carmagnola nella palude." *Il sole 24 ore*, 12 Nov. 1989. Negative review of Puggelli's *Carmagnola* on account of the text's obsolete language and symbolism, unappealing to today's youth.

Pani, Egidio. "In *Adelchi*, sottile stimolo politico." *Gazzetta del mezzogiorno*, 25 Apr. 1992. Very positive review of Tiezzi's *Adelchis*.

Pieri, Romano. "Tanti personaggi in cerca di Bene." *Il resto del carlino*, 1 Nov. 1984. Positive review of Bene's *Adelchis*.

Polacco, Giorgio. "Questo sì è Manzoni." *Il piccolo*, 6 Dec. 1989. Positive and descriptive review of Puggelli's *Carmagnola*.

Polese, Ranieri. "Tutte le voci di *Adelchi*." *La nazione*, 29 Nov. 1984. Positive review of Bene's *Adelchis*.

Possente, Eligio. "L'Adelchi nel giardino di Boboli." *Corriere della sera*, 5 June 1940. Positive review of Simoni's *Adelchis*, which proves beyond any doubts that Manzoni's tragedy was written for the stage.

Prosperi, Giorgio. "Adelchi è Manzoni." *Il tempo*, 15 Mar. 1992. Mixed review of Tiezzi's *Adelchis*. Historical-biographical account about Manzoni highlights the surmised resemblance between the tragic hero and the tragedian himself.

Raboni, Giovanni. "Un Carmagnola che va dritto al cuore." *Corriere della sera*, 29 Oct. 1989. Very positive review of Puggelli's *Carmagnola*, with the sole objection to the chorus being recited for the second time by an actor in bourgeois attire.

———. "Se due *Adelchi* vi sembran pochi." *Corriere della sera*, 27 Mar. 1992. In positively reviewing Tiezzi's *Adelchis*, the author thinks that the competition between the two directors (in

1992 Bene proposed again his *Adelchis* to vie with Tiezzi) is all to the advantage of a much neglected masterpiece of Italian literature.

———. "La fine di Ermengarda: strazio e rivolta." *Corrieredella sera*, 1 Jul. 1995. Positive review of the third Brescia production of *Adelchis*, this one directed by N. Garella.

Rigotti, Domenico. "Il Conte di Carmagnola." *Rivista del cinematografo*, Dec. 1989. Very positive descriptive and scholarly review of Puggelli's *Carmagnola*.

———. "Manzoni si recita per strada." *Avvenire*, 15 Jul. 1993. Descriptive review of the Brescia project for the yearly staging of *Adelchis* in the streets of the historical city center. Brief interview with the director, Mezzadri; she says that she interprets the Lombard siblings as "sacrificial Lambs."

Ronfani, Ugo. "S'ode a destra il coro verdiano." *Il giorno*, 29 Oct. 1989. Fairly positive review of Puggelli's *Carmagnola*; slight objection to the sophisticated theatrical apparatus, which might distract the audience from Manzoni's text.

———. "C'è anche il melodramma nei Magazzini di Tiezzi." *Il giorno*, 18 Mar. 1992. Positive review of Tiezzi's *Adelchis*.

Rosati, Carlo. "Tragedia della solitudine." *Giornale di Sicilia*, 16 Feb. 1992. Positive review of Tiezzi's *Adelchis*. Recalls Croce's analysis of tragic hero.

Salvini, Celso. "*Adelchi* del Manzoni rappresentato al giardino di Boboli." *Il popolo d'Italia*, 5 June 1940. Positive and descriptive review of Simoni's *Adelchis*.

Savioli, Aggeo. "Manzoni più Shakespeare più Verdi. E *Adelchi* si trasforma in melodramma." *L'Unità* 10 Mar. 1992. Fairly positive review of Tiezzi's *Adelchis*. Verdi's music suits the tragedy, although a little too abundant. The tableaux vivants are too rigid, though, as if made of puppets. Manzoni's work is valid, however, with its pessimism about history dictated by his Catholic faith and his study of Shakespeare.

Scorrano, Osvaldo. "Carmelo e Manzoni, un'attrazione fatale." *La gazzetta del mezzogiorno*, 3 Oct. 1997. Descriptive review of Bene's 1997 *Adelchis* with excerpts of an interview with the actor, who quotes Croce to support his view of Manzoni's tragedy as superior to the novel and states that Manzoni wrote *Adelchis* in his "anti-Catholic" period.

Secchi, Claudio Cesare. "Le tragedie del Manzoni sul palco." *L'Italia*, 5 Mar. 1931. The lack of fortune of the stage renditions of Manzoni's tragedies is ascribed to the excessive control over passions in the too morally minded characters. The future might however bring new and better attempts at stage performances.

Soddu, Ubaldo. "La scena italiana? Va riscoperta." *Il giornale di Sicilia*, 1 Oct. 1991. Appreciation of attempts by theaters of Palermo and Rome to put on stage works by Italian playwrights, including Manzoni's *Adelchis*.

———. "Assolo per Manzoni." *Il messaggero*, 23 Feb. 1992. Negative, scholarly review of Bene's 1992 *Adelchis*. Objection to the missing notes of Christian faith, eliminated by Bene. In such a rendition, the Lombard prince's weakness appears mere narcissism.

Tei, Francesco. "Adelchi sconfitto dalla Storia." *La città*, 27 Nov. 1984. Bene's 1984 *Adelchis* occasions an interesting essay taking issue with the *figura Christi* reading of Adelchis's character but still asserting the simplistic view of that the hero's greatness is in his defeat and in his awareness of the injustice supposedly inherent in political power.

Tian, Renzo. "Manzoni da recuperare." *Il messaggero*, 29 Oct. 1989. Positive and scholarly review of Puggelli's *Carmagnola*.

Tomasino, Renato. *"Adelchi,* capolavoro ritrovato." *Il giornale di Sicilia,* 1 Mar. 1992. Scholarly review of Tiezzi's *Adelchis.* The critic appreciates Manzoni's text and provides a fairly good judgment on the director's work. The excessive tidiness of the scenic sequences creates an impression of coldness, but Ermengarde's death makes up for the few defects.

Torresani, Sergio. "Recita per voce solista." *La provincia* (Cremona), 2 Mar. 1984. Negative, scholarly review of Bene's 1984 *Adelchis,* criticizing Bene's egocentrism in reciting all the parts and therefore paradoxically reproducing nineteenth-century narcissistic overacting by the leading actor, instead of a would-be avant-garde performance,. Manzoni's beautiful tragedy is eclipsed by such noisy performance.

———. *"Il Conte di Carmagnola." Sipario,* Nov.–Dec. 1989. Very positive, scholarly review of Puggelli's *Carmagnola.*

Vallauri, Carlo. "Da Manzoni a Bernhard." *Ore 12. Il globo,* 12 Apr. 1992. Positive review of Tiezzi's *Adelchis.*